中国参与制定多边投资规则问题研究

邓瑞平 等 著

厦门大学出版社 国家一级出版社
XIAMEN UNIVERSITY PRESS 全国百佳图书出版单位

图书在版编目（CIP）数据

中国参与制定多边投资规则问题研究 / 邓瑞平等著
. -- 厦门：厦门大学出版社，2023.9
ISBN 978-7-5615-9095-9

Ⅰ．①中… Ⅱ．①邓… Ⅲ．①国际投资-规则-研究
Ⅳ．①F831.6

中国版本图书馆CIP数据核字(2023)第156260号

出 版 人　郑文礼
责任编辑　李　宁
美术编辑　李嘉彬
技术编辑　许克华

出版发行　厦门大学出版社
社　　址　厦门市软件园二期望海路 39 号
邮政编码　361008
总　　机　0592-2181111　0592-2181406(传真)
营销中心　0592-2184458　0592-2181365
网　　址　http://www.xmupress.com
邮　　箱　xmup@xmupress.com
印　　刷　厦门市明亮彩印有限公司

开本　787 mm×1 092 mm　1/16
印张　19.5
插页　1
字数　520 千字
版次　2023 年 9 月第 1 版
印次　2023 年 9 月第 1 次印刷
定价　88.00 元

厦门大学出版社
微信二维码　　　厦门大学出版社
微博二维码

目 录
CONTENTS

引　言

　　经过改革开放 40 余年、加入世界贸易组织 20 余年,我国经济高速发展,参与国际经贸竞争力大增,成为世界经济发展中强劲的经济体。我国经济发展成就的重要组成部分是我国国际投资(外国投资和对外投资)的迅猛发展,我国目前不仅成为世界最大资本输入国之一,也成为世界最大资本输出国之一。我国国际投资的发展不但要求我国国内法对外资和海外投资予以充分保护,更需要国际法制特别是多边投资规则①的促进和充分保护。这必然决定我国应积极、全面参与多边投资规则的制定。因此本书对我国参与国际投资法制建设、建立健全多边投资法律规则,以促进和保护我国国际投资特别是对外投资、维护国家利益,具有重大理论价值和实践价值。

　　2000—2019 年,在国内公开刊物上发表的与本书相关的文献有 200 余篇,绝大多数探讨的是 WTO 体系内的多边投资规则、多边投资框架(multilateral framework on investment,简称 MFI)、多边投资协定(multilateral investment agreement,简称 MIA)、OECD 的《多边投资协定》(multilateral agreement on investment,简称 MAI)、构建多边投资规则(multilateral investment rules,简称 MIRs)、区域性投资协定(regional investment agreements)等,只有极少数论文探讨中国如何参与多边投资协定或规则的谈判,且仅从单一领域进行探讨,如多边投资框架与中国战略利益或经济战略、世界贸易组织多边投资协定谈判与我国的战略选择、我国应对多边投资协定谈判的策略、国际多边投资法律框架与中国基本策略等,对中国参与多边投资规则或协定的谈判或制定缺乏整体性研究,对特殊领域的投资规则缺乏建设性、可操作性研究。即使在对我国战略、策略、基本原则等问题的研究上,也缺乏系统性、深入性和实证性。

　　与本书相关的英文论文有近 300 篇,90% 以上集中在 MIA 的构建、OECD 的 MAI 条文、外国投资政策与 MAI 和发展权、MAI 与全球化、MAI 的合理性与存在的问题、政

---

　　①　多边投资规则的含义有广义、狭义之分。广义是指三个及以上国家或地区缔结或参加的国际投资条约中规定的有关投资权利义务的规则。狭义是指区域性和普遍性投资条约中规定的有关投资的权利义务的规则。本书采广义。

治平衡中的 MIA、MAI 对国家的影响、WTO 体系内《与贸易有关的投资措施协定》(TRIMs)和《服务贸易总协定》(GATS)的规则等,对不同发展水平的国家或地区是否应当及如何参与 MAI 或 MIA,缺少整体、深入、系统研究;极少数论文涉及 MAI 与发展中国家,但鲜有人提出符合发展中国家特殊情况的参与策略与路径。在收集到的多种专著中,绝大多数论题或涉及的领域为 WTO 的投资规则、MAI、MIA、投资条约法与实践、外国投资的国际法等,只有一人从中国人视野研究 MAI[①]。其指出 MAI 存在的诸多问题,认为 MAI 在每一方面都体现了发达国家对国际投资协定高标准的诉求,值得发展中国家研究,但作者没有就中国参与 MAI 谈判提出可供参考的系统性意见或见解。

本书拟研究的主要内容为:(1)当代国际投资的发展与多边投资规则的调整。重点研究国际投资的发展与多边投资规则的关系、多边投资规则的类型及其相互关系与发展规律、存在的主要问题,分析有关多边投资规则的国际与国别政治、经济、外交、法律、文化背景,指出现存主要类型的多边投资规则在调整国际投资关系中的优势与缺陷,提出多边投资规则的总体发展趋势与未来主要方向。(2)我国国际投资的发展及其对多边投资规则的需求。重点研究中国对外投资现状、发展趋势及其对不同类型的多边投资规则的需求、中国参与多边投资规则的理论与实践及经验教训,分析中国对外投资格局所面临的具有规律性的法律问题特别是多边投资规则问题、中国应主要参与制定的多边投资规则的类型。(3)我国参与制定多边投资规则应坚持的基本原则。重点研究我国参与制定多边投资规则应坚持的国家经济主权、公平互惠、促进投资自由化、投资与投资者待遇平等等原则。(4)我国参与制定多边投资规则的总体战略。重点研究我国参与制定多边投资规则的总体战略及其原因。(5)我国参与制定的总体策略。重点研究我国参与制定多边投资规则的总体策略及其原因。(6)我国参与制定的基本方式。重点研究有规律性的基本方式,为我国未来采取的参与方式提供理论和实践依据。(7)我国参与制定的工作机制。重点研究我国参与制定多边投资规则的内部体制和工作机制、职责与分工。在分析我国和其他主要国家或地区现行体制、机制利弊的基础上,提出我国参与制定的工作机制未来改革建议。(8)我国参与制定的规则内容。在重点研究双边、区域性、普遍性和其他类型现存投资规则的基础上,探讨多边投资规则包含的一般条款和不同性质、不同类型的多边规则所具有的特殊条款,分别提出主要类型多边投资规则谈判条文的学者建议稿。

通过对以上各部分的研究,试图在以下方面予以创新:多边投资规则的主要分类及其相互关系、发展规律、发展趋势、调整国际投资关系的优劣,我国参与制定多边投资规则面临的主要法律问题特别是多边投资规则类型问题,我国参与制定多边规则应坚持的基本原则、采取的总体战略和策略、基本方式、工作机制及其改革、规则的内容和主要条文的学者建议。

本书拟采取的主要研究方法为历史分析法、比较分析法、实证分析法和规范分析法。

---

① Chen Huiping, *OECD's Multilateral Agreement on Investment—A Chinese Perspective*, Kluwer Law International, 2002.

前三种方法在每部分中均会运用,规范分析法主要运用于第八章的研究。

　　拟以中国参与制定多边投资规则的理论与实践为基点,采取政治、经济、外交、法律、文化等多视角对中国参与制定多边投资规则的问题进行较全面、系统、深入的研究,以期得出尽可能科学、合理,具有可操作性的指导性结论。

　　在研究过程中,视不同部分,拟分别采取"古今中外、理论与实践"的论理(逻辑)方法,尽可能使本书的研究成果在结构和层次上具有合理性、清晰性,在引用数据、资料上具有准确性,在推理上具有严密逻辑性,所得出的结论或提出的观点具有科学性。

　　拟以国际投资发展与多边投资规则的关系为起点,首先研究当代国际投资发展状况及其对多边投资规则的需求、多边投资规则的类型及其发展历程和其在调整当代国际投资关系中存在的主要问题,然后论证我国国际投资发展对多边投资规则的需求和我国积极、全面参与制定多边投资规则的相关基本理论,再系统、深入研究我国参与制定多边投资规则的基本原则、总体战略和策略、基本方式和工作机制、规则的基本条款与我国取向,最后提出有关多边投资规则谈判条文建议稿,供有关部门参考。

第一章

国际投资的发展与多边投资规则的调整

投资与投资规则是经济基础与上层建筑的关系,不同时期的国际投资决定了相对应时期投资规则的特征。经历了五个历史发展阶段后的国际投资已经呈现出多向流动的特性,这在客观上要求多边投资规则对其予以调整。当代多边投资规则主要有区域性与普遍性两种,其形成有明显的规律性。多边投资规则已经展现出制定场所多样、谈判范围广泛和内容细致的总体发展趋势。对多边投资规则形成的规律及其各自优劣的分析,有助于我国在不同类型多边投资规则构建过程中进行战略定位与策略选择。

第一节 国际投资与多边投资规则的历史发展关系

国际投资与多边投资规则是经济基础与上层建筑的关系,是规律决定规则、规则反映规律的关系。随着投资资本从商品资本发展到金融资本直至生产力资本形态,多边投资规则经历了从无到有、从有到多的发展变化过程。

一、国际投资的产生与国际投资规则的雏形期

国际投资的产生与国际投资规则的雏形期是指 1870 年以前。

国际投资保护规则的早期雏形可追溯到欧洲文艺复兴早期。此时的跨国交易形式仍然是以贸易为主,并没有专门的投资保护条约,仅仅是一些国家单方颁布并冠以"特许"(concession)或者"准许"(grants)字眼,涉及对外国商人在本国的交易以及对其财产

的保护的国内法令。① 这些国内法中有关外国商人人身及财产安全保护的标准成为现代国际投资条约中有关投资待遇及保护标准的雏形。

随着国际贸易的发展,国际资本形态逐渐从商品资本向货币资本和生产资本转化。早在 14 世纪后期,意大利佛罗伦萨就建立了梅迪西银行,其在欧洲各大主要城市均有分支机构,这标志着货币资本(间接投资)的产生。② 到 16 世纪,欧洲金融中心逐渐转移至英、法、德等国,发达国家货币资本迅速向海外扩张,资本运动要求采取更高级的国际生产资本的形式,于是其逐渐与商业行会相结合。随着西方资本主义国家对世界各地的殖民扩张,一方面,发达资本主义国家通过国内法授予本国商业公司特许令状的方式允许财团对外进行投资③;另一方面,发达资本主义国家运用武力等手段迫使不发达国家签署形式上"互惠、平等"的商事条约来保障其在殖民地的贸易与投资利益。1536 年,法兰西王国与奥斯曼帝国之间签订了《贸易互惠及航海权利条约》,规定有关法国商人在奥斯曼帝国的贸易与投资自由以及治外法权等不平等的内容。随后的英国东印度公司在中东地区通过投资手段进行的经济掠夺更是有过之而无不及。④ 因此在 16 世纪末至 19 世纪中叶,在殖民统治下,殖民者没有必要诉诸国际法和外交保护的手段,而是通过治外法权对本国国民的投资进行保护。⑤

二、国际投资的初步发展与国际法规则的产生期

国际投资的初步发展与国际法规则的产生期是指 1870—1946 年。

1870—1914 年期间,资本主义自由竞争高度发展并逐渐向垄断阶段过渡,发达资本主义国家的大型企业以跨国公司的形式开始向海外投资,标志着现代意义的国际投资出现。据统计,1913 年,美、英、法、德四国对外私人投资总额为 410 亿美元,其中英国 170 亿美元、法国 120 亿美元、德国 90 亿美元、美国 30 亿美元。⑥ 这一阶段主要是以私人资

---

① 例如,在公元 991 年,拜占庭国王巴兹尔二世和康斯坦八世都颁布 chrysobull 法令,赋予威尼斯商人在港口免税贸易和在本国购买房产的权利;公元 1157 年,英格兰国王亨利二世颁布法令保护来自德国科隆的商人及其财产安全。See Jeswald W. Salacuse, *The Law of Investment Treaties*, Oxford University Press, 2010, p.80.
② 陈坤等编:《国际投资法》,哈尔滨工程大学出版社 2003 年版,第 9 页。
③ 在中世纪后期的欧洲,行会(company)并不能自由设立,需要通过皇室的特许令状才能设立。特许令状是行会承担某些公共职能的对价或是国家对行会已作出的奉献所给予的回报。参见方流芳:《中西公司法律地位历史考察》,载《中国社会科学》1992 年第 4 期。
④ J. W. Salacuse, Foreign Investment and Legislative Exemption in Egypt: Needed Stimulus or New Capitulations, in I.D. Michalak and J. W. Salacuse, *Social Legislation in the Contemporary Middle East*, University of California International & Area Studies Press, 2009, pp.61-241.
⑤ 但值得注意的是,这些殖民地国家不包括拉丁美洲,这似乎说明了为何外交保护最先在拉丁美洲产生。See Andrew Newcombe, Lluis Paradell, *Law and Practice of Investment Treaties——Standards of Treatment*, Wolters Kluwer Press, 2009, p.11.
⑥ 吴承明编:《帝国主义在中国的投资》,人民出版社 1955 年版,第 27 页。

本的形式流入北美洲、拉丁美洲、大洋洲以及亚洲、非洲等殖民地与半殖民地国家的资源开采和铁路建设等领域。[①] 此时有关国际投资的法律规范,主要是散见于宗主国基本法中的调整本国公司在外国或者国外公司在本国活动的国内涉外法律规范。[②]

1914—1946 年期间,两次世界大战和资本主义国家爆发经济危机导致国际投资环境恶化,工业国家产量下降 17%,世界贸易量下降 25% 以上,国际投资资本急剧短缺。全球主要投资国家在 1945 年的投资总额为 380 亿美元,其中美国 170 亿美元、英国 140 亿美元、法国 60 亿美元、日本为零。[③] 这一时期,在美国国务卿查尔斯·埃文斯·休斯(Charles Evans Hughes)领导下对友好通商航海条约(FCN)加以改造,专门规定了投资保护、投资待遇和征收补偿条款,而后各国纷纷效仿,使之成为调整国际投资的主要国际法规则。[④]

三、国际投资的逐步增长与多边投资规则的形成期

国际投资的逐步增长与多边投资规则的形成期是指 1947—1981 年。

1947—1981 年期间,美国凭借其政治和经济实力继续充当主要债权国。其于 1947 年实行"马歇尔计划",向欧洲提供了 130 多亿美元的援助,主要国家投资规模逐渐恢复。1970 年,五大投资国家投资总额达到 2402 亿美元,其中美国 1486 亿美元、英国 490 亿美元、法国 200 亿美元、德国 190 亿美元、日本 36 亿美元。[⑤] 到 1969 年,发展中国家的跨国公司达到 1100 个,阿根廷、巴西、新加坡等国家成为新兴市场国家中的主要对外投资国。1980 年,美国对外投资额达到 6069 亿美元,引进外资额为 5009 亿美元,全球投资呈现以美国为主导、逐步增长的特点。

在国际投资逐步恢复和美国主导国际投资的背景下,美国商界迫切期望在《建立国际贸易组织的哈瓦那宪章》(以下简称《哈瓦那宪章》)中加入投资议题,以形成一个具有较高保护标准的多边投资规则。[⑥] 但是由于发展中国家极力反对,约文草案令发达国家大失所望:该宪章没有给发展中国家施加任何国际法义务,将当地政策目标凌驾于国际投资政策标准之上。[⑦]《哈瓦那宪章》的失败可以归于两个主要原因:一是,宪章未达到美

---

① 这一阶段投资的主要特征是:(1)私人资本为主要来源;(2)投资期限较长,99 年的贷款期间并不罕见;(3)投资国仅是发达国家,其中以英国为首。

② 如《德国民法典》(1907 年)第 23 条、《日本民法典》(1898 年)第 36 条、第 49 条。

③ 蒲罗尔:《美帝国主义论》,陈羽纶译,五十年代出版社 1953 年版,第 20 页。转引自杨树明等:《国际投资法原理》,重庆大学出版社 1992 年版,第 4 页。

④ Kenneth J. Vandevelde, *U.S. International Investment Agreements*, Oxford University Press, 2009, p.28.

⑤ 陈坤等编:《国际投资法》,哈尔滨工程大学出版社 2003 年版,第 11 页。

⑥ Kenneth J. Vandevelde, A Brief History of International Investment Agreements, *U. C. Davis Journal of International Law and Policy*, 2005, Vol.12, p.157.

⑦ Dattu, A Journey from Havana to Paris, *Fordham International Law Journal*, 2000, Vol.24, p.286.

国商界所期望的投资自由化目标,不可能在美国众议院获得通过,因此杜鲁门总统(民主党)没有将宪章提交至共和党占据多数的国会请求批准,转而利用自己的"行政协定"权致力于促使贸易自由化的关税与贸易总协定(GATT)的谈判。[①] 二是,东西方之间意识形态斗争和南北国家在经济利益上的争夺促使宪章必然失败,预示未来十余年间社会主义国家和民族独立国家对发达国家投资的国有化浪潮。

虽然《哈瓦那宪章》以失败告终,官方和非官方多边规则草案的制定脚步并未停止。德意志银行主席阿布斯(Abs)和壳牌能源公司总裁肖克罗斯(Shawcross)在1959年联手起草了著名的《外国投资公约草案》(阿布斯-肖克罗斯草案),涉及投资待遇、投资保护与投资安全、直接征收、间接征收和争端解决等国际投资条约的核心内容。[②] 这一完全有利于资本输出国的草案尽管未生效,但极大影响了后来反映发达国家的多边立法活动。[③] 发达国家投资规模的迅猛发展直接催生了经济合作与发展组织(OECD)频繁起草多边投资规则的活动。1961年出台了具有现实拘束力的《资本移动自由化法典》和《无形交易自由化法典》两个投资自由化法典,对发达国家之间的资本移动自由化有着重要意义。但有学者指出,两个法典的执行力度长期被成员国大打折扣,直到20世纪80年代才有所好转。[④] 由于南北阵营的激烈矛盾,发展中国家也寻求自己的立法场所,与发达国家展开对抗。拉美一些国家依据1969年签署的《卡塔赫纳协定》成立了安第斯共同市场。为排除发达国家资本流入,带有强烈保护主义情绪的安第斯条约组织委员会第24号决议以严格管制外资为其主要特色,强调东道国的外资管辖权、征收权和卡尔沃主义救济途径。世界银行考虑到发达国家与发展中国家在投资问题上的激烈矛盾,寻求更为务实的程序性多边条约。一些国家于1965年签署了《解决国家与他国国民间投资争端公约》(简称《华盛顿公约》或ICSID公约)并依据该公约成立"解决投资争端国际中心"(简称ICSID),以此调和在争端解决方面的矛盾。

---

① 《1934年互惠贸易协定法》授予总统和外国展开贸易谈判及签订贸易协定的权力,因此对GATT的签订并不需要国会三分之二的批准。参见徐泉:《美国外贸政策决策机制的变革——美国〈1934年互惠贸易协定法〉述评》,载《法学家》2008年第1期。

② 在投资待遇方面,成员国应确保投资者的公平公正待遇(第7条)。在投资保护方面,除非紧急情况,30年内东道国不得征收外国投资财产且征收必须伴有公平、有效、及时补偿(第3条)。在投资争端解决方面,就公约争议,提交国际法庭,当事人可立即求助于该法庭或先求助于当地司法救济;就征收补偿争议,提交国际仲裁委员会解决(第10条、第7条)。See UNCTAD, *International Investment Instruments—A Compendium*, UNCTAD/DITE/4(Vol.V),2000,p.395.

③ 如1961年由哈佛法学院索恩教授和巴克斯教授应联合国之邀起草的《国家侵害外国人之国际责任公约草案》,就在补偿标准上对其进行细化与延伸。

④ Sol Picciotto, Linkage in International Investment Regulation: The Antinomies of the Draft Multilateral Agreement on Investment, *University of Pennsylvania Journal of International Economic Law*,1998, Vol.19, p.745.

四、国际投资的高速稳定增长与区域性多边投资规则的发展期

国际投资的高速稳定增长与区域性多边投资规则的发展期是指 1981—2000 年。

从规模看,进入 20 世纪 80 年代,以美国为首的主要西方国家投资呈缓慢增长态势,投资总规模不断扩大但增速明显放缓。1983 年至 1989 年,全球对外直接投资增长率每年平均为 28.9％,共计 15000 亿美元。① 进入 20 世纪 90 年代,因西方发达国家经济衰退,国际投资增长率有所下降,但其投资流入与流出额仍是同期全球固定资产形成总额及世界生产总值年平均增长率的一倍多,国际投资已成为世界经济的支柱之一。

从结构看,国际投资已不再是一家独大的局面,区域集团化趋势愈加明显。1982 年年底,美国以 1470 亿美元的国外净资产投资额执世界投资国家之牛耳。但随后其投资增长速度极为缓慢,至 1985 年第二季度,美国丧失了保持 67 年的债权国地位,成为头号债务国,而日本同年的国外净资产额达到 1300 亿美元。发展中国家也逐渐向外投资。截至 1991 年 8 月,我国海外投资遍及 90 多个国家和地区,实际投资额超过了 10 亿美元。② 整个世界投资形成了以北美(美国为首)、欧盟和日本为首的国际直接投资大三角结构,而发展中国家以地缘或者投资历史积淀为基础,聚集在大三角结构周围。

基于国际投资的稳定增长态势,国际投资法律规范如雨后春笋般蓬勃发展,并在整体上呈现出从区域国际法到普遍国际法发展的趋势,主要表现在以下方面:

第一,区域投资带动了相关国际投资的立法步伐。1981 年阿拉伯国家签署《阿拉伯国家间阿拉伯资本投资联合协定》③,东南亚国家于 1987 年签署《东南亚国家联盟促进与保护投资协定》,安第斯条约组织成员国发布了替代 220 号决议的 290 号决议,美国、加拿大、墨西哥于 1992 年签订《北美自由贸易协定》(NAFTA)。区域性国际投资法体现出区域投资高度自由化的特征。

第二,普遍性国际投资立法活动逐渐复苏。乌拉圭回合成功调和了发展中国家与发达国家的矛盾,将《与贸易有关的投资措施协定》(TRIMs 协定)纳入 WTO 体系中,形成了一个合格投资部分内容的国际投资法典。④ 与此同时,东欧剧变后的社会主义阵营的能源国家唯恐错失(miss out)国际投资的利益,以《欧洲能源宪章》为蓝本与欧洲发达国家缔结《能源宪章条约》(ECT)。值得注意的是,OECD 在 1998 年再一次进行了《多边投资条约草案》(MAI 草案)的立法尝试,但由于欧盟国家与美国在文化产业保护等问题上

---

① 《对外投资将成为 90 年代经济主力》,载《国际经贸消息报》1991 年 10 月 6 日,第 1 版。

② 杨树明等:《国际投资法原理》,重庆大学出版社 1992 年版,第 5 页。

③ League of Arab States, Unified Agreement for the Investment of Arab Capital in the Arab States, 1982, http://unctad.org/Sections/dite/iia/docs/compendium/en/36％20volume％202.pdf, last visited on 22 Nov. 2022.

④ 张严方主编:《与贸易有关的投资措施协定解读》,湖南科学技术出版社 2005 年版,第 4～15 页。

的无法调和而流产。[①]

五、国际投资的发展调整与普遍性综合投资规则的滞后期

国际投资的发展调整与普遍性综合投资规则的滞后期是指 2000 年至今。

当前国际投资资本多向流动,处于结构性调整阶段。在直接投资流出量方面,发展中国家直接投资流出量从 2002 年的 496 亿美元(占当时全球总量 9.2%)攀升至 2011 年的 3838 亿美元(占全球总量 23%),虽然 2011 年因拉丁美洲与加勒比地区的撤资而导致数额下降 4%,但依然在全球总量中占据较高比例。在直接投资流量流入方面,从 2002 年的 1710 亿美元(占全球总量 27.4%)攀升至 2011 年的 6844 亿美元(占全球总量 44.9%)。[②] 无论是数据的绝对增长还是百分比的相对增长,近 20 年来,国际直接投资资本的流动(无论是流出还是流入)都逐步从发达国家之间的双向流动转向发达国家、发展中国家和转型经济体国家之间的多向流动,国际直接投资呈现出多向流动的态势。联合国贸易与发展会议(UNCTAD)谨慎地认为:越来越多的发展中国家跨国公司正在作出贡献,它们占全球外国直接投资流量的比例从 20 世纪 80 年代中期的不到 6%,增加到 20 世纪 90 年代后 5 年的约 11%,2002—2003 年期间则降到 7%(年平均为 460 亿美元)。它们约占全球外国直接投资外流存量的十分之一,该存量 2003 年增长了 8%,达到 8590 亿美元。按占固定资本形成总额比例衡量,某些发展中国家的对外投资已超过了部分发达国家。例如,在 2001—2003 年,与美国(7%)、德国(4%)和日本(3%)相比,新加坡为 36%、智利为 7%,马来西亚为 5%。随着经济稳定复苏,这些国家和其他发展中国家的外国直接投资可望恢复增长。一种作为新的贸易地理格局补充的新型外国直接投资流向地理格局正在形成。[③] 在此意义上,除了最不发达国家外,纯粹的资本输入国与资本输出国的概念已经不能适应当前国际投资环境,更为广泛的国际投资市场已经形成,投资结构发生了重大变化。

但在国际法律层面,调整国际投资的国际法律规则仍然依靠双边投资条约(BITs)、区域性投资协定和 WTO 下的投资规则,普遍性综合投资规则处于停滞状态。有学者认为,全球 2600 多个双边投资协定尽管是双边的形式,但并不是严格依据双边谈判形成的,而是一些国家通过已准备好的模式或者范本进行细节磋商形成的,毋宁说是已经形成了一套不同于传统的"会谈多边主义"(conference multilateralism)的"系列多边主义"(serial multilateralism)机制(regime)。[④] 因此,用普遍性综合多边投资规则代替碎片化的 BITs 体系,已经十分必要。

[①]　UNCTAD, *Lessons from the MAI*, UNCTAD Series on Issues in International Investment Agreements, United Nations, 1999, pp.12-13.

[②]　联合国贸易与发展会议:《2012 年世界投资报告》(中文版),第 3 页;《2008 年世界投资报告》(中文版),第 13 页。

[③]　联合国贸易与发展会议:《2004 年世界投资报告》(中文版),第 8 页。

[④]　Andrew Newcombe, Lluis Paradell, *Law and Practice of Investment Treaties—Standards of Treatment*, Wolters Kluwer Press, 2009, p.13.

第二节　当代多边投资规则的主要类型

多边投资规则的历史演进表明,若按地理标准分类,可以将多边投资规则分为区域性、普遍性的多边投资规则。二者在内容、调整范围上各有特点,是受到经济、政治等多种因素的影响而形成的,具有较为明显的规律性。

一、区域性多边投资规则

区域性投资规则是随着 1948 年《哈瓦那宪章》项下投资规则失败而迅速发展起来的新形式。现有十余个区域性多边投资规则,其法律性质与效力各不相同。例如,APEC项下的投资规则仅具有倡议性质,无法律拘束力。以下仅简述具有代表性的区域性多边投资规则。

(一)阿拉伯国家联盟的投资规则

1980 年 11 月 26 日,以科威特、沙特阿拉伯和阿联酋为代表的中东资本国与以苏丹、叙利亚、埃及为代表的资本需求国签订了《阿拉伯国家间阿拉伯资本投资联合协定》。[1]该协定在实体内容上未包含诸如充分保护与安全、公平公正待遇等高水平保护标准[2],在争端解决方面未包含 ICSID 仲裁管辖条款。2003 年建立阿拉伯投资法庭后,缔约方之间的投资争端可以提交该法庭解决。

(二)东南亚国家联盟的投资规则

1987 年 12 月 15 日,东盟创始成员(文莱、印度尼西亚、菲律宾、马来西亚、新加坡、泰国)达成《关于促进与保护投资的协定》。[3] 该协定在投资待遇方面,规定了公平公正待遇和持续安全与保护、最惠国待遇和协商基础上的国民待遇;在征收方面,基本向西方国家看齐,即根据法律程序、基于公共利益,方可为之,且给予充分、及时、有效、不限制移转的补偿;在争端解决方面,ICSID、UNCTAD 和 KLRCA(吉隆坡地区仲裁中心)及其他机构都是在 3 个月内无法协商一致下可诉诸的法律救济机构。

东盟国家还于 1998 年签署《东盟投资区域框架协定》,进一步明确了各国的资本、人

---

① 　League of Arab States，Unified Agreement for the Investment of Arab Capital in the Arab States Economic Documents，1982，No.3，p.21.

②　随后在 1988 年伊斯兰会议组织外长会议上,产生了《伊斯兰会议组织成员国间促进、保护和保证投资的协定》,包含了最惠国待遇、征收补偿、协议仲裁、岔路口条款等内容。

③　The ASEAN Agreement for the Promotion and Protection of Investment of 1987，(1988)27 ILM 612.

员的自由流动以及投资行业的开放时间表:到 2010 年对东盟内的投资者开放所有行业,到 2020 年对所有投资者开放所有行业;各缔约国保证缔约国间资本、熟练劳动力和管理人员的自由流动。该协定在东盟区域内正式建立起了区域性投资法律制度,但该协定总体上仍是一个框架性协定。

(三)安第斯共同体的投资规则

由于南北阵营的激烈矛盾,发展中国家寻求自己的谈判场所,与发达国家展开对抗。拉美国家依据 1969 年《卡塔赫纳协定》成立了安第斯共同市场。为限制发达国家资本流入,带有强烈保护主义情绪的该共同市场委员会通过第 24 号决议,严格管制外资,强调东道国的外资管辖权、征收权和卡尔沃主义救济途径。自 20 世纪 70 年代末,由于拉美国家发生外债危机,筹资能力下降,投资环境急剧恶化,部分安第斯条约组织成员开始反省并逐渐背离限制发达国家外资准入的第 24 号决议。1987 年第 220 号决议正式替代第 24 号决议,不但将外资利润转移比例限制、投资领域限制逐渐放松,而且废除了"卡尔沃条款"在投资争端解决中的强制性。

(四)北美自由贸易区的投资规则

美国、加拿大、墨西哥于 1992 年签订《北美自由贸易协定》(NAFTA),将曾高举"卡尔沃主义"旗帜的墨西哥纳入其中。其被认为是南北国家投资趋同、全球投资自由化里程碑式的区域性投资规则。[①] 该协定第 11 章"投资",内容几乎照搬了美式 BIT 范本,除了规定绝对待遇、相对待遇、征收补偿和资本转移自由,还将"投资"概念的外延极大扩张,将投资保护延伸至投资准备、投资进行与投资后的经营三个阶段。有学者认为NAFTA 投资规则是迄今为止最具代表性的区域性投资规则。

随着时间推移,NAFTA 已经不适应时代要求,特别不符合美国国际贸易发展利益。三国于 2018 年 9 月 30 日就更新 NAFTA 达成一致,新协定被命名为《美国—墨西哥—加拿大协定》(简称《美墨加协定》或 USMCA),同年 11 月 30 日三国领导人在阿根廷首都布宜诺斯艾利斯签署该协定,取代 NAFTA,2020 年 7 月 1 日生效。[②] 该协定第 14 章"投资"成为新一代北美区域投资规则,预示北美区域投资进一步自由化、保护投资的标准更高、投资者及其投资的义务更多。

(五)《能源宪章条约》的投资规则

以《欧洲能源宪章》为基础的《能源宪章条约》于 1994 年在欧洲发达国家与独立国家联合体(简称"独联体")主要国家之间签署。东欧剧变后,缺乏能源开发技术、资本的前

[①] See Daniel M., Price, An Overview of the NAFTA Investment Chapter—Substantive Rules and Investor-State Dispute Settlement, *The International Lawyer*, 2018, Vol.27, No.3, pp.722-738.

[②] 美墨加协定参见 https://baike.baidu.com/item/美墨加三国协议/22908942? fr=aladdin#4,最后访问日期:2022 年 11 月 20 日。

社会主义国家与有能源需求的欧洲一拍即合。该条约中的投资待遇与争端解决方式都具有典型"南北合作"的特征。有学者认为,与其他南北国家之间的"指南""宣言""守则"不同,该条约是一个"有牙齿的老虎":允许私人径直向国际仲裁机构提请仲裁而不需要事先合意。① 值得注意的是,当前多数缔约国已成为 WTO 成员方,在 WTO 体系下建立一个能源投资和贸易体系,《能源宪章条约》具有极大的参考价值。

(六)南方共同市场的投资规则

南方共同市场(MERCOSUR)成员国于 1994 年 8 月和 11 月分别签署了《南方共同市场投资议定书(外部)》《南方共同市场投资议定书(内部)》,但均未生效。2017 年 4 月 7 日,成员国阿根廷、巴西、巴拉圭和乌拉圭东岸共和国在阿根廷布宜诺斯艾利斯市举行的世界经济论坛拉美峰会上签署了《南方共同市场合作和便利投资议定书》,以期促进诸缔约国可持续发展、经济增长、减少贫困和扩大其生产能力。该议定书于 2019 年 7 月 3 日生效。其由 26 条正文和 1 个附件组成,特色条款有:各缔约国的义务(待遇、非歧视、直接征收、损失补偿、透明度、转移、税收措施、审慎措施、安全例外、打击腐败和违法、环境与劳工和健康),投资者的义务(反腐败、企业社会责任),机构性治理和争端解决机制(本议定书管理、信息交换、受保护信息的处理、与私营部门的互动、投资促进组织间的合作、争端预防程序、缔约国间争端解决),合作和便利投资的基准,合作和便利投资议程。② 该议定书无论在形式上还是内容上,均体现出巴西的国际投资条约模式。

(七)欧亚经济联盟的投资规则

俄罗斯联邦、白俄罗斯共和国和哈萨克斯坦共和国总统于 2014 年 5 月 29 日签署、2015 年 1 月 1 日生效的《欧亚经济联盟条约》③是苏联解体后独联体主要国家建立欧亚联盟过程中的重要条约。其第三部分第 XV 节"服务贸易、组建、活动和投资"和附件 16《关于服务贸易、组建、活动和投资的议定书》的相关规定,构成了欧亚经济联盟的投资规则。这些投资规则的特色内容有:适用于诸成员国对投资采取的任何和全部措施;单个国别限制、例外、附加要求与条件清单(即"国别清单"),应当由本联盟最高理事会批准;成员国不应当将降低其法律规定的保护人类生命健康、环境、国家安全、劳工标准的任何要求,用于吸引其他成员国和第三国人员在其境内组建的机制;"投资"指一成员国投资者根据另一成员国法律在该另一成员国领土内向经营活动主体投入的有形和无形资产;在支付和转移方面,另有规定除外,各成员国应当废除与投资有关的全部限制措施的效力,

---

① Thomas W. Waelde, International Investment under the 1994 Energy Charter Treaty: Legal Negotiation and Policy Implication for International Investor within Western and Commonwealth of Independent States/Eastern Countries, *Journal of World Trade*, 1995, Vol.29, p.5.

② 参见 Protocolo De Cooperación Y Facilitación De Inversiones Intramercosur, 2017.

③ 亚美尼亚、吉尔吉斯斯坦分别于 2014 年 10 月 10 日、12 月 23 日签署本条约,本条约分别于 2015 年 1 月 2 日、8 月 6 日对两国生效。

且不应当采取此方面的新限制措施;组建构成一种投资形式,本议定书另有规定除外,本议定书的全部规定适用于此种投资;特别注重投资的法律待遇与保护,即各成员国给予他国投资及其投资者的待遇为公平与公正待遇,而公平与公正待遇不低于国民待遇或最惠国待遇,投资者可以选择待遇标准;对战争等造成的投资者的损失进行赔偿和担保;对征收中投资者的权利进行担保;已将拟解决的争端提交规定的一国内法院或一仲裁院的投资者,无权将该争端再提交其他任何法院或仲裁院。①

二、普遍性多边投资规则

(一)ICSID 公约

ICSID 公约是历史上最早的具有法律效力的普遍性投资公约,其核心是解决东道国与外国投资者之间的投资争端。按照该公约成立的 ICSID 是迄今为止最为重要的国际投资争端解决机构。

20 世纪 60 年代,南北矛盾使发达国家与发展中国家在投资待遇和征收等问题上分歧两极化,世界银行为避开实体性条约路径,转向试图在两大阵营间达成争端解决的程序性规则,以改变恶劣的投资环境。在世界银行牵头下,该公约达成并于 1965 年根据该公约正式成立 ICSID。② 1987—2008 年,全球 288 起投资争端解决案件中有 150 起提交了 ICSID 仲裁。③ 该中心通过裁决对国际投资中的重要法律问题所作的阐释,成为后续裁判的"证据"甚至是"法律渊源"。UNCTAD 认为,ICSID 裁决本身是一种造法行为(rule-making)。④

(二)《多边投资担保机构公约》(MIGA 公约)

1988 年生效的 MIGA 公约的最大成就在于,南北国家在外资政策无法调和的情况下,成立了多边投资担保机构,为国际投资中面临的征收、货币转移限制、违约、战乱等政治风险提供担保。

《哈瓦那宪章》多边实体投资规则失败后,世界银行于 1961 年开始着手制定多边投资担保规则,分别于 1966 年、1968 年、1972 年形成了三次草案。但是草案中的担保机构仅作为专门承担机构业务的金融风险的赞助会员国的代理人,并且代表发达会员国的利

---

① 见《欧亚经济联盟条约》附件 16《关于服务贸易、组建、活动和投资的议定书》第 2、5、6(7)、8、66、67、68、69、70、71、77~81、86 款。

② Note by the President of the Executive Directors,R 61-128(28 Dec. 1961)ICSID,*History of the ICSID Convention*,1968,Vol.2,part 1,pp.4-6.

③ UNCTAD,*International Investment Rule-making—Stocktaking*,*Challenges and the Way Forward*,UNCTAD/ITE/IIT/2007/3,2008,p.17.

④ UNCTAD,*Investor-State Dispute Settlement and Impact on Investment Rulemaking*,Sales No. E.07.11.D. 10,2007.

益。发展中国家特别是拉丁美洲强烈反对该建议案。① 直到 1983 年南北斗争趋于缓和，世界银行才重启普遍性投资担保规则的研究，重点研究了七类问题，并认识到"所有资本输出国为另一个类别，会出现一些困难，因为潜在的东道国可能也是或者正在变为资本输出国"②。在勉强平衡了南北国家的利益后，MIGA 公约迟了近三十年才出现。

（三）WTO 体系中的多边投资规则

《与贸易有关的投资措施协定》（TRIMs 协定）、《服务贸易总协定》（GATS）和《与贸易有关的知识产权协定》（TRIPs 协定）共同构成了 WTO 多边投资规则体系。有学者认为，TRIMs 协定虽然被冠以"与贸易有关"的前缀限定，但其实是发达国家为避免发展中国家将不相关的问题纳入多边贸易谈判中而采取的障眼法，③把字头缩略词 TR 的意义看作不是与贸易有关的（trade-related）而是无关的（tangentially related）才合乎实际。④

客观地看，20 世纪 80 年代以来，国际贸易与国际投资的同向性发展和相互影响，对国际贸易与国际投资理论产生了重大挑战，主要原因在于跨国公司构成了投资与贸易的共同载体，二者在理论上互不相容的预设前提为国际生产体系一体化的国际实践逐步消除。⑤ 具体而言，服务贸易晚近发展的主要动力来自国际投资，国际投资的净收益本身构成了广义国际服务贸易的一项重要内容（资本要素服务）。投资与贸易的关系成为"鸡"与"蛋"的关系。⑥ 跨国公司作为当今国际投资的主要力量，无形财产特别是知识产权是其生存与发展的灵魂与生命。知识产权保护存在国别差异，而且《伯尔尼公约》《巴黎公约》等国际公约因缺乏有效的争端解决机制使知识产权成为投资领域的重大障碍，这使得 TRIPs 协定的"硬法性质"有着非凡的意义。⑦ 总之，WTO 多边投资规则体系为国际投资提供了一个非完整的普遍投资法典，对各国的国内投资立法产生重大影响。

三、多边投资规则的发展规律及其理论阐释

考察多边投资规则的发展，可以总结出以下发展规律。

---

① 易卜拉欣·F. I. 西哈塔:《多边投资担保机构形成的早期历史（上）》，黎晖译，载《南京大学法学评论》1996 年春季号，第 72 页。

② 易卜拉欣·F. I. 西哈塔:《多边投资担保机构形成的早期历史（下）》，黎晖译，载《南京大学法学评论》1996 年秋季号，第 66 页。

③ 刘笋:《WTO 法律规则体系对国际投资法的影响》，中国法制出版社 2001 年版，第 288 页。

④ Jagdish Bhagwati, *The World Trade System at Risk*, Prentice Hall-Harvester Wheat sheaf Publishers Press,1991, pp.71-72. 转引自张向晨:《发展中国家与 WTO 的政治经济关系》，法律出版社 2000 年版，第 150～151 页。

⑤ 徐泉:《国际贸易投资自由化法律规制研究》，中国检察出版社 2004 年版，第 134～140 页。

⑥ 刘笋:《WTO 法律规则体系对国际投资法的影响》，中国法制出版社 2001 年版，第 216 页。

⑦ 曾华群主编:《国际投资法学》，北京大学出版社 1999 年版，第 712～714 页。

（一）先区域性规则后普遍性规则

综观多边投资规则发展，其规律之一是从区域性向普遍性发展。

在区域性投资规则出现前，OECD除了1961年推出的具有拘束力的《资本移动自由化法典》和《无形交易自由化法典》，其余（包括1998年MAI草案）涵盖南北国家的区域性综合投资规则均以失败告终。但制定区域性和普遍性投资规则的努力仍在继续，呈现出从区域向普遍的发展规律。[①]

从地缘角度看，无论是"南南合作"的安第斯共同市场还是"南北合作"的《北美自由贸易协定》《能源宪章条约》，都展现出了地缘区域经济对国际投资规则的需求。区域性投资规则的形成原因比较复杂，每个区域国际经济组织都有自己的形成过程和形成原因；每个成员在加入某一个区域国际经济组织时所考虑的因素不同，加入一个区域国际经济组织并不表示就赞同该区域国际经济组织的每一部分的具体规则。从宏观实践看，一些共通的原因仍然是客观存在的。

从政治角度看，恰如著名学者John H. Jackson指出的那样，在第一次区域浪潮下，"除非有强烈的政治目标去驱动经济整合，否则经济整合不可能在原定的经济目标方面获得成功。在欧洲，这个强烈的政治目标充分展现在煤钢共同体条约和罗马条约，旨在于防止第三次世界大战和法德之间的冲突……其他经济组织的建立过程中这种因素可能并不凸显，但这种背景的存在是无疑的"[②]。有学者进一步指出，"第二次区域主义浪潮与第一次（欧盟一体化）相比，美国改变了其坚定的多边主义立场，转向了在NAFTA框架下就贸易、投资等多维经济关系进行优惠协定谈判，这一方面是在为乌拉圭回合铺平道路"，另一方面是在为下一次与拉美国家合作铺平道路。[③]

从经济角度看，早期区域经济共同体是在贸易领域的比较优势理论指导下建构的。[④]但是随着区域贸易发展，区域成员发现纯粹贸易问题的解决并不能达到区域经济整合的目标。国家之间为促进自由和公平竞争建立了关税联盟，但仅凭削减乃至免除关税，难以实现原有目的，因此欧洲共同体条约和欧洲经济共同体条约都包含了关于限制性措施、滥用市场主导地位、隐性贸易壁垒、政府补贴和垄断等纵向经济整合措施的规定。[⑤]

[①] UNCTAD, *World Investment Report* 2012：*Towards a New Generation of Investment Policies—the Regional Trends in FDI*，UNCTAD/E.12.II.D.3，2012，p.84.

[②] John H. Jackson, Perspectives on Regionalism in Trade Relations，Law and Policy in International Business，1996，Vol.27，pp.874-875.

[③] Richard Baldwin, Patrick Low, *Multilateralizing Regionalism*，Cambridge University Press，2009，pp.21-25.

[④] Richard H. Steinberg, Antidotes to Regionalism：Responses to Trade Diversion Effects of the North American Free Trade Agreement，Stanford Journal of International Law，1993，Vol.29，pp.318-319.

[⑤] Ignaz Seidl-Hohenveldern, *International Economic Law*，Kluwer Law International Press，1999，pp.91-92.

因此,在普遍性投资规则建构失败的情况下,经济整合措施的多维性促使各方将投资规则纳入其中,投资规则作为经济整合手段之一首先以区域性投资规则出现。

(二)先程序性规则后实体性规则

多边投资规则另一发展规律是先程序性规则后实体性规则。

《哈瓦那宪章》的失败没有冷却国际社会对普遍性投资规则的热情。根据世界银行《外国直接投资待遇指南》起草过程中的专家调查报告,到 20 世纪 90 年代初期,有影响的多边投资条约或国际问题文件达到 26 个。[①] 在二战结束至 20 世纪 90 年代中期,国际投资领域的斗争重心主要体现在东道国(发展中国家)与投资国(发达国家)之间的立法层面,即围绕着作为争端解决法律依据的国际法应如何对外国投资保护作出规定的问题,明显表现出了"国际投资争端政治化"的特性。[②]

由于南北阵营对立,各自寻找自己的立法场所,在实体规则的立场上随时间推移呈现出钟摆式的从两极走向趋同的发展过程。南方国家作为资本输入国坚持经济主权原则,在内容上要求外资准入的管理权和控制权、东道国征收权、卡尔沃主义及东道国法律适用。实际上,当地救济优先权、逐案审批同意权、东道国法律适用权和重大安全例外权为南方国家投资立法的"四大安全阀"。南方国家在国际上掀起了"建立国际经济新秩序运动",旨在通过国际立法来对主权原则这一国际法基本原则进行重申。但是发达国家凭借其对政府间国际组织和非政府间国际组织的控制,极力否认诸如《自然资源永久主权宣言》(1962)、《建立新的国际经济秩序宣言》(1974)等一系列文件的国际习惯法性质。[③] 世界银行认识到南北双方在实体规则方面的矛盾难以在短期内调和,为降低发展中国家的敏感程度,成功促成有关争端解决的《华盛顿公约》诞生。

在 1990 年以后,投资领域主要矛盾发生了深刻变化。"南北矛盾"作为传统的主流分析范式,认为发达国家企图推动全球投资自由化而发展中国家试图保有对外资的限制。[④] 但该种观点已不能对当前国际投资现象作出合理解释:(1)截至 2008 年 1 月 1 日,在外国投资者根据 NAFTA 提起的 49 起国际投资争端仲裁案中,除 17 起针对墨西哥之外,其他 32 起的被诉对象均为美国和加拿大,其中美国 14 起,加拿大 18 起。[⑤] 这种诉求个体化的投资争端解决,使发达国家意识到他们在当前情势下所面临的地位与发展中国家一样,都是"资本输入国"。(2)由于跨国公司逐利性损害东道国社会利益,各国间新签订的国际投资协定中出现了一些平衡投资者和国家权利义务、平衡经济目标和诸如环境

---

① 刘笋:《WTO 法律规则体系对国际投资法的影响》,中国法制出版社 2001 年版,第 16 页。

② 徐崇利:《晚近国际投资争端解决实践之评判:"全球治理"理论的引入》,载《法学家》2010 年第 3 期。

③ M. Sornarajah, *The International Law on Foreign Investment*, Cambridge University Press, 2010, pp.19-33.

④ 陈安:《国际经济法学专论》,高等教育出版社 2007 年第 2 版,第 659 页。

⑤ 徐崇利:《晚近国际投资争端解决实践之评判:"全球治理"理论的引入》,载《法学家》2010 年第 3 期。

保护等其他公共政策目标的新条款,以确保国际投资协定和国家其他公共政策目标的一致性。[1] 联合国贸易与发展会议指出,国际投资协定要在促进增长与发展方面发挥更有效和有利的作用仍需要长期的努力,其中一个重要的努力方向是"增强国际投资协定与其他处理社会、广泛的经济和环境关切问题领域的公共政策的互动"[2]。因此,晚近NAFTA、ECT、WTO体系均证实了南北矛盾逐渐被"公私冲突"(东道国—跨国公司)所替代,钟摆从两极走向趋同。

正因为国际经济与国际政治局势的深刻变化,各国投资法出现趋同化现象。20世纪90年代以来,发展中国家的外资政策逐步出现单边自由化特征,不断调整国内外资法,竞相吸引外资,在许多方面呈现出自由化与趋同化的趋势。在2011年,有44个国家调整外资政策、67个国家变动政策,其中利于投资的有52个,不利于投资的仅有15个。2019年,有54个经济体至少出台了107项影响外国投资的措施,有四分之三是朝自由化、促进和便利化的方向发展;其中亚洲的发展中国家和新兴经济体最为活跃,在采矿、能源、金融、运输和电信等领域采取了自由化措施。一些国家简化了投资者的行政手续,或扩大了投资激励机制。[3] 事实上,由于各国外资立法与政策理念逐步趋同,每年新签双边投资协定的数量继续减少,而区域层面制定的投资政策日益增多,[4]区域协定同化的多边实体规则已经生成。席勒认为,当前的国际投资法已在双边协定基础上呈现出多边性,它构成了国际法的一个"子系统"(sub-system)并产生了一般性的原则和适用规则。[5]

(三)先独立于贸易规则后综合于自由贸易区规则

与20世纪80年代之前的国际投资规则比较,当前的国际投资规则,无论是NAFTA、ECT、东南亚国家联盟(东盟,ASEAN)、欧亚经济联盟(EAEU)还是WTO体系,在形式上都呈现出一种贸易与投资相混合的模式。这种现象不是立法场所综合的偶然性结果,而是国际经济关系深刻变化的结果。根据传统国际贸易理论,其前提假设是,各国的生产要素在质上是相同的且在国内可以自由流动,但在国际间不能自由流动。而国际投资是以资本的非同质性及在国际间的自由流动为预设前提。因此在传统国际经济关系中,二者展现出较强的次序性:先贸易后投资或者先投资后贸易。诚然,之前的跨国公司未能在企业组织优势、产业聚集和知识产权方面形成巨大规模,传统的国际经济理论对当时情况的解释是科学的。

---

① 就环境、自然资源等方面的要求,参见美国2004年BIT范本第12条、第13条,《北美自由贸易协定》第11章第6条。

② 联合国贸易与发展会议:《2004年世界投资报告》(中文版),第20页。

③ 联合国贸易与发展会议:《2020年世界投资报告——疫情后的国际生产》(要旨和概述)(中文版),第Ⅻ页。

④ 联合国贸易与发展会议:《2012年世界投资报告》(中文版),第7、18页。

⑤ Stephan W. Schill, *The Multilateralization of International Investment Law*,Cambridge University Press,2009,p.17.

二战后,自美国经济学家里昂惕夫提出著名的"里昂惕夫之谜"①,全球经济学界就解答贸易与直接投资的关系建构了大量模型,产生了丰硕成果。② 首先,经济学家波特在其名著《国家竞争优势》中提出了国家在国际市场上取得竞争优势的钻石模型理论,认为:在地理上的相互接近、在技术上的相互支持、在人才上的相互补充,存在国际竞争产业链,是一国国际竞争优势的重要因素;资本逐利性要求要素禀赋好的国家,该国的优势商品为投资积累大量顺差;本国愈加苛刻的市场需要要求当期企业的技术创新和产业升级,而国际投资是技术、资本等企业发展要素的"一揽子转移",因此逐利性驱使投资转向该类国家。③ 波特特别强调了地缘关系在其模型中的重要性,这很好地解释了为何该种同向化发展最先在区域自由贸易区中出现。④

　　其次,当代经济学表明,经济要素在不同国家是异质的。劳动力分为普通劳动力、技术型劳动力和知识型劳动力,这三种类型都具有典型的专用性特征,不能简单地用类比关系进行推演。基于不同要素价格在不同禀赋国家的区别,资本的逐利性要求跨国公司运用要素价格进行经营,最初会出现不同国家商品之间的交换;一旦超过价格极限,企业就将普通劳动力转移至资本需求国,而在本土进行资本密集型运作,最终的形态是交换差别和同质产品,而不是仅仅出口差别产品。此时的国际贸易与投资同向性发展。

　　反映上述经济规律的乌拉圭回合协定标志着多边投资规则的重大变化。由于世界贸易的很大部分是在关联企业间进行的,贸易与投资不再被看作获取资源或者为市场提供服务的替代手段,而是被当作互为补充的手段。⑤ 着手解决并力图便利贸易和投资交易的双边、区域、区域间、诸边等协定越来越多地将国际投资规则作为它们的组成部分。这些协定除了规定一批多边化的放宽及促进贸易条款,还包含放宽、保护和促进缔约国之间投资流动的承诺。

---

　　① 里昂惕夫之谜是指根据传统国际贸易学的要素禀赋理论,一个国家出口的应是密集使用本国丰富的生产要素生产的商品,进口的应是密集使用本国稀缺的生产要素生产的商品。根据此理论,一般认为,美国是资本相对丰富、劳动相对稀缺的国家,理所当然应当出口资本密集型商品,进口劳动密集型商品。但是二战后,里昂惕夫运用投入产出方法,对美国经济统计资料进行验证,结果与要素禀赋理论预测相悖。

　　② 参见陈洁蓓、张二震:《从分歧到融合——国际贸易与投资理论的发展趋势综述》,载《经济学研究》2003 年第 3 期;向铁梅:《国际贸易与直接投资的关系及其中国情况的实证分析》,载《世界经济研究》2003 年第 3 期;李荣林:《国际贸易和直接投资的关系:文献综述》,载《世界经济》2002 年第 1 期;李荣林:《国际贸易和直接投资的替代性和互补性》,载《2001 年中国经济学年会论文集》,北京大学中国经济研究中心。

　　③ 迈克尔·波特:《国家竞争优势》,李明轩、邱如美译,华夏出版社 2002 年版,第 4～23 页。

　　④ 在投资与贸易的回归性分析的经济学"引力模型"中,相互距离($DIST_{cj}$)是一个重要的参数因素。参见郭飞等:《贸易自由化与投资自由化互动关系研究》,人民出版社 2006 年版,第 293 页,表 1。

　　⑤ Tim Buthe, Helen V. Milner, The Politics of Foreign Direct Investment into Developing Countries: Increasing FDI through International Trade Agreements?, *American Journal of Political Science*, 2008, Vol.52, No.4, pp.741-762.

第三节　多边投资规则主要类型的优劣分析

当前多边投资规则的基本类型是区域性和普遍性两种,由此形成了多边投资规则二元模式,但它们不是一个自洽的投资规则,不同类型的规则具有相应的优势与劣势。

一、区域性投资规则的优势与缺陷

如前述,区域性投资规则首先是地缘政治经济推动下的产物,它满足了不同经济要素、禀赋的区域内相近国家的资本流动,但仍有其固有缺陷,并不能完全取代普遍性投资规则。

(一)优势

区域性投资规则是对普遍性投资规则的狂热追求及国家对地缘安全与经济现实进行考虑的综合结果。

1.区域性投资规则促进了区域内成员国内投资立法的趋同

根据区域一体化的要求,成员国必须按照区域投资规则的要求,对国内投资立法作出相应的补充、修改与废止,以满足区域协定赋予它的国际义务。同时,区域投资规则整合了由 BITs 形成的错综复杂的网状投资规则,促使成员国内部签订的 BITs 在内容要求上同向发展。欧盟在 2010 年后积极展开研究,目的在于在现有的资本自由流动的基础上,进一步确立统一的投资规则。① 国际投资法制由最初的国内单边调整,到网状发展的双边调整,再到区域性的多边调整,逐步实现世界性的多边调整,符合国际法律规则的发展规律。

2.为普遍性国际投资规则的建立积累经验

当今区域经济一体化组织规模最大、影响最广的仍是发达国家间的或是以发达国家为主导的区域性组织。这些组织在国际投资法律安排上的影响力相对较广,对未来多边投资规则的走向会产生不可低估的作用。多边投资规则中的投资自由化特征已是不争的事实,采取何种程度的保护标准已成为摆在发展中国家与发达国家面前的难题,但区域性投资规则提供了一个好的范例。以 NAFTA 为例,作为继受美式 BIT 范本的典型,较高的保护标准并不必然受到墨西哥这样的发展中国家的反对。

---

① Carolinn Hjalmroth, Stefan Westerberg, A Common Investment Policy for the EU, http://www.kommers.se/In-English/Analyses/Analysis-The-contribution-of-trade-to-a-new-EU-growth-strategy-/, last visited on 13 Oct. 2022.

(二)缺陷

区域性多边投资规则作为普遍性多边投资规则缺位时的现实替代产物,有以下两个方面的缺陷。

1.适用范围和作用限于区域内

与双边投资规则相比,区域性投资规则虽然在一定程度上能减少不同双边投资条约的冲突,促进双边投资条约的相互协同,有力促进区域经济一体化的进程,但是区域投资规则仍是局限于区域范围。由于不同地区的区域投资规则没有遵循一个统一的模式,因而区域投资规则呈现出的种种差异,不能完全消除双边投资条约所具有的局限性,容易形成区域性投资壁垒。[①] 在不进行任何体系内协调的情况下,国家间以双边或区域方式缔结投资条约,会延续并强化现有的国际投资协定大杂烩格局。

2.不同区域性投资规则之间、普遍性投资规则之间存在冲突或重叠

投资者需要适应不同地区的差异性投资规则,难以减少其在投资准入、开业和经营整个过程中的实际成本。各区域间经济、社会、文化发展差异造成的投资规则不统一,会使各区域内的各东道国继续维持一种无序竞争状态,以吸引外国直接投资。[②] 例如,一个欧盟成员国有可能根据双边投资条约、《欧洲联盟条约》、《能源宪章条约》或者根据国际货币基金组织和世贸组织规则,对其他欧盟成员国承担与投资有关的义务。随着各国更加频繁地缔结含有投资条款的自由贸易协定,这些协定将越来越多地与双边投资条约、其他自由贸易协定发生冲突或重叠;涉及某种投资的某项交易,有可能适用多项国际投资协定。这就出现了冲突、重叠条约之间的一致性问题,将会造成各方竞相提高保护标准以吸引外资,形成国际投资领域"劣币驱逐良币"的现象。

经济学研究表明,不是每一种区域经济都可以获得经济增长的好处。根据中国自身投资与贸易结构的特点,在 ASEAN＋3(东盟＋中日韩)的模式下,中国国内生产总值(GDP)实际受到了负面影响。为使中国在区域经济中获得更大的益处,需要同时促进中国同其他构架特别是 EU 和 NAFTA 之间的投资、贸易自由化。[③] UNCTAD 考察最不发达国家、大陆国家和岛屿国家等不同类型的国家后得出的结论是,区域化投资协定是一种脆弱的(weak)和易受攻击的(vulnerable)投资结构形式。[④] 中国的区域性多边合作也存在一个问题,即 ASEAN 成员与 NAFTA 成员所接受的双边投资规则不尽相同,造成中国在多个区域组织成员国进行投资时面临着不同的投资规则。更为严重的是,当前

① UNCTAD, *International Investment Rule-making—Stocktaking*, *Challenges and the Way Forward*, UNCTAD/ITE/IIT/2007/3, 2008, pp.47-50.

② 叶兴平:《外国直接投资最新趋势与变迁中的国际投资规则——宏观考察》,载《法学评论》2002年第4期。

③ 郭飞等:《贸易自由化与投资自由化互动关系研究》,人民出版社2006年版,第410页。

④ UNCTAD, *World Investment Report 2012: Towards a New Generation of Investment Policies—the Regional Trends in FDI*, UNCTAD/E.12.II.D.3, 2012, p.64.

国际投资实践中出现了最惠国(MFN)待遇条款扩大适用于程序性事项的情况。[①]如果MFN扩大适用在未来成为国际习惯法,我国与两个或两个以上自由贸易区的投资保护标准,将会始终以较高的为准,而且国际仲裁机构对我国的管辖权将会大大扩张,与我国有关的案件数量也将激增。

二、普遍性投资规则的优势与缺陷

理想状态的法律规则是具有确定性和统一性的,在国际投资领域也是如此。透明的、可预见的普遍性投资规则是降低投资风险的重要保障。但普遍性投资规则也有自身难以克服的缺陷。

(一)优势

在一定意义上,普遍性投资规则的优势恰是双边与区域投资规则的劣势。

1.实体性权利义务具有确定性和统一性

从实体性条约的整合情况看,在当前国际投资协定体系高度分散化的前提下,区域与双边投资协定下的国家只能在他们的条约制定工作中寻求个体解决方案而不是具有一致性的外资政策。一项双边协定的谈判,特别是发展中国家与发达国家间缔结的协定,可能会因为两国之间不平等的政治、经济力量关系而受到影响。大多数发展中国家因为其有限的议价能力而处于不利地位,而这种风险在多边谈判中则会降低。[②]各国可能觉得很难做到:在他们的国际投资协定网络中建立一致性,在国际投资规则制定中实现私有和公共利益的适当平衡以及确保充分考虑到发展问题;只要国际投资协定领域继续保持高度分散,就很难实现更大限度的同一性、透明度,很难重视合理的发展,而根据定义,只有通过国际投资协定体系自身发展才能有效地解决这些缺陷。[③]以WTO为例,WTO多边投资协定谈判一旦达成,其可以保证多边投资规则与GATS、TRIMs和其他WTO条款相一致。

从规则的使用看,多边协定还使规则具有更广泛的协调性和可预见性,因为若想改

---

① 该实践最早见于 ICSID 2010 年 Maffezini v. Spain 案,随后 2010 年斯德哥尔摩仲裁院在 RosInvest v. Russia 案中再次确认这种观点。2011 年 Ekran v. China 案是我国首次被诉至 ICSID 案件,原告理由中有 MFN 条款的扩大适用问题。See Maffezini v. Spain Decision on Objections to Jurisdiction, CASE No. ARB/97/7, 25 January 2000, paras.54-56;RosInvest v. Russia, Stockholm, Sweden SCC ARBITRATION V (079/2005), Final Award, 12 Sept. 2010, paras. 39-124;Ekran v. China, ICSID Case No. ARB/11/15.

② 美国、德国等资本输出国草拟了双边投资协定范本,使诸多发达国家只能在现有的范本中进行议价,实质上存在不公平。Andrew Newcombe, Lluis Paradell, *Law and Practice of Investment Treaties—Standards of Treatment*, Wolters Kluwer Press, 2009, pp.14-17.

③ Andrew Newcombe, Lluis Paradell, *Law and Practice of Investment Treaties—Standards of Treatment*, Wolters Kluwer Press, 2009, p.35.

变规则,需要得到各方的同意。与现有的众多双边投资协定相比,对多边框架的条款进行定期审查也是更节省资源的办法。不同的双边或区域投资协定包含许多不同的规则,而一项普遍性多边投资协定只存在单一的规则,这增强了投资者的可预见性。普遍性多边投资规则的建立还扩展了规则适用的地域范围,因为加入该协定的国家要一揽子地接受其他所有贸易纪律。

2.程序性权利义务规则具有普遍公正性

从争端解决角度看,当前的区域与双边投资协定存在案件所涉事实相同且当事人相关联和投资权利相似、案件所涉商业背景和投资权利相似、案件所涉当事人和商业背景不同但所涉投资权利相同情况下,争端解决结果却不一致的现象。[①] 造成争端解决结果的不一致性的原因本身就蕴含在了程序性规定中。现有的国际投资仲裁体系有 ICSID 公约、《联合国贸易法委员会仲裁规则》、《国际商会仲裁规则》和《斯德哥尔摩商会仲裁规则》等,这些仲裁规则互有不同。虽然这些不同为争端各方提供了程序上的不同选项,但是程序性规则的不一致性势必影响裁决结果的不一致性。仲裁庭组建的临时性、仲裁过程的保密性、仲裁员的独立性和一裁终局机制,使在同一仲裁机构和同一仲裁规则下在不同时期组建的仲裁庭,很难寻求先例的指引或形成相对稳定和成熟的法律解释文化,而跨机构的法律解释文化的整合或趋同更加困难。[②] 值得注意的是,久负盛名的 ICSID 争端解决机制出现了因发展中国家的不信任而引发的信任危机,[③]直接导致玻利维亚(2007 年)、厄瓜多尔(2010 年)正式退出 ICSID 机制。[④]

总体上,普遍性多边投资规则的形成有助于提高争端解决结果的可预测性,与区域、双边投资规则相比,普遍性规则在案件的公开、先例的遵守和后果的可预见性方面都有明显的优势。

(二)劣势

1.灵活性受到限制

与双边投资规则和区域投资规则相比,普遍性多边投资规则的灵活性受到较大限制。有学者对普遍性规则的具体内容适用于发展中国家时进行成本和收益分析,认为国家在国际投资中必须付出两类成本:第一类是为吸引外资而过度保护跨国公司利益而损失的成本,第二类是国家为提出激励措施和业绩要求而遵守相关义务的让渡国家政策制定自主权的成本。在对成本进行控制从而达到获益目标的过程中,政策灵活程度是一个重要的工具。但是,普遍性多边投资规则留给国家的权力空间显然极为有限,成本和收

---

① 刘笋:《国际投资仲裁裁决的不一致性及其解决》,载《法商研究》2009 年第 6 期。

② 刘京莲:《国际投资仲裁体制的困境与出路》,载《福建论坛》2011 年第 5 期;刘笋:《国际投资仲裁裁决的不一致性及其解决》,载《法商研究》2009 年第 6 期。

③ 刘京莲:《国际投资仲裁正当性危机之投资仲裁员独立性研究》,载《河北法学》2011 年第 9 期。

④ ICSID News release of 16 May 2007;ICSID News Release of 9 July 2009.

益变得更加难以控制。① 另外,发展中国家通过吸引跨国投资而获得的技术转移的利益与成本的关系也难以确定。根据近来多边谈判的经验,宣称普遍性投资规则项下所有的拘束条款能够包容各国国情的差异的看法,不具有合理性。②

2.存在实质不公平

普遍性多边投资规则是在世界主要国家间达成的具有拘束力的国际规则,任何缔约国国内法均不得与其相抵触。以权力导向为特征的投资规范一旦形成,就对发展中国家在投资政策方面的灵活性上产生了较大的拘束作用。尽管在形式上,较为稳定的普遍性投资规则能够带来投资政策可预见性,但是受国家力量对比关系的影响,如果该规则在设立之初就存在着实质上的不平等,很难说该种投资规则是一种国际公平治理下形成的标志和"良法之治"的理想选择。

第四节　多边投资规则的总体发展趋势

21世纪的投资变化标志着二战后国际投资规则制定历程第三个阶段的到来。第一阶段以南北国家之间的矛盾为核心,各自寻找自己的制定场所。第二阶段是各国达成一些普遍共识,赞成为保护国际投资构建一个普遍性协定体系。第三阶段是各国观点更加多样化,有可能在某些核心的问题上达成共识,但在其他一些外缘性问题上存在分歧。

一、制定场所多样

考虑到国际直接投资对经济的不可替代性以及其与贸易的交互关系,各国均认识到制定多边投资规则的必要性,但场所的选择问题依旧成为一个主要问题。

(一)WTO

基于WTO已经取得的成就,对TRIPs协定、GATS、TRIMs协定进行系统化和纵深化扩展,可以形成一个对各国均有拘束力、争端解决法律化和具有投资贸易互补性的法律体系。WTO是一个普遍性的国际组织,能够提供发达国家和发展中国家共同参与制定的机会,达成的协定能一步到位地普遍适用,而且有WTO成员方的集体压力、审查监督机制以及争端解决机制保障WTO内多边投资协定顺利实施。③ 当然,是直接取消掉

---

① Drabek Z., *A Multilateral Agreement on Investment—Convincing the Skeptics*, WTO Staff Working Paper, 1998, p.5.

② WTO, *Report of the Working Group on the Relationship between Trade and Investment to the General Council*, WT/WGTI/4, 2000.

③ 刘笋:《从多边投资协定草案看国际投资多边法制的走向》,载《比较法研究》2003年第2期。

"与贸易有关"这样一个前缀,还是重新整合一套具有普遍性的投资规则,甚至对 WTO 进行改革,形成一个"世界贸易投资组织",学者们存在分歧。① 当前多哈回合仍处于僵局,不知能否顺利完成这一回合的谈判,因此 WTO 框架内完善的投资规则能否成功,仍有很大变数。

(二)泛太平洋伙伴关系

多哈回合僵局使各国重新寻找谈判场所(regime shifting)。最引人瞩目的是美国曾主导的 TPP (Trans-Pacific Partnership,即泛太平洋伙伴关系)协定。该协定突破了地缘性和南北阵营的划分,包括了日本、韩国、马来西亚、印尼、越南、菲律宾等国家和中国台湾地区。在内容上表现为"WTO 递增"(WTO-plus)的趋势。美国众议院筹款委员会主席里文指出,TPP 的设想是形成整合以及放大自由贸易协定的统一协定。在投资方面,TPP 给予投资者更高的保护要求以及包含更为宽泛的投资议题,②但 TPP 谈判因秘密性和未邀请我国参与谈判而饱受诟病。美国退出后,其他 11 个亚太国家继续谈判,于 2018 年 3 月 8 日在智利首都圣地亚哥签署《全面与进步跨太平洋伙伴关系协定》(Comprehensive and Progressive Agreement for Trans-Pacific Partnership,简称 CPTPP)。中国在 2020 年 12 月 16 日至 18 日召开的中央经济工作会议提出,中国要积极考虑加入 CPTPP。③

(三)OECD

OECD 成员国仍然占据着国际资本流动的主导地位,OECD 仍然具有成为多边投资议题主要谈判场所的可能。OECD 自成立以来,长期致力于处理国际投资问题,在多边投资规则制定方面有丰富的经验,而且成员国在劳工、环保等领域的分歧较小,更容易在价值观上产生集体认同。④ 当前制定场所选择并不像南北斗争范式下各自寻找合适的立法场所,而是在南北外资政策逐步趋同的过程中寻找共同的、议价能力相当的制定场所。如果 OECD 能够在发展中国家和发达国家之间不持立场或者兼顾双方的利益,未尝不是一个合适的多边投资规则制定场所。

---

① 参见金成华:《国际投资立法发展现状与展望》,中国法制出版社 2009 年版,第 272 页;刘笋、李国赓:《关于"与贸易有关的问题"及 WTO 调整范围的若干思考》,载《法商研究》2003 年第 5 期;盛斌:《国际投资协定:多边安排是唯一的途径吗?》,载《南开经济研究》2003 年第 3 期。

② Levin, TPP Could Serve to Alter Existing FTAs on Environment and Investment, http://insidetrade. com/200912152308746/WTO-Daily-News/Daily-News/levin-tpp-could-serve-to-alter-existing-ftas-on-environment-investment/menu-id-948.html, last visited on 20 Dec. 2022.

③ 中国新闻网:《已签署 RCEP 的中国为何还积极考虑 CPTPP?》,2020 年 12 月 18 日发布,https://baijiahao.baidu.com/s? id=1686428575460315908&wfr=spider&for=pc,最后访问日期:2022 年 12 月 20 日。

④ Wesley Scholz, International Regulation of Foreign Direct Investment, *Cornell International Law Journal*,1998,Vol.31,No.3,pp.485-491.

二、谈判范围广泛

发展中国家与发达国家在普遍性投资规则方面长达数十年的斗争充分体现了双方在实体规则方面利益难以调和。随着区域性投资规则的不断建立，南北国家逐渐在较高的保护标准上形成一些共识，但随着经济一体化与贸易投资同向自由化发展，越来越多的问题不是投资本身的问题，而是贸易、知识产权、产业政策、劳工、人员流动、环境保护、政府采购以及其他事务不断与投资相互融合。[①] 当前国际投资规则制定的矛盾不是国际投资协定体系的核心非一致性，而是外缘性差异正在扩大，也就是，尽管对投资保护的关键要素已经达成相当程度的共识，但在涉及国际投资协定的其他事务方面依然存在重大分歧。发展中国家对温室气体排放、能源利用率等提出较严苛要求，环境问题甚至成为"绿色保护主义"的工具，直接或者间接地对投资产生了消极影响。例如，在公用设施领域，发展中国家已经不单纯地追求资本和专有技术（know-how），对环境友好的作业提出了更高的要求，直接影响到跨国公司的投资信心。一国对产品的环境影响提出更高要求，会间接影响到投资者在另一国的投资，因为另一国即东道国是该国的重要贸易伙伴，极有可能在贸易领域面临更大的风险成本。[②]

三、谈判内容细致

在晚近投资协定谈判中，传统的投资规则日渐细化，主要表现在以下主要方面。

（一）国民待遇适用范围扩大

以日本、韩国和美国 BIT 范本（2012）、NAFTA 和 MERCOSUR 为代表的双边协定和区域投资协定都将投资者的国民待遇扩展至准入或设业前（pre-establishment）。[③] 该种投资规则要求东道国通过否定式清单的方式允许投资和投资者在进入相关市场之前就享有不低于东道国国民的待遇。否定清单模式意味着缔约方几乎全面开放未来的投

---

① Rafael Leal-Arcas，The Multilateralization of International Investment Law，*North Carolina Journal of International Law*，2009，Vol.35，Iss.1，pp.33-135.

② 这种情况在政府采购领域的体现更明显。政府采购作为重要的政策执行工具，对环境、中小企业、本国自主创新激励方面有着无可替代的重要作用，发达国家的有些企业的产品流向最终是发展中国家的政府采购。See UN News Center，Countries Agree to Extend Negotiations on Rio＋20 Outcome Document，5 May 2012，http://www.un.org/apps/news/story.asp? NewsID＝41933&Cr＝sustainable #.UNBwA5upYds，last visited on 18 Dec. 2022；OECD，Harnessing Freedom of Investment for Green Growth，5 May 2011，http://www.oecd.org/investment/ internationalinvestmentagreements/47721398. pdf，last visited on 18 Dec. 2022.

③ 在设业后，国民待遇的对象仅包含已经根据东道国法设立的投资而不包括投资者。Andrew Newcombe，Lluis Paradell，*Law and Practice of Investment Treaties—Standards of Treatment*，Wolters Kluwer Press，2009，p.159.

资监管体制,包括缔约时国内尚不存在的产业。有学者指出,"准入前国民待遇对一个国家外资监管权的真正挑战不在于放开投资准入权,而在于高水平的透明度要求。这种要求既体现在按照规定的格式提供所有不符措施的详细信息,也体现在实施这些措施时要保持高度透明的环境,它远远超出了一般国际协定中信息披露的要求,也超出了 WTO 对透明度的要求"[①]。在第五次中美战略经济对话和 TPP 成员的谈判过程中,此问题均被作为重点谈判领域并取得一定成果。

(二)东道国的业绩要求受到限制

东道国的业绩要求(performance requirements),即东道国为实现各种经济与社会目标而施加给投资者或其投资的各种要求。例如当地劳动力的雇用水平、优先购买当地产品、在外商企业与本土企业竞争中的当地保护和外币兑换限制等要求。该要求曾在 20 世纪 70 年代的发展中国家盛极一时。[②] 投资领域中的业绩要求对当地经济资源配置优化的阻碍已经深深地影响到了贸易。WTO 体系下 TRIMs 协定和 GATS 均对此禁止,认为其违反了国民待遇和一般取消数量限制的 WTO 义务。印度尼西亚案和欧共体香蕉案的专家组报告均表明,有条件地使用当地产品、将关税优惠和税收刺激与当地成分要求相联系的措施,均不符合 TRIMs 协定。[③]

(三)国有企业问题日趋突出

相关资料显示,中美在投资协定谈判中,对国有企业的法律地位进行了激烈磋商。美国 2012 年 BIT 范本第 2 条第 2 项明确规定,国有企业或者其他人在行使管理性、行政性或其他政府权力时,应当遵守第一部分的义务。[④] 换言之,如果国有企业在行业内的任何行为被视为代表政府颁布立法、指令或者其他行使政府权力的行为,其行为将被视为政府行为。我国一旦在该问题上让步,不但将使国家违约行为的概率大增,而且会导致国有企业海外投资具有"政治色彩",因为投资协定仅仅保护私人直接投资而将国家投资排除在外,我国多数海外投资极有可能不被投资规则所保护。

---

① 赵玉敏:《国际投资体系中的准入前国民待遇——从日韩投资国民待遇看国际投资规则的发展趋势》,载《国际贸易》2012 年第 3 期。

② UNCTAD, *Foreign Direct Investment and Performance Requirement—New Evidence Form Selected Countries*, UNCTAD/ITE/IIA/2003/7.

③ See WTO Panel Reports:WT/DS44/R, WT/DS27, WT/DS139, WT/DS142.

④ 原文是:A Party's obligations under Section A shall apply: (a) to a state enterprise or other person when it exercises any regulatory, administrative, or other governmental authority delegated to it by that Party; and (b) to the political subdivisions of that Party.

本章小结

　　19 世纪以来,国际投资不同发展阶段对多边投资规则产生了不同的需求,在地缘政治、国际矛盾和经济发展需求多重因素的影响下产生了不同类型与特色的多边投资规则。在当代国际投资力量多极化背景下,产生了文本形式与贸易综合、内容逐步丰富、区域性与世界性并存的多边投资规则。但无论是区域性还是普遍性、特殊性还是一般性的多边投资规则,均有其自身的无可替代的优点与难以克服的缺点。多边投资规则的总体发展趋势是制定场所多样、范围涵盖广泛、内容细致。

第二章

中国当代国际投资的发展及其
对多边投资规则的需求

中国是当代国际投资的主要国家,近年来的外国直接投资和对外直接投资均居世界各国前列、在发展中国家居首位,已经成为资本输入大国和资本输出大国;但不断增长的国际投资面临诸多法律问题,其中之一是:国内法和双边投资条约的缺陷导致对不同类型多边投资规则的需求,如何实现在多边规则的层面上对我国国际投资的规制,促进中国投资自由化,充分保护中国海外投资。

第一节   中国当代国际投资的现状与发展趋势

中国国际投资由中国境内的外国(商)投资和中国对其他国家或地区的对外投资两部分有机构成。对中国国际投资的现状与发展趋势分析,需从这两方面进行。

一、中国外国投资现状与发展趋势

自改革开放以来,我国先后采取了一系列法律、法规和政策措施,大力吸引外国投资,中国境内外商投资额逐年增长,目前已经成为全球外国直接投资的主要目的地之一。

(一)中国是最大东道国之一

联合国贸易与发展会议《2012年世界投资报告》指出,中国2011年吸引外国直接投资再创历史新高,达到1240亿美元。在总量增加的同时,中国吸引外国直接投资(FDI)

的结构开始呈现出新现象,进入服务业的 FDI 首次超过了制造业。[①]

联合国贸易与发展会议 2013 年 1 月 23 日在日内瓦总部发布的《全球投资趋势监测》报告指出,2012 年全球外国直接投资流入量下降了 18%,中国吸收外国直接投资小幅下降 3.4%,但仍是外商投资的主要目的地国。[②]

根据《2012 年世界投资报告》,2012—2014 年跨国公司最具投资前景的 10 个东道经济体中,中国仍然位居榜首。[③] 换言之,未来中国仍然是跨国公司投资的首选地。中国 2011 年 FDI 流入量增长 8%,达到 1240 亿美元,世界排名第二,仅次于美国(2269 亿美元)。[④] 截至 2011 年年底,中国 FDI 流入存量约为 7120 亿美元。[⑤]

又据《2020 年世界投资报告》,中国 FDI 流入量 2018 年、2019 年分别为 1380 亿美元、1410 亿美元,均仅次于美国(分别为 2540 亿美元、2460 亿美元),均居世界第二。[⑥] 截至 2019 年年底,中国 FDI 流入存量为 17894.86 亿美元,[⑦]居世界第三。

据中国商务部外资司统计数据,2020 年 1—8 月,全国实际使用外资 6197.8 亿元人民币,同比增长 2.6%(折合 890 亿美元,同比下降 0.3%;不含银行、证券、保险领域)。8 月当月,全国实际使用外资 841.3 亿元人民币,同比增长 18.7%(折合 120.3 亿美元,同比增长 15%)。[⑧]

(二)中国吸收外资已经处于成熟期

中国吸引外资进入了成熟阶段,吸引的外资将很难重现过去经济起飞阶段的高速增长。中国吸引外资将更多地从数量增长转向质量和结构的提升与优化。高附加值、高技术含量的外国投资以及高端制造业和服务业吸引的外资比重将进一步上升。

(三)中国需对外资进行监管和鼓励

外资对我国经济与社会发展具有双重作用,即促进作用和经济控制作用。这需要中国对外资采取监管和鼓励并重的投资措施。但世界投资理论与实践的发展对东道国的

---

① 联合国贸易与发展会议:《2012 年世界投资报告》(中文版),http://www.unctad-docs.org/files/UNCTAD-WIR2012-Overview-en.pdf,最后访问日期:2013 年 7 月 25 日。

② 商务部:《联合国贸发会议报告:中国吸引外资能力不减》,http://tjtb.mofcom.gov.cn/article/y/ab/201301/ 20130100012028.shtml,最后访问日期:2013 年 7 月 19 日。

③ 联合国贸易与发展会议:《2012 年世界投资报告》(中文版),第 5 页。

④ 商务部、国家统计局、国家外汇管理局:《2011 年度中国对外直接投资统计公报》,http://finance.jrj.com.cn/2012/08/30165814315468.shtml,最后访问日期:2022 年 5 月 14 日。

⑤ 商务部:《〈2012 年世界投资报告〉解读》,http://www.mofcom.gov.cn/article/difang/anhui/201210/20121008397996.shtml,最后访问日期:2013 年 7 月 25 日。

⑥ UNCTAD,World Investment Report 2020,June 2020,p.12.

⑦ UNCTAD,World Investment Report 2020,June 2020,p.243.

⑧ 《商务部外资司负责人介绍 2020 年 1—8 月全国吸收外资情况》,2020 年 9 月 21 日发布,http://www.mofcom.gov.cn/article/tongjiziliao/v/202009/20200903003821.shtml,最后访问日期:2020 年 10 月 25 日。

要求越来越高,对外国投资的保护标准不断加强,这使我国作为东道国在利用外资过程中产生了一系列法律问题,例如国家主权、环境保护、劳工保护等问题越来越凸显,对我国提出了更大的挑战。

在当前国际经济形势持续不明朗,金融市场动荡以及缓慢发展的背景下,需继续将鼓励外国投资作为我国促进经济增长和发展的手段,并强化对外国投资的监管。

二、中国对外直接投资现状与发展趋势

我国规模性对外直接投资始于 20 世纪 70 年代末,此后每年额度呈上升趋势且近年来迅速增长。虽然在不同年代或不同时间段,与世界对外投资大国诸如美国、日本等相比,差距较大,但近年来,中国已经成为对外直接投资大国。

(一)对外投资现状

以下是中国近 10 多年来几个重要年份对外投资发展基本情况:

2007 年,中国对外直接投资净额 265.1 亿美元,较上年增长 25.3%。其中,新增股本投资 86.9 亿美元,占 32.8%;当期利润再投资 97.9 亿美元,占 36.9%;其他投资 80.3 亿美元,占 30.3%。[①]

2009 年中国对外直接投资额为 565.3 亿美元,较上年增长 1.1%。其中,新增股本投资 172.5 亿美元,占 30.5%;当期利润再投资 161.3 亿美元,占 28.5%;其他投资 231.5 亿美元,占 41%。截至 2009 年年底,中国 12000 家境内投资者在境外设立对外直接投资企业 1.3 万家,分布在全球 177 个国家(地区),对外直接投资累计净额 2457.3 亿美元,其中:股本投资 769.2 亿美元,占 31.3%;利润再投资 816.2 亿美元,占 33.2%;其他投资 872.1 亿美元,占 35.5%,年末境外企业资产总额超过 1 万亿美元。[②] 2009 年中国对外直接投资分别占全球当年流量、存量的 5.1% 和 1.3%,名列全球国家(地区)排名的第五位,发展中国家(地区)的首位。[③]

2010 年,中国对外直接投资净额 688.1 亿美元,较上年增长 21.7%。其中,新增股本投资 206.4 亿美元,占 30%;当期利润再投资 240.1 亿美元,占 34.9%;其他投资 241.6 亿美元,占 35.1%。中国 2010 年海外投资的规模居发展中国家首位,全球第五,并首次超过日本、英国等传统对外投资大国。[④] 截至 2010 年年底,中国对外直接投资累计净额达

① 商务部等:《2007 年度中国对外直接投资统计公报》,http://hzs.mofcom.gov.cn/article/date/200811/20081105895467.shtml,最后访问日期:2022 年 7 月 25 日。

② 商务部等:《2009 年度中国对外直接投资统计公报》,http://www.mofcom.gov.cn/article/zt_zhcjd/zcjdwz/201009/20100907121464.shtml,最后访问日期:2022 年 7 月 25 日。

③ 商务部等:《2009 年度中国对外直接投资统计公报》,http://images.mofcom.gov.cn/hzs/accessory/201009/1284339524515.pdf,最后访问日期:2022 年 5 月 8 日。

④ 商务部等:《2010 年度中国对外直接投资统计公报》,http://www.mofcom.gov.cn/article/tongjiziliao/dgzz/201208/20120808315019.shtml,最后访问日期:2022 年 7 月 25 日。

到 3172.1 亿美元,是 2002 年 299 亿美元的 10 倍多,境外企业资产总额超过 1.5 万亿美元。[①]

2011 年,中国对外直接投资净额为 746.5 亿美元,同比增长 8.5%。[②] 截至 2011 年年底,中国对外直接投资累计净额(存量)达 4247.8 亿美元,位居全球第 13 位,较上年末提升 4 位。[③] 但根据《2012 年世界投资报告》,2011 年中国 FDI 流出量减少 5%,为 651 亿美元,全球排名从 2010 年的第 6 位降到 2011 年的第 9 位,居于美国、日本、英国、法国、中国香港、比利时、瑞士和俄罗斯之后。这是 2003 年以来的首次下降。截至 2011 年年底中国外向 FDI 存量约为 3660 亿美元。[④]

2018 年、2019 年,中国 FDI 流出量分别为 1430 亿美元、1170 亿美元,分别居世界第二位、第四位;[⑤]截至 2019 年,中国 FDI 流出存量为 20994 亿美元,[⑥]居世界第三位。中国在全球外国直接投资中的影响力不断扩大,流量占全球比重连续四年超过一成,2019 年占 10.4%;存量占 6.4%,与 2018 年持平。[⑦]

2002—2019 年,中国对外直接投资年均增长速度为 26%,2013—2019 年累计流量 10110.3 亿美元,占对外直接投资存量规模 46%。[⑧] 存量突破 4000 亿美元,[⑨]但与发达国家仍有较大差距。根据《2020 年世界投资报告》数据,中国 2018 年流出量增幅较大,但 2019 年中国 FDI 流出量降幅较大。

为了促进我国对外投资,2013 年 2 月,国家发展和改革委员会宣布把资源、能源类的海外投资项目的国家核准限额从过去的 3000 万美元提高到 3 亿美元,大额用汇类的海外投资项目的国家核准限额从 1000 万美元提高到 1 亿美元。[⑩] 自此,上述项目以外的海外投资项目具有了较宽松的国内审核程序。

① 商务部等:《2010 年度中国对外直接投资统计公报》,http://china.ec.com.cn/article/cnhongguan/201109/1161101_1.html,最后访问日期:2022 年 7 月 25 日。
② 商务部等:《2011 年度中国对外直接投资统计公报》,http://www.mofcom.gov.cn/article/tongjiziliao/dgzz/201208/20120808315019.shtml,最后访问日期:2022 年 7 月 20 日。
③ 商务部等:《2011 年度中国对外直接投资统计公报》,http://finance.jrj.com.cn/2012/08/30165814315468.shtml,最后访问日期:2022 年 5 月 14 日。
④ 李红光:《全球外国直接投资 2012 年增速放缓》,http://intl.ce.cn/specials/zxgjzh/201207/06/t20120706_23466585.shtml,最后访问日期:2013 年 6 月 25 日。
⑤ UNCTAD, World Investment Report 2020, June 2020, p.15.
⑥ UNCTAD, World Investment Report 2020, June 2020, p.243.
⑦ 《商务部等部门联合发布〈2019 年度中国对外直接投资统计公报〉》,2020 年 9 月 16 日发布,http://www.mofcom.gov.cn/article/tongjiziliao/dgzz/202009/20200903001523.shtml,最后访问日期:2022 年 11 月 2 日。
⑧ 商务部、国家统计局、国家外汇管理局:《2019 年度中国对外直接投资统计公报》,第 8 页。
⑨ 商务部等:《2011 年度中国对外直接投资统计公报》,http://www.gov.cn/gzdt/2012-08/30/content2213920.htm,最后访问日期:2022 年 6 月 25 日。
⑩ 国家发展与改革委员会:《国家发展改革委副主任张晓强在 2011 年夏季达沃斯论坛开幕式后接受记者采访》,http://www.sdpc.gov.cn/xwzx/xwtt/t20110914_434026.htm,最后访问日期:2022 年 6 月 25 日。

以上事实和数据表明,中国一直注重大力发展海外投资,尽管不同年份流量有增有减,但总体呈上升趋势。

(二)中国对外投资发展趋势

近年来,中国对外投资额逐年上升,东道国由发达国家向发展中国家转移,投资主体中非国有企业增多,投资领域逐渐多样化。"十二五"期间,中国企业"走出去"的步伐进一步加快。

1.海外投资规模剧增,成为重要资本输出国

中国2011年FDI流出量降低5%,为651亿美元,世界排名第九;FDI流出存量约为3660亿美元。[①] 自2017年,中国经济发展速度放缓,对外直接投资增幅也放缓,2019年出现下降趋势(同比下降4.3%)。尽管如此,2019年中国FDI流出量和流出存量分别占全球当年流量、存量的10.4%和6.4%,流量位列全球第二位、存量列全球第三位。[②]

虽然中国对外贸易受全球政治经济波动的影响,但总体良好。数据显示,金融危机爆发至2009年,中国对外直接投资降至低谷,但在2010年全球经济止跌时快速回升,且对外直接投资额增长了1万亿美元以上。[③] 自此以后,中国各年对外直接投资流量和存量总体上不断增长。

随着国际投资环境的变好,中国企业已成为国际投资市场上的一支重要力量。据官方统计,2011年上半年,我国境内投资者共对全球117个国家和地区的2169家境外企业进行了直接投资,累计实现非金融类对外直接投资239亿美元,同比增长34%;[④]截至2019年年底,中国2.75万家境内投资者在国(境)外共设立对外直接投资企业4.4万家,分布全球188个国家(地区),年末境外企业资产总额7.2万亿美元,对外直接投资存量21988.8亿美元。[⑤]

2.投资区域由发展中国家转向发展中国家与发达国家并重

中国对外投资区域在不同时期具有不同重点,先后经历了重点向发达国家投资、重点向发展中国家投资、发展中国家与发达国家并重的不同发展阶段,目前为发展中国家与发达国家并重阶段。

中国在对外投资初期阶段,主要投向发达国家和地区。2011—2016年,投资对象有了一些新的变化,主要投向发展中国家。除了对美国的投资有了显著的提升外,FDI总体流向了东亚、东南亚、拉美和非洲,东亚和东南亚增长了30%,拉美增长了14%。中国

① 商务部:《〈2012年世界投资报告〉解读》,http://www.mofcom.gov.cn/article/difang/anhui/201210/20121008397996.html,最后访问日期:2022年6月20日。
② 商务部、国家统计局、国家外汇管理局:《2019年度中国对外直接投资统计公报》,第4页。
③ 《中国对外投资新趋势》,http://fec.mofcom.gov.cn/article/zljy/zjsj/201109/1250827_1.html,最后访问日期:2022年6月25日。
④ 商务部合作司:《2011年上半年我国对外直接投资简明统计》,http://www.mofcom.gov.cn/aarticle/tongjiziliao/dgzz/201107/20110707661512.html,最后访问日期:2013年6月20日。
⑤ 商务部、国家统计局、国家外汇管理局:《2019年度中国对外直接投资统计公报》,第4页。

国际贸易促进委员会《2011年度中国企业"走出去"发展报告》显示,非洲成为吸引中国投资的新热点。① 这段时期,中国对外直接投资向发展中国家转移,除了国内经济政策的引导和优惠政策的原因外,主要是美国经济危机和欧洲债务危机所致,后者市场逐渐萎缩,使得中国投资者不得不将目光转向发展中国家。自2017年,对外投资向发展中国家和发达国家(地区)投资并重转变。以2019年海外并购为例,中国企业对外投资并购十大目的地分别为:荷兰、德国、英属维尔京群岛、法国、巴西、中国香港、开曼群岛、英国、秘鲁、新加坡。②

3.投资领域、方式、主体多元化

中国实施"走出去"战略已有多年,积极发展对外投资已经成为中国利用国际资源的重要途径。但是由于政策引导以及经济实力等因素,以前的对外投资主要侧重于资源领域。

《2011年度中国企业"走出去"发展报告》显示,中国企业对外投资涉及的产业门类多样,其中投资最多的是制造业,在发达国家和发展中国家的投资比例分别达78%和71%。③ 国际直接投资由资源领域转向产业领域,尤其是制造和基础设施领域。这正是处于深度工业化时期的中国的优势所在。

投资领域不断拓宽,以能源、矿产资源为主,电子信息、工业制造、金融、物流等行业和交通基础设施的投资快速增长。通过海外投资拥有的油气、铁和铜等重要矿产权益资源量和产量已具有一定规模。

在国有企业保持对外投资主导地位的同时,民营企业的境外投资比重逐步提高,投资主体多元化。

投资方式更加多样,除新建型投资外,大量出现并购、参股、交叉换股以及投资基金等方式。投资方式多元化主要表现为海外并购和对外工程承包等。以2010年为例,据商务部统计,2010年中国以收购方式实现的直接投资238亿美元,占投资总额的40.3%,收购领域主要涉及采矿业、制造业、电力生产和供应业、专业技术服务业等。④ 主要项目有中石化集团(通过香港公司)71.39亿美元收购雷普索尔公司巴西公司40%股权,中石油集团联合壳牌能源公司以23.71亿美元共同收购澳大利亚Arrow能源有限公司,浙江吉利控股集团公司17.88亿美元收购瑞典沃尔沃轿车公司100%股权,国家电网公司9.89亿美元收购巴西7家输电公司及输电资产30年经营特许权项目等。⑤ 对外工程承包是

---

① 《中国对外投资新趋势》,http://fec.mofcom.gov.cn/article/zlyj/zjsj/201109/1250827_1.html,最后访问日期:2022年6月25日。

② 商务部、国家统计局、国家外汇管理局:《2019年度中国对外直接投资统计公报》,第10页。

③ 《中国对外投资新趋势》,http://fec.mofcom.gov.cn/article/zlyj/zjsj/201109/1250827_1.html,最后访问日期:2022年6月25日。

④ 商务部:《2010年中国海外收购占投资总额40.3%》,http://zcq.mofcom.gov.cn/article/zcqxwdt/201101/1185854_1.html,最后访问日期:2022年6月23日。

⑤ 商务部:《2010年中国海外收购占投资总额40.3%》,http://www.chinanews.com/cj/2011/01-18/2794295.shtml,最后访问日期:2022年6月1日。

中国的主要竞争优势,近年来都以30％左右的速度在增长。例如,2010年中国对外承包工程稳步发展,全年完成营业额922亿美元,同比增长18.7％;新签合同额1344亿美元,同比增长6.5％。有人认为,对中国承包商,这些都是好消息:一方面表明对外承包项目的机会增加,另一方面承包商还可以BOT(build-operate-transfer)的方式做投资人,进一步促进了投资方式多元化。①

4.投资效果良好

中国的对外投资,使企业得到了锻炼,培养了海外经营人才,积累了海外投资经验,提升了国际化经营水平。与此同时,投资所在国的资源优势正转化为经济优势,实现了经济发展,税收增加,就业增加。据统计,截至2010年年底,境外中资企业就业人数约110万,其中为当地创造了近80万人的就业机会;②2019年年末,中国境外企业从业人员总数374.4万人,其中外方员工226.6万人,占60.5％,较2018年末增加38.9万人。③ 一些企业还为当地居民无偿提供医疗设备及服务,捐助当地教育,免费供水供电等,积极履行社会责任,实现了互利共赢、共同发展。④

第二节　中国国际投资发展对多边投资规则的需求

全球经济自由化程度不断提高,使消除投资障碍和加强投资保护的愿望日趋强烈。随着投资自由化与贸易自由化相互依托、相互协调趋势的不断扩大,高标准的贸易自由化规则需要投资自由化规则与之相配合。但国际投资领域一直缺乏一套为发达国家和发展中国家一致认可的、调整国际投资关系的综合性多边投资规则,这与国际投资的迅速发展不相适应。为进一步推进投资自由化和回应经济全球化的要求,为跨国投资者创造更有利的投资环境,加强国际投资的全球性多边规则制定是必然趋势。

国际投资发展必然会对国际投资法制提出更高的要求,因为普遍性投资实体规则的缺乏对资本输入国、资本输出国和国际投资者都不利,该类规则的缺失会增加投资成本和风险。⑤

我国不断增长的国际投资,要求能够拥有一个公平的、能为我国的外国投资和对外投资带来更安全、更可靠的市场的多边投资规则。在对外投资方面,要从根本上解决中

① 《我国对外承包工程营业额达＄922亿规模不断扩大》,http://intl.ce.cn/specials/zxxx/201105/11/t20110511_22413323.shtml,最后访问日期:2022年6月1日。

② 国家发改委:《2011年前三季度非金融类对外投资约410亿美元》,http://finance.people.com.cn/GB/16254175.html,最后访问日期:2022年6月25日。

③ 商务部、国家统计局、国家外汇管理局:《2019年度中国对外直接投资统计公报》,第5页。

④ 《发改委副主任张晓强:中国对外投资水平不断提升》,http://www.chinanews.com/ga/2011/11-15/3462490.shtml,最后访问日期:2022年6月1日。

⑤ 刘笋:《从多边投资协定草案看国际投资多边法制的走向》,载《比较法研究》2003年第2期。

国企业开展海外投资的不利影响,无不需要政府在政策、管理服务体系和国际性规则上进一步完善和创新。为给中国企业海外投资营造更加安全的环境,应继续推进双、多边的投资保护协定、税收协定以及在建自由贸易区(FTA)中有关"投资协定"的谈判与签署工作进程。[①]

中国对多边投资规则的需求,基于以下多边投资规则的优势。

一、完善中国国际投资法律环境

多边投资规则能进一步完善中国国际投资法律环境,增强外国投资者信心,继而进一步吸引外国直接投资,加强我国海外投资者的法律保护和管理,促进海外投资发展,维护国家海外利益。

二、克服双边投资条约的缺陷

多边投资规则可以降低签署双边投资条约的成本。据统计,截至 2020 年 12 月,中国已经缔结的双边投资条约达 145 项[②],但中国多数 BIT 文本谈判是以美国等发达国家 BIT 范本为基础,在谈判中往往无法体现中国作为资本输出大国和资本输入大国双重身份的利益考量,且这些国家 BIT 范本对投资保护的标准很高。

与多边投资规则相比,双边投资协定有较大劣势,主要者如下。

(一)涉及范围有限

各国双边投资条约虽然存在着一些差别,但基本原则和核心内容大体相同,主要包括:适用范围,投资促进措施,投资待遇标准即最惠国待遇、国民待遇、公平公正待遇等,征用、战乱赔偿,利润转移,争议处理等,对投资者特别是跨国公司的行为准则和责任问题基本不涉及,也回避市场准入和所有权控制问题。其主要功能是保护投资,为投资提供便利条件,而不是促进投资自由化。

(二)保障性差

双边投资条约虽设立了一些争端解决机制,但它远不如多边机构更有保障。第一次世界大战以前的国际贸易秩序主要就是由双边条约加以保障的,但很快就土崩瓦解了,二战后建立的多边贸易体系才使国际贸易按约定秩序顺利发展,这充分说明多边机制的重要性。

---

① 周升起:《中国对外直接投资:现状、趋势与政策》,载《东亚论文》2009 年第 75 期。

② 其中已终止 16 项,未生效 20 项。https://investmentpolicy.unctad.org/international-investment-agreements/countries/42/china,最后访问日期:2022 年 12 月 25 日。

(三)制定成本高

双边投资条约在两国之间谈判、缔结、实施的成本很高,有许多是重复劳动;而一般的多边投资条约,特别在很多国家间达成的多边条约,可以替代成百上千个双边投资条约。

(四)谈判地位不对等

当发达国家与发展中国家谈判双边投资条约时,发展中国家容易处于弱势的谈判地位,即出现谈判力的不对等,一些重要条款对包括我国在内的发展中国家不利。①

三、克服区域性投资规则的缺陷

2011 年各国共签署国际投资协定 47 项,其中双边投资协定 33 项,其他协定 14 项。② 截至 2011 年年底,国际投资协定共计 3164 项,其中双边投资协定 2833 项,其他国际投资协定 331 项。③ 截至 2020 年 12 月 24 日,全球共有国际投资协定 3293 项,其中双边投资条约 2901 项(2342 项有效),含投资条款的条约④ 392 项(321 项有效)。2020 年新签署各种投资条约 6 项。⑤

当前,签署传统的双边投资协定缺乏动力,主要原因如下:(1)逐步转向区域性协定的制定;(2)国际投资协定愈发饱受争议并具有政治敏锐性。

从上述数据可以看出,虽然双边投资条约仍占主导地位,但从国际经济政治角度看,随着区域主义发展,区域投资协定的重要性将更加突出。

区域政治经济重要性的不断增强,必然需要制定区域投资协定。目前专门的区域投资协定主要有《非洲大湖国家经济共同体投资法典》(1982 年)、《南部非洲发展共同体投资议定书》(2006 年)、《东部与南部非洲共同市场投资协定》(2007 年)、《东非共同市场投资协定》(2007 年)、《西非国家经济共同体关于投资的补充法案》(2008 年)、《中美洲共同市场投资与服务贸易协定》(2009 年)、《东盟全面投资协定》(2009 年)、《南方共同市场内部促进与便利投资的议定书》(2017 年)等。包含"投资"章节的区域经贸协定有《能源宪章条约》(1994 年,第Ⅲ部分"投资")、《欧洲自由贸易联盟公约》(2001 年,第Ⅸ章)、《南部非洲海关同盟—欧洲自由贸易联盟自由贸易协定》(2006 年,第 4 章"服务、投资与政府采

---

① 卢进勇等主编:《国际投资条约与协定新论》,人民出版社 2007 年版,第 217 页。

② 联合国贸易与发展会议:《2012 年世界投资报告》(中文版),第 18 页。

③ 联合国贸易与发展会议:《2012 年世界投资报告》(中文版),第 18 页。

④ 包括含投资条款的自由贸易协定、经济伙伴关系协定和区域贸易协定等。

⑤ 分别为 Singapore-United Kingdom FTA(2020-12-10)、RCEP(2020-11-15)、Fiji-United States of America TIFA(2020-10-15)、Hungary-Kyrgyzstan BIT(2020-9-29)、Brazil-India BIT(2020-1-25)、Japan-Morocco BIT(2020-1-8)。UNCTAD, International Investment Agreements Navigator,https://investmentpolicy.unctad.org/international-investment-agreements,last visited on 24 Dec.2022.

购"）、《中欧自由贸易协定》（2006 年，第 B 部分"投资"）、《东盟澳大利亚新西兰自由贸易协定》（2009 年，第 14 章"投资"）、《欧盟及其成员国—南部非洲发展共同体经济伙伴关系国家经济伙伴关系协定》（2016 年，第Ⅸ章"服务贸易与投资"）、《欧亚经济联盟条约》（2014 年，第 ⅩⅤ 节和附件 16）、《美国墨西哥加拿大协定》（2018 年，第 14 章"投资"）、《全面与进步跨太平洋伙伴关系协定》（CPTPP，2018 年，第 9 章"投资"）、《区域全面经济伙伴关系协定》（RCEP，2020 年，第 10 章）等。目前大西洋沿岸国家正在商谈超大型区域投资协定即《跨大西洋贸易与投资伙伴关系协定》（TTIP），欧盟、东盟等区域国际组织代表其成员谈判其他区域经贸投资协定。

有关国家通过全面探寻区域性国际经济活动中的贸易和投资元素，使宽泛的区域自由贸易（含投资）协定能较好地应对当今的区域经济现实，使区域性国际贸易与投资关联度日益提高。区域性协定能在一定程度上整合和统一区域投资规则，成为迈向多边主义的第一步，但新区域协定并没有淘汰旧条约。

区域化虽然增加多边协定层面，但并非导致区域协定简化和趋同，而是促使国际投资协定网络更加复杂以及倾向于重叠和不一致。当代国际投资法的一个趋势是要综合平衡政府行政和维护发达国家、发展中国家与投资者之间的利益。这种趋势要求将目光从传统的保护投资者利益转到环境、人权和可持续发展的方向上来。在此意义上，国际投资法制多边化推动的原因有许多。[①]

我国已经达成的区域性自由贸易（含投资）协定主要有 2009 年《中华人民共和国政府与东南亚国家联盟成员国政府全面经济合作框架协定内投资协定》（简称《中国—东盟投资协定》或 CAFTAI）、《中华人民共和国政府、日本国政府及大韩民国政府关于促进、便利和保护投资的协定》（简称《中日韩投资协定》）、《区域全面经济伙伴关系协定》（简称 RCEP）等。以 CAFTAI 为例，其主要内容和目的是：通过双方相互给予投资者国民待遇、最惠国待遇和投资公平公正待遇，提高投资相关法律法规的透明度，为双方投资者创造一个自由、便利、透明和公平的投资环境，并为双方投资者提供充分的法律保护，从而进一步促进双方投资便利化和逐步自由化。该协定是我国签署的第一个专门性区域投资协定，其意义重大，但在市场准入、国民待遇、投资便利化、保护外国投资者合法利益等方面均存在缺陷。

为适应我国区域发展战略，我国需要在现有区域投资协定的基础上进一步发展，制定和完善以我国为重要成员的多种区域多边投资规则。

四、普遍性投资规则制定的国际协作

普遍性投资规则谈判有助于各国（地区）在世界多边层次加强规范投资措施方面的

[①]　金学凌、赵红梅：《国际投资法制多边化发展趋势研究》，载《河南司法警官职业学院学报》2011 年第 9 卷第 1 期。

国际协调和合作。①

国际投资领域普遍性国际法律协调的缺位主要表现在：(1)国际投资领域一直缺少世界范围内的综合性多边投资规则或"游戏规则"(普遍性综合多边投资则)。过去30多年,世界FDI流量总体上显著增长,在一些年份远远超过了同期世界贸易和世界GDP的增长,已成为组织国际化生产和服务国际市场的重要方式。但是,与国际贸易和国际金融领域已经分别建立的以世界贸易组织为核心的国际贸易体制和以国际货币基金组织、世界银行为核心的国际货币金融体制相比,国际投资的国际性协调极为滞后,既没有一个统一协调的组织机构,也没有制定出类似货物贸易领域GATT和服务贸易领域GATS的协定。(2)尽管世界贸易组织中TRIMs协定、GATS和TRIPs协定的制定和实施,在某种程度上推动了国际投资领域国际协调的发展和国际规范的制定进程,但因其天生缺陷,没有从根本上解决诸如投资定义、投资待遇、投资促进与保护措施、政治风险及其范围等问题。

中国是发展中大国,促进本国经济发展是整个中国经济政策的核心目标之一,但对外资的过分依赖以及对外资监管的乏力,势必妨碍中国经济发展目标的实现,甚至有可能损害中国的根本利益。因此,中国需从规范外资和加强外资监管的角度来考虑中国在多边投资规则谈判中的利益和风险。

第三节　中国参与制定普遍性多边投资规则的理论与实践

尽管普遍性投资规则对促进和保护国际投资具有重要意义,但因其涉及各国根本利益,较难以成功制定综合性规则。目前有效的普遍性投资规则体现于世界银行主导下的有关公约和WTO框架下的有关协定。

一、中国参与普遍性多边投资规则的理论争议

有学者反对包括中国在内的发展中国家过快地参与多边投资规则,理由是:(1)在短期内,很难说流入主要发展中国家的FDI会因为它们是否加入多边投资框架而受到很大的影响。(2)多边投资框架所要求的义务显然超出了发展中国家当前的承受能力。发展中国家现阶段并不急需一个多边投资框架,但从长期需要考虑,建立多边投资框架可以采取渐进的态度,即选择通过FDI政策单边自由化,并辅以双边和区域协定来改善其投

---

① 卢进勇、杨立强:《多边投资框架谈判与中国》,载《国际商务(对外经济贸易大学学报)》2004年第5期。

资环境,逐步向一个全面的、具有法律约束力的多边投资框架迈进。[1]

有学者认为,中国亟须参与多边投资规则制定:"现存国际投资的制度安排缺乏一致性、连贯性和综合性,使从事跨国投资与国际化经营的企业仍面临形形色色的投资壁垒、歧视性待遇、政策法规的不确定性以及由此引发的各种矛盾,没有取得在全球范围内促进投资自由化的效果。因此,制定和推动具有全球性国际投资规范性质的制度就显得尤为迫切。"[2]

二、中国参与普遍性多边投资规则的实践

中国一直重视缔结和参与普遍性多边投资规则,先后参加了有关公约和协定。

(一)中国参加普遍国际投资规则

1.《华盛顿公约》

中国已于 1992 年 11 月 1 日正式成为该公约的成员国。在该公约中,发展中国家坚持四个"安全阀",有限地让渡国家主权,同意将部分投资者与东道国间的争端提交 ICSID 解决。这四个"安全阀"是用尽当地救济、逐案审批同意、东道国国内法为准据法之一,以及国家主权与安全。但自 20 世纪 80 年代末开始,发展中国家对投资者与东道国争端解决机制的态度发生了巨大变化,背离了过去的"卡尔沃主义",也逐步放弃了上述四大安全阀。发展中国家认为,接受发达国家高标准的 BIT 是改善国内投资环境的主要手段之一,为了吸引外资发展本国经济,不顾后果地竞相与发达国家签订 BIT。[3]

2.MIGA 公约

中国于 1988 年 4 月 30 日向世界银行递交了对该公约的核准书,从而成为多边投资担保机构的创始会员国。

3.GATS

WTO 首次将服务贸易纳入多边调整的范围。WTO 包含两个与投资直接相关的主要协定:《与贸易有关的投资措施协定》(TRIMs 协定)和《服务贸易总协定》(GATS)。[4]

按照 GATS 规定,其调整的范围主要包括:跨境消费、跨境支付、商业存在以及自然人流动等四个方面,其中商业存在直接涉及对有关服务领域的投资问题。WTO 对服务贸易仍是以促进服务贸易自由化为目标,但在实施方式上采取了逐步推进的方法,即允许各国根据自身情况,对服务贸易的开放范围、开放程度以具体承诺的方式作出选择。

---

[1]　冼国明、方友林:《发展中国家加入多边投资框架的利弊及当前的抉择》,载《世界经济与政治》2004 年第 1 期。

[2]　綦建红、陈东:《关于多边投资框架的经济学分析》,载《学习与探索》2005 年第 3 期。

[3]　陈辉萍:《美国投资者与东道国争端解决机制的晚近发展及其对发展中国家的启示》,载《国际经济法学刊》2007 年第 14 卷第 3 期。

[4]　Benno Ferrarini, *A Multilateral Framework for Investment*: *Research Fellow*, World Trade Institute, University of Bern, http://www.wti.org/, last visited on 7 May 2013.

GATS 的规则依次分为两个部分。一般性义务要求各成员遵守最惠国待遇和透明度原则,每一成员对任何其他成员的服务和服务提供者的待遇,应立即和无条件地给予不低于其给予任何其他国家同类服务和服务提供者的待遇;各成员应对有关措施迅速加以公布,并至少每年向服务贸易理事会通知对有关服务贸易有重大影响的任何新的法律、法规、行政准则或现有法律法规、行政准则的任何变更。GATS 的达成对在透明和逐步实现自由化的条件下不断促进服务贸易的扩大具有巨大作用。GATS 在推进服务贸易的同时,必然会促进国际投资的发展,其对国际服务贸易所作出的一系列规定,无疑成为规范国际投资的重要依据。

4.TRIMs 协定

乌拉圭回合谈判开始后,美国为了适应国内跨国公司向外扩张的需要,提出有必要将投资措施纳入新的议题,特别是外国直接投资适用关贸总协定国民待遇和最惠国待遇原则的可行性,这对发达国家跨国公司进入东道国特别是一些对外国直接投资实行干预政策的发展中国家的国内市场,在全球范围内进行价格制定和转移,实行全球采购、生产和销售是非常有利的。这一提议得到了一些发达国家的支持。

最初,发展中国家担心 TRIMs 协定的签订,将使外国公司与本国公司在投资建厂和经营时享有同样的权利,从而使发展中国家丧失其部分国家经济主权,使国家利益被超国家的 WTO 规则所损害,因此反对将投资措施纳入议程,但发展中国家在关税与贸易总协定谈判中的作用十分有限。很久以来,由于限制性的配额体系——《多种纤维协定》的存在,占发展中国家出口很大份额的纺织品和服装被排除在关税与贸易总协定的体系之外,一直是受到歧视的;对发展中国家至关重要的农业没有被纳入谈判议程。为了换取发达国家对农业和纺织品贸易谈判的支持,发展中国家最终同意将投资措施纳入议程并签订了 TRIMs 协定。但是直到乌拉圭回合结束,发达国家在农业问题上还只是作出了很小的让步,对纺织品和服装协定的实施也采取了延迟的态度,这对发展中国家显然是不公平的。为了接受 TRIMs 协定,发展中国家必须作出重大政策调整,但其努力没有得到应有的回报,即发展中国家在乌拉圭回合中没有获得应有的利益,发达国家和发展中国家在利益分配中处于严重的不均衡状态。于是发展中国家根据 TRIMs 协定第 5 条"通知与过渡安排"要求延长过渡期,继续享受特殊和差别待遇。

由上可见,TRIMs 协定虽然在建立普遍性国际投资协定方面取得了一定进展,但它仅对与货物贸易有关的方面构成约束,涵盖的范围有限,也未涉及激励性的投资措施,只是对会产生贸易扭曲的限制性投资措施加以规范,且在执行中还存在很多问题,就建立多边投资框架而言还远远不够,更不可能替代之,这就要求 WTO 进一步朝建立一个完整的多边投资框架的方向努力。

5.TRIPs 协定

TRIPs 协定是乌拉圭回合谈判的 21 个最后文件之一,于 1994 年 4 月 15 日由各国代表在摩洛哥的马拉喀什签字,并于 1995 年 1 月 1 日起生效。

在我国参加的上述国际投资条约中,没有一项是全面规范投资待遇、投资保护、政治风险、投资争议解决等所有有关国际投资的重要问题的综合性协定,无疑是国际投资法律保障体系的一个欠缺,与国际投资进一步全球化、自由化的要求不相符。

综观普遍性投资准入规则的制定,GATS、TRIMs 协定是国际投资准入自由化立法进程的开端,在消除与贸易有关的投资障碍、促进跨国投资方面迈出了一大步,但其没有全面取消扭曲贸易的投资措施。其他协定,如 TRIPs 协定等尽管与投资有关,但都只涉及了投资准入自由化某个方面的问题,或间接地涉及投资准入自由化。因此,美日欧等发达国家普遍对 WTO 现有的与投资有关的协定不满,认为只有制定一个全球性、综合性、具有普遍约束力的国际多边投资条约,才能符合当今全球经济化、国际投资自由化的趋势。

作为世贸组织成员,我国有义务将以后达成的任何有关投资准入的共同规则纳入国内法体系,反映在不断修订的外资法中。从以往的经验,可以确切地得知,多边投资协定的最终利益取向,取决于规则由谁来制定以及通过何种途径制定。为了使今后达成共识的普遍性投资规则更多地反映发展中国家的利益和要求,照顾到发展中国家在现阶段经济发展状况,现在我们能做的就是积极参与到国际多边投资规则的谈判和制定中,以维护我国和广大发展中国家的利益。[①]

(二)中国参与制定普遍性投资规则的经验教训

总结我国参加普遍性投资规则的实践,可以得出以下经验教训:

第一,普遍性投资规则大都由发达国家制定,再由发展中国家加入。发展中国家在其制定中力量薄弱,没有体现应有的话语权。

第二,普遍性投资规则总体上体现发达国家或者资本输出国利益而忽略发展中国家或东道国利益,使投资者与东道国之间的权利义务呈现严重失衡状态。

第三,发展中国家被动接受发达国家高标准的投资保护规则,使东道国面临重大风险,威胁到国家经济主权和安全,也损害东道国的公共健康、环境、劳工等重要社会价值。

第四,谈判经验的缺乏以及对投资规则研究不深入等问题使我国的谈判水平不高,谈判实力弱。

第四节　中国参与制定多边投资规则面临的主要法律问题

无论是东道国还是投资国,参与国际投资的目标是实现自身经济社会发展。基于此目标,东道国要求通过多边投资规则发挥外资的积极作用、减少外资的消极作用、发展东道国的经济,即最大限度地利用外资发展本国经济,并对外资进行规范管理;投资国要求

---

① 闫永红、梁洪杰:《外资准入自由化趋势下中国外资准入立法取向》,载《辽东学院学报》2006 年第 1 期。

通过多边投资规则,在符合东道国发展目标、遵守其法律的前提下,减少或降低海外投资各种风险、保障投资及其利益的安全,发挥对外投资在促进本国经济海外发展中的作用、维护国家海外利益。

中国目前是一个正在成长中的海外投资大国,未来的多边投资规则应为中国对外投资创造一个稳定、可靠和透明的环境,这将极大地便利中国企业的海外投资,并有效避免东道国或区域集团对中国企业的歧视。多边投资规则应降低中国海外企业向发展中国家和地区投资时的非商业风险,有力保护中国海外投资免受征收或国有化、外汇管制和其他政治风险的负面影响。

中国作为资本输出国,面临诸多法律问题,包括海外投资安全、海外投资保护、劳工权益保护等。本节仅重点研究以下三个主要问题。

一、东道国间接征收

中国正处于"发展转型期",对外投资会面临东道国间接征收问题。

传统上较少被关注的间接征收问题,日益成为东道国、外国投资者乃至资本输出国共同面临的重要风险,成为既继续体现南北矛盾又超越南北矛盾的复杂问题。

在此,以与中国有关的两个案件为例。第一,中石化与中石油诉厄瓜多尔案。2007年厄瓜多尔政府宣布对外国石油公司超出基准石油价格的额外收入征收税率高达99%的特别收益金。这种只针对外国石油企业征收石油特别收益金的歧视性做法相当于是对外国石油企业进行了征收。这些相当于征收的措施即构成间接征收。该事件中,中石化和中石油两家企业均在厄瓜多尔石油产业中占有重要利益。[①] 第二,中国平安集团诉比利时案。[②] 比利时政府对富通集团进行强制拆分,并将其购买的富通比利时银行的股份转让给巴黎银行。据比利时政府与巴黎银行所签订的转售协议,欧盟境内的个人投资者可以获得上述转售过程中的溢价款,而作为富通集团第一大股东的中国平安保险(集团)股份有限公司不能获得此项收益。在这一事件中,比利时政府的强制拆分和转售行

---

① 梁咏:《间接征收与中国海外投资利益保障——以厄瓜多尔征收 99% 石油特别收益金为视角》,载《甘肃政法学院学报》2009 年 9 月第 106 期。

② 基本案情:2007 年至 2008 年间,平安集团通过在公开市场收购富通集团(Fortis Group)价值 20 余亿欧元的股票,成为富通集团的单一最大股东。2008 年经济危机期间,富通集团下属银行业务出现严重的流动性风险,比利时、荷兰、卢森堡政府以"国家援助"为名,实施了增资、收购、担保、强制转让股权等一系列干预措施,将富通集团银行业务全部变卖,致使平安集团投资大幅缩水近 90%,但平安集团未获得相应补偿。2012 年 9 月,平安集团在多次与比利时当局沟通无效后,选择依据中国和比利时签订的双边投资协定,向 ICSID 提起仲裁。平安集团主张:比利时政府的行为损害了平安集团对比利时银行业稳定、透明和可预测的法律和商业环境的合理期待;比利时政府征收了平安集团大部分投资并从中不正当获利,且未进行合理赔偿,构成对平安集团的歧视等。由此向比政府提出 7.8 亿至 10 亿欧元左右的索赔主张。参见 King & Wood Mallesons:《中国投资者状告东道国政府——平安集团诉比利时政府投资仲裁案之启示》,18 June 2015,https://www.chinalawinsight.com/2015/06/articles/dispute-resolution/中国投资者状告东道国政府——平安集团诉比利时/,最后访问日期:2019 年 7 月 20 日。

为已经构成了对包括中国平安保险公司在内的富通集团投资者的间接征收,我国投资者的利益在此事件中受到严重损害。

二、对海外投资放松监管

(一)现行放宽规定

国务院 2004 年 7 月《关于投资体制改革的决定》进一步把对外投资项目从审批制向转向核准备案制。商务部 2009 年 5 月《境外投资管理办法》进一步放宽地方对外投资审批权限,并简化审批程序和审查内容,缩短并严格明确审批时间。例如,对 1000 万美元以下的非能源、资源类对外直接投资,商务部和省级商务主管部门的核准和审查时间由原来的 15—20 个工作日缩短至 3 个工作日,并且只需在商务部的"境外投资管理系统"中填写申请表即可,不需要提交额外的申请材料。再如,在企业境外投资所需外汇的使用上,2004 年的规定要求企业在申请材料中,提交外汇主管部门出具的境外投资外汇资金来源审查意见,新的办法中不仅取消了此项要求,还规定企业在对外直接投资获得核准后,可以持《企业境外投资证书》办理外汇、银行、海关、外事等相关手续,并享受国家有关政策支持。在监督管理方面,原中国外经贸部联合其他部委在 2002 年分别发布了《对外直接投资统计制度》(该制度在 2004 年修订后于 2005 年 1 月 1 日起执行)、《境外投资联合年检暂行办法》、《境外投资综合绩效评价办法(试行)》、《成立境外中资企业商会(协会)的暂行规定》。从 2003 年起,由商务部牵头组织对外直接投资统计、境外投资联合年检、对外投资综合绩效评价和境外中商企业商会工作。商务部和国家外汇管理局 2005 年 5 月发布了《企业境外并购事项前期报告制度》,要求企业在确定境外并购意向后,须及时向国家商务部及外汇管理部门报告。

(二)现行制度存在的问题及其解决

1.管理繁多

中国目前对外投资行政管理体制和权限,仍存在明显的手续繁多、管理部门多、部门职能交叉或重叠的现象。

中国对外投资企业完成所有境外投资审批手续,需要经过商务部(负责公司核准、统计、年检等)、国家发改委(负责项目核准)、国家外汇管理局(负责外汇审查和管理)、财政部(负责对外投资专项基金使用)、国务院国有资产管理委员会(负责中央企业对外投资所有权管理)、中国进出口银行(负责对外投资的信贷、保险)、国家开发银行(负责对外投资产业投资基金使用和管理)、国家税务总局(负责对外投资税收管理)和地方政府相应职能部门的审批。由于缺少专门的协调机构,导致行政管理效率不高或者服务不到位。因此中国对外投资需要减少行政手续、简化相关程序、统一归口管理。

2.对外投资支持措施少

随着以中小规模为主的民营企业的崛起和力量的壮大,其对外投资的愿望和积极性迅速提高。且这类企业由于投资地区流向、产业分布和投资目标的"多元化",很少会因为政治、经济或社会安全原因,受到东道国政府或利益集团的特别关注。由于大多数民营企业相对缺少对外投资所需的资金、信息、经验和人才,抗风险能力较弱,更需要政府的政策支持和服务保障。政府应考虑尽快扩大"中小企业国际市场开拓专项基金"的规模,放宽企业申请和使用条件,借鉴发达国家成功经验,对中小企业设立"海外投资损失保险金制度"。

现有的海外产业投资基金、信贷、税收等领域,还有很大的政策创新空间。

政府在为海外投资企业解决对外投资所需复合型跨国经营管理人才及专业技术人才的培训上,还应当有更大的作为。商务部已经制订的以培养对外投资与跨国经营"中高级"经营管理人才为目标的培训方案,远远不能满足越来越多对外投资企业的人才需要。而且,企业对外直接投资更需要的是具有"实战"经验的跨国经营管理及专业技术人才。政府应将人才培训的政策重点,向发挥企业自身或专业培训机构的积极性转变,设立"海外投资企业人才培训专项基金",对愿意实施内部培训的对外投资企业进行补贴,应成为政府重点考虑的一项政策选择。[①]

三、中国需要参与制定多边投资规则的种类

发展中国家只有参与到经济全球化进程中、参与到经济全球化游戏规则的制定中,才能有效地表达自己的意志,才有可能打破西方发达国家对全球化主导权的垄断,而不至于被动地接受西方发达国家制定的规则,才能维护本国的经济主权利益,建立国际经济新秩序才有可能真正实现。

(一)多边投资规则的种类

如前述,多边投资规则包括区域性多边投资规则和全球性(或普遍性)多边投资规则。区域性多边投资规则主要体现于两种条约:一种是有关国家专门就投资中的一般性问题或某些特定问题所签署的条约,如《资本移动与流动性无形交易运营自由化条约》《亚太经合组织非约束性投资原则》《中国—东盟投资协定》。另一种是在经济合作和一体化的综合性协定中,投资仅作为其中的一部分,如《罗马条约》《北美自由贸易协定》《美墨加协定》《区域全面经济伙伴关系协定》等。普遍性多边投资规则主要体现于两种:一是特殊领域的投资协定,如 ICSID 公约、MIGA 公约、TRIMs 协定、GATS 等;二是综合性投资协定,目前尚缺。

(二)中国需优先参与制定区域性多边投资规则

就多边投资规则的现状和中国目前的实际情况而论,需优先参与制定区域性多边投资规则。理由如下:

---

① 周升起:《中国对外直接投资:现状、趋势与政策》,载《东亚论文》2009 年第 75 期。

1.为区域性多边统一规则发展趋势所决定

当前,世界上出现区域性多边投资统一规则的发展趋势。普遍性投资规则虽然不可避免,但是南北双方利益难以协调,统一制定的进展困难重重。与其坐等遥遥无期的普遍性多边投资协定的实现,不如针对本区域内或不同地区国家间的自由贸易区的实际情况,进行全面具体的友好磋商,创制适合本区域或自由贸易区发展状况的区域性投资协定。该区域投资协定能相应地推进区域内成员方外资法改革,促进国内法的趋同,为未来普遍性多边投规则的制定奠定基础。

2.区域性多边投资规则的制定相对成熟

区域性投资协定能带动本地区甚至跨越地缘的区域合作向更加成熟、规范和密切的方向发展。深厚密切、牢不可破的经济利益关系能使区域内成员方在未来多边投资规则的谈判中团结一心,用一个声音说话,增强在多边谈判中的实力。中国可以找到更多同盟成员,特别在一些事关中国的东亚、中亚、东南亚、南亚、泛太平洋、金砖国家等区域的切身利益的谈判领域,加强与相关国家合作的深度和力度,而不是单枪匹马、孤军奋战。

3.中国作为一个大国的主导作用

中国作为为亚洲的一个发展中大国,如果在推动本地区投资规则的制定过程中难以发挥主导作用,就不可能在相关区域性或普遍多边投资规则的谈判过程中产生重要影响。如果中国长期不参与主导属于自己可以控制的区域组织,积极推进具实质性成果的区域性投资规则的形成,单纯局限于 APEC 等非约束性机制,必然将面临全球范围内迅速发展的实质性区域投资合作机制边缘化和外围化的危险。

(三)中国需积极参与普遍性投资规则的制定

"中国应当积极参与多边投资框架的谈判,以争取在 WTO 框架下建立一个较为公平兼顾发达和发展中成员方利益的多边投资框架。这不仅符合中国目前的投资环境及其特点,也符合中国经济发展的战略利益和可持续发展的目标。"[①]中国对外直接投资的发展趋势表明,中国需积极参与普遍性投资规则制定,以更进一步改善投资法律环境,积极发展对外投资,促进经济持续发展。但在此类投资规则制定前或过程中,首先要解决与美国的双边投资协定问题。"中美双边投资协定能够提供一种平衡资本输入型东道国和资本输出型母国之间利益这一挑战方法。迎接该挑战意味着传统上立场完全不同的东道国和母国要作出一次历史性的妥协,总有一天,中美双边协定可能成为一个构建多边框架的平台。中美间的谈判之所以至关重要,不仅是因为涉及世界上最大的两个经济体间的经济关系,而且因为国际投资法制的不断发展。"[②]

---

① 冯军:《从多哈回合议程谈中国多边投资框架谈判立场》,载《政治与法律》2005 年第 2 期。

② Karl P. Sauvant、陈辉萍:《中美双边投资协定:多边投资框架的范本》,载《哥伦比亚国际直接投资展望》2012 年 12 月 17 日第 85 期。

本章小结

    我国国际投资发展使我国成为资本输入大国和资本输出大国,这种身份混同需要兼顾我国实施外资管理权和保护海外投资的多边投资规则,且我国已经缔结和参加了一些区域性投资规则和重要的国际投资公约或协定。我国参与制定多边投资规则面临诸多问题,其中东道国征收或国有化、我国放宽海外投资监管、需要参与制定多边投资规则的类型是三个重要问题。我国国际投资的特点和区域发展战略等因素决定了我国需优先参与制定区域性多边规则、积极参与制定普遍性多边规则。

第三章

中国参与制定多边投资规则的基本原则

我国作为发展中大国,兼具资本输入国和资本输出国的双重身份,在努力引进外资、大力发展国内经济的同时需要充分保护我国海外投资。寻求多边投资规则的确定,是我国应当考虑的长远对策。参与制定多边投资规则,要吸取经验教训,发挥多边投资规则的优势,避开双边投资规则的劣势,平衡东道国和外国投资者的权利义务,坚持我国应有的基本原则。我国参与制定多边投资规则应遵循的基本原则是国家经济主权原则、公平互利原则、投资自由化原则、投资与投资者平等待遇原则。

第一节 国家经济主权原则

国家经济主权原则是国家主权原则在经济领域的体现,系主权国家处理一切国际经济关系和参与任何国际经济活动的根本准则和指导思想,也是主权国家参与制定多边投资规则所必须遵循的首要原则。

一、国家经济主权原则的演进

二战后初期,有关主权的规定主要集中在独立和国家安全两方面。这是由战后初期的形势决定的。防止法西斯主义死灰复燃的迫切需要使国际社会还来不及考虑经济发展方面的问题,同时作为主导战后国际经济政治秩序的发达国家也不愿意提及经济主权问题。因此《联合国宪章》在主权问题上的规定,主要内容是以政治主权、政治独立和国家安全为主,但还是为经济主权的提出留下了足够的空间。

联合国通过的有关宣言和决议对经济主权原则的形成起到了极大的推动作用。发展中国家在赢得政治独立后,出于发展民族经济的需要,把维护主权的核心放在了以自然资源永久主权和独立的经济政策决策权为核心的经济主权方面。发展中国家通过大规模的国有化运动，巩固了国家主权，维护了国家的独立生存与发展。取得独立后的广大发展中国家充分依靠自身的力量，通过达成各种国际条约和促成国际性文件形成的方式，以联合国大会为争取经济主权的主战场，明确提出经济主权的要求。1952 年 1 月联合国大会第 6 届会议通过了《关于经济发展与通商协定的决议》，率先肯定和承认了各国人民享有经济上的自主权。1952 年 12 月，联合国大会第 7 届会议通过了《关于自由开发财富和自然资源的权利的决议》，开始把自然资源问题与国家主权联系起来，决议承认各国国有化和开采自然资源、自然财富的权利。国有化的权利与《联合国宪章》第 1 条第 2 款"民族自决权"的规定是相符合的。这是发展中国家在自然资源永久主权问题上的一次成功实践。南北双方在国有化问题的斗争是经济主权斗争的关键所在。1962 年 12 月联合国第 17 届会议通过了《关于自然资源之永久主权宣言》，正式确立了各国对本国境内的自然资源享有永久主权的基本原则。这是发展中国家维护本国经济主权、争取经济独立的重大成果。经济主权原则最终在 20 世纪 70 年代得以确立。1974 年 5 月联合国大会第 6 届特别会议通过了《建立国际经济新秩序宣言》和《建立国际经济新秩序行动纲领》，同年 12 月联大第 29 届会议又通过了《各国经济权利和义务宪章》。上述 3 个纲领性法律文件，再次确认和强调了各国不但对本国境内的全部自然资源享有完全的永久主权，而且对本国境内的一切经济活动享有完整的永久主权。[1]

二、国家经济主权的含义与基本内容

国家经济主权原则是国家主权原则的内容之一。各主权国家不但在本国内部和对外的政治、文化、社会事务上享有独立自主之权，而且在内外一切经济事务上享有独立自主之权，当家作主之权。它是由一系列国际法律文件体现并最终确定下来的。

国家经济主权是国家主权在经济领域的体现，其含义可以从狭义和广义两方面加以界定。

狭义的国家经济主权，是指主权国家对其自然资源的永久主权。这在 1962 年联合国《关于自然资源之永久主权宣言》以及其他各种国际宣言中已经得到确认。1974 年联合国《各国经济权利与义务宪章》第 2 章第 5 条第 1 款中明确规定："每个国家对其全部财富、自然资源和经济活动享有充分的永久主权，包括拥有权、使用权和处置权在内，并得以行使此项权利。"

广义的国家经济主权，是指国家在国内、国际经济活动中，有选择国家经济制度和参与、协调国际经济秩序等重大经济问题的最高独立决策权。国家经济主权具有对内最高属性和对外独立性。对内最高属性体现为：主权国家有权自主选择自己的经济制度；自主决定自己的经济发展战略；自主立法建立本国国内的市场经济运行规则；自主开发和利用本国的经济资源。对外独立性表现为：主权国家无论是否参与国际经济活动，都有

---

[1] 徐泉：《国家经济主权论》，人民出版社 2006 年版，第 12 页。

自己的生存权和发展权;主权国家可以自主决定是否参与国际经济活动;在承担国际经济规则的义务的同时,享有平等的权利;国家之间的经济交往以平等互利为基础,主权国家有权保护自己不受外来经济势力的掠夺和剥削。①

综上观之,国家经济主权原则的基本内容有:第一,有独立自主地处理本国一切经济事务的权利。第二,对本国境内一切自然资源有完全主权。第三,对境内的外国投资和跨国公司享有监督管理权。第四,对本国境内的外国资产享有国有化或征收的权利。第五,对世界经济事务享有平等的参与权和决策权。②

三、国家经济主权原则在多边投资条约中的主要表现

国家经济主权原则在多边投资条约中主要表现为两个方面:一是各缔约国将其独立行使的部分主权权利转移至缔约方共同行使,在该权利范围内各缔约国享有集体决策权、负有执行集体决定的义务,其主权行使被适当限制。典型例子是 WTO 体系内各成员的具体权利和义务,其有关投资的协定对成员方的投资措施或履行要求进行限制或禁止,要求成员方承诺开放投资领域、给予其他成员方投资或投资者以国民待遇或最惠国待遇。二是确认各缔约国仍然享有基本的经济主权,但对其行使进行限制。典型例子是各种投资条约中的征收条款和投资者与东道国投资争端解决条款。征收条款一般规定,缔约一方行使征收或国有化权利时,须遵守的条件是为了公共利益、依照正当法律程序并给予补偿。投资者与东道国投资争端解决条款一般规定,用尽东道国当地救济是进行国际仲裁解决的前提条件。

一些区域性组织如东盟、北美自由贸易区等以部分经济管理职能集体化或一体化的形式在有限的范围内转移成员某些国家经济主权权利。欧盟更是通过高度一体化实现了各成员部分国家经济主权权力和管理职能向外部转移。这种转移对处于同一经济发展水平的国家,是为了在激烈竞争中争取主动而付出的一种代价,其前提是权力共享。对于处于同一集团内经济发展水平与规模和体制相去较远的国家,要实现在主权平等基础上的部分经济主权转移需面临许多困难。对发展中国家而言,往往是付出的要比得到的多许多。③

目前在普遍性投资条约领域,除了《华盛顿公约》、MIGA 公约,还有 WTO 体系内的TRIMs 协定、GATS 等。这些协定中的统一投资法律规则既是经济全球化的先导,又是推动经济全球化进程的工具。在这些条约下,各种贸易障碍日趋减少的全球资本市场,将对国家经济主权起到约束作用。从经济主权的实践看,"各国对境内一切自然资源享有永久主权"的内容不可动摇,但"各国对境内外资的监管及国有化政策"有了很大变化,因为 WTO 体系中 TRIMs 协定等已经把各国给予外资的国际最低标准法律化了,并通

① 徐泉:《国家经济主权论》,人民出版社 2006 年版,第 11 页。
② 陈业宏、张庆麟、刘笋主编:《国际经济法新论》,华中科技大学出版社 2010 年版,第 20 页。
③ 谢晓娟:《论经济全球化过程中发展中国家的经济主权问题》,载《江西社会科学》2001 年第 4 期。

过国民待遇原则和/或最惠国待遇原则加以保障,凡缔约方均须遵守。经济主权原则因 TRIMs 协定等发生了重大变化。可见国家经济主权的内容和范围是不断发展变化的。①

四、我国应坚持的基本立场

国家经济主权原则应是中国在参与制定多边投资规则时坚持的首要原则。在经济全球化进程中,发展中国家应敢于坚持和善于运用本国的经济主权。在经济全球化加速发展的大潮流中,发展中国家面对的是机遇与风险并存的局势。要抓住机遇,就必须牢牢掌握自己手中的经济主权,以它作为主要杠杆,才能对各种内外经济因素实行必要的引导、组织和管理。要预防和抵御风险,也必须牢牢掌握经济主权,以它作为主要屏障,采取各种切实有效的措施,及时化解和消除各种潜在的和已存在的风险。

在经济全球化趋势下,国家经济主权的一些方面有所变化。过去的主权观念主要强调国家的政治独立,现在主权发展为以政治独立与经济独立并重的全方位主权观念。在经济全球化影响下,发展中国家迫切要求改变不合理的国际经济法律秩序,建立新型的平等的国际经济法律秩序,经济主权特别是自然资源主权成为各国关注的重要问题。②未来多边投资规则制定必须反映的一个原则是,投资和贸易自由化推动下的经济全球化,不应当以牺牲经济弱国的主权权利为代价,也不应当忽视资源、财富和权力的公平分配。③ 国际投资法律规则的制定要以尊重国家主权为基础,各个国家在缔结多边投资条约时要互相尊重国家主权,尊重对方国家的法律制度。

我国参与制定多边投资规则,必须坚持国家经济主权原则,在此前提下,根据我国实际情况、多边投资规则的性质和种类、参加制定的其他国家的类型及其数量,在不动摇国家经济主权基本权力的基础上,可以就具体领域的国家经济权力行使,分别作出单独、共同行使,在共同行使的情况下又分别作出保留或让步。

第二节　公平互利原则

公平互利原则是各国参与和处理国际关系的基本原则之一,其必然反映在国际经济关系领域,也必然是主权国家参与制定多边投资规则所遵循的基本原则。

① 宋冰:《从〈华盛顿公约〉看国家经济主权》,载《法学杂志》2005 年第 1 期。
② 樊静:《经济全球化趋势下的国家主权原则》,载《法学杂志》2002 年第 6 期。
③ 张艾妮:《中国应对多边投资协定谈判的策略研究》,载《广东海洋大学学报(哲学社会科学版)》2009 年第 2 期。

一、公平互利原则的历史演进

本原则是在传统的平等互利原则基础上发展起来的,是对平等互利原则的超越和发展。传统意义上的平等互利原则中的"平等",是指主权平等(主要是政治和法律地位平等),即在国际社会中,国家不分大小强弱,都具有平等的国际法律人格,享有平等法律地位,既没有高低贵贱之分,也不允许存在统治与被统治关系,任何国家都不应要求享受任何特权。在殖民主义时期,处于殖民地或半殖民地国家的主权全部或部分被剥夺,其国际法律人格要么不独立,要么不完整,对它们没有平等可言。二战后,广大殖民地或半殖民地国家取得了政治独立,具备独立的国际法律人格,享有平等的法律地位。但在国际交往中,发达国家凭借经济上的优势,肆意剥削和掠夺发展中国家的经济利益,以形式上的平等掩盖实质上的不平等。这使广大发展中国家逐步意识到,仅从政治角度上强调主权平等是远远不够的,必须进一步要求经济互利,并将平等和互利有机结合起来。只有在平等基础上,才能做到互利;只有真正实行互利,才能实现实质上的平等,这就是平等互利原则。但在实践中,平等互利原则的贯彻常常遇到阻碍。由于历史的痼疾,发达国家和发展中国家之间存在着过大的经济差距。在这些国家之间,"平等"地用同一尺度去衡量,用同一标准去要求,实行绝对的、无差别的"平等待遇",其实际效果是以"平等"的假象掩盖了不平等的实质。正是在这种背景下,广大发展中国家在强调各国在政治、法律上享有平等法律地位的同时,强调在国际经济关系中要求贯彻公平互利原则,并且借助于联合国大会通过的《宣言》和《宪章》,使它上升为建立国际经济新秩序的一项基本原则和调整国际经济关系的一项基本准则。[①]

二、公平互利原则的含义与基本内容

公平互利原则是指国家在相互关系中不论彼此大小强弱、人口多寡、政治制度如何、经济发展程度如何,都有平等地位,都应相互尊重、平等相处,不能以损害对方的利益来满足自己的要求,更不能以牺牲他国和榨取他国为目的而要求各种特权。

该原则旨在实现"双赢",即国际经济交往主体均能在相互交往过程中获利,整个国际社会和谐稳定发展。这里的"公平"一般可理解为"公正平等""公平合理"。真正的公平,不但要求形式上公平,而且要求实质上公平,是形式上的公平和实质上公平的有机统一体。这里的"互利",是指要照顾到相关各方的利益,不能为谋求单方面利益而无视甚至损害他方利益。公平与互利是不可分割的统一整体,互利是核心和基础,没有互利就谈不上公平,公平又必然要求互利,两者密不可分。没有经济上的互利就不可能有法律上的真正公平,因为获取公平最重要的目的之一是获取经济上的利益。

该原则的基本要求是:(1)国家间经济关系处于公平互利状况。反对一方只享有权

---

① 　陈业宏、张庆麟、刘笋主编:《国际经济法新论》,华中科技大学出版社 2010 年版,第 22 页。

利不承担义务、另一方只承担义务不享受权利的"片面条款"。在国际经济关系中,不仅体现在国家间经济关系上的公平互利,还体现在自然人、法人和其他经济组织间或与国家、国际组织间的关系上公平互利。在当代国际经济关系中,公平互利原则还赋予了经济援助这一新的内容,且经济援助是相互的,必须在平等的地位上进行;它承认了发展中国家在世界经济中的特殊地位。[1] (2)公平互惠。在国际贸易中,互惠一般是指两国或多国之间在贸易利益或特权方面的相互或相应给予。这种互惠包括关税方面、运输、非关税壁垒方面的削减和知识产权方面的相互保护等。互惠贸易原则是在多边贸易谈判及一成员贸易自由化过程中与其他成员实现经贸合作的主要原则之一。参加关税减让谈判的成员必须根据互惠贸易原则交换减让,即一成员将他能提供的一项减让与另一成员能给予的减让交换,这样才能使各方获益。税率互减后对扩大各成员出口有利,自然会有力地促进成员之间的贸易。通过成员对等减让和相互提供互惠的方式来保持贸易平衡,谋求贸易自由化的实现。

公平互惠原则是 GATT 的重要原则之一,是 GATT 关税减让的基础,指一成员要得到另一成员的关税减让承诺,必须以自己作出关税减让承诺为前提,即权益与特权的相互转让。在国际贸易中,双方通过"互惠"才能达到双赢效果,没有哪一个成员喜欢单方面在利益上作出让步,它总希望在让步的同时得到相应的回报。否则,在成员之间不可能达成任何协议。在 GATT 中,没有对"互惠"原则作出明确规定,但在几个条款中有相应的体现。GATT 第 28 条规定,在谈判及协议中(对其他产品所作的补偿性调整规定可能包括在内),有关成员应力求维持互惠互利减让的一般水平,使其对贸易的优惠待遇不低于谈判前本协定所规定的水平。这一规定被视为是在互利基础上的大幅度地、普遍地以降低关税水平为目标的一条重要谈判原则。第 28 条附加规定:关税谈判第 1 款规定,成员认识到关税通常成为进行贸易的严重阻碍,因此,成员应在互惠互利的基础上进行谈判,以大幅度降低关税和进出口其他费用的一般水平,特别是降低那些使少量进口受到阻碍的高关税,并在谈判中适当注意本协定的目的与成员的不同需要。[2]

三、公平互利原则在多边投资条约中的体现

在 WTO 体制中,各成员通过多边贸易谈判达成相互之间的互惠关税减让和具体承诺,然后通过信守承诺和规则来维持平衡。在承诺和规则被违反时通过争端解决机制恢复平衡。同时,对于发展中国家成员,它们无须对发达成员作出对等的减让,就可以享受其他成员的关税减让成果。

公平互利原则在 GATS 中的体现最明显。其第 4 条"发展中国家更多地参与"之第 1 款规定,应通过由不同成员方根据本协定第三、四部分而承担的具体义务,促使发展中国家

---

[1]　陈业宏、张庆麟、刘笋主编:《国际经济法新论》,华中科技大学出版社 2010 年版,第 20 页。

[2]　李斯:《WTO 规则对中国农业的影响评价与发展对策实用手册》,世图音像电子出版社 2002 年版,第 50 页。

成员方更多地参与世界贸易,这些义务涉及:(1)特别要通过引进商业性技术,增强发展中国家国内服务业的生产能力、效率和竞争力;(2)改善发展中国家进入销售渠道和信息网络的机会;(3)对各部门的市场准入和有利于发展中国家成员方的出口部门的供给方式实行自由化。该条第 2 款规定,发达国家成员方及其他有能力的成员方,应在自世界贸易组织协定生效日起的 2 年内建立联系点,以便发展中国家成员方服务提供者能够获得与其各自市场有关的:(1)关于服务提供的商业和技术方面的信息;(2)有关专业资格方面的注册、认可和获得的信息;(3)获得服务技术的可能性的信息。该条第 3 款规定,在履行上述第 1、2 款时,应特别优先考虑最不发达国家成员方。鉴于他们的特殊经济状况及其在发展、贸易和财政方面的需要,应对最不发达国家成员方在接受商定的具体义务方面的严重困难予以特别的考虑。第 5 条"经济一体化"之第 3 款规定,如果发展中国家属于双边或多边自由贸易协定的参与方,则对本条第 1 款,特别是子款(2)规定的条件,应有灵活性的规定,以符合这些国家总体的和个别部门及分部门的发展水平;双边或多边自由贸易协定仅涉及发展中国家的情况下,也可以给予由协定参与方的自然人所拥有或控制的法人以更为优惠的待遇。

在有关区域性投资协定中,缔约方是相互给予对等的保护和待遇。即使一国是资本输入国,本国国民无法享受投资协定中规定的相应好处,该国在决定对方投资的市场准入时,通常以准入能否促进本国的经济和社会发展或能否使本国国民获益为条件。[①]

四、我国应坚持的基本立场

大部分多边投资条约草案以尽可能保护外国投资者权益为目的,因而遭到资本输入国的反对。[②] 一味地强调保护外国投资者利益而忽视资本输入国利益势必使得二者权益失衡,从而违背公平互利这一基本原则。因此我国在参与制定多边投资规则时,应当坚持公平互利原则,对发展中国家利益予以特别考虑,给予特别待遇。

第三节　投资自由化原则

鉴于国际投资对东道国经济社会发展具有利和弊的双重属性,东道国出于自身利益考量,在不同时期会分别采取鼓励、限制或两者结合的法律与政策,使外国投资符合本国阶段性和长远性发展目标。在当代,投资便利化与自由化是国际投资法发展的总趋势。作为资本输入和资本输出大国的中国,在参与制定多边投资规则时,必然适应这种国际

---

① 左海聪:《国际经济法基本问题论纲》,载《法学评论》2009 年第 1 期。
② M. Sorharajah, *The International Law on Foreign Investment* (3rd ed.), Cambridge University Press,2010,p.236.

趋势,坚持投资自由化原则。

一、投资自由化原则的历史演进

早在二战后的布雷顿森林会议上,贸易投资与货币金融议题成为全球规范的焦点,当时制定的建立国际贸易组织(1948 年)的《哈瓦那宪章》中就有关于外国直接投资的专门条款(例如第 12 条等)。跨国投资法律规范已纳入对战后国际经济体系的总体设计和考虑中。国际贸易组织的流产,使有关投资的条款没能生效。但国际社会,尤其是发达国家,试图规范全球投资活动的努力并未却步。规范投资活动从双边走向多边发展的趋势与资本跨国界流动和投资自由化有着某种程度的"默契"。而投资自由化不但是发达国家生产资本寻求利润最大化的内在要求,而且是发达资本主义国家垄断资本要求消除阻碍其追逐全球利润的各种形式堡垒的外在表现。发达国家选择《外国直接投资指南》的形式推行投资自由化。该指南是 1991 年由法国等发达国家倡议后,由世界银行和国际货币基金组织联合设定的行政委员会(即"发展委员会")认为有必要制定一个旨在促进外国直接投资、涵盖面广泛的法律框架。该指南对晚近发达国家在传统国际投资重大法律问题上所取得的成果进行了全面的提炼和总结,为推行投资自由化、外资准入等设计了一套指导性规则。它完全按照发达国家的标准从中抽出的"最好实践"制定而成,其实质是建议广大发展中国家实现外资准入自由化。所不同的是其采用"指南"这种不具有法律约束力的"软法"形式提出。经合组织提出了《多边投资协定》,但以失败告终。目前促进投资自由化的主要国际法律规范形式有:各国缔结的双边投资条约、区域组织制定的投资规范和全球多边国际机构制定的国际投资规范。

在历史上,外国直接投资领域的规则,无论是双边还是多边规则,都以单方面约束资本输入国(东道国)的政府行为,为外国投资及投资者提供有利待遇和有效保障为主要目的和内容。发达国家在制定多边投资规则时,为拓展其海外市场、保护其海外投资利益,总是试图把资本输入国的投资准入限制减少,把投资保护的规格提得很高,以利发达国家资本在东道国获取更多的保护。据联合国统计显示,发达国家是世界上最主要的资本输出国,占全球资本输出总额的绝大部分;发达国家也是世界上主要的资本输入国,吸收的资本流入量占全球总量的 65%。发展中国家随着晚近经济活力的持续增长,吸收外国直接投资的比例也在不断攀升。制定促进投资自由化的规范性文件的更多主动权落在了发达国家一边。1995 年 5 月,由美国倡议、经合组织启动了《多边投资协定》(MAI)。MAI 的主要目标是:建立国际投资多边框架,为投资的自由化和保护设置高标准,并建立有效争端解决程序。其从发达国家立场出发,在注重提高对外国投资的法律保护的同时要求东道国对外资准入实行自由化政策。虽然 MAI 最终未能有效产生,但发达国家推动投资自由化的热情和实践一直没有中断,推动投资自由化的企图仍在继续。欧盟、加拿大、美国等建议将 MAI 谈判移植于世界贸易组织重新进行。

投资自由化是经济全球化最具实质性的内容。与贸易自由化相比,投资自由化是经济全球化的一个更高阶段。只不过直到 20 世纪 70 年代末,投资自由化才作为一种观念和政策出现,并逐渐在世界范围内展开。20世纪80年代,越来越多的发展中国家开始吸引外资,引进外国技术。到了20世纪末,经济全球化已是大势所趋。在这一进程中,以中国、印度、俄罗斯和巴西等国为代表的一大批新兴经济体成就卓然,实力大增。但这一时期的国际资本流动,如激流汹涌,泥沙俱下。1997年亚洲金融风暴危害惨重,俄罗斯、土耳其、巴西和阿根廷等国先后爆发了金融危机,给世人留下了深刻的警示。现实提醒,对各种投资唯有规制得当,才能趋利避害。进入21世纪,投资自由化进程有了新的发展,尤其是国际金融市场和金融机构,与以前相比已是旧貌换新颜。其间发生的巨大变化,虽然面目朦胧,难以窥其全貌,但有大量的事实表明,目前的国际金融和货币体系,仍处在一个不稳定时期。各国竞相开放外国投资市场,并对外资实行较为宽松的优惠政策。而发达国家为了促进直接投资及其随带的各种生产要素在国际间的流动,以便在"比较利益"基础上实现全球资源的最合理或有效的配置,积极谋求通过双边和多边努力,以实现最大限度的投资自由化和利润最大化,特别是在发达国家的积极倡导下,一些投资措施已被纳入WTO多边管制内。

二、投资自由化原则的含义与基本内容

　　根据联合国贸易与发展会议的解释,投资自由化主要包括以下几个方面的内容:(1)减轻或者消除市场扭曲(market distortions)的影响。造成市场扭曲的原因可能是外资法中专门针对外国投资者的限制性措施,如外资准入及经营方面的障碍,也可能是外资法中有关给予或不给予外国投资者某种优惠措施及补贴的规定。(2)提高给予外国投资者的待遇标准,如给予外国投资者以国民待遇、最惠国待遇和公平公正待遇。(3)加强对市场的监督以保障市场机制的正常运转,如制定竞争规则、信息披露规则等。

　　近年来,投资自由化观念得到了西方学者广泛支持,不断为投资自由化提供理论依据,希望这些理论尽快地反映到各层面上的立法中。美国知名国际投资法学者范德菲尔德曾指出,投资自由化是全球经济自由化的重要组成部分和推动力量,而经济自由化能最大限度地促进经济的发展。许多西方学者认为,自由经济理论倡导的核心观念之一是:自由的市场能够促成资源的最大限度利用并因此产生最大生产力。然而,自由市场的建立往往以一种政府与市场之间的特殊关系的建立为条件,这种关系有三个基本的支撑点,或称自由市场的三大基本原则:第一,国家必须保护私有财产和契约权利。换言之,政府必须创建一个有效的法律体系以保障市场参与方有效谈判契约的权利,私人财产权利和契约权利必须受到保护,不得遭受来自公共权力或私人权利的侵害。第二,国家必须服从市场对资源的配置。换言之,既然政府已经创建了一套有关市场的法律体系,就应当让市场去引导资源的分配。第三,国家必须维护市场便利,必要时可以出面纠正市场失灵。换言之,政府应当维护市场机制的正常运行,当市场机制不能有效运行时,政府就必须出面进行适当干预。例如,政府必须制止私人部门的反竞争行为对其他市场参与方进入市场的威胁或阻碍。上述原则运用于国际投资,就产生出相应的投资自由三原则,即投资安全原则、投资中性原则和投资便利原则。投资安全原则要求国家确保投

资不受来自公共权力和私人的干预。投资中性原则要求国家允许由市场决定跨国界投资的流动方向和性质。投资便利原则要求国家保障市场的运作正常,保证投资者充分知晓投资机会和有关投资法律法规。[①]

联合国贸易与发展会议提出,国际直接投资自由化是减少或消除政府对跨国公司实施的限制或鼓励措施,对其提供平等的待遇,废除歧视性的、造成市场扭曲的做法,确保市场的正常运行。关于国际直接投资自由化内涵的理解,尚存在分歧。联合国贸易与发展会议认为,国际直接投资自由化包括以下动态过程:(1)减轻或取消由于专门针对外国投资者的限制(例如进入壁垒)以及由于对外国投资者实行歧视而给予或拒绝给予鼓励、补贴所导致的市场扭曲。(2)加强对外国投资者的某些积极的待遇标准(如国民待遇、最惠国待遇、公平和平等待遇)。(3)加强市场监管,确保市场的正常运转(如竞争规则、信息披露规则和审慎监管规则)。在上述三项因素中,前两项因素是核心,但其效应的发挥在很大程度上又依赖于第三项因素。国际直接投资自由化的目标在于,建立消除歧视(或优惠)、充分竞争、有序运行的市场环境。自由化能够使跨国公司在东道国投资,但并不能保证投资一定会发生,即直接投资自由化是跨国公司在东道国投资的必要条件,而非充分条件。

自由化一般是指经济政策和法规对资源配置的负面影响最小化,政府的责任是保证市场的正常运行。一般而言,政府管制与市场是不相容的,自由化的极端是没有任何政府管制。一套法律制度对于保证市场经济的正常运行是必不可少的,这意味着政府需要运用法规和政策对市场实行一定程度的管制。自由化是朝着某一方向推进的动态过程,因而一国在特定时点相关政策和措施只能描述为比较自由化。自由化不但要求消除对市场造成扭曲的限制性和歧视性措施,而且应当包括某些积极标准的建立。自由化进程的全部积极效应在相当程度上取决于为保证市场正常运行而出台一些管制措施。例如:维护竞争、禁止滥用市场支配权力的规定是一个自由化投资体制的组成部分,一个健全的保护知识产权的体制也是必不可少的。从最终目标讲,国际直接投资自由化是指消除所有造成市场扭曲的外资政策,其中既包括外资限制政策,也包括外资鼓励政策。尽管理论上鼓励政策会扭曲市场行为,但是现实中鼓励政策的作用比较复杂,而且各国采用鼓励政策争取外资流入的趋势不会立即改变。

三、投资自由化原则在多边投资条约中的体现

放松投资管制、提高投资待遇的立法趋向在晚近的一些多边投资条约中有不同程度的反映。在区域性多边投资条约层面,1992 年《北美自由贸易协定》堪称自由化多边投资条约的典范。该协定虽然被冠之贸易协定,但其设立专章全面确定了投资准入、投资待遇、投资保护和投资争议解决等各方面的规范,实际上是一个多边投资条约。该协定关于准入自由、禁止履行要求、相互给予缔约国投资者在投资各阶段的国民待遇和最惠国

---

① 刘笋:《投资自由化规则在晚近投资条约中的反映及其地位评析》,载《法学论坛》2002 年第 1 期。

待遇以及绝对待遇、提高投资者在争端解决中的主动性、加强投资争端的非东道国解决机制等方面的规定,充分说明该协定对美式双边投资条约倡导的投资自由精神的不折不扣传承,表明 20 世纪 80 年代以来美国推行的旨在进一步削弱东道国外资管辖权的双边投资条约实践已经在区域性多边投资规则层面得到了全面肯定。

20 世纪 90 年代,投资自由化开始在部门性多边投资条约中取得了不少突破。作为第一个部门性投资自由化条约的《能源宪章条约》(ECT),将独联体成员国、东欧国家与主要西方发达国家纳入一个高度自由化的能源贸易和投资法律体制,较典型地、较全面地反映了近年来发达国家关于投资保护、投资准入、投资待遇方面的高标准、严要求。值得注意的是,ECT 可以称得上第一个赋予投资者直接针对缔约国违反条约义务提请国际仲裁的多边投资条约。它对 ICSID 体制下同意机制(即仲裁必须经由争端当事人双方的同意)的突破,比 NAFTA 更具影响,反映出投资争端仲裁机制的晚近变化。ECT 作为一个投资条约,最引人注目的地方在于其第 26 条的仲裁规则,它给予投资者发起仲裁程序的单方面选择权,且不需要任何事先存在的仲裁协议。这意味着投资者可以就 ECT 第 3 部分(关于投资待遇、投资保护、代位求偿权等内容的规定)所涉东道国违反条约义务,径直对任何 ECT 成员国提起仲裁要求。能源领域达成一项具有投资自由化特色的多边条约,应当被视为是国际投资自由化的多边立法方面的一个重要突破,在某种意义上 ECT 可以作为国际投资自由化立法日益纵深发展的一个标志。

从全球性多边投资立法层面看,乌拉圭回合谈判所产生的一系列多边条约在推动投资自由化方面形成了投资自由化规则,其地位、发挥的作用要远远大于《北美自由贸易协定》和《能源宪章条约》,因为这些条约系在 WTO 这一全球范围内最具影响国际经济组织的监督下实施的,在贯彻执行方面有 WTO 争端解决机制这一准司法性质的争端解决机制作为强有力的保证。WTO 框架中的一些协定直接或间接地涉及投资规则,在抑制东道国外资政策和立法对国际贸易和投资自由化的妨碍方面发挥着重大影响。例如,依据 TRIMs 协定,各国引导和管辖外资的权利开始受到多边纪律的约束。WTO 成员方不得违背 GATT 1994 第 3 条(国民待遇)和第 11 条(一般取消数量限制),采取对贸易有扭曲作用的投资措施,尤其不得维持对外国投资和投资者的当地成分要求、外汇平衡要求、贸易平衡要求、不得以当地销售为条件限制企业出口和以出口为条件限制企业进口(TRIMs 协定解释性清单第 1、2 款)。又如,GATS 首次将服务贸易纳入多边管制。由于 GATS 中规定了以商业存在的方式提供服务必须遵守多边纪律,而以商业存在方式提供服务实际上是服务业的国际直接投资,因此 GATS 作为多边规则对投资自由化有直接影响。依据该协定,只要成员承诺允许市场准入,就不得要求外国服务提供者必须通过特定的法人实体或合营企业才可提供服务,也不得对参加投资的外国资本限定最高股权比例或对个人的或累计的外国资本投资额予以限制。可以说,自 WTO 成立,国际投资法已经向多边法制化方向迈进了实质性的一步,国际投资问题已不再单纯地受各国外资法、双边投资条约和 WTO 体制外的多边投资公约的约束,还要在实体法和程序法上受现代多边贸易体制的制约。[①]

四、我国应坚持的基本立场

国际投资自由化可以视为不同程度的、在世界许多地方同时发生的世界市场自由化和生产要素跨国界自由移动进程的一部分。这一进程促进了正在形成的一体化国际生产体系的进一步发展,并从中获得动力:一方面,国际经济活动的自由化是经济全球化、区域一体化的必要条件;另一方面,随着全球化、一体化程度的加深,各国FDI政策会成为国际关注和需要加以协调的问题。国际投资自由化进程导致各国外资体制的趋同,但各国的外资体制仍存在着许多差异,这些差异成为跨国公司进行投资时需要考虑的重要因素。[②]

我国在坚持投资自由化的前提下,需根据不同类型的国家及其发展水平、利益需求、参与国际投资活动的规模、资本流向、外资政策宽严等因素,制定和调整战略、策略,采取灵活多样、务实的做法,分阶段、分步骤地实现高水平的投资自由化。

第四节　投资与投资者平等待遇原则

投资与投资者平等待遇原则是现代国际投资法的基本原则之一。中国无论作为吸收外国投资的大国还是作为对外投资的大国,在参与制定多边投资规则时,基于参与国之间公平、平衡的考量,均宜坚持此原则。

一、投资与投资者平等待遇原则的历史演进

在国际投资领域,投资与投资者平等待遇原则主要体现为国民待遇原则和最惠国待遇原则。前者的实质是东道国在本国实现外国投资者及其投资与本国投资者及其投资之间的平等待遇,后者的实质是东道国在本国实现外国投资者及其投资之间的平等待遇。因此考察国际投资法中的国民待遇(national treatment)原则、最惠国待遇(most-favored-nation treatment)原则的演进即可说明投资与投资者平等待遇原则的历史演进。

纵观关贸总协定的历史,各成员间的许多争议均与国民待遇义务相关。二战以后,国民待遇原则成为国际投资法律领域的一项重要原则,是国际经济关系发展的结果。战

---

① 刘笋:《投资自由化规则在晚近投资条约中的反映及其地位评析》,载《法学论坛》2002年第1期。

② 苏旭霞:《国际直接投资自由化与中国外资政策——以WTO多边投资框架谈判为背景》,中国商务出版社2005年版,第19页。

后的非殖民化运动、国际经济相互依赖关系的加强以及区域性经济合作安排的发展等，是使国民待遇成为国际投资待遇原则的直接动因。如果没有欧洲共同体、经济合作与发展组织(OECD)等的推动，国民待遇至今还限定在贸易领域。因此，国民待遇原则与国际贸易和包括区域性组织在内的国际组织直接相关。

传统上，最惠国待遇主要涉及货物进入外国国境过程中和入境后的待遇问题。这一情况随着服务贸易的跨境提供而变得复杂。在国际投资活动中，国民待遇和最惠国待遇经常交互或同时适用。例如，国有化外国人财产的法律效力以及当事国的赔偿责任既涉及最惠国待遇又关乎国民待遇。现代国际投资条约通常规定，同时适用国民待遇和最惠国待遇标准。

国民待遇原则是基于国际经济关系的主体，特别是主权国家的认可。事实上，没有主权国家的明示同意或授权，国际社会无法将国民待遇义务强加于任何成员。这是由国际法的性质使然，也因为国民待遇原则主要是保护货物及资本输出国家的利益。虽然几乎所有双边和多边条约均规定最惠国待遇和国民待遇的提供以相互原则为基础，但不可否认的事实是，每个貌似平等的条约都隐藏着不平等。因此，国民待遇和最惠国待遇作为待遇原则必须得到相关国家的明示同意。

国民待遇原则最早适用于国际贸易关系。关贸总协定等对国民待遇原则的解释直接影响该原则在国际投资活动中的适用。现实中，贸易和投资有时很难区分。以服务贸易为例，某银行在国外设立一分支机构是属于服务贸易还是国际投资？又例如，政府的有些措施表面是针对国际投资但亦直接影响外国货物的进口，此类措施是属于国际贸易法还是国际投资法的范畴？因此，关于国际投资活动中国民待遇原则的研究必须兼涉其在国际贸易关系中之适用。如前所述，国民待遇原则对东道国的投资环境、与外国投资相关的法律等有直接影响。

以关税与贸易总协定和世界贸易组织关于国民待遇原则的解释、经济合作与发展组织的《国际投资与跨国企业宣言》、经济合作与发展组织理事会关于国民待遇的决议、《北美自由贸易协定》、世界银行的《国际投资指南》《能源宪章条约》、TRIMs 协定等为基础，探讨国民待遇、最惠国待遇在国际投资中的具体适用及存在的问题，以及国民待遇与最惠国待遇原则和国际最低标准待遇的关系及相互作用。[①]

二、投资与投资者平等待遇原则的含义与基本内容

投资与投资者平等待遇是指东道国对外国投资者及其投资在法律上给予平等待遇。目前，投资与投资者平等待遇原则的基本内容包括不歧视、公平公正、最惠国待遇和国民待遇等。最惠国待遇和国民待遇是将不歧视、公平公正原则具体化。西方发达国家亦有人主张国际最低标准待遇。但何谓国际最低标准待遇历来颇有争议。无论是哪一项原则都与其他原则相互作用，都涉及国际投资的各个阶段和各个方面，包括外资的进入、外

---

① 　王贵国：《国际投资法》，北京大学出版社 2001 年版，第 151 页。

国投资企业的经营、资本和投资利润的汇出等。在各项原则中,最惠国待遇和国民待遇原则对国际投资有直接和重要影响,两者中又以后者最为重要。

最惠国待遇原则是历史上最早的平等待遇原则。在历史上主要体现于国际政治与国际贸易领域。但随着时代的发展,最惠国待遇原则适用于国际投资领域。最早反映在双边投资条约中,在当代体现于双边、区域和普遍性投资条约中,因此它是一项重要的国际投资待遇原则。其基本内容是,东道国给予一国投资者及其投资的待遇不低于其给予任何第三国投资者及其投资的待遇。

国民待遇原则的起始者为美国。美国通过与其他国家签订的通商航海条约使国民待遇原则广为传播。第二次世界大战之前,国际贸易和投资主要是在殖民地和宗主国之间进行;来自宗主国的货物、资本和投资者享有很多特权、享有充分的保护。无论是双边的、多边的条约还是国际法规范对国际贸易和投资的直接影响都相当有限。因此国民待遇作为国际经济交往的原则并在实践中发挥重要作用,被纳入关贸总协定。国民待遇原则的基本内容是东道国给予外国投资者及其投资的待遇不低其给予本国国民及其投资的待遇。

有关国民待遇、最惠国待遇基本内容的阐述另见以下第三部分。

三、投资与投资者平等待遇原则的确定标准

纵观国际投资待遇制度的实践,关于投资与投资者平等待遇原则,国际上常见的确定标准有国民待遇、最惠国待遇、公平公正待遇。

(一)国民待遇标准

国民待遇是指外国投资者及其投资在东道国享受的待遇与东道国赋予本国国民享受的待遇相同,即外国人与本国国民在享受权利和承担义务方面具有同等地位。根据国民待遇原则,东道国赋予外国人所享有的权利,不得低于本国国民所享受的同等权利。东道国不得对外国投资者实行歧视性或不公正待遇。外国投资者在东道国应当服从该国的法律管辖,在法律上与东道国国民享受同等的待遇和保护,承担同等的义务和责任,不能要求享受更多的权利,也不承担更多的义务。[①]

国民待遇因有确切的标准可循,成为国际上关于外国人待遇的最重要制度之一。

对国民待遇,历史上乃至现在,资本输出国和资本输入国均持有不同态度。资本输出国极力想为其投资者及其投资争取到国民待遇,资本输入国特别是发展中国家因历史传统、经济发展水平与发展目标的不同而采取否定或肯定态度。

对大多数资本输出国或发达国家,国民待遇是一个重要原则,因而其大多数双边投资条约中有国民待遇条款。大多数发展中国家对国民待遇采取保留态度,在其与其他发展中国家签订的双边投资协定中一般不规定国民待遇,在与发达国家订立的双边投资条

---

① 高凛、任丹红等:《国际经济法热点问题研究》,中国民主法制出版社 2007 年版,第 39 页。

约中对国民待遇予以限制。在我国与外国签订的绝大多数双边投资条约中没有国民待遇条款,只在少数双边投资条约中有国民待遇条款,且一般实行有限制的国民待遇。

近年来,在国际文件中逐渐出现了国民待遇。如经合组织《关于国际投资与跨国公司的宣言》中规定:各成员在维护公共秩序,保护本国基本安全利益的条件下,对境内由其他成员国国民拥有的跨国公司,应给予国民待遇,并努力保证在本国各行政区域适用国民待遇。此国民待遇要求的效力在1991年被进一步加强,自此年,经合组织各成员国均有义务向该组织通报其各级政府采取的与国民待遇原则相悖的措施。世界银行《外国直接投资待遇指南》中规定,整体上外资待遇以"公正、公平"待遇为基准,以国民待遇为补充,即东道国给予外国投资者的待遇,在符合"公正、公平"标准下,应和本国投资者在同等条件下享受相同优惠待遇。

经合组织MAI草案中的国民待遇适用范围非常广泛:既适用于投资设立前,也适用于投资设立后;适用于所有与投资有关的活动,包括投资的设立、获取、扩大、经营、管理、维持、使用、享有、出售及以其他方式处置。MAI允许各国将本国不对外国投资者实行国民待遇的经济部门或其他措施作出保留。

在WTO框架下,TRIMs协定禁止成员方实行违反国民待遇原则的与贸易有关的投资措施,第一次在WTO框架下将国民待遇引入投资领域。但其国民待遇的适用有很大的局限性,仅适用于与货物贸易有关的特定投资措施,且列明投资措施为当地成分要求与贸易平衡要求等。GATS中规定了国民待遇,但其适用受制于具体承诺部门,成员方依其承诺表所列部门、条件与限制给予国民待遇,而不是普遍自动地适用。

从近年来各国外资法、双边投资条约和多边投资协定可以看出,国民待遇标准正在被越来越多的国家接受,其在国际投资领域的地位有逐步增强的趋势,同时其适用受到很多限制。

(二)最惠国待遇标准

最惠国待遇是指缔约一方将已经或将要给予任何第三方的优惠待遇,也给予缔约另一方。大多数投资保护协定纳入了最惠国待遇条款。一些拉美国家长期坚持"卡沃尔主义",只同意给外国投资者以国民待遇。它们认为最惠国待遇有可能使外国投资者获得特权,因而反对在投资保护协定中引入该待遇标准。但是只要最惠国待遇不会带来这种消极结果,它们也在投资协定中纳入这一标准。20世纪80年代以来,尤其是90年代以后,拉美国家对外资的政策趋于开放,最惠国待遇得到了普遍认同。与国民待遇相比,在当前的投资协定谈判中,发达国家和发展中国家在最惠国待遇上的分歧并不大。[①]

最惠国待遇标准是多边贸易谈判的重要议题。非歧视原则是多边贸易体制的基石,是各成员间平等从事贸易的重要保证,也是避免贸易歧视、贸易摩擦的重要基础。有人认为,非歧视行为缓解了不签署贸易协定国家之间潜在的紧张关系,而非歧视原则的核心是最惠国待遇原则;数百年来,最惠国待遇一直是贸易政策的重要支柱;多边主义是一

---

① 张庆麟:《国际投资法问题专论》,武汉大学出版社2007年版,第86页。

种国际谈判方式,包括多个国家之间的相互作用,但最惠国待遇是谈判遵循的一项重要原则,不管谈判是多边、诸边还是双边的。①

在当前,最惠国待遇是规范多边贸易体制参与者国内贸易政策的原则,是落实互惠原则的具体保障措施,不但能够使多边贸易体制中双边谈判的博弈利益进一步扩大,而且能够保障利益的实现和多边贸易体制的顺利进行。在多边投资规则谈判中,最惠国待遇同样是一个重要原则和待遇标准,最惠国待遇原则与互惠原则共同发挥重要作用。

(三)公平公正待遇标准

公平公正待遇标准最早、最多出现于双边投资协定,但目前国际社会对其仍没有明确的定义,对其理解存在分歧。这种标准作为发达国家和发展中国家妥协性产物的出现,在投资条约谈判史的早期较为常见。发达国家和发展中国家在适用上都能各司其利地加以解释。

发达国家主张,在公平与公正标准的适用上,应以"国际法或国际文明"标准为准,适用的效果无疑由它们来判断。如美国 BIT 范本规定:"各种投资在任何情况下,均应获得公平合理的待遇,享有充分的保护和安全,所获得的待遇在任何时候不得低于国际法的要求。"英国 BIT 范本有类似的规定。发展中国家主张,在不违背主权国家自愿承担国际义务的前提下,公平与公正待遇应依其国内法加以适用。

目前,国际学说和国际实践对公平公正待遇争议的焦点在于,它是否包括传统的所谓最低国际标准。虽然有的学者认为国际最低标准应属于公正公平待遇的一部分,但发展中国家对此表示异议。其实,公平与公正在个案中很大程度上是解释性问题,将其纳入投资条约中的目的是:它作为一个基本的标准可以确定条约的基调;它可以作为解释条约中特定规定的辅助因素,或者为了填补条约以及有关国内立法或国家契约的漏洞。正是由于这一标准的模糊性,使其可以灵活解释,达到保护外国投资者及其投资的目的。

四、我国应坚持的基本立场

我国参与多边投资规则的制定,必须坚持投资与投资者平等待遇原则,在此前提下,视多边投资规则的性质、类型、对我国经济社会发展的影响程度、对发展中国家利益诉求的反映程度,分别采取以下组合性待遇标准:国民待遇、公平公正待遇;最惠国待遇、公平公正待遇;国民待遇、最惠国待遇、公平公正待遇。

---

① 联合国贸易与发展会议:《2007 年世界贸易报告》,中国世界贸易组织研究会、对外经济贸易大学中国 WTO 研究院译,中国商务出版社 2008 年版,第 166 页。

本章小结

　　我国既是资本输入大国又是资本输出大国,在参与制定多边投资规则中首先应当坚持的基本原则是国家经济主权原则。只有坚持这一首要原则,才能保障我国和其他发展中国家的国家主权和安全。在此前提下,还应当坚持公平互利原则、投资自由化原则、投资与投资者平等待遇原则。在各原则下,我国应当有基本的立场和观点。

第四章

中国参与制定多边投资规则的总体战略

一个国家参与制定多边投资规则的前提是基于本国利益对多边投资规则的议题所持有的基本立场与达到的最终目标。各国为达到其最终目标,无不根据其面临的国际政治经济形势,制定其发展总体战略,确定不同时期或不同阶段参与多边投资规则制定的优先顺序和工作重点。

多边投资规则有地缘性(区域性)、自由贸易区、发展中国家和普遍性四种基本类型,目前我国宜据此确立参与制定的总体战略,即优先参与制定地缘性多边投资规则、重点参与制定多边自由贸易区投资规则、主导制定发展中国家间多边投资规则、积极参与制定普遍性投资规则。

第一节　优先参与制定地缘性多边投资规则

当代国际经贸法律关系整体上呈现出普遍性与区域性齐头并进的趋势,以地理资源为前提的区域一体化要求我国优先参与制定地缘性多边投资规则。

一、中国地缘性经济贸易地位突出

(一)地缘性经济层次明显

从地缘经济看,中国的主要经贸伙伴大致可以划分为三个层次:欧盟、北美、俄罗斯、非洲、拉美属于全球层次,日本、韩国、东盟、中亚和澳大利亚属于亚太地区层次,中国香港、澳门、台湾地区属于自然经济区域层次的"大中华经济圈"。[①]

(二)资本流入地缘性明显

以 2012 年为例,对华投资前十位国家和地区(以实际投入外资金额计)依次为:中国香港(712.89 亿美元)、日本(73.8 亿美元)、新加坡(65.39 亿美元)、中国台湾(61.83 亿美元)、美国(31.3 亿美元)、韩国(30.66 亿美元)、德国(14.71 亿美元)、荷兰(11.44 亿美元)、英国(10.31 亿美元)和瑞士(8.78 亿美元)。前十位国家和地区实际投入外资金额占全国实际使用外资金额的 91.4%。[②] 可见,中国在亚洲地区层次上的外资来源地主要是日本、韩国,其他国家和地区对华直接投资所占比例较小。

(三)中国对外投资地缘性明显

以我国 2012 年资本流出为例,向亚洲地区的直接投资为 448.9 亿美元,占总投资的 65.3%。在区域层面主要是新加坡(11.19 亿美元)、缅甸(8.76 亿美元)、泰国(7.00 亿美元)、柬埔寨(4.67 亿美元)、土库曼斯坦(4.51 亿美元)和阿联酋(3.49 亿美元);在周边自然经济区域主要是中国香港,占 385.05 亿美元,位居全球和亚洲第一。[③]

随着我国成为亚洲第一、全球第二大经济体,虽然说将形成以我国为中心的"轮辐式"地缘经济格局的论断为时尚早,但稳定与广泛的地缘经济空间成为必须优先考虑的问题之一。与我国有关的资本流入与流出均集中在了少数、特定的几个国家和地区,其他所有国家或经济体都是中国投资发展的潜在地缘空间。因此,优先参与制定统一、广泛的地缘性多边投资规则就成为我国首要的战略选择。恰如有的学者指出的那样,虽然在数量方面,双边协定仍占主导地位,但经济意义上的区域主义日益重要,这种转变能巩固和统一投资规则,表明迈出了多边主义的第一步。[④]

二、中国需要地缘性投资规则是必然趋势

以下仅以亚太经合组织为例。

亚太地区未如北美、欧洲那样形成一个统一的地缘性投资规则,投资自由化主要依靠 APEC 项下的单边行动计划(IAP)和集体行动计划(CAP)的共同推进。APEC 是一个由"议程"(agenda)推动的论坛,而非结构完备的组织,除无实权的秘书处外,没有其他日常组织架构,因此 APEC 又被称为"软组织"、"弱组织"或"论坛"。[⑤]

---

① 潘忠岐、黄仁伟:《中国的地缘经济战略》,载《清华大学学报(哲社版)》2008 年第 5 期。

② 商务部:《2012 年 1—12 月全国吸收外商直接投资情况》,http://www.mofcom.gov.cn/article/tongjiziliao/ v/201301/20130100009582.shtml,最后访问日期:2013 年 1 月 23 日。

③ 商务部:《中国对外投资合作发展报告(2011—2012)》,第 10 页。

④ 詹晓宁、葛顺奇:《2012 年世界投资报告:迈向新一代的投资政策》,载《第一财经日报》,2012 年 7 月 9 日第 A06 版。

⑤ 路建人:《APEC 20 年:回顾与展望》,载《国际贸易问题》2010 年第 1 期。

1994 年 APEC 部长会议通过了"APEC 非约束性投资原则"(NBIPs),虽规定了 12 条原则,但只规定了投资自由化的一般原则,对诸如国民待遇、最惠国待遇、利润汇回与外汇兑换等有关投资者待遇的核心问题的要求较弱,APEC 的自愿原则使有关争端解决机制没有较强的制度保障。

APEC 实行以"自主自愿,协商一致"为核心的独特的行事原则,创造了独一无二的"APEC 方式",与 WTO 和其他多边贸易集团所采用的谈判、强制、法律约束的原则根本不同,其主要内容包括:(1)承认成员的多样性,强调灵活性、渐进性;(2)相互尊重、平等互利;(3)协商一致,自主自愿;(4)协调的单边主义;(5)开放的地区主义。①

对 APEC 上述独特合作模式,大部分学者表示赞同,认为这一独特模式符合亚太地区各成员经济发展水平存在巨大差异以及政治、社会制度复杂的实际情况,具有相当的灵活性,是对传统国际组织原则的一个创新,突破了如欧盟等区域经济合作组织强调的贸易政策基本一致、政治价值观的相对统一的传统。② 但是,随着区域主义浪潮对区域经济一体化更高的要求,APEC 这种松散的联合必然会从一种"成员驱动"走向"规则驱动"。换言之,APEC 下的区域投资规则将会成为未来地缘性多边投资规则的首要制定场所,理由如下:

首先,APEC 2010 年"横滨愿景"提出的首要目标是实现经济一体化,而达到该目标的重要途径是达成《亚太自由贸易协定》(Free Trade Agreement of the Asia Pacific),建设亚太自由贸易区(Free Trade Area of the Asia Pacific,简称 FTAAP),并强调"APEC 应对 FTAAP 所涵盖的'下一代贸易和投资问题'的定义、制定及阐释等起重要作用",就此提出了"下一代贸易和投资问题"。2010 年 12 月,美国高官 Kurt Tong 表示"未来 APEC 会议的核心任务将是加强经济整合,并致力于定义、制定及阐释将列入 21 世纪区域贸易协定中的下一阶段贸易与投资事务"。③

其次,数量众多的自由贸易协定(Free Trade Agreements,简称 FTAs)及依其建立的自由贸易区(Free Trade Area,简称 FTA)使 APEC 下的投资环境更加复杂,极像一个"意大利面条碗"式的规则网络,这对区域经济一体化产生严重的阻碍作用。笔者认为,投资自由化和经济一体化程度的加深,在 APEC 内建立一个具有法律拘束力的统一地缘性多边投资规则是一种必然趋势。

最后,美国在"亚太战略再平衡"中已经提出制定地缘性投资规则。2011 年 11 月 13 日 APEC 第 19 次领导人非正式会议上,美国总统奥巴马宣布,美国已与其他 8 个国家就跨太平洋战略经济伙伴关系(Trans-Pacific Strategic Economic Partnership,简称 TPSEP)的纲领达成一致,并随后展开了热烈的谈判,其中包含了一个统一的、高水平的地缘性投资

① 陆建人主编:《亚太经合组织与中国》,经济管理出版社 2007 年版,第 22~24 页。
② 路宇立:《APEC 合作的理论基础:新区域主义的视角分析》,载《国际贸易问题》2011 年第 4 期。
③ 刘重力、王丽华:《2011 年 APEC 重要议题评析及中国策略》,载《亚太经济》2011 年第 6 期。

66

规则。①

我国积极并优先参与制定地缘性多边投资规则,不仅有利于区域经济一体化,也是我国抵消 TPSEP 对我国不利影响的重要战略选择之一。

第二节　重点参与制定多边自由贸易区投资规则

在当代区域多边投资规则的一大发展趋势是,多边自由贸易区协定包括了该区域的投资规则条款。这种趋势必然要求中国重点参与制定多边自由贸易区投资规则。

一、多边自由贸易区投资规则是深化区域一体化的重要手段

随着 WTO 多哈回合谈判停滞不前,许多国家逐渐认识到由于谈判方众多、关注领域的分歧巨大,导致多边国际合作机制无法获得进一步成果,通过建立双边、多边的自由贸易区(FTA)的方式推进国际经济关系的发展。进入 21 世纪后,FTA 作为 WTO 附加型(WTO-Plus)的进一步延伸,其条款逐渐从贸易转向了投资、知识产权保护、政府采购和劳工等领域。欧盟认为,"竞争驱动型"的 FTA 战略对欧盟是至关重要的,这是深度一体化的重要手段。②

根据近年来新区域主义浪潮的发展实践,可以按涉及的内容、依照一体化深度的不同,将全球自由贸易协定分为以下几个层次:最基本的层次是货物贸易自由化;第二个层次是包括货物贸易、服务贸易和投资三个方面的贸易投资一体化;第三个层次是在贸易投资一体化基础上包括更广泛的内容,如竞争政策、知识产权、政府采购、金融合作、能源合作、电子商务等。涉及第二个和第三个层次的一体化协定通常称为"深度一体化"协定。③ 与地缘性投资规则不同,自由贸易区的投资规则是基于多边参与方在经济方面合作的需求,并不一定要求满足地缘性质。

二、中国参与多边自由贸易区投资规则制定的成功实践

(一)中国—东盟投资协定

《中国—东盟投资协定》在 2009 年第 8 次中国—东盟经贸部长会议上签署。此协定

---

①　田海:《TPP 背景下中国的选择策思考——基于与 APEC 的比较分析》,载《亚太经济》2012 年第 4 期。

②　European Commission, Global Europe: Competing in the World, COM(2006)567 final, 4 October 2006.

③　东艳:《深度一体化:中国自由贸易区战略的新趋势》,载《当代亚太》2009 年第 4 期。

签署后,直接投资资本呈现出快速增长的态势。以 2012 年为例。中国和东盟双向投资累计 940 亿美元;东盟对我国的投资规模不断扩大,截至 2012 年 6 月底,对中国的直接投资累计达 738 亿美元,占中国吸引外资总额的 6%,是中国的第三大外资来源地。中国企业对东盟各国投资势头方兴未艾,东盟已成为中国企业国外投资的第一大市场,中国是东盟的第四大外资来源地。又据统计,2013 年,中国在东盟累计投资 229.4 亿美元,年均增速达 68%。①

(二)中国—海湾合作委员会框架协定

2004 年 7 月,我国与海湾合作委员会(简称"海合会")6 个成员国签署了《中国—海合会经济、贸易投资和技术合作框架协定》,并共同宣布启动中国—海合会自由贸易区谈判。截至 2016 年 12 月,中国与海合会举行了 9 轮自由贸易协定谈判,双方就 15 个谈判议题中的 9 个结束谈判,并就技术性贸易壁垒、法律条款、电子商务等条款内容基本达成一致,在核心的货物、服务等领域取得积极进展。② 就投资而言,双方在能源方面的投资合作尤为重要,我国的石油进口已经突破 50% 的红线,如何利用多边自由贸易区投资规则促进能源领域的投资,保证我国在能源方面的稳定供应成为当前的重要议题。

(三)中日韩投资协定与自由贸易区谈判

中日韩三国不仅在地理上接近,其经济总量之和占亚洲经济总量的 70%,三国的经济发展对于东亚乃至整个世界经济的复苏具有重要意义。鉴于中日韩三国在经济上具有很强的互补性,20 世纪 90 年代中期,日本和韩国一些学者提出创建中日韩共同体的主张,有关中日韩区域经济一体化的想法首次被提出。在 2002 年 11 月举行的中日韩领导人会议期间,中方向日韩两国提出了建立中日韩自由贸易区的构想。以后的十余年间,中日、韩日之间经历了一系列领土纠纷,设立自由贸易区的谈判被一再搁置。2010 年 5 月 29 日在韩国济州岛召开的第三次中日韩领导人会议通过了"2020 中日韩合作展望",三国承诺努力在 2012 年前完成中日韩自由贸易区的联合研究。根据中日韩三方约定,中日韩在 2013 年举行自由贸易区三轮谈判,第一轮谈判于 2013 年 3 月 26 日至 28 日在韩国首尔举行。2013 年 3 月 26 日,中日韩自由贸易区首轮谈判正式如期在韩国首尔开启。③ 截至 2019 年 12 月,中日韩举行了 16 轮自由贸易区谈判。第 16 轮谈判在货物贸

---

① 许宁宁:《中国与东盟经贸合作 2012—2013 年度报告》,http://news.hexun.com/2012-12-28/149611086.html,最后访问日期:2022 年 1 月 23 日。

② 《中国—海合会自贸区第九轮谈判在沙特利雅得闭幕》,http://fta.mofcom.gov.cn/article/chinahaihehui/haihehuinews/201612/33882_1.html,最后访问日期:2022 年 12 月 12 日。

③ 《中日韩自由贸易区谈判开启 十一年努力终掀大幕》,http://www.dzwww.com/xinwen/xinwenzhuanti/2008/ggkf30zn/201303/t20130327_8298396.htm,最后访问日期:2022 年 5 月 10 日。

易、服务贸易、投资和规则等重要议题上取得积极进展 。①

中日韩投资协定谈判自 2007 年启动以来,历时 5 年,先后进行了 13 轮正式谈判和数次非正式磋商,于 2012 年 3 月下旬圆满结束,2012 年 5 月 13 日于北京正式签署《中日韩投资协定》。该协定由 27 条和 1 个附加议定书组成,囊括了国际投资协定通常包含的所有重要内容,包括投资定义、适用范围、最惠国待遇、国民待遇、征收、转移、代位、税收、一般例外、争端解决等条款。《中日韩投资协定》的签署在中日韩三国经贸合作中具有里程碑意义。这是中日韩第一个促进和保护三国间投资的法律文件和制度安排,为中日韩自由贸易区建设提供了重要基础。该协定将为三国投资者提供更为稳定和透明的投资环境,进一步激发三国投资者的投资热情,促进三国间经贸活动更趋活跃,推动三国经济的共同发展和繁荣。三国将尽快履行国内法律程序,使投资协定早日生效并发挥作用。②该协定已于 2014 年 5 月 17 日生效。③

(四)金砖国家经贸投资合作框架

2013 年 3 月 26 日,金砖国家第三次贸易部长会议发表《金砖国家贸易投资合作框架》,其主要内容为:合作框架的目标是促进金砖国家间贸易、投资和经济合作;鼓励强化金砖国家间贸易和投资联系,发挥经济互补性,促进可持续发展和包容性增长;在成员国之间共享贸易和投资发展经验;鼓励金砖国家间构建相关机制,增强生产能力和多种经济部门的价值提升;加强沟通与合作。具体合作领域有多边场合的合作与协调、贸易投资促进和便利化、技术创新合作、中小企业合作、知识产权合作、基础设施和工业发展合作。④

该框架中虽未明确规定开展自由贸易区的谈判,但根据合作目标与具体领域,可以预见,金砖国家间的合作必将向自由贸易区方向发展。

(五)《区域全面经济伙伴关系协定》

《区域全面经济伙伴关系协定》(RCEP)是亚太地区规模最大、最重要的自由贸易协定,其覆盖世界近一半人口和近三分之一贸易量,成为世界上涵盖人口最多、成员构成最

---

① 《中日韩自贸区第十六轮谈判在韩国首尔举行》,http://fta.mofcom.gov.cn/article/chinarihan/chinarhnews/201912/41938_1.html,最后访问日期:2022 年 12 月 15 日;《中日韩自贸区谈判首席谈判代表会间会在京举行》,http://fta.mofcom.gov.cn/article/chinarihan/chinarhnews/201912/41938_1.html,最后访问日期:2022 年 12 月 15 日。

② 《中日韩三国正式签署投资协定》,http://www.chinanews.com/gn/2012/05-13/3884252.shtml,最后访问日期:2022 年 3 月 10 日。

③ China-Japan-Korea, Republic of Trilateral Investment Agreement (2012), https://investmentpolicy.unctad.org/international-investment-agreements/countries/42/china, last visited on 27 Dec. 2020.

④ 《金砖国家经贸部长会议发表贸易投资合作框架》,http://news.163.com/13/0327/10/8QVE28R700014JB6.html,最后访问日期:2022 年 5 月 2 日。

多元、发展最具活力的自由贸易区。① 其第 10 章"投资"规定促进、保护投资的具体实体规则。其中有些规则属于投资领域新规则,代表了国际投资实体规则的新发展。

综观我国已经或即将参加的自由贸易区,除少数投资规则外,我国深度一体化自由贸易区投资规则仍然停留在"纲领性"的层面,主要表现在两个方面:(1)在市场准入的具体投资领域开放上,投资协定未作出具体规定。根据当前投资协定实践,一般是缔约各国针对本国较为成熟的开放领域,拟定具体的承诺义务,列出市场开放的范围和时间表,并通过例外清单、敏感清单、过渡期等方法解决各成员方经济发展水平不均衡而导致的开放领域差异问题,而我国当前的自由贸易区协定未作出规定而是交由各缔约国国内法律根据各自吸引外资的需求进行规定。(2)在争端解决上,无论是《中国—东盟投资协定》还是《中日韩投资协定》,都未建立类似于 NAFTA、EU 等的投资争端解决机构,而是交由 UNCTAD 和 ICSID 解决,未体现出自由贸易区的封闭性与"优惠"性质。

自由贸易区所涵盖的议题除投资之外,还包括货物贸易、服务贸易、争端解决机制等,虽然每个议题具有独立性,但在总体上又是相关联的,参与主体在一个议题上的分歧,可以在一定程度上从另外一个议题上进行弥合甚至通过交换来实现,各参与方在进行一个议题谈判时会将考虑其他议题的利益得失,因此在谈判议题的交换、妥协的作出和利益的让渡建立在国家整体利益基点上的前提下,重点参与多边自由贸易区投资规则的建构是我国的重要战略之一。②

第三节　主导制定发展中国家间多边投资规则

鉴于中国国际投资在发展中国家或地区流量与存量的占比很大,中国宜主导制定中国作为成员的发展中国家间多边投资规则。

一、发展中国家需"同类国家"的多边投资规则

在国际投资自由化浪潮下,发展中国家对待外资的态度从逐渐抵触走向开放,在发达国家主导下,国际投资规则逐渐趋同,发展中国家迫切需要形成一个"同类国家"间的投资协定,以提高多边投资协定谈判过程中的议价能力。"同类国家"是指在政治制度、经济体制、意识形态、法律体系、文化传统、宗教信仰以及语言等方面具有一致性或相似

---

① 《区域全面经济伙伴关系协定》,https://baike.sogou.com/v174023874.htm? fromTitle＝rcep,最后访问日期:2022 年 12 月 5 日。
② 张庆麟、彭忠波:《晚近多边投资规则谈判的新动向——兼论我国多边投资谈判策略的选择》,载《国际经济法学刊》2005 年第 3 期。

性的不同国家。[1] 正是基于发展中国家的同类性,其与发达国家就投资规则的磋商过程中,陷入发达国家所提供的"范本"式的讨价还价中。发展中国家在与发达国家的投资协定谈判过程中,都面临限制性商业行为、转移定价、技术转让、环境标准和政府采购等方面的较高要价,而这也正是双边谈判无法解决的问题。如果在发展中国家之间有相对统一的多边投资规则,则有助于在发展中国家之间就共同关切的问题提早进行谈判并明确互相认可的出价底线,在未来与发达国家进行投资规则的谈判过程中,不仅能对议题认识更为明晰,也能在发展中国家间形成底线相同的"谈判联盟",从而提高在相关问题上的议价能力。

二、为中国与其他发展中国家合作与发展所必需

进入 21 世纪,中国成为影响国际投资关系最为重要的发展中国家之一。

20 世纪以前,我国参与多边投资规则的基本态度和立场是"随势而动",积极与发达国家和地区建立投资关系并合理接受相应的投资规则。在 21 世纪初,随着中国加入WTO,经济总量空前发展,国际投资的角色扮演逐渐从"资本输入国"的单一身份向"资本输入与输出国"的混同身份发展,可称"得势而为"。自 2004 年后,我国不断参与、修正对外投资和双边、多边投资规则,在"走出去"战略的背景下,正在迈入"谋势而为"的阶段。一方面,我国作为最大的发展中国家,和其他发展中国家有着长期友好的合作基础、广泛的共同关切和共同利益;另一方面,国际体系正在发生变革,中国与发展中国家的关系面临着一些新情况和新问题,甚至出现以往不曾显现的矛盾,例如对外贸易摩擦、安全诉求分歧、能源争夺、文化冲突等。因此,要想成为发展中国家间多边投资规则的主导者,应采取以下态度和立场:正确客观地认识分歧和矛盾,不回避不粉饰;重视谈判对象,加深对其研究,在深入了解的基础上拟定应对措施,不打无准备之仗;支持发展中国家的正当要求,以促进和保护投资为共同目标。我国作为国际投资关系的重要一极,利用"发展中国家"这一身份认同,主导制定发展中国家间的多边投资规则,成为我国参与制定多边投资规则的重要战略之一。

三、为中国在发展中国家的投资利益所必要

我国在发展中国家的投资份额日渐增多,领域日趋宽泛,迫切需要我国主导制定发展中国家间的多边投资规则。

从我国对外直接投资地区构成情况看,2010 年对欧洲、北美洲、拉丁美洲的投资继续保持快速增长态势,尤其对非洲的投资较上年增长超四成占3.1%,主要分布在南非、刚果(金)、尼日尔、阿尔及利亚、尼日利亚、肯尼亚等,拉丁美洲 105.4 亿美元,同比增长

---

① 张云燕:《社会建构主义与东亚区域经济合作》,复旦大学 2004 年博士学位论文。

43.8％,占流量的 15.3％;主要流向英属维尔京群岛、开曼群岛、巴西、秘鲁等。[1] 中国对非洲直接投资存量在 2002 年为 4.9 亿美元,2008 年达到 78 亿美元。在非洲进行直接投资的中国企业从 2000 年的 500 家左右上升到 2008 年的 900 多家。[2] 根据商务部 2010 年数据,我国对拉丁美洲的直接投资额较大,对非洲的直接投资总额相对较小,2010 年中国对外直接投资排在前三位的分别是中国香港、英属维尔京群岛、开曼群岛,流出量分别为 385.05 亿美元、61.2 亿美元、34 亿美元,总计共占了 75.5％的权重。中国香港、英属维尔京群岛和开曼群岛是世界著名的三大避税地,诸多国际投资仅仅是将其作为了一个投资避税跳板而已,其中的"水份"不容低估。据统计,2020 年,中国对外直接投资流量1537.1 亿美元,同比增长 12.3％;存量 25806.58 亿美元,分别占全球当年流量、存量的20.2％和 6.6％。其中对亚洲、非洲、拉丁美洲的流量和存量分别为 1123.44 亿美元和1648.96 亿美元、42.26 亿美元和 433.99 亿美元、116.57 亿美元和 6298.10 亿美元。可见,我国在发展中地区的直接投资额巨大,在这些地区的国家海外利益凸显。[3]

中国对非洲、拉丁美洲的直接投资占中国实质对外直接投资的总量是一个相当可观的比重,中国在这些国家有投资利益和国家利益,需要我国主导制定发展中国家间的多边投资规则,对我国投资者及其利益和国家海外投资利益提供规则保障。

四、中国与其他发展中国家协商一致程度高

由于我国与亚洲、非洲和拉美发展中国家间没有形成一个涵盖避税、劳工以及环境等内容的共同投资规则,导致了投资流向偏转,甚至带来西方国家对我国对这些地区的经济活动冠以"新殖民主义"的非难。我国对发展中国家的投资实践证明恰恰相反。

为改善非洲国家在吸引外商投资领域所处的劣势地位和撒哈拉以南非洲的投资法律环境为目标,2003 年非洲法律专家们在达喀尔会议上通过了非洲示范投资法。[4] 该示范法在内容上较明确体现了非洲发展中国家在若干重要议题上"稳中求进"的思路,对非洲各国的立法产生了较为重要的影响,加速了非洲发展中国家国内投资法制的趋同。在此方面,我国的基本立场上是,在遵守东道国的法律、符合东道国经济社会发展目标的前提下促进我国对非洲的投资。因此我国作为与非洲发展中国家多边投资规则制定的主导者,能够充分尊重和吸纳这些趋同的投资法律规则。

拉丁美洲政治舞台"左派"力量日渐崛起,主张在电力、能源等领域的国有化,要求国有公司对重要能源领域实行全面掌控,这与我国在经济体制方面具有相似性,有利于产

---

① 商务部等:《2010 年度中国对外直接投资统计公报》,http://hzs.mofcom.gov.cn/aarticle/date/201109/20110907741156.html,最后访问日期:2022 年 7 月 25 日。

② [毛里塔尼亚]古尔默·阿布杜罗:《非洲与中国:新殖民主义还是新型战略伙伴关系》,马京鹏译,载《国外理论动态》2012 年第 9 期。

③ 商务部、国家统计局、国家外汇管理局:《2020 年度中国对外直接投资统计公报》,中国商务出版社 2021 年版,第 6～30 页、第 50～60 页。

④ 郭莉莉:《非洲投资示范法述评》,湘潭大学 2010 年法律硕士学位论文。

生进一步对话。随着阿根廷等国家在能源投资领域陷入了发达国家投资规则下的"中等收入陷阱",在 ICSID 作为被告的案件不断涌现,促使拉美国家逐步反思并调整其国际投资政策。而中拉经贸关系形成了"贸易和投资并重,金融合作正在转型,并以援助促进经济技术合作"的多样化格局。此外,通过在拉美投资设厂,部分竞争力较强的中国企业形成了全球性的区域布局,有利于扩大市场辐射面,规避单个市场的风险。[①]

历史和现实的实践证明,发展中国家有能力以集体的力量,在多边贸易体制中遏制发达国家的漫天要价,使规则既顺应投资自由化的趋势又能反映各国利益。[②] 因此,我国主导非洲、拉美等发展中国家间多边投资规则的制定,是我国制定多边投资规则的重要战略之一。

第四节　积极参与制定普遍性投资规则

二战以后,为了保护国际投资,改善国际投资环境,由联合国、世界银行、经合组织等全球性国际组织为普遍性多边投资规则的制定持续发起造法运动,在各自领域制定了一系列的多边投资规则。虽然在全球范围内尚未建立一个跨区域的、全面的多边投资框架,但这并不意味着普遍性多边投资规则制定的停滞,相反,普遍性投资规则的制定已成为必然趋势。

一、国际投资的发展需要制定普遍性投资规则

21 世纪以前,国际投资主要集中于这两者需求的互补性上:外国投资者利用东道国生产要素并占有市场的需求和东道国期望通过外国直接投资带来就业、管理、技术、资金等一揽子要素转移需求。当前国际资本多向流动,发展中国家企业崛起,跨国性日益明显。发达国家与发展中国家企业之间的竞争更多地表现在服务与技术革新。国际投资的新趋势体现在四个方面:(1)国有公司成为重要的国际投资者。由于国有公司的投资行为在一定程度上体现了国家的战略性安排,不但其投资领域具有敏感性,而且其会被归因于国家行为,例如中海油与加拿大尼克森公司并购案。当前国际投资规则的双边体制的关涉者仅是双边协定的签署国,并无多边体制下其他成员的压力,东道国更容易采取投资保护主义。(2)跨国公司的直接投资方式从"绿地投资"向"棕地投资之跨国并购"转变,通过控制一个跨国公司而占领被并购者之前占有的跨国市场,例如联想公司对IBM 公司的并购,投资关系的特点不再是双边性而是多边性。(3)随着发展中国家进一步开放市场,服务自由化趋势更加明显,国际资本流动从传统制造业转向电信、医疗、金

---

① 郑秉文:《中国与拉美 60 年:总结与思考》,载《拉丁美洲研究》2009 年第 10 期。
② 陈畅东:《国际投资立法自由化趋势及我国的对策》,载《民主与法治》2008 年第 8 期。

融、物流等产业,国际间的多向流动性增强,双边性逐渐弱化。(4)技术革新促使资本从劳动密集型产业向技术密集型、资本密集型、资源密集型的产业流动,极大地拉动了国际投资规模。

随着投资主体、投资方式、投资领域的变化,双边投资规则对国际投资的调整能力正在逐渐下降。2010年共有178项新的国际投资协定(平均每周3个新协定),年末国际投资协定的总数达到了6092个。这些协定之间庞大的谈判量和复杂程度令政府和投资者都难以应对;但它仍无法涵盖所有可能出现的双边投资关系。如果要做到这一点,需要再缔结14100项双边条约。[①] 因此,建立多边国际投资协定框架的呼声越来越高。

二、普遍性投资规则是投资自由化与便利化的法律保障

投资自由化与便利化要求资本在国家间更自由地流动,要求各国政府减少对国际资本的监督和管制,这是经济全球化的必然趋势。尽管双边投资协定在征收及补偿、履行要求禁止和争端解决方面的立场实现了趋同,但各国在投资待遇特别是给予投资者设业前的国民待遇和敏感行业的投资准入方面仍然存有重大分歧。联合国贸易与发展会议2011年报告显示,2010年共有74个经济体设立或修正了149项投资政策措施,近三分之一的投资措施对外国私人直接投资实行了新的限制或监管程序,与2009年相比略有增加;近年来对外国直接投资增加限制性措施和行政审批程序的现象正在增多,投资自由化与便利化正面临重大障碍。[②]

造成障碍的原因之一是当前国际投资规则的机制性缺陷。当前调整国际投资的国际法律规范主要是双边投资协定,这种协定往往对投资自由化和便利化有一定程度的保留。即使一方实施了违反协定的投资保护主义措施甚至单方废止双边协定,其所面临的仅是另一签署方及其投资者的压力。但在普遍性投资规则下,成员方一旦实施违反规则的投资保护主义措施,将面临其他成员方根据多边规则对其施加报复的集团化压力,违法成本远高于其所获得的利益。因此,普遍性多边投资规则是投资自由化与便利化的法律保障。

三、中国积极参与制定普遍投资规则是谋取国际舞台话语权

2008年金融危机以后,我国迎来了谋取国际经济话语权的一大契机。在"走出去"战略背景下,国有企业对外投资额增长较快,能源领域的投资占据约16%的份额,而国有企业在一定程度上体现的是国家产业发展的战略意图,其对外投资更容易被赋予政治意味。由于双边投资协定解决的是私人投资者与东道国之间的直接投资关系,因此这种有

---

① 《国际投资趋势》,http://www.cb.com.cn/info/2011_0810/254440.html,最后访问日期:2022年7月22日。

② UNCTAD, World Investment Report 2011, pp.94-98.

可能被"归因于国家"的投资难以从双边投资协定中获得应有的保护。根据德勤会计师事务所的一份报告,中国海外并购交易的成功率只有一半,但是中国对外投资以资源为导向的不良印象已经形成。[①] 以 2010 年为例,中国对外投资年流量超过日本、英国等对外投资大国,达到 680 亿美元,位居世界第五,中国在全球外资存量(总量)居全球第九,但投资收益由于种种原因至今未能披露。

积极参加制定普遍性投资规则可以更多地表达我国在国有企业以及其他问题上的利益诉求,尽可能使普遍性投资规则在最大程度上符合我国利益,保证我国投资的合法收益。在融入国际投资自由化的过程中,中国可根据本国经济发展水平决定自由化进程,坚持投资自由化、便利化与规范化并重,合理兼顾投资者、东道国和投资母国三方利益的原则,化解各方分歧,在共谋发展的基础上推动国际经济的发展和国际经济新秩序的形成。[②]

本章小结

随着国际资本多向流动,发展中国家日渐成为国际投资的新生力量,国际投资规则已经从双边和区域规则为主向区域性与普遍性并进的发展趋势。区域性规则下的地缘性规则已逐步完善,区域经济一体化带动了贸易与投资规则的迅猛发展。我国在多元类型的投资规则构建过程中,应当采取不同的身份定位,将地缘性规则置于优先位置,将多边自由贸易区投资规则作为重点谈判议题,利用身份认同主导发展中国家间的规则构建,并积极参与普遍性投资规则的谈判,争取不同场所下的话语权,保证区域性与普遍性规则协同发展,充分保护我国海外投资利益。

[①] 《国际投资趋势》,http://news.hexun.com/2011-08-09/132259511.html,最后访问日期:2022年 7 月 15 日。

[②] 李本:《对国际多边投资立法从回应到参与——中国外商投资立法的嬗变分析》,载《法学杂志》2009 年第 8 期。

第五章

中国参与制定多边投资规则的总体策略

各国为实现战略目标,需采取行之有效的策略。策略是预先根据可能出现的问题制订的若干应对方案,是实现战略目标的具体方案的集合,是战略目标实现过程中具体的趋利避害的方法与手段。多边投资规则的形成是国家合意的产物,但国家在谈判过程中的态度与立场受到政治、经济、地缘、安全等因素的影响。我国在参与多边投资规则制定过程中应当在多维标准的视角下,区分不同国家类型,采取不同的策略,以促成多边投资规则的最终达成。具体而言,我国宜遵循先特殊后一般、先区域后普遍、先近邻后远邻、先同类国家后不同类型国家的策略,求同存异,制定出较大程度符合我国利益的多边投资规则。

第一节　先特殊后一般的策略

辩证唯物主义认为,特殊与一般反映的是客观世界规律的个性与一般性。一般是指各种门类事物内部的统一性乃至世界的统一性,特殊是指某个种类所属事物共同具有的特殊性和各个单一事物独有的特殊性。客观规律总是经由特殊向一般转化,因此需要根据特殊问题的特点特殊对待。我国参与多边投资规则的制定,在策略上首先要区分特殊问题和一般问题,采取灵活变通的做法先解决特殊问题。在多边投资规则制定中主要关注以下特殊问题。

一、特殊谈判对象

多边投资规则涉及多方利益博弈,每个谈判主体都有自己不同的利益,需要根据不同国家的类型、不同类型国家的立场寻求共同利益点或者采取不同的策略来应对。如新兴经济体(例如巴西、中国、印度和南非)在最近几年内已经成为重要的投资输出国。这标志全球化进程的一个新阶段的开始。[①] 这些新兴经济体曾经为了吸引外国投资而勉强接受国际投资准则,随着本国对外投资规模的增大,它们越来越希望其海外投资受到国际投资法律体系的保护,同时作为主要的资本输入国不得不考虑外资与本国公共利益的平衡。因此参与和推进多边投资规则有着共同的利益要求,基于这些共同利益可以在谈判中结成利益共同体。但文化和地区方面的差异又可能使各国在多边投资规则应当涵盖哪些具体内容的问题上出现较大分歧。传统发展中国家长期与我国保持良好的政治、经济交往,随着各国参与经济全球化,利益分化开始出现,尤其是我国日渐成为资本输出大国,这些发展中国家仍然是主要资本输入国,我国海外投资与东道国的摩擦增多。[②] 因此在谈判中首先需要分析特殊国家的特点,根据具体的谈判现状作出具体的应对,采取不同的具体策略。

二、特殊谈判议题

发展、国家安全、投资措施等问题在现有大多数国际投资协定中不专门处理,或者仅仅以次要方式处理。[③]

(一)发展问题

大多数国际投资条约不涉及发展问题,即使涉及发展问题也只是在序言部分笼统提及。除序言中的表述外,国际投资条约主要通过间接方式,即通过保护东道国境内外国投资来推进发展目标,如业绩要求及环境要求。多边投资规则的制定是多方博弈的结果,各参与方均有自己的利益,如果利益严重分化,分歧不能化解和弥合,无法求同存异,则不可能达成多边投资协定。如果过分强调投资自由化而忽视东道国利益或者对东道国的外资管理权施加过分压制,则多边投资规则谈判成功的可能性小。多边投资规则的谈判成功必须建立在考虑东道国发展问题的基础上。[④] 发展中国家允许外资进入的目的是直接投资能对管理、就业、技术及资金的一揽子要素转移,无条件的自由化将会使不发达国家处于产业链的中低端,无法优化自身经济产业结构。如果不考虑环境保护的投资

---

① UNCTAD, *International Investment Rule-making—Stocktaking*, *Challenges and the Way Forward on International Investment Policies for Development*, UNCTAD Series, United Nations, 2008, p.43.

② 崇泉:《三因素致中国企业海外投资摩擦增多》,http://news.xinhuanet.com/2012-11/26/c_113805469.htm,最后访问日期:2022年1月20日。

③ Zachary Douglas, *The International Law of Investment Claims*, Cambridge University Press, 2009, p.6.

④ E.V.K. FitzGerald, R. Cubero-Brealey and A. Lehmann, *The Development Implications of the Multilateral Agreement on Investment*, A Report Commissioned by the Department for International Development, 2010, p.46.

对东道国可持续发展,对全球治理是弊大于利,无益于多边投资规则的达成与有效运转。因此,我国在参与制定多边投资规则过程中宜将不发达国家的发展问题考虑在内,给予不发达国家一定的过渡期与特殊优惠条件。①

(二)国家安全问题

在多边投资框架内,发达国家一方面推崇自由化、另一方面非常重视国家安全,一般通过国内法上的国家安全条款或条约中根本安全例外条款来实现。如:美国无论是在贸易领域还是在投资领域,在有关条约的具体条款中均采用了安全例外条款,而且在安全例外条款的判定方面使用"其认为"(it considers)这一极富主观色彩的判断标准,拥有极大的自由裁量权。② 相反,发展中国家对该问题的关注程度较低,我国参与的国际投资规则中只有少数协定明确规定根本安全例外条款。国际投资问题从开始就涉及有关国家的经济安全、生态安全,在一些特殊部门甚至会涉及政治安全与军事安全,采取必要手段进行必要关注是深入参与经济全球化和制定普遍性多边投资规则的必然考虑。

(三)投资措施

多边投资规则对投资措施的关注始于 GATT 乌拉圭回合谈判。当时纳入谈判的有13 项投资措施,③但经过各方较量、斡旋,最终确定了 4 项,并达成了 TRIMs 协定。TRIMs 协定中明确规定了禁止成员方采用四种与贸易有关的投资措施,即贸易平衡、当地成分、外汇平衡和出口实绩。④ 在 OECD 的 MAI 草案中涉及的范围更为广泛,基本上囊括了乌拉圭回合谈判时涉及的所有投资措施。⑤ 虽然发达国家和发展中国家在是否对投资措施进行限制的问题上存在分歧,但投资措施是多边投资协定不可回避的话题,尤其是在以投资自由化为目标的多边投资规则中更值得重视。

三、特殊的谈判推进方式

谈判方式的选择在一定程度上影响谈判结果。目前已有多边投资规则的谈判方式有投资协定、合作框架两种基本方式。

---

① Errc M. Burt,Developing Countries and the Framework for Negotiations on Foreign Direct Investment in the World Trade Organization,*American University Journal of International Law & Policy*,1997,Vol.12,p.1043.

② 温先涛:《〈中国投资保护协定范本〉(草案)论稿(二)》,载《国际经济法学刊》2012 年第 1 期。

③ 赵维田:《世界贸易组织的法律制度》,吉林大学出版社 2000 年版,第 416~418 页。

④ TRIMs 协定要求禁止采用与 GATT 第 2 条(国民待遇)和第 11 条(一般取消数量限制)相冲突的投资措施:贸易平衡要求、当地成分要求、外汇平衡要求和出口实绩要求。

⑤ OECD,Launch of the Negotiations of A multilateral Agreement on Investment,DAFFE/CMIT/CIME(95) 13/FINAL,5 May 1995.

(一)投资协定方式

投资协定的谈判方式中有自上而下、自下而上、一揽子谈判和分部门谈判四种。

1.自上而下的方式

自上而下(up-down)谈判方式,是指在谈判过程中,先设定高标准的投资保护和自由化规则,并以此作为谈判的基准,再允许各谈判方作出有限的保留或规定相应的例外情形,以便就高标准的多边投资规则迅速达成一致。《北美自由贸易协定》(NAFTA)、《能源宪章条约》(ECT)和MAI草案均采取该种谈判方式。在该方式中,不仅强调国民待遇是多边投资规则的基本原则,而且将其扩展至市场准入阶段,仅在特殊部门允许各国在互惠和国家安全的基础上予以保留和/或作出例外。[①]

自上而下方式反映的是一步到位的谈判思想,其优点在于能够迅速实现高标准的投资保护和投资促进的目标,缺点在于当谈判方数量众多,各方利益分化比较严重、分歧较大时难以促成谈判成功,尤其是在谈判内容设置了高标准的投资自由化目标时,一般不容易为发展中国家接受。

2.自下而上的方式

自下而上(down-up)的谈判方式,是指在谈判过程中,各方以所能接受的较低投资规则标准作为起点,并在此基础上进行后续谈判,以逐步达成高标准的投资规则。[②] 例如,TRIMs协定并未全面禁止业绩要求,在解释清单中明确禁止了5种典型的限制投资措施,与GATT第3条的国民待遇及一般取消数量限制原则对其予以弹性化约束。[③] GATS仅要求各缔约方在其承诺领域的市场准入采取国民待遇,不将其定位成一般原则。这种方式的优点是能够温和地达成一个多边投资规则的目标,但是该投资规则下的自由化程度相对较低,其后续推进会相对缓慢甚至停滞不前。

3.一揽子谈判方式

一揽子方式是"要么全有,要么全无"的方式,即谈判各方就多个领域、多个议题同时展开谈判,并接受谈判达成的所有成果,不能挑选接受其中的部分内容。[④] OECD起草的MAI草案即是如此,全面规定投资领域的核心问题,不允许各方对规则的不同内容选择性接受。

4.分部门谈判方式

分部门谈判方式是各缔约方就特殊或容易达成的多边投资规则先行制定,采取化整为零的办法。欧盟及其成员国与独联体在能源贸易与投资自由化合作领域达成的《能源宪章条约》采用了这种谈判方式。

[①]　徐崇利:《经济全球化与国际经济条约谈判方式的创新》,载《比较法研究》2001年第3期。

[②]　徐崇利:《经济全球化与国际经济条约谈判方式的创新》,载《比较法研究》2001年第3期。

[③]　张庆麟、彭忠波:《晚近多边投资规则谈判的新动向——兼论我国多边投资谈判策略的选择》,载《国际经济法学刊》2005年第12卷第3期。

[④]　徐崇利:《经济全球化与国际经济条约谈判方式的创新》,载《比较法研究》2001年第3期。

鉴于我国目前发展水平和对外投资状况,我国在参与多边投资规则制定时适合采取自下而上的谈判方式,先建立多边投资规则框架,在这个框架搭建起来以后,对不同内容的多边投资规则根据其特点选择相应的谈判方式。

(二)合作框架

并非所有的投资谈判都要达成含有权利义务条款的多边投资规则。在参与各方差异和分歧较大、难以达成具有实质权利义务的多边投资条约时,可以考虑只确立促进投资的合作框架,通过交流信息方式鼓励建立对投资有利的环境,在缔约方之间设立顾问委员会、联合小组或者某种类似的制度安排,以便就履行约定承诺采取后续行动,并且讨论和研究哪些因素有可能妨碍贸易和确定投资方面的市场准入等。金砖国家贸易部长2013 年 3 月达成的《贸易投资合作框架》即为典型实例。

第二节 先区域后普遍的策略

基于普遍性投资规则难以达成、区域性多边投资规则较容易达成的历史与现实,中国宜采取先区域、后普遍的策略。

一、制定普遍性投资规则的成功率小

国际社会进行了多次制定普遍性投资规则的努力,均未能取得全面性、实质性的进展,最多只是在某一方面获得一些普遍认同,与具有统领性、普遍性的国际投资规则尚有差距。[①]

(一)普遍性投资规则的制定概要

1929 年,由国际联盟和国际商会发起制定普遍性投资规则,但未能为各国接受。1948 年,《哈瓦那宪章》中纳入了具有国际投资法典性质的内容,因主要资本输出国不满而搁浅。1949 年,国际商会起草的《外国投资公正待遇法典》,未得到广泛认同。1972 年,国际商会又制定了《国际商会国际投资指南》(*ICC Guidelines for International Investment*),但不具约束力。经合组织于 1961 年、1962 年分别制定了对其成员国生效的《资本流动自由化法典》(*The OECD Code of Liberalization of Capital Movements*)和《关于保护外国财产公约草案》,未得到发展中国家认可。1976 年经合组织通过了对成员国有效的《关于国际投资与跨国公司的宣言》(*Declarations by Governments of OECD*

---

① Julie A. Maupin, MFN-Based Jurisdiction in Investor-State Arbitration:Is There any Hope for a Consistent Approach,*Journal of International Economic Law*,2011, Vol.14, No.1, p.158.

Member Countries on International Investment and Multinational Enterprises)。联合国大会于 1962 年通过了《关于自然资源之永久主权的宣言》、1974 年通过了《建立国际经济新秩序宣言》和《各国经济权利和义务宪章》；从 1974 年开始讨论制定《跨国公司行动守则》，但是至今没能达成有约束力的跨国公司行为规范。世界银行于 1965 年通过了 ICSID 公约，并建立了 ICSID；1981 年通过了 MIGA 公约，建立了 MIGA。这两个机构在国际投资争端解决和投资保险方面取得了突破性的进展。1992 年，世界银行与国际货币基金组织制定《外国直接投资待遇指南》(*Guidelines on the Treatment of Foreign Direct Investment*)，但不具有法律约束力。[1] GATT 乌拉圭回合试图将投资纳入多边贸易体制，借助多边贸易体制已基本搭建成功的体系架构来实现普遍适用的国际投资法制的理想，但最终只是通过了 TRIMs 协定，将与贸易有关的四种投资措施纳入规制范围，[2]影响只在投资管理方面，与真正的多边投资协定相去甚远。

鉴于以上尝试和努力都未能获得令人满意的实质性进展，OECD 于 1995 年开始了构建一个全面的、综合性多边投资协定，起草了《多边投资协定》(MAI)，内容包括投资与投资者定义、投资待遇、投资促进和投资便利、政治风险、代位求偿、争端解决和例外等，本计划于 1997 年结束，但终因谈判各方分歧较大，于 1998 年以失败而告终。[3]

2003 年，WTO 坎昆部长级会议第四次会议（新加坡会议）上再次提及投资议题，当时及以后未有收获。

(二)普遍性投资规则难以成功的原因

以上各类国际组织的各种努力收效甚微，说明制定一个普遍性的综合多边投资规则在特定条件和特定客观环境下不易实现。学者们对以上努力的失败总结出以下经验和教训。

1.制定机构难以胜任

以上规则的制定机构都不是合适的多边投资协定谈判场所，不具有统领性，难以驾驭两大阵营的国家。[4] 国际联盟自身地位岌岌可危，国际商会是非政府间国际组织，OECD 是区域间国际组织且一向被视为富人俱乐部，联合国大会在具体问题上一向难有作为，WTO 本是贸易组织，世界银行只能在专业领域有所建树。

2.各国利益差异大

各国利益差异大主要体现在以下两方面：

第一，两类国家态度两端。发展中国家和发达国家对制定统一投资规则的态度分

① Peter D. Cameron, *International Energy Investment Law*, Oxford University Press, 2010, p.24.
② Andrew Newcombe, Lluis Paradell, *Law and Practice of Investment Treaties—Standards of Treatment*, Wolters Kluwer Press, 2009, p.514.
③ Katia Tieleman, The Failure of the Multilateral Agreement on Investment and the Absence of a Global Public Policy Network, http://www.gppi.net/fileadmin/gppi/Tieleman_MAI_GPP_Network.pdf, last visited on 12 Sept. 2012.
④ 叶兴平：《WTO 内多边投资规则谈判的利弊分析》，载《深圳大学学报》2006 年第 8 期。

歧较大,可谓两极。发达国家一向极力推崇投资自由化,为实现该目标而力推多边投资领域的谈判(除联合国制定的文件外,以上多边投资规则草案基本上是在发达国家主持或推动下进行的),而发展中国家一贯对多边投资规则心存疑虑,态度消极,反对在国际会议或国际组织场所经由谈判来制定这样的规则,[1]两类国家利益难以找到契合点。

第二,发达国家间发展水平差异大。在发达国家阵营内部,各国经济发展水平高低不同和各方利益重点不同,利益分化明显,在文化产业投资和战略性产业部门(航空器制造和航空公司并购)等领域难以形成一致意见。[2]

3.东道国外资管理权受到较大限制

东道国外资管理权是其国家主权的重要体现,但多边投资规则是对该国家主权产生约束力并在许多具体领域进行限制,必然导致各国特别是发展中国家对多边投资规则(特别是普遍性投资规则)采取十分谨慎的态度,因此制定多边投资规则注定是举步维艰、命运多舛。

二、制定区域性投资规则的成功率大

普遍性多边投资规则制定裹足不前,但区域性多边投资规则呈现出遍地开花的局面。2011年6月,全球共有331项涉及投资的贸易与投资特惠协定(PTIAs),包括自由贸易区协定(FTAs)、区域经济一体化协定、经济合作框架或协定、紧密经济伙伴协定(EPAs)等。[3] 近年来,区域性投资规则的数量呈现递增趋势,对世界经济的影响力也在持续增加。[4] 目前主要区域性多边投资规则体现在《能源宪章条约》《美墨加协定》《东盟全面投资协定》《南方共同市场合作与便利投资议定书》《伊斯兰大会投资协定》《阿拉伯国家投资统一协定》等。它们在区域范围内对投资合作和促进发挥着重要作用。

区域性多边投资规则成功的原因在于,区域内参加利益博弈的国家相对较少,谈判成本低,而且区域内的国家长期存在历史、政治和经贸往来,容易达成一致意见。区域性多边投资规则的成功昭示着区域经济合作的成果,说明两个问题:第一,区域范围内基于一定的地缘政治和利益协调,制定多边投资规则是可能的;第二,区域范围内制定投资规则的难度要小于普遍性多边投资规则。

---

① A. V. Ganesan, Strategic Options Available to Developing Countries with regard to a Multilateral Agreement on Investment, *International Monetary and Financial Issues for the* 1990s, 1999, Vol.10, p.34.

② 刘笋:《从 MAI 看综合性国际投资多边立法的困境和出路》,载《中国法学》2001 年第 5 期。

③ UNCTAD, World Investment Report 2012, p.84.

④ UNCTAD, World Investment Report 2012, p.92.

三、制定区域性多边投资规则是中国的必然选择

我国参与区域经济合作虽然起步较晚,但是在全球区域经济一体化高潮时期起步的,因而发展迅速。[1] 卓有成效的是机制化的区域经济合作主要表现在以下方面:第一,中国—东盟自由贸易区等自由贸易区的建立;第二,建立了一些次区域合作组织,如图们江地区的次区域合作组织、澜沧江—湄公河次区域合作组织等;第三,搭建或参与了论坛性质的区域合作机制,如亚太经济合作组织、亚欧会议、博鳌亚洲论坛等。这些区域经济合作或紧密或松散,在不同程度上均提及多边投资安排,影响较大的是在自由贸易协定或自由贸易区协定中的投资章或投资协定。具有实质性内容的区域多边投资安排主要有三个,一是《中国—东盟投资协定》,二是《中日韩投资协定》,三是《区域全面经济伙伴关系协定》"投资"章。因中国—东盟自由贸易区和中日韩自由贸易区(谈判中)在文本选择上采取了分立模式,所以这两个协定都是作为自由贸易区谈判的重点内容,在自由贸易区正式建立之前业已生效。这些在区域层面推进多边投资规则的成功经验可以为展开新的谈判积累经验,建立模板和树立典范。

基于一定地缘关系的国家之间在不同程度的经济、文化、科技和政治的区域联合是当代国际经济合作的一大特点。不顺应这一潮流者必然会被边缘化。国家之间的较量越来越转向为区域国际组织之间的角逐,各国都需依托区域性经济合作。[2] 在普遍性多边投资规则的制定屡遭失败、道路艰难的情况下,我国参与多边投资规则的制定应当从易到难,避免直接切入普遍性规则的制定,应顺应区域经济发展大势,基于地缘政治经济利益认同,首先实现在区域范围内的多边投资合作,当区域性多边投资合作达到一定程度时在推而广之,在已有合作和磨合的基础上实现制定普遍性多边投资规则的理想。

第三节 先近邻后远邻的策略

在区域性多边投资规则的制定中,需要根据地缘政治经济因素,先与近邻国家进行投资协定谈判,在条件成熟、经验丰富之后再与远邻国家进行实践。

一、近远邻策略的他国实践

"远邻""近邻"之说在美国、俄罗斯等大国的国际政治和对外交往战略中一直受到重

---

[1] 华晓红、庄芮、杨立强:《中国参与周边区域经济合作的实践与策略》,载《云南师范大学学报》2011年第2期。

[2] 李宏岳:《中国参与国际区域经济合作的战略思考》,载《经济问题探索》2010年第1期。

视。

在俄罗斯官方文件中,一直将苏联解体后的独立国家称为"近邻"国家,将其他国家称为"远邻"国家,在外交政策和对外交往中对这些国家的对外战略和其他国家区别对待。[①]

美国将近邻的加拿大、墨西哥完全收罗囊中,建立了高度自由化的 NAFTA 和新北美自由贸易区,成为各国建立自由贸易区的典范和标杆,而在 NAFTA 运作良好,从立法、司法和执行各个机制运作的配合日渐完善之际,配合美国政府的"战略东移"和"亚太印再平衡"战略,继续推行美国一直所惬意的贸易、投资高标准的自由化。

二、中国近远邻策略确立的基础

我国治理与周边关系的研究机构——周边合作与发展协同创新中心在研究中将"周边"作"近邻"与"远邻"之分。近邻国家由于地理原因在地缘文化方面具有一定程度的相似性,许多文化要素甚至属于同一谱系,相互交往容易获得较大程度的认同,而在经济交往方面往往具有千丝万缕的历史关系,甚至在一定领域、一定程度上形成了交易习惯,可以有效降低交易成本,有利于达成共识。在与近邻国家的多边投资协定成功并取得成效后,一方面可以为在更大范围内的投资谈判提供样本,另一方面对远邻国家也具有示范效应。

(一)地缘政治经济基础

从国际政治角度看,保证与近邻国家关系的稳定,改善与近邻的地缘政治关系是建立和扩大对外经济联系的良好基础,而国家必须在一定地理区域内通过保有或控制一定地缘区域来实现自身的地缘利益诉求。[②] 我国地处亚洲,周边环境异常复杂,在与每个近邻国家交往的过程中都存在这样或者那样的历史问题。虽然各国在处理国家关系时已经日益摆脱非此即彼的零和博弈困境,充分认识到互利、合作、共赢的发展方向,但长期积累下来的矛盾并没有得到根本解决,因此要想获得认同、谋求经济利益的实现,必须具体问题具体分析,结合不同国家和我国交往的具体特点和投资结构来各个击破。

(二)地缘国际投资基础

从我国外资来源看,我国在亚洲地区层次上的外资来源地主要是日本、东盟和韩国,其他经济体对中国的直接投资较少。

从对外投资流向看,中国的主要投资对象是亚洲、太平洋地区层次上的韩国、澳大利

---

① 刘乾:《美俄新冷战　世界大国逐鹿中原》,http://finance.ifeng.com/opinion/hqgc/20121213/7424580.shtml,最后访问日期:2022 年 12 月 25 日。

② 王毅:《中国与周边国家外交关系综述:与邻为善以邻为伴》,载《求是》2013 年第 2 期。

亚、伊拉克、东盟部分国家和日本，以及自然经济区域层次上的中国香港和中国澳门。[①]在这两个层次上，其他所有国家或经济体都是中国投资发展的潜在地缘空间。具体而言，在亚洲太平洋地区层次上主要包括东亚、南亚、中亚、中东和南太平洋地区的各个经济体，以及东盟中获得中国投资份额很少的几个国家（菲律宾、文莱、老挝、缅甸和柬埔寨）；在自然经济区域层次上主要包括已经有所发展的澜沧江—湄公河次区域经济合作和图们江流域开发计划，以及尚待推进的东北地区、西南地区和西北地区的跨境自然经济区域。[②]

由上可以看出，我国在亚洲的主要外资来源和投资地区基本上是我国的近邻国家和地区，这些国家或地区与我国在历史、文化、经济交往上一直有着很深的历史渊源，在地缘经济上，理论上容易达成协议，但是也有不利的方面，如历史积怨、领海、领土、地区影响力等因素的影响。

(三)近远邻策略的实践基础

我国在亚洲、太平洋地区开展的区域经济合作发展迅速，结果虽不很理想但仍取得一定的突破和成就，尤其是在机制性区域合作方面，目前具有实质意义有 CAFTAI、全面经济伙伴关系协定(CEPA)和 RCEP。

1.近邻策略的实践与走向

虽然我国在 2020 年以前建立机制性自由贸易区方面实质性进展不大，但是在自由贸易区协定文本选择上采取了分立模式，即与区域贸易安排对象分别签署货物贸易协定、服务贸易协定、投资协定、争端解决机制协定等，待各分项协定达成后再成立自由贸易区，因此区域性投资协定的达成早于自由贸易区。例如，CAFTAI 投资协定于 2008 年达成而 CAFTAI 正式成立于 2010 年；中日韩自由贸易区谈判的设想自 2002 年被提起就一直处于研究阶段，未有实质性进展，直到 2012 年 5 月正式签署投资协定，而自由贸易区的正式谈判启动因受领土问题的影响直到 2012 年 11 月才宣布开始，第一轮谈判于 2013 年 3 月 26 日开始，但这不影响三国投资协定的生效。此做法为我们提供一条思路，即使在与某些国家的自由贸易区协定未达成或正在进行中，只要在自由贸易区文本选择上采取了分立模式，即先搁置政治、历史、军事的争议，而在投资领域先达成协定。我国在继续推进其他自由贸易区的过程中可以推广这种模式。

基于以上，我国与主要近邻的东盟、日本、韩国已建立起区域投资框架，与中国香港的投资在 CEPA 的适用范围内。但与中国台湾地区的合作目前仍需找到一个合适的切入点，海峡两岸暨香港、澳门建立自由贸易区的建构固然有学者进行了关注和论证，但是受到有关台湾地区的一些敏感问题，未能有实质性的进展。与近邻的其他一些国家，如印度、俄罗斯等，虽然设立深度自由贸易区的条件不成熟，但可以在金砖国家合作机制、

---

① 潘忠岐、黄仁伟：《中国的地缘经济战略》，载《清华大学学报(哲社版)》2008 年第 5 期。
② 朱凯兵：《中国维护与发展中国家合作关系的战略前瞻》，载《南京政治学院学报》2012 年第 3 期。

上海组织合作机制或者双边投资协定的基础上,在"增长三角"或次区域经济合作的模式下进行区域多边投资协定的实践尝试。[①]

2.远邻策略的思考

从远邻看,南亚、中亚、中东和东部与南部太平洋地区的经济区,都可以成为我国对外投资中亚太地区内有合作空间的区域,与有关国家的投资规则的制定可以参照比较成熟的与近邻达成的投资协定作为范本提出报价和要价,实现投资促进和投资便利。

需要关注的是,为了防止某些国家 TPP 或 CPTPP 边缘化战略,中国需要重视与美国《跨太平洋战略经济伙伴协定》(简称 TPSEP)[②]战略范围内的国家进行合作与交流,尤其要重视中日韩自由贸易区和 CAFTAI 的建设,根据具体情况,权衡自身利益后,适时地参加 TPSEP 谈判,从内部瓦解构成的针对中国的自由贸易体系性壁垒,避免被排除在"亚太自由贸易区"的发展进程之外。[③]

北美、拉美地区和欧盟地区是中国在全球层次上的主要地缘经济空间,中国经济成长在很大程度上得益于改革开放以来中国在这些地区中从贸易、投资、金融、制度等领域与全球经济体系的积极互动。因此在远邻策略上,我国在坚持国家利益并服从我国基本原则和立场的前提,应当与这些国家和地区谈判多边投资规则。

3.近远邻并重的实践

2020 年 11 月,RCEP 的达成是中国参与制定跨区域多边自由贸易区投资规则的成功典范,标志着我国成功实施近邻与远邻并重且大型集团化谈判多边投资规则的策略,为正在和未来与"一带一路"沿线国家、非洲区域集团谈判多边自由贸易协定、制定跨区域多边投资规则提供了成功实践经验。

第四节　先同类国家后不同类型国家的策略

同类国家在经济发展中所面临的经济、社会问题具有相通性,在国际经济合作方面有着共同的利益需求,容易达成共识,缔结投资条约的成本相对较少。因此,在进行多边投资规则制定中可以考虑先与同类国家达成共识,在此基础上再与不同类型国家进行谈判。

————————

① 李强:《中国周边的地缘政治经济环境》,载《世界经济与政治》2007 年第 8 期。

② 《跨太平洋战略经济伙伴协定》(TPSEP)谈判最初由智利、新加坡、新西兰、文莱四个环太平洋国家于 2005 年 6 月发起。TPSEP 最初没有在亚太地区引起太多关注。直到 2009 年年底美国高调宣布加入 TPSEP 谈判,这一多边贸易谈判才引来各方瞩目。目前除这五国外,还有澳大利亚、秘鲁、越南、马来西亚。

③ 田海:《我国应对 TPP 的策略思考》,载《中国国情国力》2012 年第 11 期。

一、同类国家的界定

所谓同类国家,依不同的标准来考量会得出不同的结论,如政治体制、意识形态、经济发展水平、经济体制、文化背景、宗教信仰、历史渊源等,但是和国际投资有关的考量标准主要是经济体制和经济发展水平。依照此标准,我国的同类国家应当是经济发展水平相当、经济体制类似的国家以及广大发展中国家。

二、与同类或不同类型国家的主要策略

(一)与发展转型期国家和新兴发展中国家推进多边投资则规则的制定

发展转型期国家、新兴发展中国家与我国经济发展水平相当、经济体制类似,有着相同的发展目标与层次。发展转型期国家主要是指从计划经济向市场经济转轨的国家或者刚刚转轨不久的国家,如俄罗斯、越南、缅甸等国。新兴发展中国家主要是指由中国、俄罗斯、巴西、印度和南非构成的金砖国家。

发展转型期国家和我国在历史或现实中有着相同的政治体制和由政治体制决定的经济体制,在经济全球化背景下纷纷开始了从计划经济向市场经济的改革,在改革中面临的很多相似问题,在对外交往中有一些共同利益需求和焦点,如外资需求、非市场经济国家地位、参与国际经济合作的需求。这些共同利益或焦点即可成为多边合作的基础,我国与东盟国家的实践证明了这一点。虽然目前与俄罗斯及其他独联体国家的自由贸易区建设尚无明显建树,但 2009 年 9 月中俄两国首脑正式批准的《中华人民共和国东北地区与俄罗斯联邦远东地区及东西伯利亚地区合作规划纲要(2009—2018)》为建立远东自由贸易区奠定了基础,同年 11 月国务院批复了《中国图们江区域合作开发规划纲要——以长吉图为开发开放先导区》推动图们江区域合作开发,将俄罗斯、朝鲜、蒙古等国家纳入图们江次区域合作的范围,揭开了该区域多边合作的序幕,进一步需要在相互经济交往的基础上进行多边规则的制定,多边投资规则应当作为自由贸易区建设的重头戏和贸易规则的制定并重。[①]

新兴发展中国家作为新兴经济体的代表,在经济状况上具有明显的共同特点,如国土面积大、人口多、具有资源或要素优势、经济快速增长潜力巨大、消费市场发展日益扩大等,而且在参与应对国际金融危机冲击、二十国集团(G20)峰会进程、国际金融机构改革、粮食安全、气候变化等重大紧迫问题上,具有共同的立场和共同的利益。加之各国的要素禀赋不同,在经济交往中可以进行优势互补,具有良好的合作基础。近年来,金砖五国在政治、经济上多有对话与交流,尤其是面对八国集团(G8)的精诚合作,更有实质性经

---

① 李靖宇、韩青:《中俄两国边境区域合作开发文件落实问题探讨》,载《俄罗斯中亚东欧市场》2011 年第 4 期。

济合作的空间与可能。金砖五国在现有合作的基础上,进一步利用法律化、机制化的多边规则合作将更有力促进各国的经济发展。因此在金砖五国合作机制框架内推进多边投资规则制定和实施具有可能性和必要性。

(二)积极推进与广大发展中国家多边投资规则的制定

国际投资的南南合作不断发展,越来越多的发展中国家正在成为对外投资的来源地。发展中国家的这种新动向会增强它们在未来国际投资协定谈判中的议价能力。[①]

我国作为发展中的大国,与广大发展中国家有着深厚的历史情感和共同发展目标,在国际社会有着共同的利益,主要表现在两个方面:第一,自 20 世纪 50 年代开始,在南北矛盾激烈的斗争中,我国一直和广大发展中国家保持良好的外交关系和国际合作关系。随着全球化进程加快,尽管各发展中国家参与全球化的范围和程度不同,加之国情差异,国别利益开始凸显,但在经济结构和发展定位方面仍然是共性大于个性,求同存异的合作仍然有很大空间。第二,从我国对外投资结构看,对发展中国家的直接投资保持在全部对外直接投资的 80% 以上,对发展中国家投资是我国对外直接投资的主要流向之一。因此我国需要与广大发展中国家进行投资促进和保护的谈判,通过法律机制保护我国对外投资。与发展中国家进行多边投资规则谈判,既是保护我国海外投资的有力手段,又是掌控多边投资规则谈判主动权的历史机遇。

(三)在积累经验的基础上与发达国家谈判多边投资规则

在与同类国家多边投资规则成功制定或者积累了丰富经验之后,一方面在发展中国家之间形成了多边投资规则谈判的集团化立场,形成集团化议价能力;另一方面丰富了我国在多边投资规则谈判方面的经验。我国可将这些成功的范例或者经验适用于与发达国家谈判多边投资规则的实践中可获得事半功倍的效果。

本章小结

在多边投资规则发展进程中,既有发达国家和发展中国家之间的分歧,又有发达国家之间、发展中国家之间的矛盾,试图在单一场合"毕其功于一役"地解决多边投资规则构建问题显然不实际。我国在参与多边投资规则制定中,应当在多维标准下,区别不同的谈判对象、议题,采取先特殊后一般、先区域后普遍、先近邻后远邻、先同类国家后不同类型国家的策略。

[①] M. Sornarajah, *The International Law on Foreign Investment*, Cambridge University Press, 2010,pp.19-33.

第六章

中国参与制定多边投资规则的基本方式

当前多边投资规则主要类型有普遍性、非普遍性两种。普遍性投资规则是在全球领域内多数国家或者重要国家都参与的投资规则。该种规则有 WTO 框架下的投资规则、有关公约的投资规则。非普遍性投资规则是指在特定国家之间达成的投资规则,可以区分为金砖国家间的投资规则、我国与其他三个国家以上的自由贸易区投资规则、我国与其他发展中国家之间的多边投资规则。我国参与制定多边投资规则的方式,宜根据投资规则的不同性质、类型与特征采取不同的方式。总体上有主导型和接受型两种基本方式。

第一节 主导型方式

主导型方式是指在规则的倡议、条文的草拟、谈判的推动与相关辅助机制方面起全面主导地位的方式。

我国在特定对象与特定领域内有关多边投资规则的主导主要是依赖于我国在特定情势下的角色扮演。就当前国际经贸关系而言,我国应当在金砖国家、自由贸易区和与发展中国家间的多边投资规则制定中起主导者作用,积极推动此类多边投资规则的建构与形成。

一、主导金砖国家多边投资规则

"金砖国家"是取巴西、俄罗斯联邦、印度、中国和南非五个新兴经济大国的英文名称首字母,组成缩写 BRICS,因其发音与英文单词 BRICK 相似,故被称为"金砖国家"。

金砖国家在全球经济中居重要地位。从经济体量看,金砖五国的 GDP 总和,按购买力计算,超过全球 GDP 的 1/4,而美国和欧盟均只占 1/5 左右。金砖国家作为一种合力和集体,从经济规模上讲,已成为不弱于美国和欧盟的一股力量。金砖五国稳定的政治经济环境以及持续发展的能力,不断吸引着国际资本,尤其是直接投资的流入。中国是目前世界上 FDI 净流入第二大国,占 GDP 的 5% 左右,其他四国是重要的外资净流入国。在金融危机期间,金砖五国是全球外资青睐之地。以 2009 年为例,全球 FDI 为 11140 亿美元,同比下跌 37%,超过 2008 年的 16% 跌幅。其中,发达国家吸引的 FDI 下降了 44%,欧洲下降 25%,美国下降 50%。在金砖五国中,除俄罗斯 FDI 下降较多之外,中国、印度、巴西、南非均保持稳定增长。其中,中国 2009 年同比增长 7%。随着经济的发展和外汇储备的上升,金砖国家对外投资和并购的力度显著增强。又以 2010 年主要数据为例,金砖五国海外并购金额达到 4020 亿美元,同比上升 74%,是 5 年前的 4 倍多,占全球 2.23 万亿美元并购总额的 22%,创历史新高。① 金砖各方之间在投资领域有着广阔的多边投资合作前景。

2012 年以前,五国一直未能在经贸合作方面形成一个机制化的合作模式。2013 年 3 月 26 日,金砖国家第三次贸易部长会议发表联合公报和《金砖国家贸易投资合作框架》,重申了五国以 WTO 为多边合作的基础,在其他涉及贸易与投资的多边场合展开深入合作,认可了经贸联络组草拟的《金砖国家贸易投资合作框架》,指示经贸联络组落实并在今后继续完善该框架。在与投资有关的两大领域达成合作意愿,即多边场合的合作与协调、贸易投资促进和便利化,包括 10 项具体措施。②

此框架协定标志着金砖国家间多边投资规则的合作框架初步形成,但仍需在该框架下进一步细化、完善具体规则。在这种情况下,我国应当随势而动、谋势而为,积极主导金砖国家间投资规则的建构与细化,不仅要对五国之间的投资便利化创造较好的法律环境,还应当积极推动投资协定的谈判和签署,进一步地完善争端解决等具体法律机制。

二、主导自由贸易区或经贸合作区的投资规则

晚近多哈回合的停滞,使各国将视角从理想的普遍主义转向了更为务实的区域主义。根据近年来新区域主义浪潮的发展实践,可以按所涉及的内容、依照一体化深度的不同,将全球自由贸易协定分为以下几个层次:第一层次是货物贸易自由化;第二个层次是包括货物贸易、服务贸易和投资三个方面的贸易投资一体化;第三个层次是在贸易投资一体化基础上包括更广泛的内容,如竞争政策、知识产权、政府采购、金融合作、能源合作、电子商务等。涉及第二个和第三个层次的一体化协定通常称为"深度一体化"协定。③甚至在欧盟这样的超国家看来,"竞争驱动型"的自由贸易区战略对欧盟而言是至关重要

---

① 龚斌恩:《金砖五国合作政策》,载《中国外资》2011 年第 6 期。
② 金砖国家第三次贸易部长会议发表联合公报和《金砖国家贸易投资合作框架》。
③ 东艳:《深度一体化:中国自由贸易区战略的新趋势》,载《当代亚太》2009 年第 4 期。

的,这是深度一体化重要手段。[①] 通过多边自由贸易区方式推进制定多边投资规则,已经成了主流趋势之一。

我国已经达成多项自由贸易区框架或构架下的投资协定或具有投资内容的协定,有如:2004 年与海湾合作委员会的《经济、贸易投资和技术合作框架协定》,2009 年与东盟的《全面经济合作框架协定内投资协定》(简称《中国—东盟投资协定》),2012 年与日本、韩国的投资协定。目前真正意义上的自由贸易区下的多边投资协定为《中国—东盟投资协定》、RCEP 第 10 章,正在与海湾合作委员会[②]、日本—韩国谈判自由贸易协定中的投资章。

在上海合作组织中,投资合作的规模日益扩大。根据商务部统计,2008 年中国对上海合作组织直接投资达 9.6 亿美元,同比 2003 年增长 26.3 倍。2009 年,中国成为俄罗斯的第四大投资伙伴;俄罗斯和中国成为哈萨克斯坦的主要投资伙伴;中国、俄罗斯和哈萨克斯坦成为吉尔吉斯斯坦直接投资的主要来源国。2010 年,中国成为塔吉克斯坦的最大债权国。据不完全统计,成员国之间的相互投资已超过 150 亿美元。[③] 但上海合作组织迄今未能形成一个法律化的条约合作制度,而是通过部长级的磋商和联合声明对经贸合作予以推动。如果设想以上海合作组织成员为基础建立自由贸易区,中国不仅要主导自由贸易区协定的制定,还主导其投资协定的制定。如果在短时期内没有考虑建立自由贸易区,可先行倡导制定上海合作组织投资协定或经贸投资合作框架协定。

无论是在自由贸易区框架下,还是在经贸合作区框架下,我国均应当在投资规则建构过程中明确自身的主导作用。我国应当在政治互信的基础上,充分尊重谈判各方的战略选择的前提下,积极推动在直接投资、金融类的间接投资、跨国运输工程和能源投资方面的制度建构,主动承担相应的辅助性工作的成本。

三、主导我国与其他发展中国家间的多边投资规则

自"入世"以后,我国日渐成为影响国际投资关系最为重要的发展中国家之一。我国在国际投资的角色逐渐从"资本输入国"的单一身份向"资本输入与输出国"的混同身份发展。2004 年后,我国不断参与、修正对外投资和双边、多边投资规则,逐步与国际接轨,已经具备了主导发展中国家多边投资规则建构的能力。

(一)主导发展中国家所需同类国家多边投资规则的制定

未与中国建立自由贸易区或非中国经贸合作区域的发展中国家,目前或不久的将来

---

① European Commission,Global Europe: Competing in the World,COM (2006) 567 final, 4 October 2006.

② 关于中国—海合会自由贸易区谈判情况,见《中国—海合会自由贸易区》,http://fta.mofcom.gov.cn/gcc/gcc_special.shtml,最后访问日期:2022 年 12 月 23 日。

③ 王健:《上海合作组织发展进程研究》,上海社会科学院世界经济研究所 2012 年博士论文。

也需要一个"同类国家"主导其直接资本流动的多边投资协定。同类国家是指在政治制度、经济体制、意识形态、法律体系、文化传统、宗教信仰以及语言等方面具有一致性或相似程度高的国家。① 包括我国在内的发展中国家在与西方发达国家投资规则谈判中,都面对着限制性商业行为、转移定价、技术转让、环境标准和政府采购等方面的较高要价,为应付发达国家所开具的投资范本而疲于应付,无法提出符合其自身利益的要价。相反,如果由我国为主导,尊重各方国情和利益的前提下,在发展中国家之间形成在重大议题上"同进退"的多边投资规则,并在此相关方面已经形成的共同立场,在未来的以发达国家为主导的普遍性投资规则谈判中,形成"议价联盟",提高发展中国家的议价能力。

(二)主导制定拉美、非洲等地区多边投资规则

我国在拉美、非洲等地区的规模巨大、领域宽泛的海外投资迫切需要形成一个明确的多边投资规则以保障我国投资安全。

在非洲,进行直接投资的中国企业从 2000 年的 500 家左右上升到 2008 年的 900 多家,2008 年对非洲直接投资存量达到 78 亿美元。② 2010 年,我国对非洲的投资较上年增长超四成占 3.1%,主要分布在南非、刚果(金)、尼日尔、阿尔及利亚、尼日利亚、肯尼亚等。

在拉美,2010 年的直接投资额为 105.4 亿美元,同比增长 43.8%,占流量的 15.3%,主要流向英属维尔京群岛、开曼群岛、巴西、秘鲁等,2010 年年底的总存量 438.8 亿美元(占 13.8%)。③

因中国香港、英属维尔京群岛和开曼群岛是世界著名的三大避税地,我国诸多国际投资先在三地设立"离岸公司"而后将资本转移,仅仅将三地作为"投资跳板"以规避税收的中转地,其最终流向多数都集中在非洲、拉丁美洲等发展中国家,中国对非洲、拉丁美洲的直接投资量占中国实质对外直接投资总量的比例相当可观。

上述两方面阐明我国主导制定符合发展中国家自身利益的多边投资规则已具备了现实条件。

综上,如果我国在发展中国家之间形成一个多边投资规则,发展中国家有能力以集体的力量,在未来普遍性多边投资规则的建构中遏制发达国家的漫天要价,使规则既顺应投资自由化的趋势又能反映发展中国家的利益。④ 因此,我国主导发展中国家间多边投资规则的建构已势在必行。

---

① 张云燕:《社会建构主义与东亚区域经济合作》,复旦大学 2004 年博士学位论文。
② 古尔默·阿布杜罗:《非洲与中国:新殖民主义还是新型战略伙伴关系》,马京鹏译,载《国外理论动态》2012 年第 9 期。
③ 商务部等:《2010 年度中国对外直接投资统计公报》,http://hzs.mofcom.gov.cn/aarticle/date/201109/ 20110907741156.html,最后访问日期:2013 年 3 月 20 日。
④ 陈畅东:《国际投资立法自由化趋势及我国的对策》,载《民主与法治》2008 年第 8 期。

第二节　接受型方式

接受型方式是指在多边规则的倡议、条文的草拟、谈判的推动与相关辅助机制方面不起主导作用而接受主导者发起的倡议、文本草案、谈判进程等的方式。在此种方式下，接受者有权提出本国的诉求和愿意、表达自己立场和观点、参与谈判过程等具体实质性和程序性事项。根据当代国际实践，我国采取接受型方式应用于普遍性国际组织和主要区域性国家组织（如 OECD）主持下的多边投资规则制定活动。

一、WTO 体制下的多边投资规则

当前 WTO 中与投资有关的是 TRIMs 协定、TRIPs 协定、GATS 和 ASCMs 协议。上述四个协议由于均冠以"与贸易有关"的前缀，对多边投资的规则显得非常有限，存在诸多缺陷。① （1）各协定的调整范围有限。TRIMs 协定作为 WTO 项下直接调整多边国际投资关系的协议，其范围仅限于货物贸易，并不适用于服务贸易，也未能考虑外国自然人和法人在东道国的投资待遇问题。GTAS 的基本原则虽然是国民待遇和最惠国待遇，但是由于各国的《承诺减让表》中只对特定部门提供保障，投资保护范围相当有限。ASCMs 虽然对投资激励措施进行规范，但仅限于"货物贸易补贴"。（2）由于四个协定是相对独立的协定，在投资待遇、例外情况等问题上存在着本质冲突，未能在法理上予以协调。（3）WTO 下的"投资"仅仅限于与贸易有关的直接投资，与晚近国际投资法的投资定义扩大趋势不符。在 2001 年 WTO 多哈回合启动之初，《多哈回合宣言》第 20 段至第 22段对投资问题作了说明。在此后的 4 次部长级会议上对所列问题进行了谈判。② 该谈判在 2003 年的第 5 次部长级会议（坎昆会议）上宣告失败。2004 年，WTO 总理事会在《多哈工作计划》"贸易与投资、贸易与竞争政策互动关系及政府采购透明度"中规定：总理事会同意《多哈回合宣言》有关投资议题的讨论，但不列入《宣言》所列的工作计划之中。③因此，在多哈回合期间，WTO 将不会针对投资问题开展旨在谈判的工作，投资议题终止。

但投资议题终止不意味着 WTO 框架下建立多边投资规则的死亡，WTO 各方已经在诸多关键性议题上有着可调和的立场。主要动向是：（1）当前各国的外资立法与政策理念逐步趋同。具体数据见前述。④ （2）从各国对议题的提案立场看，当前在"投资"定义

---

① 薛荣久、樊瑛：《WTO 多哈回合与中国》，对外经济贸易大学出版社 2004 年版，第 138 页。

② WTO, Doha WTO Ministerial 2001: Ministerial Declaration, WT/MIN(01)/DEC/1, paras. 20-22.

③ WTO, Doha Development Agenda: Doha Work Programme, para-1(g).

④ 联合国贸易与发展会议：《2012 年世界投资报告》（中文版），第 7、18 页。

方面,区域投资协定与双边投资协定都呈现出一种旨在包含"资产为基础"的趋势,包括了若干间接投资的资产。① 因此从 2004 年投资议题终止后,国际投资规则已经发生了重大的变化,支持"狭义投资定义"的日本、中国等国家与支持"广义的投资定义"的美国、欧盟及其成员国之间的矛盾已经逐渐弥合。(3)在透明度方面,当前区域与双边投资协定中的透明度远远不如 WTO 框架下的纪律要求,中国、韩国等国家均认为在 WTO 既有的透明度框架内的透明度完全可以满足国际投资的需求,而且更容易为 WTO 各成员方所接受。② (4)在非歧视条款方面,欧盟、日本和我国均同意以 GATS 为立法模式,按照具体部门进行承诺,在第一产业、第二产业的多边框架内纳入最惠国待遇和国民待遇及其限制。③ (5)在发展条款方面,加拿大、欧共体及其成员国均认为,WTO 协定及其他协定都为发展中国家提供了灵活的弹性条款,发展中国家有权根据其国内法来规范外资。④

事实上,WTO 框架下的投资议题并不是各方立场的根本对立,而是因为发达国家和发展中国家在农业补贴问题上的根本分歧造成,是农业问题谈判的牺牲品。⑤ 发展中国家认为,多哈回合的核心问题是发达国家应当实质性削减农业补贴,在 WTO 现有框架下给予发展中国家相应的让步,在核心问题解决前,发达国家对发展中国家的包括投资在内的要价应当搁置。因此,投资议题的破裂是发展中国家以此作为向发达国家在农业问题上的对价,或称为牺牲品,不是因为各方对多边投资规则本身有着根本立场冲突。事实上,在 1998—2001 年工作组召开的 13 次会议中均讨论了多边投资规则的谈判问题,联合国贸易与发展会议、经合组织、世界银行、国际货币基金组织、联合国工业发展组织(UNIDO)和亚太经合组织一致支持在 WTO 内讨论多边投资规则问题,并提供了书面意见和建议。⑥

在农业问题上难以达成一致的情况下,发展中国家宜甩掉农业补贴的沉重包袱轻装上阵,接受多边投资协定的谈判,以避免浪费谈判资源。如果多哈回合的谈判重点确实从理想主义迈向现实主义,致力于达成更为务实和可能的多边投资协定,我国对此应当接受。

---

① 张庆麟:《论国际投资协定中的投资性质与扩大化的意义》,载《法学家》2011 年第 6 期。

② WTO, Working Group on the Relationship between Trade and Investment-Communication from Korea, WT/WGTI/W/70, 30 march 1999; WTO, Working Group on the Relationship between Trade and Investment, Communication from China, WT/WGTI/W/160, 15 April 2003.

③ WTO, Working Group on the Relationship between Trade and Investment-Communication from Japan, WT/WGTI/W/121, 27 July 2002; WTO, Working Group on the Relationship between Trade and Investment—Communication from European Community and its Members, WT/WGTI/W/125, 28 June 2002.

④ WTO, Working Group on the Relationship Between Trade and Investment-Communication from European Community and Its Members, WT/WGTI/W/150, 7 October 2002; WTO, Working Group on The Relationship Between Trade and Investment-Communication From Canada, WT/WGTI/W/131, 3 June 2002.

⑤ 刘勇:《WTO 坎昆会议的失败及其相关思考》,载《环球经贸》2003 年第 11 期。

⑥ 张磊:《多哈回合谈判的最新进展——2010 年度报告》,法律出版社 2012 年版,第 161 页。

二、《能源宪章条约》中的多边投资规则

《能源宪章条约》(简称 ECT)以《能源宪章》为主体,涵盖了贸易修正案、投资补充条约、能源效率议定书和能源运输议定书等多个法律文件,构成能源领域综合性法律体系。该条约是为满足独联体能源供给国与欧洲能源需求国在能源与资本之间的交易而达成的,目前拥有 53 个成员国,我国于 2001 年成为观察员国家。[①]

ECT 是迄今唯一致力于国际能源投资自由化的多边条约。其序言指出,"本条约是根据宪章的目标和原则,在互补互利的基础上,为促进能源领域的长期合作而创建的一个法律框架"。能源投资是《能源宪章条约》规则的核心部分,整个法律体系均是围绕着投资展开。能源投资、能源贸易、能源运输、能源利用效率与能源环境、能源争议解决等各环节构成投资链条上的组成部分,与能源投资活动一起构成了能源投资行业的全部价值链条,充分体现了能源投资自由化的四个要求。[②] 条约"努力改善本国条件,吸引投资者进入本国市场"(第 9 条第 1 款);"取消影响投资的限制"[第 10 条第 5 款(b)]体现了促进资金准入的要求;每个投资者"都应享受最优惠待遇"(第 10 条第 3 款)则是为了提高投资者待遇,它们共同表现了对内投资自由化的追求;"投资不能被国有化"(第 13 条第 1 款)、"保证投资可以自由转入转出,包含转移"(第 14 条第 1 款)等体现了对投资的保护。

正如 Waelde 指出的那样,有关国际投资的国际法与国内法一样,都经历了钟摆式的变化,其动因在于 20 世纪 90 年代各国外资政策的剧烈变动。现在,钟摆已经回摆:私有化、自由化、去管制化和国家间的竞争已成为当前外资政策的主流看法,ECT 就代表着回摆的高点。[③]

晚近以来,ECT 受到能源利益相关国家特别是俄罗斯的诸多批评。(1)该条约给予能源投资者过高保护,使能源价格与能源资本流动呈现此消彼长的失衡关系,造成以能源为主要产业的独联体国家出现经济波动。(2)能源宪章在运输议定书方面的谈判迟迟不能推进,其在最为核心的运输税收方面的谈判困境对协定应然功能的有效发挥产生了严重减损。(3)能源宪章是一个软法与硬法兼具的法律,其争端解决机制在实践中并不高效,而能源问题一旦产生,多数都具有紧迫性。(4)宪章签订于 20 世纪 90 年代,其规定已经在较大程度上不能适应当前能源投资的迅猛发展,诸如碳排放交易、生物能源等问题。俄罗斯宣布于 2009 年 10 月 19 日停止 ECT 条款对其适用,并积极倡导建立一个

---

① Haghighi and Sanam Salem, *Energy Security—The External Legal Relations of the European Union with Major Oil and Gas Supplying Country*, Hart Publishing Press, 2007, pp.194-192.

② Konoplyanik A, Walde T., Energy Charter Treaty and Its Role in International Energy, *Journal of Energy and Natural Resources Law*, 2007, Vol.24, pp.523-558.

③ Thomas W. Waelde, International Investment under the 1994 Energy Charter Treaty: Legal Negotiation and Policy Implication for International Investors within Western and Commonwealth of Independent States/Eastern Countries, *Journal of World Trade*, 1995, Vol.29, p.5.

普遍的(具有适用于任何国家的可能)、开放的(允许世界任何一个国家加入)、广泛的(涵盖所有的能源问题)、非歧视的、有效解决争端的世界能源组织一劳永逸地解决能源问题。[①]

尽管 ECT 在诸多方面确实存在着缺陷与不足,但是俄罗斯此举的实质并非 ECT 真正有问题,而是由欧盟成员国与乌克兰的能源合作以及其与欧盟成员国之间的能源贸易、投资问题的摩擦引起的,是一种国际经济博弈策略和手段。[②] ECT 成员国已经意识到当前能源投资领域的新发展趋势,在环境、消费者、生产者等非政府组织推动下,就多边能源投资利益再平衡的规则已经开始谈判。此外,ECT 始终坚守其与 WTO 的一致性,在一定意义上解决了 WTO 迟迟未能解决的重要问题,是"WTO 体制之外的 WTO规则",有利于国际经济规则的一体化。ECT 仍然是当前唯一一个涵盖所有能源投资问题的多边投资规则,是南北合作和能源供需国之间利益平衡的典范,十年来未有任何一个多边投资规则对其形成挑战,具有重要的法律价值。另起炉灶建立全新"俄罗斯式"的多边能源投资规则显得过于理想,困难重重。

我国是 ECT 观察国之一。随着我国能源进口日趋增长,能源供应安全迫在眉睫,在能源贸易迟迟不能推动、能源运输饱受地缘政治干扰的情况下,通过国际能源投资的方式获得稳定的能源供应未尝不是一个好的路径。随着我国能源公司的竞争力日渐强大,为保护我国海外能源投资,加入 ECT 正当其时。

三、经合组织主持的多边投资规则

经合组织在 1998 年出台了一个综合性多边投资协定(MAI)草案。MAI 不像《华盛顿公约》《汉城公约》那样仅仅局限于国际投资的某一个或者几个方面的问题,而是旨在解除国内法对投资的限制(投资自由化)、提供高水平的投资保护和创设高效的投资争端解决机制三个方面进行全方位规范。[③]

(一)MAI 的三大特性

1.投资自由化要求较高

MAI 要求各缔约国对全球所有的投资者提供一个公平的经济场所,确立非歧视待遇,提高相关政策法规的透明度;要求将国民待遇扩展适用于设业前,而不仅限于投资进入后的经营运作阶段;通过自上而下的方式取消履约要求,减弱东道国对外资的管理

---

　① A.Konoplyanik,Energy Charter Plus-Russia to Take the Lead Role in Modernizing ECT,*Oil*,*Gas & Energy Law Journal*,2009,Vol.7,p.2.

　② A.Konoplyanik,Russia-EU Summit-WTO,The Energy Charter and the Issue of Energy Transit,*International Energy Law and Taxation Review*,2005,No.2,p.188.

　③ ABA,Multilateral Agreement on Investment,American Bar Association Section of International Law and Practice Report to the House of Delegates,*The International Lawyer*,1997,pp.204-206.

权力。

2.确立高标准的投资保护标准

MAI要求各国根据国际法基于投资及投资者持续的保护和安全,将公平公正待遇作为最低保护标准;禁止非基于公共利益的征收,合法征收应根据"赫尔公式"(充分、及时、有效)的三原则补偿;投资资本及利润根据市场汇率可自由汇兑与转移。

3.高效争端解决机制

MAI综合了WTO提供的"国家—国家"的争端解决模式和有ICSID和NAFTA第11章提供的"私人—国家"争端解决模式,为多边投资规则的执行提供了高效的争端解决机制。

总之,MAI提供了一个标准高、内容全和争端解决机制高效的多边投资规则。

(二)发展中国家与发达国家共同创制 MAI

有学者认为,MAI的失败没有加固南北利益,其超出了发展中国家所能提供的市场开放和放松管制的程度,是"南北矛盾"无法调和的失败产物。[1] 对此,笔者并不赞同。尽管多数发展中国家没有参与MAI的谈判,但在参与MAI谈判的34国家、地区中,有12个是非发达国家,占总数的1/3强,参与MAI谈判的国家(地区)实际上涵盖了绝大多数国际投资的主要东道国。[2]

当时MAI谈判的主要国家是资本流动的拥有者,是资本输出国(发达国家)、发展中国家(资本输入国)所共同参与的多边投资规则。发展中国家在谈判中不可能不考虑自身的经济发展目标而通过一个只对发达国家有利的草案。南北阵营的对立与矛盾确实是国际投资关系中最为重要的一种,但这并不是全部。当时的欧共体国家(以法国为代表)与加拿大在文化产业投资方面形成了同一阵营,[3]与美国形成了尖锐的对立。在一定程度上,这两个以文化产业投资议题而形成的发达国家间不同阵营的不可调和的矛盾,才构成了MAI草案难以通过的真正动因之一。[4]

(三)我国应总体上接受 MAI

21世纪初是国际投资格局调整发展期,国际直接投资资本的流动(无论是流出还是流入)逐步从发达国家之间的双向流动转向发达国家、发展中国家和转型经济体国家多层次流动,国际直接投资呈现出多向流动的态势。越来越多的发展中国家跨国公司对国际投资正在作出贡献,我国及一些发展中国家对外投资发展迅猛,甚至已超过部分发达

---

[1]　刘笋:《国际投资保护的国际法制》,法律出版社2002年版,第56~83页。

[2]　董跃:《MAI:构建多边投资规则的未来之路》,http://article.chinalawinfo.com/ article_print. asp? articleid=22902,最后访问时期:2013年3月5日。

[3]　UNCTAD, *Lessons from the MAI UNCTAD series on Issues In International Investment Agreements*, United Nations,1999, pp.12-13.

[4]　Carolinn Hjalmroth, Stefan Westerberg, A Common Investment Policy for the EU, www. kommers.se/ trade&growth, last visited on 25 March 2013.

国家,成为重要的资本输出与输入国。① 从这个意义上,发展中国家是资本输入国、资本输出国阵营中的重要力量,承担了日益重要的双重角色。

随着国际资本多向流动,国际投资协定要在促进增长与发展方面发挥更有效和有利的作用仍需要长期的努力,其中一个重要的努力方向就是"增强国际投资协定与其他处理社会、广泛的经济和环境关切问题领域的公共政策的互动"②。我国参与多边投资规则的制定不但能在发展问题上争取有利于我国的优惠安排,而且也是参与其他国际事务全球治理过程的手段与切入点之一。

接受 OECD 制定的 MAI 及其随后的多边投资规则,对我国有两大好处:第一,成为资本输入阵营当中的一员,表明了我国在投资环境方面的改善,对外国投资人的投资信心能够产生一定的吸引作用,使我国成为投资东道国的领军国家;第二,在我国企业"走出去"战略下,中国已经成为重要的资本输出国,MAI 在实质上能为我国海外投资提供较好的法律保护。

本章小结

当前多边投资规则制定场所多样,我国应当区分不同场所和缔约方的类型,以区别对待。对我国与金砖国家之间、自由贸易区和其他发展中国家的多边投资规则,在尊重各参与方不同战略目标的前提下,我国应当积极主导。对当前已成为观察员国家的 ECT、已有草案的 MAI 和未来可能在 WTO 框架下建构的多边投资规则,在综合分析和权衡利弊的基础上,应当在总体上予以接受,在具体条款上提出符合我国利益的修改建议。

---

① 联合国贸易与发展会议:《2004 年世界投资报告》(中文版),第 8 页、附录表 1、6、7、9。
② 联合国贸易与发展会议:《2004 年世界投资报告》(中文版),第 8 页、附录表 1、6、7、9。

第七章
中国参与制定多边投资规则的工作机制

多边投资规则的谈判进程与成果往往受到谈判者推动能力的影响。若我国充分掌握谈判对手的主导者、参与者及其工作机制，就会形成信息对称博弈，对提升我国参与制定多边投资规则的议价能力有重要意义。否则，会是信息非对称的博弈，使我国陷入被动局面，造成利益空间压缩。美国与欧盟是全球最大的资本流入与流出地区，也是参与多边投资规则最多的国家和地区。本章旨在比较分析当前美国、欧盟和我国在多边投资规则制定中的主导者、参与者及其主要工作程序，提出我国未来改进建议，以期为我国机制改进和对外谈判有所裨益。

第一节 主导者

主导者是指多边投资规则谈判的主导机构，是谈判进程的主要推动力量。无论是美国还是欧盟，其主导者均呈现出单一化特征，保证了谈判的高效。

一、美国欧盟的主导机构与主要工作程序

(一)美国

1.主导机构

(1)国务院法律顾问办公室

美国国务院法律顾问办公室(Office of the Legal Adviser)是由法律顾问领导的副国务卿级直属单位。法律顾问不是公务员或职业外交官，是由国务卿直接任命的官员，通

过国务卿向总统提供所有对外事务(包括经贸事务)的法律意见,其一般与国务卿同进退。①

法律顾问办公室法律官员的一项重要职责是承担国际协定的起草、谈判、解释和相关的咨询工作,在法律领域的国际会议或国际组织中代表美国政府行事。法律顾问办公室共有 4 名副法律顾问,级别相当于我国司(局)级;设 23 助理法律顾问,其中 5 名负责非洲、近东和南亚、西半球、欧洲、东亚及太平洋五个地区的国际公法问题。国际投资、贸易、民航等国际协定的谈判起草事务(treaty affairs)主要由经济和工商事务处负责。

法律顾问办公室下设条约事务处,负责条约和其他国际协定的起草、谈判、实施、解释和公布等日常事务及美国条约的宪法问题的(国会与总统对外缔约权的划分)、其他条约法上的法律咨询与协助工作。② 在 1988 年以前,由于总统对外"贸易促进权"的扩张,涉及多边投资的《哈瓦那宪章》《华盛顿公约》《汉城公约》均是由法律顾问办公室代表国务院对外谈判。

但是,附属于行政权的法律顾问办公室的谈判主导作用往往依赖于总统"快车道谈判权"的大小。总统与国会相互斗争的情况犹如一个摇晃的巨大政治钟摆,总是撞击出令世人侧耳倾听的声音。③ 在国家面临危机时,权力的钟摆偏向总统和行政部门,当冲突和危机消减时,权力的钟摆又重新摆向国会。④ 从 20 世纪 80 年代开始,国际格局发生重大变化,经济全球化进一步纵深发展,国会认为美国贸易政策成为美国外交政策的孤儿,批评行政部门"总是通过贸易和与贸易有关的投资问题上的让步来获取国际政治特定目标"。⑤ 众议院不断对国务院是否有能力和精力进行 GATT 逐步复杂和深入的谈判提出质疑,⑥国会通过《1988 年综合贸易和竞争力法》(Omnibus Trade and Competitiveness Act of 1988),进一步分解了总统的对外经济政策权,而狄龙回合成为国务院最后一次主导的国际谈判。

(2)美国贸易代表办公室

美国贸易代表办公室(Office of the United States Trade Representative,以下简称 USTR)被《1988 年综合贸易和竞争力法》正式确认,是美国国内社会力量反抗冷战政治结构和全球化加剧带来的体系性压力的结果,体现了国家在市场与社会之间实现平衡的政策努力。该办公室首席贸易代表为大使级内阁官员,直接对总统和国会负责,处于行政中间人的角色。根据《1988 年综合贸易和竞争力法》,在由总统建立的、与对外经济关系有关的任何经济机构中,USTR 都应当成为高级代表,所有国际经济峰会、凡是与贸易

---

① Office of the Legal Adviser, http://www.state.gov/s/l/, last visited on 29 Feb.2013.

② Foreign Affairs Manual, Vol.2, http://www.state.gov/m/a/dir/regs/fam/, last visited on 12 May 2013.

③ 孙哲:《左右未来:美国国会的制度创新和决策行为》,复旦大学出版社 2001 年版,第 9 页。

④ 杰里尔·A.罗塞蒂:《美国对外政策的政治学》,世界知识出版社 1997 年版,第 273 页。

⑤ William A. Lovett, Alfred E. Eckes, Richard L. Brinkman, *U.S. Trade Policy—History, Theory and the WTO*, NM. E. Sharper Press, 1999, p.85.

⑥ I.M. Destler, *American Trade Politics* (4ᵗʰ), Peterson Institute Press, 2005, p.19.

有关的国际会议,USTR 都必须参加,USTR 成功将国际经贸决策权从国务院中剥离出来。[1] USTR 最初仅关注与国际贸易有关的问题,但随着经济部门一体化与复杂化,凡是与贸易有关的议题均由其主导,NAFTA 和 USMCA 中的投资规则、乌拉圭回合下的 TRIMs 协定由其主导谈判并完成。20 世纪 90 年代以后的双边投资条约谈判工作均由 USTR 完成。[2]

从 USTR 内部架构看,共分为双边谈判、多边谈判、部门服务、分析和法律事务协调五个部门。当前,双边投资条约谈判、涉及投资规则的区域贸易协定(RTA)谈判、经合组织和联合国贸易与发展会议提出的直接投资事务谈判,由服务与投资办公室(Office of Service and Investment)和多边谈判办公室共同负责。[3]

从 USTR 对外协调看,在经贸议题上通过以自己为核心建立了一个跨部门协调的亚内阁层级机制。这种协调工作通过贸易政策审议小组(TPRG)和贸易政策参谋委员会(TPSC)完成。这些小组由 17 个联邦机构和办公室组成,由 USTR 管理并任主席。

2.主要工作程序

凡未经与国务卿协商,任何政府部门不得代表美国参与谈判、缔结、批准任何国际协定。[4] 如果一项多边投资协定由国务院负责,国务卿一般指定法律顾问办公室相关人员进行谈判。如果一项多边投资协定由 USTR 负责,则由贸易代表批准谈判人员和开始时间,国务卿和国务卿指定的人员可以提出意见,并向美国代表发出书面文件,其法律形式为"立场文件"。[5] 上述批准或意见必须在开始与国务卿协商并在国务卿收到相关信息后 20 日内作出。

为了便利协商,USTR 应在谈判开始前将相关草案材料提交国务院。如果不能在谈判开始前提交,应在不晚于预期签署协定 50 日的谈判过程中提交。在不是由国务院主导的协定谈判过程中,任何重要的政策决定、立场变化均需要与国务院助理法律顾问协商。在签署协定之前的所有谈判进程中,未经国务卿批准,美国谈判代表不得披露谈判的任何内容。

在签署技术事项方面,若协定有数种语言文本,保存文本中英文文本在先,其他文本

---

①　美国贸易代表办公室(USTR)由美国国会根据 1962 年《贸易扩张法案》设立,依据肯尼迪总统 1963 年 1 月 15 日签署的 11075 号总统行政令落实。最初命名为特别贸易代表办公室,该机构经授权负责 1930 年《关税法案》和 1962 年《贸易扩张法案》项下的所有贸易协定项目的谈判。孙哲、李巍:《美国贸易代表办公室与美国贸易政策》,载《美国研究》2007 年第 1 期。

②　美国与世界各国所签订的双边投资条约在联合国贸易与发展会议数据库中均可查阅,http://www.unctadxi.org/ templates/DocSearch.aspx? id＝779,最后访问日期:2022 年 5 月 15 日。

③　USTR, Services and Investment, http://www.ustr.gov/trade-topics/services-investment, last visited on 23 Feb. 2013.

④　Bradley, Goldsmith, *Foreign Relations Law—Cases and Material*, Wolter Kluwer Press, 2003, pp.416-418.

⑤　*Declaration of War and Authorization for the Use of Military Force-Historical Background and Legal Implications*, CRS Report for Congress, 2007.

在后;若平行印制,英文在左,其他文字在右;若正反面印制,英文在正面,其他文本在背面。美国版本行文应当美国在先,外国在后;美方签字在左,外国在右。

(二)欧盟

欧盟是当前区域一体化最先进者,由经济一体化、外交防务一体化和司法、内务一体化三大支柱构成。与共同经贸政策①的发展相比,共同投资政策的发展相对滞后,直至2007年《里斯本条约》才将投资的专属权能(exclusive competence)赋予欧盟。这意味着欧盟在直接投资方享有参与制定多边投资规则的谈判权。

1.主导机构

(1)欧盟委员会

欧盟委员会(European Commission)是处理欧盟日常事务的"行政执行"机关,是纯粹的"超国家"独立机构,被称为大共同体条约的"保护女神"。② 欧盟委员会负责对外经贸谈判业务的部门是"对外关系总司"下的贸易处。③

根据《欧盟运行条约》④第17条,欧盟委员会是与非欧盟国家就经贸政策进行谈判的代表机构,在对外谈判起着支配性的中心作用。⑤ 具体而言,欧盟与非欧盟国家或国际组织签订的条约构成欧盟法的法律渊源之一,⑥而欧盟委员会在经贸领域具有独立提出对外条约立法动议的提案权,没有该委员会的立法动议,理事会无权直接批准对外条约谈判。欧盟委员会凭借这一权力,不仅能为谈判的走向奠定基调,还能直接介入谈判进程。

关于欧盟委员会谈判投资规则的权能范围,学界未有定论。按《欧盟运行条约》第207条规定,外国直接投资措施是对外经贸政策的组成部分之一。但就"外国直接投资"

---

① 有学者采用共同贸易政策(common trade policy)、对外贸易政策(external trade policy or foreign trade policy)、对外经济政策(foreign economic policy)等概念。在欧盟法中,"共同商业政策"(common commercial policy)是指调整欧盟与第三国和国际组织间贸易、商务和经济交往的法律、原则与政策的统称,包括了贸易协定、配额、直接投资、关税、出口信贷、出口援助、普惠制,甚至是经济制裁等内容。因此,为避免误解,笔者采用"对外经贸政策"的提法。参见刘文秀等:《欧洲联盟政策及政策过程研究》,法律出版社2003年版,309页。

② 张彤等:《欧盟法概论》,中国人民大学出版社2011年版,第66～67页。

③ 最初因《里斯本条约》之前未授权欧盟的投资职能,因此该处以贸易(trade)命名,欧盟与美国正在进行的贸易与投资谈判是由该处提请欧盟委员会而发起的。http://trade.ec.europa.eu/doclib/press/index.cfm? id＝883,最后访问日期:2022年5月10日。

④ 2009年12月1日生效的《改革〈建立欧洲共同体条约〉及〈建立欧洲联盟条约〉的条约》暨《里斯本条约》对原《欧共体条约》和《建立欧洲联盟条约》作了大幅修改,将《欧共体条约》更名为《欧盟运行条约》。See Consolidated Version of the Treaty on the Functioning of the European Union,[2010] O.J.L 83/47.

⑤ 欧共体官方出版局编:《欧洲共同体条约集》,戴炳然译,复旦大学出版社1993年版,第173页。

⑥ 邵景春:《欧洲联盟的法律与制度》,人民法院出版社1999年版,第53页。

一词的理解,主流学说主要分为与贸易有关的投资说[1]、有限的综合权限说[2]、对外谈判权说、直接投资市场准入自由化说[3]、综合权限说[4]五种学说。[5] 各种学说均支持欧盟委员会在直接投资领域具有对外谈判代表权。

(2)欧盟理事会

欧盟理事会(Council of the European Union,也称部长理事会),是欧盟的决策机构,享有欧盟是否对外进行谈判、如何谈判、条约签署等问题的最高决策权。理事会是由每个成员国派出的部长级代表组成,他们代表本国政府作出决定,代表本国政府投票。[6] 理事会的对外关系是由外交事务理事会负责,确定对外关系的战略方针,形成对外关系的一致性。对外多边投资关系,由"经济与金融理事会"(ECOFIN)就专门议题进行讨论和决定。[7]

尽管欧盟委员会对诸如一项对外国际投资协定的谈判具有立法动议权,但在欧盟是否与第三方国家或国际组织进行以缔约目的的谈判方面,理事会对委员会的动议具有排他的决定权。谈判的方式、范围和周期由理事会决定,在条约的签署与批准时,是由理事会以欧盟的名义行使权力。[8]

2.主要工作程序

一项多边投资规则的谈判首先由欧盟委员会提出立法动议案。该动议的草案由对外关系总司拟定,经上级主管部门、委员内阁、主席内阁的每周例会层层上报,最后到委员院。在此过程中,草案内容可能发生实质性修改。委员院对动议可任意处理,既可接受,也可否决,还可将其退回并责令对外关系总司重新起草,或者作出延期审议决定。

当欧盟委员会确定条约谈判草案后,需提交欧盟部长理事在 B 级议程程序下讨论。[9]

---

① Cardwell,P. J. & French,D.,The European Union and a Global Investment Partner—Law,Policy and Rhetoric in the Attainment of Development Assistance and Market Liberalization,in Brown C. and Miles,K. ed.,*Evolution in Investment Treaty Law and Arbitration*,Cambridge University Press,2011,p.6.

② Wouters,Coppens and De Meester,The European Union's External Relations after the Lisbon Treaty,in S. Griller and J. Ziller ed.,*The Lisbon Treaty-EU Constitutionalism without a Constitutional Treaty*? Spinger Press,2008,p.173.

③ Stephen Woolcock,The Potential Impact of Lisbon Treaty on European Union External Trade Policy,*Swedish Inst. For Eur. Pol & Analysis*,2008,p.4.

④ Dimopoulos,The Common Commercial Policy After the Lisbon Treaty-Establishing Parallelism Between Jnternal and Extemal Economic Relations,4th *Croatian Yearbook European Law and Policy*,2008,p.101.

⑤ 张庆麟、张惟威:《〈里斯本条约〉对欧盟国际投资法律制度的影响》,载《武汉大学国际法评论》2011 年第 1 期。

⑥ 《欧盟运行条约》第 16 条第 4 款。

⑦ 该理事会与农业、竞争、能源等不同议题的其他 21 个理事会共同称为"专门理事会"。

⑧ 刘文秀:《欧洲联盟政策及政策过程研究》,法律出版社 2003 年版,第 421 页。

⑨ 刘光华等:《运行在国家与超国家之间——欧盟的立法制度》,江西高校出版社 2006 年版,第 11 页。

部长理事会在听取经济与金融理事会、欧盟委员会动议和相关专家的意见后,对该动议予以批准或否决。欧盟委员会在理事会批准动议后,可代表欧盟对外正式谈判多边投资规则。

具体言之,欧盟对外谈判与缔约程序如下:(1)欧盟委员会向理事会提出参与或者与其他国家缔结多边投资规则谈判的立法动议。(2)理事会在 B 级程序下讨论,决定是否开始谈判。如果决定可以谈判,则通过谈判指令、指导原则或者委托权的形式授权给委员会。(3)委员会的相关部门代表委员会对外举行谈判。在此过程中,谈判人员与理事会任命的特别委员保持联系与沟通。此外,因《欧盟运行条约》没有明确"投资"议题是委员会的专属权能,因此可以推定其为成员国与委员会的共享权能,成员国就其权能范围内的事项代表本国共同参与谈判。(4)对特别困难或者重要的谈判,委员会可要求理事会澄清或者修改指令,以便继续推动谈判。(5)谈判结束后,委员会向理事会建议缔结协定,委员会可先行草签。(6)理事会采用特定多数表决机制进行表决,通过后,正式授权签署。

二、美国欧盟机制的利弊分析

(一)美国机制的优劣

1.优势

USTR 是政府的内阁成员,是美国白宫总统办公室的一部分,充当总统的贸易问题顾问、谈判代表和发言人。它在经贸议题上通过以自己为核心建立了一个跨部门协调的亚内阁层级机制。这种协调工作通过贸易政策审议小组(TPRG)和贸易政策参谋委员会(TPSC)完成。这些小组由 17 个联邦机构和办公室组成,由 USTR 管理并担任主席。由于 USTR 是美国府会之争的结果,其在政治上是一个中立的"非党派"的技术专家机构,有三个方面的政策协调任务:听取总统在贸易政策上的战略性考虑、行政体系内部各部门的意见;听取来自国会的多重声音;听取各利益团体和不同产业的政策诉求。这种同时兼容专家意见、国内利益集团意见和非政府组织意见的跨部门协调作用是其他部门无法替代的,有着高效、稳定的优势。

2.劣势

美国对外双边、区域和普遍性投资协定均属于《联邦宪法》意义上的条约,其批准权专属于国会。例如,在美国与厄瓜多尔双边投资保护协定中,美国贸易执行代表特别强调了协定的"条约"(treaty)属性[①],在确认约文内容后,尚需国会批准。因此,USTR 的谈判活动在很大程度上受制于美国国会的意图,其在谈判过程中,必须就一些重大问题向

---

① Treaty between the United States of America and the Republic of Ecuador concerning the Encouragement and Reciprocal Protection of Investment,http://unctad.org/sections/dite/iia/docs/bits/us_ecuador.pdf,last visited on 15 May 2013.

国会汇报,甚至必须得到国会批准方可继续谈判。因此,美国的府会之争始终是美国对外多边投资规则谈判的不稳定因素。一旦总统与国会在投资议题方面出现根本性分歧或对立,就会产生"分裂的政府"(divided government)这一奇特现象。特别是在总统所属党派在国会占据较少席位时,这种条约缔结的不确定性尤为明显。正是来自国会的强大压力,布什政府的历任贸易谈判代表都必须表现出强硬的谈判立场,只有迫使贸易伙伴作出让步,为美国的农业、制造业和服务业提供更多贸易机会,USTR才能在减少美国自身贸易壁垒方面获得国会支持。[①] 由于当前双边投资协定已经为美国商界提供了相对满意的保护,因此国会同意多边投资规则谈判的可能性相对较小。这也造成了美国贸易代表为绕开敏感问题,从单一议题的多边贸易向贸易与投资混合的多轨贸易体制转换的原因所在。因此,美国这样一个"弱政府"的特性会对多边投资规则的推进造成不确定性。

(二)欧盟机制的优劣

1.优势

欧盟作为一个超国家治理的组织,对外经贸政策随着欧盟的发展而不断纵深发展,主要表现在两个方面:(1)在"后里斯本时代",欧盟将"直接投资"纳入对外经贸政策中,在一定程度上形成了"对内一个步伐前进""对外一个声音说话"的现象。欧盟作为世界上资本流入量与资本流出量最大地区,投资政策的统一将强化其在多边投资规则中的谈判筹码,形成27个成员国捆绑谈判的规模效应,对投资规则的内容与标准产生举足轻重的影响。在可预计的未来,多边投资规则的谈判范本将不再是美国一家独大,会出现"欧盟投资规则范本"。(2)欧盟法律与政策使外国直接投资更加自由化,在国际投资问题上更加一致和一贯。通过欧盟内部协调可以减少国际投资关系中的不稳定因素与局部的变量,有利于欧盟与非欧盟的多边投资规则形成。

2.劣势

在《里斯本条约》生效前,欧盟及其成员国一直未能在国际投资的权能划分上形成统一规则,未产生专门负责对外多边投资规则谈判的部门,一直是由欧盟委员会对外关系总司下的贸易处负责。这种机制的劣势有:(1)欧盟与其成员职能划分不清。如前述,《欧盟运行条约》中"直接投资"的措辞仍然未能改变欧盟及其成员国在权能划分上的问题,多边投资协定的谈判将是欧盟法意义上的"混合条约"(mixed treaty)。换言之,即使欧盟根据条约享有对外谈判权能,该权能也仅仅是对市场准入问题具有谈判权能,而在谈判后的设业自由、外资管制等设业后管制,仍然是成员国的专属权能。(2)欧盟的多元治理结构使其决策过程效率低下。欧盟理事会、欧盟委员会和成员国三者之间的博弈、互相制衡,大大削弱了欧盟对外谈判的有效性与效率,在一定程度上增加了谈判难度。(3)投资的界定范围狭窄。当前国际投资协定发展趋势之一是投资定义扩大化,给予间

① 杰弗利·J.舒特:《当前美国贸易政策面临的挑战》,载弗雷德·伯格斯坦主编:《美国与世界经济:未来十年美国对外经济政策》,朱民等译,经济科学出版社2005年版,第261页。

接投资一定空间,而欧盟的对外经贸政策仅限于"直接投资"。欧盟要想在多边投资规则的建构领域发挥一定主导性,尚需通过立法进一步澄清或者改变其当前投资范围过窄的局面。

三、中国的主导机构与主要工作程序

(一)主导机构

当前我国对外经贸协定谈判的主导者为商务部。商务部有关投资协定谈判的部门众多,主要有以下具有主导职能的司(局)[1]:

1.国际经贸关系司。负责拟订并执行多边、区域经贸政策;根据分工处理与多边、区域经贸组织的关系;组织实施自由贸易区战略;牵头组织多边、区域及自由贸易区等对外经贸谈判。

2.外国投资管理司。负责建立多双边投资促进机制并开展相关工作,筹划跨地区大型投资促进和外资政策宣传活动;牵头协调多边双边、区域谈判中涉及投资议题的中方立场,拟订谈判方案,负责对外谈判工作,参与双边投资协定谈判工作。

3.对外投资和经济合作司。负责开展对外投资和经济合作方面的多边、双边交流与合作,建立相关机制。

4.世界贸易组织司。代表我国政府处理与世贸组织的关系,负责我国在世贸组织框架下的各种会议、多边双边谈判。

5.投资促进事务局。该局是商务部直属事业单位,受商务部委托代表商务部参加世界投资促进机构、协会并开展相关工作,与相关国际经济组织开展投资促进业务合作,与境外投资促进机构与协会建立合作机制,商签合作协议。

6.其他区域司局。商务部以地缘为标准设立了欧洲司、美大司、亚洲司、西亚非洲司、台港澳司6个司。各司的职能均建立双边、区域政府间经济贸易联委会、混委会等机制;组织双边、区域经贸谈判;处理国别(地区)经贸关系中的重要事务;监督外国政府履行与我国签订的经贸协定情况并承担对外交涉工作。

(二)主要工作程序

我国对外谈判及缔约权问题主要由我国1990年《缔结条约程序法》调整。根据该法第5条规定,我国有关谈判和签署条约、协定的决定程序如下:(1)以中华人民共和国名义谈判和签署条约、协定,由外交部或者国务院有关部门会同外交部提出建议并拟订条约、协定的中方草案,报请国务院审核决定。(2)以中华人民共和国政府名义谈判和签署条约、协定,由外交部提出建议并拟订条约、协定的中方草案,或者由国务院有关部门提

---

① 本部分资料来源于商务部网站,http://www.mofcom.gov.cn/,最后访问日期:2022年2月18日。

出建议并拟订条约、协定的中方草案,会商外交部后,报请国务院审核决定。属于具体业务事项的协定,经国务院同意,协定的中方草案由国务院有关部门审核决定,必要时会商外交部。(3)以中华人民共和国政府部门名义谈判和签署属于本部门职权范围内事项的协定,由本部门决定或者本部门会商外交部后决定;涉及重大问题或者涉及国务院其他有关部门职权范围的,由本部门或者本部门会商国务院其他有关部门后,报请国务院决定。协定的中方草案由本部门审核决定,必要时会商外交部。经国务院审核决定的条约、协定的中方草案,经谈判需要做重要改动的,重新报请国务院审核决定。

我国与他国之间的双边或多边投资协定均冠以"中华人民共和国政府"的称谓,由国务院授权、商务部部长或者副部长作为代表草签。

(三)主要优劣分析

我国当前参与多边投资规则的谈判部门是商务部各司局为主导的谈判架构,这种架构下的谈判既有一定优势,又有不足。

1.优势

谈判主导力量集中,能够就谈判对手在某一议题上的要价作出迅速的回应,在磋商过程中具有一以贯之的谈判立场与明确的谈判底线,避免了不同部门基于不同考量而难以形成一致的谈判立场,相对降低了谈判难度、缩短了谈判周期,更有利于形成实质性的谈判成果。

2.劣势

当前多边投资规则在内容上涵盖广泛,已不是某一部门所能解决的问题。随着经济全球化、区域一体化,投资规则向综合化方向发展,越来越多的投资规则谈判不是投资本身问题的谈判,而是投资与贸易、知识产权、产业政策、劳工、人员流动、环境保护、政府采购、能源合作甚至与政治合作、经济战略等事务相互融合的谈判。尽管对投资保护的关键要素已经达成相当程度的共识,但在涉及国际投资条约的其他事务方面依然存在重大分歧。因此,商务部单一推动的谈判模式难以对上述问题作出综合平衡,不利于投资规则制定过程中我国利益的最大化。

第二节　参与者

一、其他官方机构

(一)美国的国会

美国《联邦宪法》要求总统"根据参议院的建议和同意"缔结条约。从文意解释看,可以理解为在缔约过程中,行政部门应当事先、事中征询参议院的建议,并在事后寻求参议院的同意。但实践中,参议院通常不参与缔约谈判,但个别情况除外。例如,《北大西洋公约》的缔约倡议就出自国会议员范登堡的提案,并且该议员同时参与了该公约的谈判。[①] 又如,一战结束前夕,威尔逊总统倡议的《国际联盟条约》未能邀请参议院参与谈判,是参议院两次拒绝批准的原因之一;二战结束前,罗斯福总统和杜鲁门总统先后倡议建立联合国,由于邀请了参议院对外关系委员会主席及其主要成员参与谈判,《联合国宪章》顺利通过。[②] 除 USTR 与国务院外,参议院在特定情况下参与谈判国际条约。即使参议院未能直接参与谈判,其对谈判主导者递交的草案和相关问题仍具有建议权,以否决权制衡谈判主导者,而主导者不可能不考虑参议院的相关意见。参议院因其对国际协定的批准权而对多边投资规则的谈判内容与立场施加影响,是美国在多边投资规则建构方面的参与者。

(二)欧盟的有关机构、成员国

除欧盟委员会和部长理事会作为对外投资规则的谈判者外,欧盟的其他重要机构和成员国也参与或影响谈判。

1.欧洲议会

欧洲议会(European Parliament)是体现全体欧洲公民民主意志的机构,具有监督、咨询和部分立法职能。当欧盟委员会提出参与对外投资规则的立法动议批准前,理事会应当先向欧盟委员会征求意见,以满足咨询程序(consult procedure)要求,即对任何谈判阶段的草案进行适当性审查。对外经贸协定的谈判还需要经过合作程序(cooperation procedure),进行"二读"。委员会和理事会在形成共同立场后,议会在二读阶段的立法修正案仍然可以纳入谈判草案中。如果理事会和委员会否决了议会的修正案,除非理事会全票通过共同立场草案,仍需进行共同决策程序(co-decision procedure),进行"三读"。在该阶段,理事会和议会形成调解委员会进行立场协调。只有双方立场协调成功后,谈判内容草案方可继续,否则议会将行使其拒绝权而否认条约谈判的继续。

2.欧盟的其他机构

除欧洲议会外,欧盟的其他机构对谈判也有一定的影响。欧洲经济和社会委员会(European Economic and Social Committee,EESC)作为代表工会、中小企业、消费者和环境组织的咨询机构,享有对谈判主导者的强制咨询权、选择咨询权和主动提出建议权。

3.成员国

欧盟作为一个主权国家的国际组织,其对外缔约权来自成员国的主权让渡。在国际投资关系中,欧盟并不是完全享有专属排他权。《欧盟运行条约》中的"直接投资"表明,欧盟投资政策的统一化对晚近 BITs 将投资扩大到间接投资的做法持谨慎态度。当多边投资协定中包含直接投资和间接投资时,成员国对该类"混合协定"有权参与谈判并在相

---

① 许海云:《对〈范登堡案〉的历史反思》,载《史学月刊》2007 年第 3 期。

② 孙昂:《美国对外事务法律机制》,国际文化出版公司 2008 年版,第 242 页。

应内容上具有批准权。例如,欧盟及其成员国在参与《反假冒贸易协定》谈判中,因此协定中的刑事执法措施不属于欧盟知识产权"对外经贸政策"的范畴,欧盟委员会宣称其对该事项无代表权,无法对该内容进行谈判,需要成员国进行谈判或授权谈判。①

二、利益集团

利益集团,又称压力集团、院外集团或游说集团,是指社会中的一些成员为了共同的集团利益而结合在一起,通过积极行动达到共同目的的社会组织。

(一)美国的利益集团

美国在对外经贸关系谈判中,利益集团对条约的起草、谈判有重要影响。二战结束后,美国商界迫切期望在《哈瓦那宪章》中加入投资议题,以期形成一个高保护标准的多边投资规则,②但因发展中国家在起草过程中的博弈,约文草案令发达国家失望。《哈瓦那宪章》的失败可以归因于该宪章未达到美国商界所期望的投资自由化目标,不可能在美国代表利益集团的国会获得通过。因此杜鲁门总统(民主党)没有将此宪章提交至共和党占多数的国会请求批准,转而利用自己的"行政协定"权致力于促使贸易自由化的GATT谈判,利益集团用"结果控制"影响了多边投资规则的制定。③

美国利益集团主要为经济性利益集团和公益性利益集团。前者由来自商界的不同行业专业人士组成,主要代表商界利益。后者反映美国市民社会对议题的公益性诉求,包括环保、妇女权益等组织。商界集团凭其雄厚财力及其重要社会影响而在各类利益集团的游说组成中占重要地位。尤其在有关国家对外政策的制定和执行中,跨国公司因其存在特殊利益,更积极参与到与政府的联系和交往中。早在1897年,麦金莱总统任命芝加哥第一国家银行高级执行官林曼·盖奇(Lyman Gage)为国家财政部长。20年后,时任总统哈定提名金融家安德鲁·梅隆(Andrew Mellon)担任此项职务。此后,美国财政部长一职多次由美国知名金融家或企业家担任。这一职位除了在调整国内财政经济中发挥关键作用外,还负责处理美国应对的国际金融问题。

有学者将美国的USTR、参议院和利益集团比作同一台戏的甲、乙、丙,指出:在对华经贸政策问题上,原来甲、乙、丙演的是同一出戏,并各司其职:有的唱黑脸,有的唱白脸;有人呐喊,有人行动。总体上,演员之间配合默契、取长补短、相互搭台。当然,有时演员之间也发生"冲突",使得剧情跌宕起伏,险象环生。因此"观众"都应当成为明眼人,清楚不同演员的角色和心理,准确地理解故事,预测情节的发展,以便在出现任何精彩的"剧

---

① 尚妍:《〈反假冒贸易协定〉研究》,西南政法大学 2013 年博士学位论文。

② Kenneth J. Vandevelde, A Brief History of International Investment Agreements, *U. C. Davis Journal of International Law and Policy*, 2005, Vol.12, p.157.

③ 《1934 年互惠贸易协定法》授予总统和外国展开贸易谈判及签订贸易协定的权力,因此对 GATT 的签订并不需要国会三分之二的批准。参见徐泉:《美国外贸政策决策机制的变革——美国〈1934 年互惠贸易协定法〉述评》,载《法学家》2008 年第 1 期。

情"时都能够洞察秋毫,坦然面对。[①]

(二)欧盟的利益集团

在欧盟对外经贸政策决策过程,利益集团虽然未直接参与谈判国际协定,但其对官方谈判者施加一定的影响。与美国一样,商界代表的利益集团对欧盟的立法产生重要的影响。[②] 以欧洲企业家圆桌会议(ERT)为例,该组织是由40多个欧洲跨国公司组成的非政府组织,资产总值超过1亿欧元,全球雇员达到400多万。[③] ERT从1983年开始发布其研究报告,数十年间不断影响欧盟对外经贸协定的谈判。其2000年发布了发展中国家改善投资环境的报告,2003年向各国领导人传递信息推动了多哈回合的谈判,其中重要议题是多边投资规则。[④] 利益集团对国际协定谈判的影响体现为对欧盟委员会、欧盟理事会、欧洲议会和其他机构的欧盟决策产生不可忽视的影响,其是欧盟对外经贸协定谈判的"亲密战友"。[⑤]

在某种意义上,跨国利益集团在欧盟对外经贸关系谈判过程中要比单一的国家利益集团活跃,日益成为欧盟机构与成员国间的利益协调者。[⑥]

三、法学学者

无论在美国还是在欧盟,法学学者是一支不可忽视的重要力量。最早由学者起草的多边投资公约草案为1959年《阿巴斯-肖克罗斯外国投资公约草案》,由德国学者阿巴斯与肖克罗斯共同完成,反映了发达国家商界对多边投资规则的需求,为后续立法奠定了框架性基础。1961年,联合国秘书长邀请哈佛大学法学院索恩教授和巴克斯教授起草《国家侵害外国人的国际责任公约草案》(简称"哈佛公约草案")。该草案对征收及其补偿作了高标准的规定,对二战后多边投资规则的建立产生了重要影响。[⑦]

事实上,美国、欧盟及其成员国政坛中都存在着广泛的"旋转门"现象,学界与政界的互动非常明显。在美国,以奥巴马的外交团队为例。原常务副国务卿詹姆斯·斯坦伯格

---

① 杨国华:《异曲同工——美国对华贸易政策》,载《国际经济法学刊》2008年第3期。

② 杨光斌主编:《政治学导论》,中国人民大学出版社2000年版,第156页。

③ 刘文秀:《欧盟的超国家治理》,社会科学文献出版社2003年版,第219页。

④ Achievements:the Highlight of ERT Activities,www.ert.be/pg/eng_frame.htm,last visited on 13 Feb. 2013.

⑤ Whilhelm lehmann,lars bosche,Lobbying in The European Union,Current Rules and Practices,European Parliament,Directorate-General for Research,Working Paper,AFCO 104 EN,04-2003.

⑥ 布鲁塞尔有超过300家的私营游说公司,业务包括各种领域,以盈利为目的,为客户与欧盟机构从事专门的游说业务。

⑦ 刘笋:《国际投资保护的国际法治——若干重要法律问题研究》,法律出版社2001年版,第28页。

曾分别供职于国际战略研究所、兰德公司和布鲁金斯学会等大型智库,并在国家安全、国际关系和情报收集等领域具备丰富的研究经验。在 2001 年至 2005 年担任布鲁金斯学会副总裁期间,斯坦伯格负责学会的外交事务项目(foreign affairs program)。此外,斯坦伯格还发表过多篇专论,例如《欧洲防务与跨大西洋合作的未来》(*European Defense and the Future of Transatlantic Cooperation*)、《前方的道路:小布什政府第二任期内的中东政策》(*The Road Ahead ：Middle East Policy in the Bush Administration's Second Term*)等。在欧盟,以欧盟委员会主席巴罗佐为例,其拥有里斯本大学法学学士背景,曾在多所大学任教,是一位学者型的官员。[1]

　　除政界与学界的"旋转门"外,专家学者还通过对外交流方式潜在地促成了某些议题国际协定的达成。原因在于,对某一具体议题,不同国家在法律、经济方面存在不同立场,只有弥合观念上的差异,才能达成双方均可接受的妥协。例如:早期美国与安第斯共同市场、南锥共同体国家间就征收及其补偿等问题存在根本分歧,民间学者的跨国学术交流,极大推动了这种分歧的弥合速度。有学者将美国对拉美的法律输出称为"两次十字军东征",对转型国家的法律输出称为"密涅瓦猫头鹰猎食"。[2] 按照葡萄牙学者桑托斯的概括,美国对拉美国家和转型国家主要表现为输出者的四项共识:新自由主义的经济共识、弱国的共识、自由主义的民主政治共识、以司法为核心的法治共识。[3] 具体而言,除了美国商务部对转型国家开展的知识产权与外资企业法的官方法律援助,美国法律专家还在"中欧和东欧项目部"支持下,以各种方式影响转型国家的商事立法,例如:帮助俄罗斯、爱沙尼亚和罗马尼亚制定商业组织法,帮助爱沙尼亚和立陶宛起草确保交易安全的法律,帮助阿尔巴尼亚、保加利亚、匈牙利和罗马尼亚等国制定破产法和国有企业私有化的法律,帮助保加利亚、罗马尼亚等国制定反垄断法。此外,美国法律专家还帮助独联体和一些东欧国家制定和修改民法典。[4] 美国这一系列措施的实质在于试图构建接受国形式主义的法治,借助于具有稳定性和可预见性的法律,维护市场秩序,确保财产和交易安全,为拉美等国家在私权神圣、能源投资国际主义、吸引外资以促进发展、提供良好投资环境等的观念上产生了根本性改变。这对拉美、转型国家晚近接受美国 BIT 范本以及TRIMs 协定等多边投资规则有着重要贡献。

---

① 刘笋:《国际投资保护的国际法治——若干重要法律问题研究》,法律出版社 2001 年版,第28 页。

② 高鸿钧:《美国法全球化:典型例证与法理反思》,载《中国法学》2011 年第 1 期。

③ 四项共识的基本内容是:(1)新自由主义的经济共识。其要义是全球市场化、市场自由化、财产私有化和交易合同化。为了市场有序,必须对全球经济进行法律规制,民族国家必须服从世界贸易组织和国际金融机构的规制和协调。(2)弱国的共识。其主旨是,国家权力强大,市场无法健康发展,公民自治无法壮大,为此必须弱化国家权力,以使公民社会迅速成长壮大。(3)自由主义的民主政治共识。其核心是个人主义的选举权、参政权、表达权、结社权以及对抗政府的权力。(4)以司法为核心的法治共识。主要内容是司法强立和司法公正,强化司法效能,尤其是强化刑事司法在打击犯罪和控制社会秩序方面的效能。博温托·迪·苏萨·桑托斯:《迈向新的法律常识——法律、全球化和解放》,刘坤轮、叶传星译,中国人民大学出版社 2009 年版,第 387~391 页。

④ 高鸿钧:《美国法全球化:典型例证与法理反思》,载《中国法学》2011 年第 1 期。

四、中国参与者的现状

我国参与制定多边投资规则,主要由政府主导谈判,法学学者、企业力量和公益组织等非政府力量的参与程度严重不足。

(一)法律实务界与法学界未形成"旋转门"

在法学学者参与层面,我国未形成法律实务界与法学界之间机制化的"旋转门",谈判均由"学者型官员"直接推动,少有高校、科研机构的国际法学者直接参与到国际条约谈判。学者型官员也不会在一段时间后转换身份,进入高校从事研究工作。① 参与程度不足的现状也与法学学者自身有一定关系。

1.实务界的主流状况

我国当前负责谈判的行政部门对工作"过于保守"的态度造成了法学学者的参与不足。谈判主导部门经常以"国家利益""机密"等理由拒绝透露有关谈判的重大、疑难问题,导致学界对实务界的运作和关键争议点处于模糊认识的状态。以中美双边投资协定谈判为例,我国对外谈判预计在 18 轮结束,但我国学者对于美方的要价、我国的出价、双方最为关注的条款和领域毫不知情,自然无法提供相关的专家参考意见,法学学者的参与更无从谈起。尽管我国在一些重大问题上通过官方机构或者半官方机构平台,以横向或者纵向课题的形式召集专家进行研究,但谈判部门并不提供与谈判相关的进程信息和资料,造成法学学者"巧妇难为无米之炊",无法参与多边投资规则谈判的实质性问题。

2.法学界的主流状况

有专家对法学界主流现状进行了描述,其精要者有如:在与法治相关的问题上,"理论正确于实践""学者高明于实务人员"已成为部分法学人认识中的预设;一些法学人常以训导者或布道者的口吻表达自己的各种观点与见解;一些法学人自觉或不自觉地把自己视为法治理想的守护者、法治真理的占有者;一些法学人对于形成自实务界的一些认识和做法,付之以漠视、轻视,甚而鄙视。② 这种"居高自傲""超然物外""对现实批判"的姿态不自觉地造成了法学者与国际谈判的距离。

(二)商界及其他非政府组织力量参与程度很低

造成这种状况的原因有:(1)我国经济体制发展是从"计划经济"走向"市场经济"的过程,长期以来形成了大政府、小社会的社会格局,个人利益往往让位于国家利益。我国在对外谈判中,首先考虑的是对外资的管辖权问题,其次才考虑我国企业在"走出去"过程中的投资风险问题。这在一定程度上影响了社会力量对我国国际条约谈判的关注与

① 以李浩培和陈体强先生为例,二位国际法大师作为享誉世界的国际法大师,由于身兼外交部法律顾问之职,根据保密规定,不能以导师身份指导学生。
② 顾培东:《也论中国法学向何处去》,载《中国法学》2009 年第 1 期。

参与程度。（2）我国未在国际条约的谈判启动、草案签署和批准层面形成机制化的听证、投票或者其他公众参与制度。国内立法过程中存在着立法草案出台后，由公众写信的方式提出修改建议，在国际投资规则、贸易规则等经贸规则的谈判及签署过程中，未能形成如国内立法过程中的社会沟通渠道。尽管全国人民代表大会中，商界及其他非政府组织代表设有一定的席位，但在全国人大常委会中的代表很少。此外，正如前述分析，我国参与多边投资规则是以中央政府名义签署的，并不需要全国人大进行投票批准。因此我国参与国际投资规则制定缺乏社会力量。

第三节　对我国未来工作机制的建议

根据前述分析和有关国家或国际组织的实践，拟提出以下意见和建议。

一、建立公约类和非公约类为主的多边投资规则制定工作机制

我国《宪法》第 67 条和《条约缔结程序法》第 3 条规定，全国人大常委会"决定同外国缔结的条约和重要协定的批准和废除"。我国对条约与协定作了区分，条约一般冠以"条约"或"公约"名称，而协定则指冠以"协定""安排""换文""换函""备忘录"等名称。《条约缔约程序法》第 5 条同时赋予外交部与商务部享有多边投资规则谈判和拟定中方条文草案的权力。这种权力重合的谈判架构不利于多边投资规则谈判、制定的高效性与立场一致性。有必要对当前多边投资规则制定工作机制进行一定改革。

在条约法意义上，多边投资规则按不同标准可分为不同种类。其中按其代表者身份可以分为"公约类"与"非公约类"。前者如 ICSID 公约、MIGA 公约，后者如《WTO 协定》。此种分类的法律意义在于，"国际公约"一般在缔约国外交大会上通过，公约案文的起草、修改谈判由以国家名义的外交代表进行，其主导机构为各国外交部门；而非公约类的国际条约、协定等一般在缔约国政府间专门会议上缔结，其案文的起草、修改谈判由以政府名义的非外交代表（即非外交性质的谈判代表）进行，其主导机构是外交部门以外的政府部门。根据此种分类，我国参与多边投资规则制定的主导者分别为外交部和商务部，其职责分工为：外交部主导公约类多边投资规则的制定，商务部主导非公约类多边投资规则的制定。

（一）外交部主导的主要工作机制

由外交部主导公约类多边投资规则的制定，主要职责是：提出是否制定或参与制定某项多边投资规则的意见，提出具体规则案文草案或中方案文，主导中方谈判或作为普遍性或区域性投资规则谈判的中方首席谈判者，草签和正式签署。商务部是主要参与

者,外交部需就此类每项多边投资规则的具体问题会商商务部。

在外交部内部,因条约法律司的主要职能之一是承办国家对外缔结双边、多边条约和国际司法合作的有关事项,因此条法司应为公约类多边投资规则制定的核心机构,其他部门如国际经济司、区域性司(局)为协助和配合机构,可提供相关数据或意见,必要时参与案文的起草、修改、谈判等具体工作。

(二)商务部主导的主要工作机制

由商务部主导非公约类多边投资规则制定,其主要职责是:提出是否制定或参加某项多边投资规则的意见,提出具体规则案文草案或中方案文,主导中方谈判或作为区域性或普遍性投资规则的中方首席谈判者,签署文本。外交部是主要参与者,商务部需就此类每项多边投资规则的具体问题会商外交部。

在商务部内部,条约法律司应为非公约类多边投资规则制定的核心机构,世贸司、国际司及其他区域司(局)作为协助机构,可提供必要的相关数据或参考性意见,必要时参与案文的起草、修改、谈判等具体工作。

(三)其他政府部门的职责

在当代区域经济一体化、贸易投资自由化趋势下,多边投资规则呈现出议题广泛的特征,产业政策、劳工问题、环境保护、政府采购等议题不断与传统的投资规则相融合。无论外交部、商务部主导,也无论多边投资规则的性质和种类,凡在投资规则中所涵盖的具体领域或特殊问题,其他相关政府部门如国家发改委、农业农村部、水利部、科技部、生态环境部、教育部、财政部、人社部、自然资源部、工信部、交通运输部等在其职能范围内为重要参与者,对是否制定某多边投资规则提出肯定或否定意见,对投资规则案文草案提出具体修改建议,若涉及本部门重要事项或对本部门管辖领域产生重要影响,可直接派出代表参与具体工作,包括参与谈判。

如果其他部委与主导机构的意见存在严重分歧,应当报国务院审议,必要时可征询全国人大外事委员会的意见。

二、建立多边投资规则多元参与制定机制

我国在相关经贸条约谈判中,缺乏非政府力量的参与。建立学者、企业、公益机构参与的多元参与机制能提高我国参与制定多边投资规则的科学性、民主性、有效性。

(一)专家参与

无论是外交部、商务部,还是其他中央政府部门,都应当在本部门建立专家参与机制。

专家分两类,一类是法学专家,由国际公法、国际经济法(含国际贸易法、国际投资法等)和相关国内法(如产业法、环境资源法、劳动法、交通运输法等)专家组成;另一类是经

济、科技专家,由对有关领域有深入研究、声誉卓著的经济、科技专家组成。

专家参与的方式主要有三种:一是参加主导机构主持召开的专家论证会,提出专家论证意见;二是主持主导机构委托的具体课题研究,向主导机构提供指导性或参考性意见;三是个别符合条件的专家直接参与多边投资规则制定过程,包括参与起草工作方案、具体案文等。

(二)商界代表的参与

企业是我国海外投资的利益攸关者之一。多边投资规则不仅是国家间妥协的共同意志表达,更是跨国企业对世界资源进行再分配的规则。我国应当建立商界代表参与多边投资规则制定机制。

商界代表参与的方式可以是在某项多边投资规则谈判不同阶段不定期举行的座谈会、讨论会、专门论坛,主导机构应广泛听取商界代表的意见。为保证商界意见能够切实反映商界的意愿,与会代表应当从行业协会中通过推选产生,推选代表向行业协会负责,并在会议上享有充分表达意见和建议的权利。

(三)公益机构的参与

随着全球民权运动的兴起,21世纪国际投资规则的制定是国家、跨国公司与公益机构的多元全球治理的结果。多边投资规则制定的主导机构应当建立公益机构参与机制,充分协调投资自由化与社会利益保护之间的矛盾。

公益机构参与的方式可以是:单独参与或与商界代表共同参与主导机构定期或不定期召开的有关会议;向主导机构直接提交意见书或者民间研究报告。

本章小结

美国与欧盟均是以行政部门为主导者,前者是国务院法律顾问办公室和贸易代表办公室,后者则是欧盟委员会和欧盟理事会。在参与者方面,美国具有完善的"旋转门"制度和企业、非政府组织等公众参与制度,欧盟形成了欧盟、成员国和利益集团共同参与的多层治理、谈判及决策结构。我国应当充分了解美国、欧盟的谈判及其运转机制,在知己知彼的基础上评估谈判的前景并给出针对性的策略,与美国、欧盟进行谈判。我国还应当对当前参与工作机制进行一定程度的改革:一是建立公约类和非公约类为主的多边投资规则制定工作机制,进一步明确外交部、商务部、其他相关部委各自的职责分工与协作,确定内部核心机构;二是建立多边投资规则多元参与制定机制,包括专家、商界代表、公益机构参与机制。

第八章

中国参与制定的多边投资规则的应有内容

　　我国参与制定多边投资规则,需要在分析现有国际投资规则的基础上,结合我国国际投资现状和我国拟参与制定多边投资规则的类型来确定具体的规则内容。

　　现有国际投资规则的一般条款包括:序言和宗旨,投资与投资者的定义,投资与投资者的待遇,投资促进与保护,投资争端解决等。具体内容因不同时期、国家发展水平和缔约主体的不同而差异较大。总体上,发达国家参与的国际投资规则倾向于投资自由化以争取更多的投资利益,发展中国家对投资自由化采取较为保守的态度以争取东道国利益的实现。①

_____

① 关于国际投资规则新发展综合性研究的国内外成果,如董静然:《国际投资规则中的国家规制权研究》,载《河北法学》2018 年第 12 期;何芳、邓瑞平:《当代国际投资条约中的新型条款与我国未来取向》,载《河北法学》2016 年第 3 期;霍建国:《国际投资规则的发展与启示》,载《国际经贸探索》2017 年第 8 期;李锋:《国际投资保护主义的发展态势及应对策略》,载《现代经济探讨》2015 年第 5 期;李玉梅:《国际投资规则比较、趋势与中国对策》,载《经济社会体制比较》2014 年第 1 期;刘艳:《国际投资协定中的发展权原则及其实现的法律机制研究》,武汉大学 2014 年博士学位论文;桑百川:《新一轮全球投资规则变迁的应对策略——以中美投资协定谈判为视角》,载《人民论坛·学术前沿》2014 年第 2 期;石静霞:《国际贸易投资规则的再构建及中国的因应》,载《中国社会科学》2015 年第 9 期;孙英哲:《国际投资协定规则发展趋势研究——以 CETA 投资章节为视角》,载《经济问题》2018 年第 4 期;唐海涛:《论国际投资条约规则的精准化发展——以 CETA 和 TTIP 为视角》,载《中国海洋大学学报(社会科学版)》2018 年第 1 期;肖军:《国际投资条约的复杂化与多元化——晚近国际投资条约发展趋势之辨及我国应对策略》,载《法学评论》2014 年第 5 期;曾华群:《论双边投资条约范本的演进与中国的对策》,载《国际法研究》2016 年第 4 期;张庆麟、郑彦君:《晚近国际投资协定中东道国规制权的新发展》,载《武大国际法评论》2017 年第 2 期;张庆麟:《论国际投资协定中东道国规制权的实践及中国立场》,载《政法论丛》2017 年第 6 期;朱易 等:《国际投资新规则:趋势、影响与应对》,载《经济论坛》2018 年第 3 期;Alberto Alvarez-Jimenez, The Great Recession and the New Frontiers of International Investment Law: The Economics of Early Warning Models and the Law of Necessity, *Journal of International Economic Law*, 2014, Vol.17, pp.517-550; Alessandra Arcuri, International Economic Law and Disintegration: Beware the Schmittean Moment, *Journal of International Economic Law*, 2020, Vol.23, pp.323-345; Andrew D Mitchell, etc., Good Governance Obligations in International Economic Law: A Comparative Analysis of Trade and Investment, *Journal of World Investment & Trade*, 2016, Vol.17, No.1, pp.7-46; Anthea Roberts, etc., Toward a Geoeconomic Order in International Trade and Investment, *Journal of International Economic Law*, 2019, Vol. 22, pp. 655-676; Jose E. Alvarez, Beware: Boundary Crossings—A Critical Appraisal of Public Law Approaches to International Investment Law, *Journal of World Investment & Trade*, 2016, Vol. 17, No. 2 pp. 171-228; Junianto James Losari, Michael Ewing-Chow, A Clash of Treaties: The Lawfulness of Countermeasures in International Trade Law and International Investment Law, *Journal of World Investment & Trade*, 2015, Vol.16, No.2, pp. 274-314; Maria Laura Marceddu, International Investment Policy-Making: Are The Times A-Changing?, *Journal of International Economic Law*, 2018, Vol.21, pp.681-702; Mitchell Moranis, Between Power and Procedure: the Changing Balance of Investment Treaty Protections, *Arbitration International*, 2016, Vol.32, pp.81-110; Muthucumaraswamy Sornarajah, Disintegration and Change in the International Law on Foreign Investment, *Journal of International Economic Law*, 2020, Vol.23, pp.413-430; Rodrigo Polanco Lazo, Missing Investment Treaties, *Journal of International Economic Law*, 2018, Vol. 21, pp. 703-732; Srikar Mysore and Aditya Vora, Tussle for Policy Space in International Investment Norm Setting: The Search for a Middle Path, *Jindal Global Law Review*, 2016, Vol. 7 pp. 135-156; UNCATAD, Investment Policy Framework for Sustainable Development, IV. —Framework for International Investment Agreements: Options, 2015; Zeng Huaqun, Balance, Sustainable Development, and Integration: Innovative Path for BIT Practice, *Journal of International Economic Law*, 2014, Vol.17, pp.299-332.

除了以上一般条款,当代国际投资规则中还涉及一些发达国家倡导的特殊条款,主要有:实现投资自由化的履行要求禁止条款、透明度条款和国际社会立法相关的环境条款、劳工或人权保护条款、例外条款等。当然,环境和劳工条款体现着投资自由化和国际社会立法双重价值目标。由于发达国家的影响力和国际社会问题的凸显,这些特殊条款长期以来受到广泛关注,我国在参与多边投资规则制定时也应考虑其相关影响。

第一节 我国对多边投资规则中一般条款的取向

国际投资规则有三种基本类型,即双边投资规则、区域性投资规则和普遍性投资规则。现有国际投资规则以双边投资规则和区域性规则为主,仅有的普遍性投资规则①均只涉及某些具体问题,尚无普遍性综合投资规则。双边投资规则最为丰富,截至 2011 年年底,全球共有 2833 项双边投资协定(BITs)达成,涉及 176 国家。另有 331 项涉及投资的贸易与投资特惠协定(PTIAs),包括自由贸易区协定(FTAs)、区域经济一体化协定、经济合作框架或协定、紧密经济伙伴协定(EPAs)等。② 据《2020 年世界投资报告》,截至 2019 年,各种国际投资协定总数为 3284 项,其中新增 22 项、终止 34 项(截至 2019 年实际终止 349 项)。③

从规则发展的趋势看,双边规则的数量仍在增加但增幅减缓,而区域性规则增速明显,对经济的影响力也在持续增加。④ 双边投资规则以美国的 BITs 为典范,区域性投资规则以 NAFTA、USMCA、RCEP 为代表。无论是哪种类型的投资规则,在内容上都主

---

① 现存普遍性投资规则有三种:一是 WTO 体系内的投资规则,如 TRIMs 协定、GATS 等,涉及投资准入与履行要求禁止;二是 1965 年《解决国家与他国国民间投资争端公约》,涉及投资争端的解决;三是 1985 年《多边投资担保机构公约》,涉及投资保险。

② UNCTAD, World Investment Report 2012, July 2012, p.84.

③ 联合国贸易与发展会议:《2020 年世界投资报告——疫情后的国际生产》(要旨和概述)(中文版),第Ⅻ页。

④ UNCTAD, World Investment Report 2012, July 2012, p.78.

要包括以下一般性条款①。

一、序言条款

(一)总体状况

序言条款包括各缔约方缔约的意愿和目的,说明各缔约方订立条约的意图。由于序言部分只是表达、描绘缔约方的愿景,不给缔约方确定实体性权利义务,不规定违反义务时应当承担的法律责任,各缔约方完全靠自愿遵守。② 因此其法律价值在传统上未引起高度关注和重视。

根据《维也纳条约法公约》第 31 条第 1 款③,条约的宗旨和目标条款阐明了条约签订的背景,是条约解释的重要依据。近年来,国际投资条约的仲裁实践表明,越来越多的仲裁庭在案件审理过程中常将条约目的作为判断争端方行为是非曲直的依据。④ 因此,序言条款对投资条约具体权利义务条款的指导性、准则性作用和对条约解释功能是我国在参与多边投资规则制定时首先需要关注的问题。

序言条款的具体内容因缔约目的和宗旨不同而有差异,而缔约目的和宗旨受国际经济大环境和国际政治背景的影响,在不同历史阶段侧重点不同。

20 世纪 60—70 年代,因发展中国家大量采取国有化措施,发达国家为保护本国海外投资,试图通过投资条约为海外投资保险制度寻找国际法依据,以拓展国际市场,促进资本向发展中国家流动。在此阶段的国际投资规则,无论是程序性的以东道国承认母国海外投资保险机构的代位求偿权为主要内容的"美式双边投资协定",还是程序、实体并重

---

① 除了以下研究的主要条款外,还有一些实质性条款,如保护伞条款(Umbrella Clause)、其他义务条款、适用条款等。其中,保护伞条款指缔约一方应当遵守其依据本条约或协定对缔约另一方投资者有关投资作出承诺的条款。该条款于 20 世纪 50 年代由英国著名国际法学家劳特派特首推,于 1959 年在原联邦德国与巴基斯坦双边投资协定中第一次规定(第 7 条),目前约 40% 的双边投资条约中有此条款。2006 年中国—俄罗斯投资协定中规定了此条款(第 11 条"适用"第 2 款)。关于保护伞条款的近期国内外学术成果参见邓瑞平、董威颉:《论中国双边投资条约中的保护伞条款》,载《河北法学》2018 年第 2 期;Jude Antony, Umbrella Clauses Since SGS v. Pakistan and SGS v. Philippines—A Developing Consensus, *Arbitration International*, 2013, Vol.29, No.4, pp.607-639; Raúl Pereira de Souza Fleury, Umbrella Clauses: a Trend towards its Elimination, *Arbitration International*, 2015, Vol.31, pp.679-691; Shotaro Hamamoto, Parties to the "Obligations" in the Obligations Observance ("Umbrella") Clause, *ICSID Review*, 2015, Vol.30, No.2, pp.449-464。

② Kojo Yelpaala, Fundamentalism in Public Health and Safety in Bilateral Investment Treaties (Part I), *AJWH*, 2008, Vol.3, p.325.

③ 《维也纳条约法公约》第 31 条第 1 款规定,条约应依其用语按其上下文并参照条约之目的和宗旨所具有之通常意义,善意解释之。

④ 如 Gas Natural 诉阿根廷、SGS 诉菲律宾等案中,仲裁庭在参照了相关双边投资协定的序言后认定,有关双边投资协定的意图是创造良好的投资环境,因此对条约作出有利于投资者的解释。

的内容较全面的"德式双边投资协定",①均体现了国际投资规则最基本的宗旨和目标——投资保护。但此阶段的投资保护水平较低,条文相对简单,表明在互惠的基础上促进投资和经济合作,通常表述为:实现经济合作,对相互间的投资予以认可,给予投资以一定合理待遇。②

20 世纪 80—90 年代后,越来越多的国家卷入全球化浪潮,发展中国家普遍出现债务危机,对外资需求激增,发达国家借机开始推行投资自由化,高标准的投资保护条款开始出现在投资条约中,投资保护的目的直接体现在投资条约的序言中。有的国际投资条约的序言部分开始增加了投资促进和投资便利的内容。③ 随着全球化不断深入和拓展,全球化带来的影响冲击到社会发展的各个领域,引起了一系列的社会问题,波及国际投资领域,表现为环境保护、劳工保护、社会公共利益等问题开始体现在投资条约的序言部分。

(二)类型

当代国际投资条约的序言部分所体现的目的有两类。一类是阐明投资条约的目的在于促进缔约方经济合作和相互投资,投资保护、投资促进和投资便利,为投资创造良好条件。如 2003 年我国和德国投资协定序言规定:缔约双方"愿为缔约一方的投资者在缔约另一方境内投资创造有利条件,认识到鼓励、促进和保护投资将有助于激励投资者经营的积极性和增进两国繁荣,愿加强两国间的经济合作。又如《中国—东盟投资协定》序言规定:为建立中国—东盟自由贸易区和促进投资,建立一个自由、便利、透明及竞争的投资体制,各缔约方同意尽快谈判并达成投资协定,以逐步实现投资体制自由化,加强投资领域的合作,促进投资便利化和提高投资相关法律法规的透明度,并为投资提供保护。另一类是除投资促进和投资保护目标外还需要尊重其他重要的公共政策目标,如环境保护、人权和可持续发展等社会公共利益。例如:美国 2004 年 BIT 范本规定,"迫切希望通过与保护国民健康、安全、自然环境和推动国际认可的劳工权利相一致的方式实现以上目标";加拿大 2004 年 BIT 范本规定,"认识到促进和保护缔约一方在缔约另一方的投资有利于刺激商业活动、促进相互间的经济合作和可持续发展";比利时与韩国 BIT 规定,"认识到缔约国任何一方都有权利建立本国的环境保护规则,并有权修订其环境与劳工立法"。

值得注意的是,根据基于国际投资条约的仲裁实践,如果条约的序言部分所体现的条约目的和宗旨仅在于保护投资、为投资提供充分保护,则解决投资争端的仲裁庭有可能在裁决时仅考虑条约的投资保护目的,而忽略东道国的社会公共利益,并由此裁决东

---

① 余劲松:《国际投资法》,法律出版社 1999 年版,第 286 页。

② 如德国—苏联、德国—南斯拉夫等 BIT 的序言。

③ 如 WTO-TRIMs 的序言规定:期望促进世界贸易的扩大和逐步自由化,并便利国际投资,以在确保自由竞争的同时,促进所有贸易伙伴,尤其是发展中国家成员的经济增长。

道国的公共利益保护措施违反条约义务,作出对东道国不利的裁决。①

(三)我国的实践与未来取向

在我国近年来缔结或参加的国际投资条约中,大部分在序言部分采取了第一种类型,即强调为投资者提供优良的投资环境,着重于投资保护和投资促进,不涉及第二种类型,主要原因是我国政府有关部门在劳工等问题上过于敏感,不愿在投资条约中涉及健康、安全、环保、人权等普适性概念,担心引进其中会作茧自缚。② 在我国 2000 年以后缔结或参加的投资条约中体现尤其突出。③

在我国海外投资数量和吸引外商投资数量已经日趋持平④、我国作为投资母国与投资东道国的双重身份日重之际,缔约宗旨和目的选择具有现实和战略意义。尤其是在与发展中国家交往中,明确投资促进和投资保护有利于我国海外投资利益的保护和实现。但是,无论是与发达国家还是与发展中国家制定国际投资规则,都应当将考虑东道国社会公共利益,理由如下:(1)在与发达国家制定国际投资规则过程中,我国相对处于弱势,将社会公共利益目标作为缔约的序言部分在条约解释时可考虑我国社会公共利益目标诉求。(2)在与发展中国家制定投资规则时需要考虑东道国的社会公共利益。第一,国际投资自始关涉发展问题,环境和人权等可持续发展问题是人类社会面临的共同课题,需要共同面对和解决;第二,虽然我国经济总量位居世界第二,但我国仍是发展中国家,和发展中国家有着同样的发展问题和发展目标,由己推人,需要将社会公共利益目标在国际投资规则制定中予以确认。(3)就我国海外投资的现实看,我国很多海外投资企业名声不佳,和当地频发因劳工、环境问题引起的冲突,海外投资企业的社会责任意识需要加强,企业行为需要约束。(4)党的十八大报告中提出"要将发展的成果惠及其他发展中国家",党的十九大报告提出"坚持和平发展道路,推动构建人类命运共同体"、"秉持正确义利观和真实亲诚理念加强同发展中国家团结合作",体现了我国作为发展中大国的风范,也是互利共赢的明智之举。因此具体到多边投资规则的制定,我们需要自始至终考虑投资利益和东道国社会公共利益的平衡。

基于以上分析和我国目前在整个国际投资体系中所处的特殊地位,在参加多边投资规则制定时,在序言条款中既要考虑投资自由化和投资促进,又要考虑东道国的社会公共利益,将环境保护、劳工保护等可持续发展要素纳入。因此,序言条款至少包含以下内

---

① 如 Siemens 诉阿根廷案中,仲裁庭认为,阿根廷—德国投资协定的序言表明"缔约双方同意条约中的条款之目的在于为缔约两国中一国国民或公司在另一国境内的投资创造有利的条件……缔约双方的意图是明确的。其为投资创造有利的条件并激励私人的投资积极性",最终支持了 Siemens 主张的最惠国待遇扩张适用。

② 温先涛:《〈中国投资保护协定范本〉(草案)论稿(一)》,载《国际经济法学刊》2011 年第 4 期。

③ 例如 2006 年中印、2006 年中俄、2005 年中德、2007 年中韩等双边投资协定的序言,基本上是以给投资创造有利条件、鼓励和保护投资为内容,均未提及劳工、环境保护等主题。

④ 根据《2011 年度中国对外直接投资统计公报》,我国 2011 年对外直接投资 746.5 亿美元,居全球第 13 位;而 2011 年我国外商直接投资为 1160.11 亿美元。

容：(1)促进彼此间的国际经济合作，尤其是相互间的投资；(2)投资促进和保护应以不损害东道国社会公共利益的方式进行。

由于多边投资规则的类型、缔约对象不同，在不同类型和国别的多边投资规则中，序言条款内容应做适当调整。具体而言，在地缘性多边投资规则的序言条款中应加入地区合作和安全，实现共同繁荣的目的；自由贸易区投资规则如果是采用分立模式，序言条款应加入促进自由贸易区建立和良性运作，实现贸易和投资共同促进的目的；与发展中国家制定多边投资规则时，序言条款应当加入建立自由、便利、透明与良性竞争的内容；参与普遍性投资规则制定时，序言条款需要考虑投资自由化和社会公共利益平衡。

二、投资与投资者定义条款

"投资"与"投资者"是国际投资规则中的关键术语，其定义直接关涉国际投资规则适用范围的宽窄。[①] 国际投资规则的精髓在于限制东道国公权力对投资者私权利的肆意侵蚀，因此"投资"与"投资者"的定义决定了投资规则对东道国行为的限制程度和东道国为投资者能够提供的保护程度。[②] 就东道国而言，"投资"与"投资者"的定义越狭窄，投资规则适用范围越窄，则责任越小，反之则相反。

(一)"投资"的定义

1.定义的主要方式

在现存国际投资规则中，给"投资"进行定义的方式主要有以资产为基础、以企业为基础和两者相结合三种方式。

(1)以资产为基础的投资定义

通过列举投资者投入的资产来界定投资含义，是最为传统的方式，为大多数国际投资协定所采用。这种投资定义又有开放式和封闭式之分。

封闭式的定义方式采取穷尽式列举，给投资以精确的定义，充分列举投资涉及的资产形式，不包含对投资下概括性的定义和避免使用"包括，但不限于……"等开放性词汇。如1991年中国—葡萄牙投资协定中，"投资"一词系指缔约一方投资者依照缔约另一方法律和法规在后者领土内投资的各种财产，主要是：①动产和不动产的所有权及其他财产权利，如抵押权、留置权或质权；②公司的股份或该公司中其他形式的权益；③金钱请求权或具有

---

① 张庆麟：《论国际投资协定中投资的性质与扩大化的意义》，载《法学家》2011第6期。

② 关于投资与投资者定义的有关论述，可参见黄世席：《国际投资条约中投资的确定与东道国发展的考量》，载《现代法学》2014年第5期；张建：《国际投资仲裁中投资者国籍的认定标准探析》，载《长江论坛》2018年第3期；Carlos Correa and Jorge E. Viñuales, Intellectual Property Rights as Protected Investments: How Open Are the Gates, *Journal of International Economic Law*, 2016, Vol.19, pp. 91-120；Ines Willemyns, Disciplines on State-Owned Enterprises in International Economic Law: Are We Moving in the Right Direction, *Journal of International Economic Law*, 2016, Vol.19, pp.657-680。

经济价值的行为请求权;④著作权、工业产权,如专利、工艺流程、工业设计和专有技术,公司或常设机构名称和商誉;⑤依照法律授予的特许权,包括勘探、研究和开发自然资源的特许权。

开放式的定义方式通常先概括性界定投资定义,然后按照资产类型进行列举,再加上开放性词汇"包括,但不限于……"。这种定义方式频繁出现于晚近国际投资规则中。如2001年中国—荷兰投资协定中,"投资"一词系指缔约一方投资者在缔约另一方领土内所投入的各种财产,特别是,包括但不限于:①动产、不动产以及其他财产权利如抵押权、质押权。②公司股份、债券、股票和任何其他形式的参股。③金钱请求权或其他具有经济价值的与投资有关的行为请求权。④知识产权,特别是著作权、专利权、商标权、商名、工艺流程、专有技术和商誉。⑤法律或法律允许依合同授予的商业特许权,包括勘探、耕作、提炼或开发自然资源的特许权;投资财产发生任何形式上的变更,不影响其作为投资的性质。这种开放性投资定义过于宽泛,给扩大解释规则的适用范围埋下了隐患,有可能将那些不利于东道国经济发展的投资[如类似于组合投资(portfolio)的具有明显投机性的资产]也包括在内。因此许多国际投资协定对该定义设定一些限定条件,如,"依照东道国的法律、法规一致"①,"必须在东道国实际投入"②,"必须是在东道国实际拥有或控制的"③,"但不包括来自贸易或服务的金钱请求权"④等。

(2)以企业为基础的定义

将"投资"定义的范围集中在企业的对外投资,而不是外国在东道国不同投资资产的构成。1990年丹麦—波兰投资协定中,"投资"是在既定投资者对公司的管理事宜具有直接影响前提下,使投资者和公司之间建立一种可持续的经济联系的所有投资。1988年《美国—加拿大自由贸易协定》中,投资是指:(a)新建企业的投资;(b)企业收购的投资;(c)投资者在建立或收购过程中进行的投资;(d)企业投资者能控制的企业的股份或其他

---

①　如1990年意大利—摩洛哥投资协定第1条。该条款实质上缩小了投资的定义,将其限制在符合东道国法律的范畴内,否则不能获得保护。国际仲裁实践确认了这一限定条件的效力。如新加坡国际商会仲裁院2007年仲裁的Fraport诉菲律宾案,该案涉及德国—菲律宾双边投资协定,该协定第1条第1款规定,投资"为每一缔约方各自的法律与法规所认可"。

②　如阿尔及利亚—印度尼西亚投资协定第1条。

③　如比利时—卢森堡与沙特阿拉伯投资协定第1条。

④　例如NAFTA第1139条,投资是指:(a)企业;(b)企业的股票;(c)企业的债券,但(i)企业是投资者的联属机构,或(ii)企业债券的原始偿还期不少于3年,但不包括一个国有企业的债券;(d)企业的贷款,但(i)企业是投资者的联属机构,或(ii)企业贷款的原始偿还期不少于3年,但不包括对一个国有企业的贷款;(e)所有者有权分享企业所得或利润的企业利益;(f)所有者有权分享企业解散时资产的企业利益;(g)为经济目标或其他商业目标预期或使用的房地产或其他财产,有形资产或无形资产;和(h)来自一缔约方领土上资本或其他资源的许诺在这个领土上经济活动产生的利益,例如,(i)涉及一个投资者的财产在缔约方领土上到位的合同,包括交钥匙或建设合同或特许权,或(ii)实质上取决于一个企业产量、收入或利润的回报合同;但投资不包括:(i)金钱请求权,该请求权来自(i)只是由于出售货物或服务的商业合同或(ii)与商业交易有关的信用延期,例如贸易融资,但不包括(d)中的贷款所产生的金钱请求权;或(j)任何其他金钱请求权但不包括(a)至(h)利益在内。

投资收益。

（3）两者相结合

以企业为基础的定义方式常和以资产为基础的定义方式结合使用。如前文 NAFTA 第 1139 条，是典型的以企业为基础和以资产为基础的结合，而 2005 年中国—德国投资协定议定书中用企业特征补充了协定中以资产为基础的定义，其第 1 条第 1 款规定，"投资，系指为了与企业建立持续的经济关系，尤其是那些能够对企业的管理产生有效影响的投资"，排斥了投机性的证券投资和其他形式的组合投资。在美国 2004 年 BIT 范本中，"投资"指投资者直接或间接所有或控制的具有投资特征的资产，包括资本或其他价值资源的投入、获得收入或利润的预期以及对风险的预估，投资形式包括经营实体；经营实体的股份、股票或其他形式的股权参与；债券、债务或其他债务工具和贷款；期货、期权和其他衍生品；交钥匙、建筑、管理、生产、特许权、收入分成和其他类似合同；知识产权；根据国内法授予的批准、授权、许可和类似权利；其他有形资产或无形资产、动产或不动产以及相关财产权利，例如租赁、抵押、留置和质押。1995 年 MAI 草案中也采用了这种方式，先作宽泛的定义然后采取列举式，即投资是指"由投资者直接或间接拥有或控制的各类资产"，包括：(a)企业；(b)股票，股份或其他参股形式及由此产生的权利；(c)债券，贷款和其他债务形式及由此而产生的权利；(d)由合同产生的权利，包括交钥匙合同、建设合同、管理合同、产品或利润分享授予的权利（如特许、许可、授权和准许等）；(e)任何其他有形财产和无形财产、动产和不动产及相关的财产权利，如租赁、抵押、留置与质押等权利。

2.投资定义的趋势

从国际投资规则发展看，投资的财产范围发展大致经过如下过程：有形财产—无形财产（主要指与自然资源有关的合同权利、股份）—知识产权——一般商业合同权利、行政特许权等，[1]明显有不断扩大的趋势。从最初的直接投资到目前涵盖股权、合同甚至期权、期货等各种间接投资在内，范围日趋广泛。[2]尤其以发达国家为主导的国际投资规则中，如前文所述的 NAFTA 第 1139 条、MAI 第一部分、美国 2004 年 BIT 范本投资定义条款等中，几乎没有限制性定义条款。[3] 这种扩大是市场逻辑在国际投资协定实践中的必然反映，也是国际投资法价值取向（有效保护投资者利益）的反映。[4] 这种宽泛的、不断扩大的"投资"定义的优点在于：(1)具有灵活性。能够对尽可能大范围的资产提供保护，还可以使东道国自行决定如何处理某些敏感性资产。(2)具有开放性、前瞻性。可以适应新型或混合型投资的发展，自动涵盖新型外国直接投资，避免在未来为保持相关性而重开关于定义的谈判，节约谈判和缔约成本。(3)有助于保证不同层次的国际投资规

---

① M. Sornarajah, *The International Law on Foreign Investment. Cambridge*, Cambridge University press, 1996, p.17.

② 郭丽梅：《国际投资法中投资定义研究》，厦门大学 2009 年硕士学位论文。

③ 陈辉萍：《论多边投资法律框架发展的新动向》，厦门大学 1999 年博士学位论文。

④ 张庆麟：《评晚近国际投资协定中"投资"定义的扩大趋势》，载《全球化时代的国际经济法：中国的视角国际研讨会论文集》。

则间的兼容和协调。但是其缺点也非常明显:(1)投机性资产可能被包括在内,鱼目混珠危及东道国经济安全;(2)东道国的主动权减小,尤其在涉及投资争端解决中,外国投资者可按广义的投资定义将任何形式和任何范围的投资争端诉诸国际仲裁庭。[①]

3.我国未来取向

在我国参加的国际投资规则中普遍采用开放式的定义方式,"包括,但不限于……"的宽泛性定义得到普遍适用,投资范围由传统的直接投资扩展到知识产权和间接投资,特许权范围从原有的矿产权增加到耕作、开采自然资源的特许权等。

基于以上对宽泛投资定义的利弊分析,我国在参与多边投资规则制定时比较可取的做法是:以国家利益优先为原则,考虑到东道国国内经济发展的政策目标,针对不同的谈判对象采用不同的投资定义方式。

在制定普遍性投资规则时,因谈判对象的不确定性和复杂性,面临多方博弈,在谈判时更需谨慎,针对不同的谈判对象,在投资定义方面采取更为谨慎的定义方式,以获得更大的主动权。具体而言,根据缔约对象的不同,采取不同的投资定义条款。如果缔约对象是发达国家或者主要是资本输出国,考虑"符合缔约国法律法规的限制"或采取以企业为基础的定义方式;如果缔约对象是发展中国家或者主要是资本输入国,则采用开放性的、宽泛的以资产为基础的定义加上对资产特征的描述即可。

(二)投资者的定义

1.现有国际实践

在现有国际投资规则中,有些不使用"投资者"一词而用"所涉投资"来代替。大多数投资规则对"投资者"一词进行了界定。"投资者"一般是指缔约国的自然人、法人或不具有法人资格的企业或者其他组织。

在某些国际投资规则中,采取资本控制说,将本国公民或法人控制的非本国企业视为投资者,如中国—瑞典投资协定第 2 条第 2 款规定,"在瑞典方面,系指符合瑞典法律规定的瑞典公民,及所在地在瑞典境内或由瑞典公民或瑞典企业控制的任何法人"。至于何为缔约国的"法人"或"自然人",通常在国际投资规则中未做明确的确定,由缔约国的国内法确定。[②]

在国际投资规则中,并未将所有的依缔约方国内法认定的缔约一方法人作为条约中所指的"法人"。有两种例外情形:(1)将某种类型的法人排除于"投资者"的范围,如 1988 年中日投资协定中采取了列举式的定义方式,"投资者"在日本国方面是指社团法人、合伙、公司和团体,不论其是否有限责任、是否法人或是否以营利为目的,财团法人被排除在外;(2)将在缔约一方设立的但由第三国投资者控制且未在成立地从事实际商务活动的实体排除在外。该类排除被称为"拒绝利益"条款,[③]主要用于确保投资协定不被第三

---

① 季烨:《国际投资条约中投资定义的扩展及其限度》,载《北大法律评论》2011 第 1 期。

② UNCTC, *Bilateral Investment Treaties*, 1988, p.83.

③ 余劲松:《国际投资法》,法律出版社 2007 版第 3 版,第 222 页。

国投资者通过"邮箱公司"所利用,①防止第三国公司通过注册公司"免费搭车"而获得条约保护,对缔约国具有"潜在的"保护性。② 该条款在双边、区域性投资规则中均有所体现。例如,美国 2012 年 BIT 范本第 17 条第 1 款 a 项规定,"一缔约方可拒绝将本协议的利益给予另一缔约方的投资者,如作为另一缔约方企业的该投资者是由非缔约方且拒绝给予利益一方的投资者所拥有或控制,且拒绝给予利益的缔约方与该非缔约方之间没有正常的外交关系"。又如 2008 年中国—墨西哥投资协定第 31 条规定:"缔约双方可以共同磋商决定拒绝将本协定之利益授予缔约另一方之企业及其投资,如果该企业系由非缔约方之自然人或企业拥有或控制。"在区域投资协定中,NAFTA、ECT、CAFTAI 中均有相关条款。2012 年《中日韩投资协定》规定,"缔约一方可以拒绝将本协定的利益给予缔约另一方的投资者,若作为缔约另一方企业的该投资者是由非缔约方和拒绝给予利益缔约方的投资者所拥有或控制,且拒绝给予利益的缔约方与该非缔约方之间没有正常的经济关系"。拒绝利益条款是将在法律上包括在投资规则下但在实际运作中不能产生国际直接投资本应产生的经济价值和社会价值的投资排除在外,防止非缔约第三方国家的投资者搭便车,防止第三方受惠于投资条约施加给缔约方的义务,不仅是条约互惠原则的重要体现③,在某种程度上也是对缔约方的保护。④ 因此,在投资定义呈现扩大化趋势的现状下,在多边投资条约中增加"利益拒绝条款",可以防止投资者规避法律、挑选条约。我国在制定多边投资规则时应当考虑将该条款纳入。

2.我国未来取向

因投资和投资者的定义涉及投资规则的适用范围,在我国参与制定多边投资规则时考虑到身份混同的现状,在投资定义部分既要宽泛、开放,又要防止投机性资产和游资假借投资规则来实现投机利益,还要考虑定义条款和其他相关条款的关联性,可以采用开放性的以资产为基础的定义方式,采取列举式加"包括但不限于"的模式,但是为了防止过于宽泛造成东道国利益的损害,尤其是为了与根本安全例外条款相配合,可以仿照美国 BIT 范本和 MAI 对资产的特征进行描述,这些特征包括"资本或其他价值资源的投入、获得收入或利润的预期以及对风险的预估"。⑤

投资者应包括自然人、法人和其他组织。自然人和法人的国籍依各缔约方国内法确定。由于有的国家在法人国籍确定上采取注册地说,有的国家采取资本控制说,因此可以将不在缔约国注册但实际为缔约国国民所控制的企业视为合格投资者,同时排除虽在

---

① 漆彤:《论国际投资协定中的利益拒绝条款》,载《政治与法律》2012 第 9 期。

② Herman Walker Jr., Provisions on Companies in United States Commercial Treaties, *American Journal of International Law*,1956,Vol.50,Iss.2,p.373.

③ J. W. Salacuse, BIT by BIT: The Growth of Bilateral Investment Treaties and Their Impact of Foreign Investment in Developing Countries,*Int'L Law*,1990,Vol.24,p.655.

④ Rudolph Dolzer, Christoph Schreuer, *Principles of International Investment Law*,Oxford Univ. Press,2008,p.55.

⑤ 美国 2012 年 BIT 范本第 1 条"条约用语"中,"投资"指投资者直接或间接所有或控制具有投资特征的资产。这些特征包括资本或其他价值资源的投入、获得收入或利润的预期以及对风险的预估。

缔约国设立但被非缔约国自然人或法人控制并且未在缔约国从事实际商业活动的企业，即加入"拒绝利益"条款，防止非缔约方投资者搭便车的行为。

三、投资与投资者待遇条款

现存国际投资规则中设定的投资或投资者待遇有三种：国民待遇、最惠国待遇和公平公正待遇。最惠国待遇和国民待遇是传统待遇标准，用于整平由不同国际投资协定造成的国际投资法律场所的不平，[①]基本含义明确，但在不同国家、不同层次的国际投资规则中表达方式有差异，适用范围的差异较大。公平公正待遇则是晚近才被广泛认同的绝对待遇水平。

（一）国民待遇

国民待遇虽是所有国际投资规则中投资待遇部分首要的待遇标准，但是其适用范围差异较大，核心问题是国民待遇能否适用于准入前，反映了不同层次的国际投资规则对投资自由化的态度。

在以投资自由化和为投资提供高标准待遇水平为目标的 NAFTA、2018 年 USMCA、美国 BIT 范本和 MAI 草案中，国民待遇的适用范围包括"准入前"和"准入后"，要求缔约一方在"设立、获取、扩大、管理、运营、转让或其他投资处置"等各个方面给予缔约另一方投资或投资者的待遇在同等情况下不低于给予本国国民享有的待遇。[②] 这种高标准待遇水平并不为国际社会普遍接受或更多的国际投资规则所采纳，尤其不被发展中国家认同，因为外资准入限制是发展中国家对本国产业进行保护的第一道屏障，国民待遇适用于准入前预示着东道国在外资准入方面给予外资以本国投资相同的待遇，外资就有可能进入事关国计民生的关键部门，对国家安全和经济安全造成损害或威胁。在大部分发展中国家参加的国际投资规则中，国民待遇仅限于准入后的"管理、经营、运营、维护、使用、出售、清算"等行为，而不包括准入前"设立"行为和与准入有关的"扩大、收购"等行为[③]，即将国民待遇适用于准入后，不涉及准入前。[④] 甚至有的双边投资协定中加上限定词"在不损害其法律法规的前提下"[⑤]，隐含着国民待遇要受到东道国法律法规的限制，

---

① Julie A. Maupin，MFN-based Jurisdiction in Investor-State Arbitration-Is There Any Hope for a Consistent Approach，*Journal of International Economic Law*，2011，Vol.14，No.1，p.158.

② NAFTA 第 1102 条第 1 款、第 2 款；美国 2004 年 BIT 范本第 3 条第 1 款、第 2 款；MAI 第 3 条第 1 款。

③ 设立是准入前行为，收购和扩大虽然是准入后行为，但可能会违背东道国的有关在某些领域限制外资股权的相关法律。

④ 如 CAFTAI 第 4 条："各缔约方在其境内应当给予缔约另一方投资者及其投资在管理、经营、运营、维护、使用、销售、清算或此类投资其他处置形式方面的待遇，不低于其在同等条件下给予其本国投资者及其投资的待遇。"

⑤ 如 2006 年中俄投资协定第 3 条第 2 款。

一旦可能损害东道国法律法规,则拒绝给予,主动权完全在东道国。

由于外资准入可能对本国产业造成冲击,即使在将国民待遇适用于外资准入阶段的国家,也设置了外资准入限制,如美国采取"负面清单"模式,将禁止外资进入的部门采取目录管理的方式公布,不在目录内的即为允许的部门。这种做法对东道国产业目录分类技术和产业发展预测要求很高,难免挂一漏万,不适合产业分类技术不成熟的发展中国家采用。包括我国在内的大多数发展中国家采取"肯定式清单"方式。与"负面清单"相反,该方式只确定了允许和鼓励的部门,除此之外即为禁止,因此对外资限制较大,不被发达国家接受。无论采取何种外资限制方式,都不宜作为国际投资规则附件,因为一旦在条约中固化,即意味着丧失产业调整的空间,目录调整时需要和其他缔约国家再协商。

在 2018 年 CPTPP、2020 年 RCEP 中,出现了新动向,即将国民待遇适用于投资的"准入前":每一缔约方应当就其领土内投资的设立、获取、扩大、管理、运行、营运和出售或其他处置,给予缔约他方投资者和涵盖投资的待遇,不低于该缔约方在类似情形下给予其本国投资者及其投资的待遇;[1]是否在"类似情形"[2]下给予待遇取决于客观情况的整体性,包括相关待遇是否以合法公共福利目标为基准在投资者或投资之间进行区分。[3]

需注意的是 WTO-TRIMs 协定和 GATS 中的投资国民待遇问题。在 TRIMs 协定中,国民待遇是一项普遍义务,基于对所有缔约方产品的国民待遇而对东道国涉嫌贸易扭曲的投资措施加以禁止,主要包括当地成分要求和贸易平衡要求[4],对其他与贸易无关的投资措施则无要求。但在美国 BIT 范本和 OECD 的 MAI 草案中,将这些投资措施扩大到强制向东道国国民转让技术、完成出口业绩等。对投资措施的限制和禁止,实质是禁止对外资采取这些措施,在这些方面对外资实行国民待遇。在 GATS 下,以"商业存在"方式进行的服务贸易涉及投资,国民待遇被安排为一种具体承诺,由缔约方在加入GATS 时就具体部门作出承诺,在这些作出承诺的部门给予外资以国民待遇。但是GATS 涉及的范围只关乎服务业的投资,不涉及其他部门,因此其影响范围较小。

(二)最惠国待遇

尽管有些国家在国际投资规则中排斥最惠国待遇[5],但总体上该待遇被认为是国际投资规则中的普适性待遇标准。它给了投资者以反对东道国歧视性待遇的保证,在不同

---

① CPTPP 第 9.4 条第 1、2 款,RCEP 第 10.3 条第 1 款。

② 关于"类似情形"的学术阐述,可参阅刘芳:《国际投资协定国民待遇条款"相似情形"的认定》,载《首都经济贸易大学学报》2018 年第 6 期。

③ CPTPP 第 9.4 条"国民待遇"标题的脚注 14,RCEP 第 10.3 条"国民待遇"标题的脚注 17。

④ TRIMs 协定禁止采用和 GATT 第 2 条(国民待遇)和第 11 条(取消一般数量限制)相冲突的投资措施,与国民待遇冲突的主要是当地成分要求、出口实绩要求。

⑤ 例如 RCEP 第 10.4 条"最惠国待遇"脚注 18 规定,本条不应当适用于柬埔寨、老挝人民民主共和国、缅甸和越南;本条下的待遇不应当给予柬埔寨、老挝人民民主共和国、缅甸和越南的投资者和此等投资者的涵盖投资。

国家的投资者间建立起相同的竞争条件。[①] 国际投资规则不一致的影响有可能被最惠国条款减轻,而最惠国条款实际上几乎是所有国际投资协定的标准特征。[②] 和国民待遇类似,最惠国待遇的表述和适用范围是不确定的,不同层次的国际投资规则界定的最惠国待遇差异较大。[③]

1.表述方式的差异

表述方式上的差异有两方面:一是最惠国待遇是否被"在相同或类似情况下"所限制。"在相同或类似情况下"被称为同类原则。从国际法律实践看,对最惠国待遇条款进行解释应遵循的一个基本原则是"同类原则",即只有在第三方条约与基础条约规定的事项属于同一类别,且该事项本身必须与最惠国待遇相关时,才能援用最惠国待遇条款。[④] "在相同或类似情况下"构成最惠国待遇适用的核心要件。但是否在约文中使用"在相同或类似情况下"一词,国际投资条约表现出明显的差异。NAFTA 第 1103 条、ECT 第 10 条、CAFTAI 第 5 条、USMCA 第 14.5 条、CPTPP 第 9.5 条、RCEP 第 10.4 条等均使用了"在类似情形下"(in like circumstances)词语;而在另一些国际投资条约中没有强调"在相同或类似情况下",但不意味着这些投资条约在适用最惠国待遇时不考虑相同性或同类性。"在相同或类似情况下"的立法意旨在于强调而非排除。[⑤] 二是最惠国待遇是否同时适用于"投资者"和"投资"或"涵盖投资"。其有两种情形:第一种,将最惠国待遇适用于"投资者及其投资",既包括对人的适用,又包括对投资或投资活动的适用,如 NAFTA 第 1103 条、美国 2004 年范本第 4 条、加拿大 2004 年范本第 4 条、USMCA 第 14.5 条、CPTPP 第 9.5 条、RCEP 第 10.4 条。第二种,将最惠国待遇的适用表述为"投资和与投资相关的活动",如 2003 年中国—德国 BIT 等。但从国际投资仲裁实践看,到目前为止,这两种方式并未产生实质性影响,在 Siemens 诉阿根廷案、Plama 诉巴拉圭案中,仲裁庭都表达了同样的观点。[⑥]

2.适用阶段的差异

此种差异体现为最惠国待遇是否适用于准入前。发达国家普遍主张将最惠国待遇适用于准入前阶段。美国 BIT 范本、NAFTA、USMCA、CPTPP 和 MAI 草案无一例外

① Most-Favored-Nation Treatment, Report of UNCTAD, http://unctad. org/en/Docs/diaeia20101_en.pdf, last visited on 25 Dec. 2017.

② UNCTAD, *International Investment Rule-making—Stocktaking*, *Challenges and the Way Forward*, UNCTAD Series on International Investment Policies for Development, 2008, p.66.

③ 关于利用最惠国条款的国外近期学术研究,可参阅 Facundo Pérez Aznar, The Use of Most-Favoured-Nation Clauses to Import Substantive Treaty Provisions in International Investment Agreements, *Journal of International Economic Law*, 2017, Vol.20, pp.777-806。

④ S. Fietta, Most-Favored-Nation Treatment and Dispute Resolution under Bilateral Investment Treaties: A Turing Point, *International Arbitration Law Review*, 2005, Vol.5, p.136.

⑤ Azlan Mohamed Noh, Establishing Jurisdiction Through a Most-Favoured-Nation Clause, *International Trade & Business Law Review*, 2012, Vol.15, p.298.

⑥ 徐崇利:《从实体到程序:最惠国待遇适用范围之争》,载《法商研究》2007 年第 2 期。

地规定①,缔约一方在投资的设立、获取、扩大、管理、经营、运营、维护、使用、清算、出售或其他处置方面给予缔约另一方投资者及其其涵盖投资的待遇,应不低于其在类似情形下给予其他任何缔约方或第三国(非缔约方)投资者及其涵盖投资的待遇。发展中国家长期采取较为保守的态度,但和国民待遇不同的是,近年来最惠国待遇适用于准入前阶段逐渐被发展中国家普遍接受。我国近年来缔结或参加的国际投资协定体现了这一倾向,如 2007 年中国—韩国 BIT、2008 年 CATFA、2020 年 RCEP 将最惠国待遇的范围扩及至准入前。②

近来,最惠国待遇在国际投资规则中的适用出现了新问题:如果基础条约中约定了最惠国待遇,第三方条约在投资争端解决方面约定将投资者与东道国之间的争端交由投资仲裁庭解决,则受惠国投资者能否根据基础条约中的最惠国待遇条款和第三方条约中投资争端解决条款,将投资争端交由国际仲裁庭解决,即最惠国待遇能否适用于程序阶段?该问题最早出现在 2000 年 Maffezini v. Spain 案③,随后多个仲裁机构受理了十几起类似案件。仲裁庭的态度飘忽不定。④ 有的仲裁庭支持最惠国待遇可适用于程序问题的观点,有的仲裁庭的态度截然相反。甚至同一申请方针对不同东道国的类似行为基于类似条约和类似诉求的案件在不同仲裁庭作出不同的裁决⑤,如同一扇打开了的特洛伊之门,影响到了投资条约的平衡,⑥难以形成统一的、持续性的做法。学者们对此问题的看法也莫衷一是,此问题一时难以解决。根据最惠国待遇案件和对有关条约文本的实证研究,解决问题的最佳途径在于,在投资协定中避免采用模糊的最惠国待遇条款术语,而是

---

① 美国 2012 年 BIT 范本第 4 条第 1 款、NAFTA 第 1103 条、2018 年 USMCA 第 14.5 条第 1 款和第 2 款、CPTPP 第 9.5 条第 1 款和第 2 款、MAI 草案第 3 条第 2 款。

② 中韩 BIT 第 3 条第 3 款:在投资和商业行为方面,包括投资准入上,每个缔约方将在其领土上给予缔约另一方投资者、他们的投资及由缔约另一方投资者作出的投资相关的活动不低于类似条件下其给予任何第三国投资者、他们的投资及与投资相关活动的待遇。CAFTAI 第 5 条第 1 款规定,各缔约方在准入、设立、获得、扩大、管理、经营、运营、维护、使用、清算、出售或对投资其他形式的处置方面,应当给予另一缔约方投资者及其相关投资,不低于其在同等条件下给予任何其他缔约方或第三国投资者及/或其投资的待遇。RCEP 第 10.4 条第 1、2 款规定:每一缔约方应当就其领土内投资的设立、获取、扩大、管理、运行、营运和出售或其他处置,给予缔约另一方投资者的待遇,不低于其在类似情形下给予其他任何缔约方或非缔约方投资者的待遇;每一缔约方应当就投资的设立、获取、扩大、管理、运行、营运和出售或其他处置,给予涵盖投资的待遇,不低于该缔约方在类似情形下给予其领土内其他任何缔约方或非缔约方投资者投资的待遇。

③ Maffezini v. Spain, ICSID Case No. ARB/97/7.

④ 梁丹妮:《国际投资条约最惠国待遇条款适用问题研究》,载《法商研究》2012 第 2 期。

⑤ SGS 诉巴基斯坦案和 SGS 诉菲律宾案。

⑥ Yannick Radi, The Application of the Most-Favoured-Nation Clause to the Dispute Settlement Provisions of Bilateral Investment Treaties—Domesticating the "Trojan Horse", *The European Journal of International Law*, 2007, Vol.18, Iss.4, p.758.

直接确定最惠国待遇是否适用于投资争端解决。[①] 最新动态是,一些区域性投资条约直接拒绝将最惠国待遇适用于国际争端解决程序。例如:CPTPP 第 9.4 条第 3 款[②]规定,本条中所述的待遇不包括国际争端解决程序或机制,诸如第 B 部分(投资者—国家争端解决)中包含的那些程序;RCEP 第 10.4 条第 3 款[③]规定:第 1、2 款中所述的待遇不包括其他现存或未来国际协定下的任何国际争端解决程序或机制。

(三)公平公正待遇

国际投资领域的公平公正待遇最早见于 1948 年《哈瓦那宪章》[④],与此同时代的《友好通商航海条约》(FCN)中出现类似条款。此后 OECD 主持起草的多份 MAI 草案中涉及该条款,最有影响的是 1995 年 MAI 草案"一般待遇"[⑤]中的规定:"各缔约方应给予其境内的外国投资以公平与公正待遇和充分、持续的保护与安全。在任何情况下,缔约一方给予的待遇不能低于国际法的要求。"

双边和区域性投资协定中也陆续将该条款作为投资待遇水平。美国 2004 年、2012 年 BIT 范本[⑥]、NAFTA 和 2018 年 USMCA、2018 年 CPTPP 中的公平公正待遇条款安排在"最低待遇标准"条款下。NAFTA 第 1105 条"最低待遇标准"第 1 款规定:每一缔约方应给予缔约另一方投资者的投资以符合国际法的待遇,包括公平公正待遇和充分保护与安全。USMCA 第 14.6 条"最低待遇标准"第 1、2 款规定与上述规定基本相同,但在表

---

① Scott Vesel，Clearing a Path Through a Tangled Jurisprudence：Most-Favored-Nation Clauses and Dispute Settlement Provisions in Bilateral Investment Treaties，*The Yale Journal of International Law*，2007，Vol.32，p.421.

② 原文如下:3. For greater certainty, the treatment referred to in this Article does not encompass international dispute resolution procedures or mechanisms，such as those included in Section B (Investor-State Dispute Settlement).

③ 原文如下:3. For greater certainty, the treatment referred to in paragraphs 1 and 2 does not encompass any international dispute resolution procedures or mechanisms under other existing or future international agreements.

④ 《哈瓦那宪章》第 11 条第 2 款(a)。

⑤ MAI 附件第 5 条第 1 款第 1 项。

⑥ 其第 1、2 款规定如下:

1.每一缔约方应当按照国际习惯法要求赋予涵盖投资公平公正待遇、充分保护与安全。

2.为避免产生歧义,第 1 款规定将国际习惯法外国人最低待遇标准作为涵盖投资的最低待遇标准;"公平公正待遇"和"充分保护与安全"概念既不能超出最低待遇标准,也不创设额外实体权利。第 1 款中规定的缔约方义务:

(a)"公平公正待遇"包括保证刑事、民事或行政裁决程序符合世界主要法律体系中正当程序和正义要求的义务;和

(b)"充分保护与安全"要求每一缔约方根据国际习惯法要求标准给予的治安保护。

述上存在一些差异。① 其中，明确界定了"国际习惯法"和"国际习惯法外国人最低待遇标准"，即：国际习惯法源自诸国家产生于法律义务感的普遍和一致实践，国际习惯法外国人最低待遇标准指保护外国人投资的全部国际习惯法原则。② 2018 年 CPTPP 第 9.6 条"最低待遇标准"第 1、2 款和附件 9A 的规定，与上述 USMCA 的规定总体上相同。

2020 年 RCEP 第 10.5 条"投资待遇"第 1、2 款和附件 10A"国际习惯法"规定：每一缔约方应当根据国际习惯法外国人待遇最低标准，给予涵盖投资公平公正待遇；公平公正待遇要求每一缔约方不否认任何法律或行政程序中的正义；充分保护与安全要求每一缔约方采取合理必要措施确保涵盖投资的实体保护和安全；公正与公平和充分保护与安全的概念不要求给予涵盖投资额外的或超出国际习惯法外国人最低待遇标准下所要求的待遇，且不要求创设额外实体权利；国际习惯法，包括与国际习惯法外国人最低待遇标准有关的，源自诸国家产生于法律义务感的普遍和一致实践。这些规定与上述 USMCA、CPTPP 的规定总体上相同。

MAI 中的公平公正待遇是一种"不低于国际法的待遇"。"不低于"一词说明公平公正待遇至少要和国际法一致，甚至应当是一种高于国际法的待遇水平，至于什么是"国际法"或者"国际法标准"，含义模糊不清。根据《国际法院规约》第 38 条，国际法是指条约、国际习惯法、一般法律原则和其他国际法渊源，范围相当宽泛。美国 BIT 范本、NAFTA

_____

① 其规定如下：

1.每一缔约方应当根据国际习惯法赋予涵盖投资的待遇，包括公平与公正待遇和充分保护与安全（Each Party shall accord to covered investments treatment in accordance with customary international law，including fair and equitable treatment and full protection and security）。

2.为了更加明晰，第 1 款将国际习惯法外国人最低待遇标准规定为提供给涵盖投资的待遇标准。"公正与公平"和"充分保护与安全"的概念不要求额外或超出该标准要求的待遇，且不创设额外实体权利。第 1 款中规定的以下义务（For greater certainty, paragraph 1 prescribes the customary international law minimum standard of treatment of aliens as the standard of treatment to be afforded to covered investments. The concepts of "fair and equitable treatment" and "full protection and security" do not require treatment in addition to or beyond that which is required by that standard，and do not create additional substantive rights. The obligations in paragraph 1 to provide）：

（a）"公平公正待遇"包括根据世界主要法律体系中体现的正当程序原则不否认刑事、民事或行政程序中正义的义务（"fair and equitable treatment" includes the obligation not to deny justice in criminal, civil，or administrative adjudicatory proceedings in accordance with the principle of due process embodied in the principal legal systems of the world）；和（and）

（b）"充分保护与安全"要求每一缔约方提供国际习惯法下要求的治安保护水平（"full protection and security" requires each Party to provide the level of police protection required under customary international law.）。

② ANNEX 14-A Customary International Law

The Parties confirm their shared understanding that "customary international law" generally and as specifically referenced in Article 14.6（Minimum Standard of Treatment）results from a general and consistent practice of States that they follow from a sense of legal obligation. The customary international law minimum standard of treatment of aliens refers to all customary international law principles that protect the investments of aliens.

和 USMCA 将其放在"最低待遇标准"项下,NAFTA 将其和国际法挂钩,美国 BIT 范本和 USMCA 将其限于国际习惯法且做了具体要求和解释,摒弃了模糊的公平公正待遇条款。ECT、安第斯共同投资规则、CAFTAI 和 RCEP 中均规定了公平公正待遇。大多数双边投资条约涉及该条款。① 我国缔结的大多数 BIT 中有该条款。尽管公平公正待遇的表达和标准总体上是模糊的,但它仍被国际投资条约普遍接受,原因在于公平公正待遇可以在不歧视待遇(国民待遇和最惠国待遇)的基础上,在国际层面上为投资者提供一定标准的保护。②

对公平公正待遇的解释虽有不同的观点,但学者普遍认同它是一种绝对待遇标准,而且是一种实体待遇标准,是对国民待遇和最惠国待遇的一种补充,在实体性规则和争端解决方面都发挥着解释和补充国际投资规则的作用,能够为投资者提供更切实的保护。③

(四)我国未来取向

综上观之,在我国参与制定的多边投资规则中,将国民待遇和最惠国待遇作为传统待遇标准纳入,自不待言,即"各缔约方给予缔约他方投资者及其投资的待遇,应当不低于其给予其本国投资者及其投资或任何第三国投资者及其投资的待遇"。其适用范围,可以根据不同类型的多边规则的特点分别确定。与发展中国家制定多边投资规时,可以

---

① UNCTAD, Fair and Equitable Treatment, UNCTAD Series on Issues in International Investment Agreements II, http://unctad.org/en/Docs/unctaddiaeia2011d5_en.pdf, last visited 20 Dec. 2015.

② UNCTAD, Fair and Equitable Treatment, UNCTAD Series on Issues in International Investment Agreements, http://unctad.org/en/Docs/psiteiitd11v3.en.pdf, last visited 20 Dec.2015.

③ 关于公平公正待遇的国内外学术成果,可参见陈正健:《国际最低待遇标准的新发展:表现、效果及应对》,载《法学论坛》2015 年第 6 期;陈正健:《投资条约保护和安全标准的适用及其启示》,载《法商研究》2013 年第 5 期;梁开银:《公平公正待遇条款的法方法困境及出路》,载《中国法学》2015 年第 6 期;莫雪:《"一带一路"之国际投资条约中公平与公正待遇标准的新发展——以 White Industries v. India 案为例》,载《广西政法管理干部学院学报》2018 年第 2 期;王晓晓:《公平公正待遇条款的革新及对中国的启示——以欧盟最新国际投资协定为视角》,载《中国商论》2018 年第 5 期;肖威:《国际投资中的"公平与公正待遇"研究》,复旦大学 2014 年博士学位论文;张苏锋:《BIT"公平公正待遇"条款中保护投资者合理期待的主观层面标准研究》,载《中国外资》2018 年第 9 期;Anastasios Gourgourinis, Fair and Equitable Treatment in International Investment Law: The Art of Watching out for Both the Elephants and the Fleas in the (Normative) Room of Investment Protection, *Journal of World Investment & Trade*, 2015, Vol.16, No.2, pp.335-360; Andrew C. Blandford, The History of Fair and Equitable Treatment before the Second World War, *ICSID Review*, 2017, Vol.32, No.2, pp.287-303; Eric De Brabandere, Fair and Equitable Treatment and (Full) Protection and Security in African Investment Treaties between Generality and Contextual Specificity, *Journal of World Investment & Trade*, 2017, Vol.18, No.3, pp.530-555; Federico Ortino, The Obligation of Regulatory Stability in the Fair and Equitable Treatment Standard: How Far Have We Come, *Journal of International Economic Law*, 2018, Vol.21, pp.845-866。

考虑将国民待遇适用于准入前和准入后阶段,即适用于"设立、获取、扩大、管理、运营、维护、使用、销售、清算转让或其他投资处置";而在其他投资规则中,国民待遇应控制在准入后阶段,即只适用于"投资的管理、运营、维护、使用、出售、清算、转让或其他处置"。在参与制定普遍性投资规则、区域性投资规则和地缘性投资规则时,需要继续实施我国已参加制定的投资规则中国民待遇的例外,沿袭冻结、回撤条款①,以使我国既可以保持并维持现行给予外资的超国民待遇或低国民待遇,又承诺以后取消现有不符国民待遇的措施。最惠国待遇则在各个类型的多边投资规则都可考虑适用于准入前和准入后,但需要明确最惠国待遇不适用于争端解决程序。

公平公正待遇作为绝对待遇水平可以弥补国民待遇和最惠国待遇的空缺,也应当在多边投资规则中予以体现。为防止其模糊性带来的不确定性,需要界定公平公正待遇的内涵,可以用"审慎尽职、正当程序、透明、善意、非歧视"等因素来解释和限定公平公正待遇。

四、投资保护条款

投资保护是国际投资规则中最主要的实体性条款,包括各种政治风险条款和代位求偿权条款。

海外投资面临重重风险,有商业风险和政治风险。从风险学角度看,商业风险是经营性风险,其风险事故可能造成损害也可能带来收益,如国际市场价格的涨跌、交易对象的资信等,而政治风险属于纯损失性的风险,一旦风险事故发生,只能带来损失,不可能产生利益。

关于政治风险的定义,迄今为止没有确切的定义,②但一般认为它是一种非商业风险,和东道国政治、经济、社会、法律等人为因素有直接关系,③引起风险事故发生的主体是东道国,风险事故的发生是由于东道国管理外资的行为或者实施了其他影响到投资者正常经营的行为,事故一旦发生会导致投资者重大损失。投资者作为一种私主体,在庞大的拥有主权的国家面前,力量薄弱,无法与之抗衡,即使利益受到了损害,难以以平等主体的身份寻求救济。投资母国如果在国际法律上缺乏依据,难以对投资者实施有效保护④,因而必须借助其他制度来对海外投资进行保护。

20世纪50年代,为满足海外投资保护的需求,海外投资保险制度应运而生。海外投

① 例如中德BIT议定书中,国民待遇不适用于:任何现存的在其境内维持的不符措施;这种不符措施的持续;对这种不符措施的任何修改,但修改不能增加措施的不符程度。
② 理查德·谢弗等:《国际商法及其环境》,邹建华译,人民邮电出版社2003年版,第476页。
③ Erhraim Clark, Valuing of Political Risk, *Journal of International Money and Finance*, 1997, p.477.
④ 投资母国能采取的主要手段是外交保护。外交保护的行使在国际习惯法上要满足两个条件,一是国籍持续,二是用尽当地救济,因此外交保护手段并不方便。另外,经过殖民时代,发展中国家对外交保护一向心有余悸。

资保险制度是指由投资国对海外投资者在东道国可能遇到的政治风险提供保险,如果承保的政治风险发生使海外投资者遭受损失,则先由投资国国内承保机构补偿其损失并取得代位索赔权,再由承保机构向东道国追偿的一种制度。该制度在发达国家海外投资保护史上发挥着不可替代的重要作用,双边投资条约最初创设就是为了配合该制度,通过条约为海外投资保险机构提供代位求偿权的国际法依据。例如 20 世纪 60 年代之前的美式双边投资协定只涉及程序性的内容,以东道国承认美国海外投资保险机构〔美国海外私人投资公司(oversea private investment company,OPIC)〕的代位权为核心内容。即使在内容比较全面的现代双边投资协定即德国式双边投资协定中,也有关于海外投资保险机构代位求偿权的相关条款。由于该制度在对海外投资者实施保护方面的有力保障,使该制度在发达国家普遍推行。到 20 世纪 60、70 年代,主要发达国家普遍建立了海外投资保险制度,也进一步催生了双边投资协定的蓬勃发展。双边投资协定发展至今从宗旨到形式、内容都发生了重大变化,但是海外投资保险机构的代位求偿权仍是每个条约必不可少的内容。

1985 年 MIGA 公约在普遍性层面建立了投资保险制度。根据该公约成立的多边投资担保机构(MIGA)对成员国海外投资面临的政治风险提供担保,尤其是为一成员国投资者在另一发展中国家成员国境内的投资提供政治风险保险服务。其承包的政治风险主要有货币兑换险、征收和类似措施险、违约险、战乱险。[1] 与各国海外投资保险制度相比,MIGA 避免政治化倾向,尽量只为投资提供便利和服务,而不愿沦为政治工具,在承保范围上相较于各缔约国的海外投资保险增加了政府违约险,在机构设置上引入公司制的做法,使成员国具有双重身份,既是机构的股东又是可能引起政治风险发生的东道国,双重身份使各成员对自己的行为有所收敛,一定程度上达到了风险预防的目的。MIGA 作为世界银行集团的一员,使东道国在采取不利于 MIGA 的举措之前三思而后行。[2] 因此,MIGA 在政治风险防范方面有制度设计上的优势。此外,该公约约文中确定了 MIGA 的代位求偿权[3],为 MIGA 在给投资者进行赔付之后可以向引起风险事故发生的东道国进行追偿提供了明确的国际法律依据。

(一)政治风险条款

1.政治风险的种类

关于政治风险的种类,在双边投资协定、区域投资协定和 MIGA 公约中有不同的规定和表述。综观不同类型的国际投资规则,政治风险主要有以下几种:

(1)征收风险

A.关于征收范围与条件的实践

---

① 《多边投资担保机构公约》第 11 条(a)款。

② I. Seidl-Hoheveldern, Subrogation under the MIGA Convention, 2 *ICSID Review—Foreign Law Journal*, 1987, p.111.

③ 《多边投资担保机构公约》第 18 条。

征收又称国有化,是指通过立法行为和为了公共利益,将某种财产或私有权利转移给国家,目的在于由国家利用或控制他们,或由国家将他们用于新的目的。①

征收问题是国际投资规则谈判中的重要议题。各类国际投资规则几乎无一遗漏地涵盖了征收问题,区别在于征收概念和范围的不同、是否补偿和补偿标准的差异。

美国 2004 年 BIT 范本第 6 条规定:"缔约方不得直接或间接地通过征收或国有化措施对涵盖投资进行征收或国有化,但满足以下情况除外:(a)为公共目的;(b)以非歧视的方式;(c)支付及时、充分和有效的补偿;并(d)符合法律正当程序和第 5 条'最低待遇标准'第 1 款至第 3 款的规定。"中国—韩国 BIT 第 3 条第 1 款规定:"缔约一方对缔约另一方的投资者在其领土内的投资,除非符合下列条件,不得采取征收、国有化或其他类似措施(以下称'征收'):(a)为了公共利益;(b)依照国内法律和法律正当程序的国际标准;(c)非歧视性的;和(d)符合第 2 款,给予补偿。"

在 MAI 草案中,征收条款的内容为:"一个成员国不得以直接或间接的方式对位于其领域范围内的另一成员方的投资者的投资进行征收或者国有化,或者采取与国有化有同等效果的措施,除非:(a)其目的是保护公共利益;(b)非歧视;(c)符合法律正当程序;(d)给予及时、充分、有效的补偿。"在其附件中,将"管制权利"规定为:一缔约方可以采取、维持或实施其认为对确保投资活动采取关切健康、安全或者环境的方式是适当的任何措施,只要此等措施与本协定一致。世界银行《外国直接投资待遇指南》第 4 条规定:"一国不得征收或变相取得其境内外国私人投资的全部或部分,或者采取具有相同效果的措施,除非其依据可适用的法律程序、诚信地追求公共目的、不因国籍而予以歧视,并且给予适当赔偿。"在 MIGA 公约中"征收险"部分,征收险承保的是"因东道国政府的责任所采取的任何立法或行政措施或懈怠行为,其作用为剥夺投保人对其投资的所有权或控制权,或剥夺其投资中产生的大量效益"。

NAFTA 第 1110 条规定:"任何缔约方不得直接或间接国有化或征收缔约另一方投资者在其境内的投资,或者对该投资采取相当于国有化或征收之措施('征收'),除非:为了公共目的;以非歧视为前提;符合法律正当程序和第 1105 条第 1 款之规定;和(d)按照第 2 款至第 6 款的规定支付补偿。"ECT 第 13 条规定:"不得对缔约一方投资者在任何其他缔约方境内的投资采取国有化、征收,或者具有等同于征收或国有化效果的措施或系列措施。除非该措施在此问题上是依照相关国际习惯法规则的(公共目的、正当程序、非歧视和赔偿)。"CAFTAI 第 8 条规定:"任何缔约方不应当对缔约另一方投资者的投资实施征收、国有化或采取其他等同措施('征收'),符合下列者除外:(a)为公共目的;(b)符合可适用的国内法,包括法律程序;(c)以非歧视方式实施;和(d)按照第 2 款规定给予补偿。"CPTPP、USMCA 和 RCEP 对征收的规定与上述规定相同。②

从以上国际投资规则看出,虽然表述不同,基本上都采取了"否定加例外"的形式确定了征收及其构成要件,构成征收的要件是:公共目的、非歧视、正当法律程序、补偿。

---

① 余劲松:《跨国公司的法律问题研究》,中国政法大学出版社 1989 年版,第 28 页。
② 例如:CPTPP 第 9.8 条第 1 款,USMCA 第 14.8 条第 1 款,RCEP 第 10.13 条第 1 款。

关于征收是否包括间接征收,有两种做法:一种是明确规定征收包括"征收和间接征收",例如 MAI、NAFTA、USMCA、CPTPP、RCEP[1];另一种是不直接规定间接征收,比较简单地规定"征收、国有化或者类似措施""等同于征收的措施",如中韩 BIT、CAFTAI。至于"类似措施、等同于征收的措施"是否包括了间接征收,从约文本身无法辨识。事实上,无论是否明文规定"间接征收",在这些投资规则中间接征收的含义是模糊的,"无论如何,现行投资条约文本没有一丁点阐明了间接征收问题;相反,他们提出了问题,并假定认为一般国际法可以为此提供答案"[2],在适用时需要进一步澄清。这给国际投资仲裁实践留下了很大自由裁量的空间,出现了用"判例法"来确定是否构成间接征收的方法。判例法对间接征收的判定具有重要性。有学者认为,只能通过逐案判断是否发生了对外资的间接征收,但直至今日,学界没有比上述论断更为接近间接征收的精确定义。[3]

在世界范围的条约实践中,判断是否构成间接征收的标准有三种[4],在国际投资仲裁实践中标准判断有两种。后者的两种标准分别是,"唯一效果测试法"(sole effect test)[5],即将政府采取的措施对投资者财产(权)产生的影响效果作为唯一的判断标准而

---

①　其中,CPTPP 第 9.8 条第 1 款,USMCA 第 14.8 条第 1 款,RCEP 第 10.13 条第1款。

②　Dolzer and Rudolf, Indirect Expropriations: New Developments, *New York University Environmental Law Journal*, 2002, Vol.11, p.79.

③　关于间接征收的国内代表性学术成果,可参见寇顺萍:《国际投资中间接征收法律问题研究》,西南政法大学 2014 年博士学位论文;寇顺萍:《国际投资领域"间接征收"之条约实践》,载《经济研究导刊》2014 年第 3 期。

④　Indirect Expropriation: Is the Right to Regulate at Risk? Symposium Co-organised by ICSID, OECD and UNCTAD, in *Making the Most of International Investment Agreement—a Common Agenda*, 12 December, 2005. 在区域贸易协定中规定了间接征收的 3 种主要判定因素,例如 CPTPP 附件 9-B"征收"第 3 款,USMCA 附件 14B"征收"第 3 款、RCEP 附件 10B"征收"第 2 款(b)项和第 3 款。其中,RCEP 附件 10B"征收"第 2 款(b)项和第 3 款规定:

2.第 10.3 条(征收)处理两种情况:

……

(b)缔约一方的一项行为或一系列相关行为虽未通过所有权正式转移或完全没收的方式,但具有与直接征收同等效果。

3.确定缔约一方的一项行为或一系列相关行为在特定事实情况下是否构成第 2 款(b)项中所述种类的征收,要求以事实为基础的个案调查,此调查尤其考虑以下因素:

(a)政府行为的经济影响。即使一项行为或一系列相关行为对投资的经济价值有负面影响,这种影响本身不能单独证实已经发生此类征收;

(b)政府行为是否违反政府以前通过合同、许可证或其他法律文书向投资者作出的具有约束力的书面承诺;和

(c)政府行为的性质,包括其目标和背景。

对韩国,相关考虑可能包括投资者是否承担了不成比例的负担,例如超出投资者或投资为了公共利益所应承受的一项特殊牺牲。

⑤　Dolzer and Rudolf, Indirect Expropriations: New Developments, *New York University Environmental Law Journal*, 2002, Vol.11, p.79.

不考虑其他因素;"目的测试法"(purpose test)①,在将效果作为主要或首要的考虑因素的同时考虑政府采取这些措施时的目的。两种方法最大的差异是有关措施产生的效果在判定间接征收的构成时所起的作用异同。就效果因素本身,有很大争议,何种程度算是达到征收的程度,仲裁庭有不同的判断标准,使间接征收问题的不确定性在一定范围内得以解决。

间接征收标准的不确定性给国际投资仲裁庭以充分自由裁量权,会导致政府在征收争端仲裁案中难以依据已有的条约规定作出合理的辩护、维护国家外资管理权,因此在有些条约中明确界定了间接征收的含义和范围。在这方面,加拿大2004年范本和2006年中印BIT议定书为典范,对间接征收及其认定标准作了详细的澄清。例如:2006年中印BIT议定书中将间接征收解释为"缔约一方为达到使投资者的投资陷于实质上无法产生收益或不能产生回报境地,但不涉及正式移转所有权或直接没收,而是有意采取的一项或一系列措施"②。并将歧视和歧视的程度作为认定间接征收的标准,"该措施在范围或适用上歧视某一方或某一投资者或某一企业的程度"。还将目的因素作为认定的重要依据之一,"该措施或该一系列措施的性质和目的,是否是为了善意的公共利益目标而采取,和在该等措施和征收目的之间是否存在合理联系"。这种规定,平衡了东道国的社会公共利益和投资者的利益,体现了关注目前国际投资规则日渐重视的利益平衡价值。加拿大范本虽然在认定间接征收的稳定性和确定性方面值得称赞,但在为利益平衡和东道国利益的保护方面少有提及③,体现了加拿大作为发达国家在征收问题上的立场。我国在参与多边投资规则制定时有必要沿袭中印BIT的做法,将间接征收的含义和范围明确化。

B.关于补偿范围与条件的实践

多边国际投资规则还关注补偿问题。发达国家长期坚持"充分、及时、有效"的赫尔三原则。这在发达国家主导的国际投资规则中有突出体现,如MAI、NAFTA、CPTPP、USMCA和美国BIT范本中直接将"充分、及时、有效"的补偿作为征收合法的必要条件。而发展中国家主张在评估征收补偿时,应当考虑征收国的支付能力。在当代国际社会,不容否认的事实是,国家越贫穷,越需要改革,而"充分、及时、有效"的补偿义务使穷国无法采取任何征收措施,④主张"适当、合理的补偿"。

我国在2000年前签订的BITs中,基本上主张"适当、合理"标准,如1982年中国一

---

① L.Yves Fortier and Stephen L. Drymer, Indirect Expropriation in the Law of International Investment:I Know It When I See It, or Caveat Investor, *ICSID Review—Foreign Investment Law Journal*, 2004, Vol.19, No.2, p.313.

② 2006年中印BIT议定书第3条。

③ 加拿大2004年范本附件B(1)。

④ Dolzer and Rudolf, Indirect Expropriations:New Developments, *New York University Environmental Law Journal*, 2002, Vol.11, p.79.

瑞典 BIT[①]、1989 年中国—保加利亚 BIT[②] 等。但在晚近签订的 BITs 中,虽然没有明确使用"充分、及时、有效"文字,但从相关条款分析,已经基本实践了该原则,只是采取一种不明确形式出现,显示出我国在身份混同条件下参与国际投资规则制定时的矛盾心理。例如,中印 BIT 规定:依照法律在非歧视性的基础上采取并给予公平和公正的补偿;此等补偿应等于采取征收前即刻或征收为公众所知时(以较早者为准)被征收投资的真实价值,并应包括支付前按公平和公正的利率计算的利息,补偿的支付不应不合理迟延,并应有效实现和自由转移。CAFTAI 规定:此补偿应以征收公布时或征收发生时(以较早者为准)被征收投资的公平市场价值计算;补偿应允许以可自由兑换货币从东道国自由转移。补偿的偿清和支付不应有不合理的延迟;公平市场价值不应因征收事先被公众所知而发生任何价值上的变化;一旦发生延迟,补偿应包括按主要商业利率计算的从征收发生日起到支付日之间的利息;包括应付利息在内的补偿,应当以原投资货币或应投资者请求以可自由兑换货币支付。[③] 事实上,我国目前国内形势稳定,对外资进行征收的可能性不大,反观我国海外投资,大部分是在政局和经济发展不稳定的发展中国家或地区,遭受征收的概率高,因此在参与制定多边投资规则时,宜将征收补偿标准确定为"充分、及时、有效",以充分保护海外投资。

C.我国未来取向

在我国参与制定多边投资规则时,关于征收条件,(a)应确定在满足"公共利益""依照国内法律程序和相关正当程序""非歧视性的""给予补偿"的条件下允许征收措施存在。(b)明确征收包括直接征收和间接征收,不再采取"与征收和国有化有相同或类似效果的措施"的方式来表示间接征收,而是明确界定间接征收的概念和范围,可采用中印 BIT 文本中对征收的解释,即:各缔约方确认以下共识:第一,除了通过正式移转所有权或直接没收的形式进行的直接征收或国有化,征收措施还包括缔约一方为达到使投资者投资陷于实质上无法产生收益或不能产生回报境地而有意采取的一项或一系列措施,但不涉及正式移转所有权或直接没收。第二,在某一特定情形下确定缔约一方的一项或一系列措施是否构成上述措施,需进行以事实为依据的个案审查,此审查需考虑以下各因素:(a)该项或系列措施的经济影响,但仅有缔约一方的一项或一系列措施负面影响投资经济价值的事实不足以推断已经发生了征收或国有化;(b)该项或系列措施在范围或适用上歧视某一缔约方或某一投资者或某一企业的程度;(c)该项或系列措施违背明显、合理、以投资为依据的预期之程度;(d)该项或系列措施的性质和目的是不是善意的公共利益目标所采取,以及在该等措施与征收目的之间是否存在合理联系。

---

① 1982 年中国—瑞典 BIT 第 3 条:缔约任何一方对缔约另一方投资者在其境内的投资,只有为了公共利益,按照适当的法律程序,并给予补偿,方可实行征收或国有化,或采取任何类似的其他措施。补偿的目的,应使该投资者处于未被征收或国有化相同的财政地位。征收或国有化不应是歧视性的。补偿不应无故迟延,而且应是可兑换的,并可在缔约国领土间自由转移。

② 1989 年中国—保加利亚 BIT 第 4 条第 2 款:本条第 1 款(3)所述的补偿,应等于宣布征收时被征收的投资财产的价值,应是可以兑换的和自由转移的,补偿的支付不应无故迟延。

③ CAFTAI 第 8 条第 2、3 款。

关于征收的补偿问题,我国已经缔结或参与的国际投资规则已基本认同"充分、及时、有效"原则,在未来参与多边投资规则制定时不适宜、也不需要采取与之相左的措施,可以继续采用如下表述,"补偿应等于采取征收或征收为公众所知的前一刻被征收投资的价值,以较早者为准。补偿的支付不应不合理迟延,应包括直至付款日按当时商业利率计算的利息,并应有效地兑换和自由转移"。

(2)利润汇回风险

利润是投资者的终极目的,利润的汇回是投资者投资目标实现的必需途径。如果东道国禁止或限制外国投资者将利润等合法收入按照公平市场价格兑换成可自由兑换的货币汇出东道国,则无异于征收。保护利润返回权是国际投资规则的重要任务,一般会在国际投资协定中以专门条款约定。

A.利润汇回条款的实践

利润汇回条款的主要内容为:缔约方应当允许利润自由汇回,投资者有权利将利润兑换成自由货币,汇回的汇率应当以转移当日外汇市场现行汇率兑换。

现有国际投资条约对利润汇回总体上采取更自由和开放的态度,允许汇回汇率按市场最高价汇回。例如美国2012年BIT范本第7条第3款:"各缔约方应当允许与涵盖投资有关的资金,以按照市场最高汇率的自由使用货币形式进行转移。"

在发达国家主导的国际投资规则中,对汇回权采取非常肯定而强硬的用词,如"毫不迟延""迅速"等。在发展中国家参与的投资规则中,用词相对温和,避免使用绝对的、态度强硬的表达方式。例如:CAFTAI第10条"允许此类转移不延误地自由汇入或汇出该方领土",中印BIT中第7条"无不合理延迟地转移其资本和收益"。这体现了发展中国家和发达国家在投资自由化问题上的一贯不同态度。

利润汇回条款的另一重要问题是可汇回的利润范围,即哪些利润可以汇回。通常情况下,可汇回的利润包括本金、收益、利润等合法收入。有的包括了征收的补偿款和从争端解决中产生的应收款,例如美国2012年BIT范本。我国近年来缔结或参加的投资条约中明确规定了可汇回的利润的范围。

在有的投资条约中,关于利润汇回,从约文上看是绝对的利润汇回权,没有规定利润的阻止汇回条款,如中印2006年BIT、中德2003年BIT。事实上绝对的利润汇回权是不现实的。

根据现有国际投资规则,利润汇回的限制有以下两种情形。

第一,基于东道国国内法律法规的阻止。东道国有外资管辖权,外资在东道国的活动必须遵守东道国法律法规,在东道国的各类法律施加给投资者的法定义务未履行或者未完全履行前,东道国可以限制外资利润的汇出。这种阻止无论是在发达国家主导的还是发展中国家缔结或参与的国际投资规则中都很普遍,区别在于所包含的内容简繁。USMCA第14.9条第4款的规定比较详细,"缔约一方可通过公平、非歧视和善意适用其与以下有关的法律来阻止或延迟转移;(a)破产、无力偿还债务或保护债权人权利;(b)证券或衍生品的发行、交易或买卖;(c)犯罪或刑事违法行为;(d)协助执法或金融监管当局所必要时对转移的金融报告或保存记录;或(e)确保遵守司法或行政程序中的命令或判决"。CAFTAI第10条第3款的规定应属最详细:缔约一方可以通过公平、非歧视和善意适用其与以下有关的法律和规章,阻止或延迟转移:(a)破产、丧失支付能力或资格,或保护债权人权利;(b)未履行东道国缔约方关于证券、期货、期权或衍生工具交易或买卖的转让要求;(c)未履行税收义务;(d)犯罪工或刑事违法行为和追缴犯罪所得;(e)社会保障,公共退休或强制储蓄计划;(f)遵守司法或行政程序中的判决;(g)尤其涉及外国投资项目停业的与劳工赔偿有关的工人遣散利益;和(h)协助执法或金融监管当局必要时对转移的金融报告或保存记录。《中韩投资协定》第6条第3款的规定较简略,"缔约一方可以通过公平、非歧视、善意地适用其以下相关的法律迟延或者阻止转移:(a)破产、倒闭或保护债权人权利;(b)证券的发行、买卖或交易;(c)犯罪或者触犯刑法或保证遵照司法程序中的判决或命令;(d)货币转移或者其他金融工具的报告"。

第二,基于国际收支平衡的阻止。如果外资撤离是无序撤离,会对东道国尤其是金融体系不稳定的发展中国家国际收支产生不良影响,因此在发展中国家缔结或参加的国际投资规则中,大多加入了国际收支平衡和金融汇率政策管理困难的限制,例如中韩BIT、中英 BIT、CAFTAI存在利润汇回权受制于国际收支困难和类似情况限制的条款。[1] 当国际收支平衡发生困难时豁免东道国资金转移义务,在 GATS 第12条有所体现,在自由贸易协定实践中不乏其例。但是何谓"国际收支平衡或外部财政危机",缺乏统一的国际判断标准,有待通过博弈逐渐形成共识。[2]

B.我国未来取向

我国未来参与制定多边投资规则时,应当特别注重以下三方面的内容。

第一,明确被允许汇回的利润及其范围。可以采取列举式但应加上"包括但不限于",即:可汇回的利润包括但不限于资本出资;利润、分红、资本收益以及涵盖投资全部和部分转让或清算的收入;利息、特许权使用费、管理费、技术指导费等费用;合同应收款。

第二,对特殊情况下利润汇回进行限制。限制的情形有两种:一是我国国内法的限制,即在投资者未履行国内法规定的义务时禁止转移。例如:(a)破产、丧失偿付能力或保护债权人权利;(b)未履行东道国关于证券、期货、期权或衍生产品交易的转移要求;(c)未履行税收义务;(d)刑事犯罪和犯罪所得的追缴;(e)社会保障、公共退休或强制储蓄计划;(f)遵守司法判决或行政决定;(g)与外商投资项目停业的劳动补偿有关的工人遣散费。二是国际收支平衡例外,即在国际收支遇到严重问题或受到严重威胁时,可以在公平、无歧视和善意的基础上暂时限制转移。

第三,考虑发展中国家金融状况。在与发展中国家制定的多边投资规则中应明确汇回的利润范围应包括投资争端解决中所得赔偿和国有化的赔偿,并且在汇回利率和汇率上由市场自由调节。

(3)战乱风险

综观有关国家的国内法和国际投资协定,其对"战乱险"的定义、分类各不相同。但

---

[1]　中韩 BIT 第9条第4款、中英 BIT 第6条第4款、CAFTAI 第10条第5款。
[2]　温先涛:《〈中国投资保护协定范本〉(草案)论稿(二)》,载《国际经济法学刊》2012 年第1期。

传统理论和各国的基本观点是,"战乱险"包括战争险和内乱险,是指外国投资者在东道国的投资因当地发生战争或类似战争等军事行动或内乱导致损失的风险。[①] 其中,"战争等军事行动"是指国家、军队或团体、武装部队之间的战争或武装冲突;"内乱"是指革命、骚乱、暴动,旨在推翻东道国现任政府在全国或部分地区统治的暴力行为,但不包括罢工、学潮等运动。

A.战乱险条款的实践

在美国,海外私人投资公司(OPIC)的保险产品中先是笼统地将"战争、内乱、政变和其他政治动机的暴力行为包括恐怖主义"作为一种政治风险,在有关政治风险保险的涵盖范围中又以"政治暴力险"(political violence)为名具体界定了其涵盖范围,主要包括以下事件:a.宣布或未宣布的战争;b.国家或国际武装的敌对行为;c.革命、起义和内战;d.恐怖主义和破坏。[②]

在日本,NEXI(Nippon Export and Investment Insurance)的战乱险主要是指战争、革命和恐怖主义。[③]

在中国出口信用保险公司(SINOSURE)[④]《投保指南》中,"战争与暴乱险"的范围为:战争指投资所在国发生的战争、革命、暴动、内战、恐怖行为以及其他类似战争的行为。战争项下的保障范围包括因战争造成的项目企业有形财产的损失和因战争行为导致项目企业不能正常经营的损失。[⑤]

MIGA 公约中使用"战争与内乱"一词,是指"东道国境内任何地区的任何军事行动或内乱"[⑥],但"任何"(any)将这一范围扩大至不可预见,便于投资担保机构基于业务需要灵活掌握。在 MIGA 业务说明中,"战争与内乱"是指"出于政治动机的战争和内乱",包括"革命、暴动、政变、阴谋破坏和恐怖主义"。[⑦]

虽然各国、MIGA 的战乱险涵盖范围不尽相同,但是基本认同的是"战乱"的动机应当是政治动机,而非经济动机,一般不包括劳资纠纷、经济矛盾所引起的骚乱冲突风险招致的损失。

B.我国未来取向

我国海外投资蓬勃发展之时正是世界局势动荡加剧之势,如利比亚战争、叙利亚危机、遍布全球的恐怖主义等,战乱风险随处可见。为使投资者利益免受战争和类似于战

---

① 史晓丽、祁欢:《国际投资法》,中国政法大学出版社 2009 年版,第 315 页。

② OPIC, Political Risk Insurance Types of Coverage-Political Violence, http://www.opic.gov/what-we-offer/ political-risk-insurance/types-of-coverage/political-violence, last visited on 28 May 2022.

③ http://www.nexi.go.jp/en/products/types/investment/, last visited on 28 May 2022.

④ 其于 2003 年成立,专门从事出口保险,也涉及投资保险业务。

⑤ 中国出口信用保险公司:《投资保险的历史与发展》,http://www.sinosure.com.cn/sinosure/cpyfw/tzbx/gytzbx/gytzbx.html,最后访问日期:2022 年 5 月 28 日。

⑥ 《多边投资担保机构公约》第 11 条第 4 款。

⑦ MIGA, Investment Guarantees-Types of Coverage, http://www.miga.org/investmentguarantees/index.cfm? stid＝1797♯toc3, last visited on 28 May 2022.

争行为的风险损失,我国应当尽可能地扩大战乱险的范围。较严重的"骚乱"和"敌对行为"能产生与战争相似的后果,且比战争更易发生,但中国出口信用保险公司《投保指南》中的"战乱险"中未包括"骚乱""敌对行为""政变"。我国在参与多边投资规则制定时应将较严重的"骚乱""敌对行为""政变"列入战乱险的范围。

(4)违约风险

违约风险即政府违约险,是指东道国政府对外国投资者违约且投资者无法求助于东道国司法或仲裁部门对违约索赔作出裁决,或司法或仲裁部门未能在合理期限内作出裁决,或其裁决不能实施的风险。该风险通常表现为:a.直接违反契约,指东道国政府实施的行为直接违反了与投资者签订的契约。b.东道国制定或修改法律,其规定与契约内容相冲突以致事实上废止契约。

A.违约风险的实践

政府违约险被单独作为一种政治风险最早出现在 MIGA 公约第 11 条。其规定:政府违约险是指"东道国政府不履行或违反与被保险人签订的合同,且被保险人无法求助于司法或仲裁机关对其提出的有关诉讼作出裁决,或该司法或仲裁机关未在担保合同根据该机构条例规定的合理期限内作出裁决,或虽有这样的裁决但不能执行"。[1]

中国出口信用保险公司《投保指南》规定,"政府违约险"是指东道国政府违反或不履行与被保险人或项目企业就投资项目签署的有关协议,且拒绝按照仲裁裁决书中载明的赔偿金额对被保险人或项目企业赔偿的行为。[2]

一些国家未将政府违约险单列为一种政治风险,而是将合同权利作为征收的对象。如美国 OPIC 未将之单列,而是放在"征用"中的"征用和其他政府非法干预行为",包括了"废除、抛弃或/和损害合同,包括强制重新谈判合同条款,政府违反仲裁裁决和拒绝正义"。[3] 有些国际仲裁实践也将合同权利作为征收的对象。[4]

B.我国未来取向

中国出口信用保险公司的违约险包括两个层次:一是东道国政府违反合同;二是违反针对东道国政府的不执行裁决的情形。基于充分保护海外投资者利益的需求,我国在参与制定多边投资规则时应考虑比较宽泛的政府违约险,可以 MIGA 为参照标准,明确将"拒绝司法"作为政府违约险的一种情形,并将其扩展至投保人无法求助于东道国司法或仲裁机关作出裁决、该司法或仲裁机关未在合理期限内作出裁决以及裁决不能执行。

(5)其他政治风险

各国海外投资保险机构承保的政治风险范围,除了以上四种典型风险,还有一些其

---

① 《多边投资担保机构公约》第 11 条第 5 款。

② 中国出口信用保险公司:《投资保险的历史与发展》,http://www.sinosure.com.cn/sinosure/cpyfw/tzbx/gytzbx/gytzbx.html,最后访问日期:2022 年 5 月 28 日。

③ OPIC, Arbitral Award Default,http://www.opic.gov/what-we-offer/political-risk-insurance/types-of-coverage/arbitral-award, last visited on 28 May 2022.

④ Phillips Petroleum Co. Iran v. Iran,Award No.425-39-2 of 29 June 1989,21 Iran-U. S. Cl Trib.

他政治风险,但各有其侧重点。

A.关于其他政治风险的国内国际实践

美国承保的其他政治风险最丰富,主要有"营业中断险"和"特殊产品"。营业中断险的基本含义是:不论发生禁兑保险事故,或征收保险事故,或战乱保险事故,致使海外私人投资者投保的投资企业营业中断而遭受损害者,应由承保人给予赔偿。OPIC 的"特殊产品"(specialty products)还为一些特定类型的国际投资"量身定做"了一些政治风险的保证,主要有以下几种:(a)为国际建筑工程中提供重型设备、涡轮机、医疗设备和服务的承包商和出口商提供的禁兑、征用和政治暴力险;(b)为美国银行和其他金融机构在发展中国家的有关金融业务提供广泛的政治风险保证;(c)为在发展中国家进行的资本市场交易提供政治风险保证;(d)不尊重主权担保(non-honoring of a sovereign guaranty),指对信用等级评估在 BB 及以下的主权国家的贷款,在这些主权国家无法履行其主权担保的债务时,由 OPIC 予以保证;(e)再保险;(f)为在发展中国家开发的石油和天然气以外自然资源提供担保;(g)为跨境租赁方式的金融投资提供的政治风险保证;(h)为在发展中国家石油和天然气开发和勘探提供的征用和免于干扰的保证。① 从以上内容可以看出,OPIC 提供的特殊保险产品主要分为两大类:一是为间接投资的政治风险提供保证,主要是针对金融及其衍生品投资;二是对自然资源投资的政治风险提供保证。

日本 NEXI 承保的海外投资风险包括政治风险和一些商业风险。在承保的政治风险中,除了禁兑和战乱险,还包括惩罚性的高关税、码头罢工和恐怖主义。承保的商业风险主要是自然灾害等不可抗力风险。除了对一般海外投资企业提供保险外,还有针对自然资源和能源的投资和贷款提供保险,主要有两种:一是对高级贷款即日本企业或银行为外国政府或公司提供的自然资源开发中长期贷款,提供因战争、革命、禁兑、迟延汇兑、不可抗力、借款人违约或破产而造成损失的保险;二是针对能源投资和次级贷款提供因战争、国有化、恐怖主义和不可抗力而造成营业中断的保险。②

在 MIGA 中,设置了"不遵守金融义务险"(non-honoring of financial obligations),承保因政府、地方政府或国有企业不履行无条件偿付义务而造成损失的风险。③

B.我国未来取向

由上观之,海外投资保险扩展到了间接投资和能源投资领域,并针对这些部门的不同特点提供不同的政治风险保证。中国出口信用保险公司的保险没有涉及金融投资和能源投资的政治风险保证。鉴于我国海外投资中能源型投资所占比例较大,而能源是各国的经济命脉,属重点管控的部门,发生政治风险的可能性相当大,需要对能源投资的政治风险提供保证。随着我国越来越深入参与国际金融交易中,尽管对有些金融工具及其

---

① OPIC, Specialty Products, http://www.opic.gov/what-we-offer/political-risk-insurance/types-of-coverage/specialty-products, last visited on 31 May 2022.

② NEXI (Nippon Export and Insurance), NEXI's Action Guideline, http://nexi.go.jp/corporate/booklet/pdf/nexi-2011_e.pdf, last visited on 31 May 2022.

③ MIGA, Investment Guarantees-Types of Coverage, http://www.miga.org/investmentguarantees/index.cfm? stid=1797♯toc5, last visited on 31 May 2022.

衍生工具的使用不很娴熟,但间接投资的蓬勃发展是必然趋势,我国应考虑对金融投资的政治风险提供保证。

(二)代位求偿权条款

如前文所述,海外投资保险是母国保护海外投资的制度工具,嫁接了商业风险的运作原理,在保险事故发生后海外投资保险机构对投资者予以赔偿,赔偿后即可取得代位求偿权向引起风险事故的东道国进行追偿。

1.代位求偿权的实践

MIGA 之类的代位求偿权来源于 MIGA 之类的国际条约、有充分的国际法依据除外,各国保险机构的代位求偿权因其海外投保险制度是国内法制度而缺乏国际法据。如果没有国家间的相互约定或者国际法施加给国家的义务,东道国没有义务承认其他国家国内法施加给自己的义务,其他国家的法律不具有域外效力,除非这些义务来自国际法律规范。为了给海外投资保险机构的代位求偿权寻找国际法依据,各国在国际投资规则制定中约定互相承认对方国家海外投资保险机构的代位求偿权。该条款成为国际投资规则中鲜有争议的条款。

根据 MIGA 公约,代位是"在对投保人支付或同意支付赔偿时,投保人对东道国其他债务人所拥有的有关承保投资的权利或索赔权应由本机构代位",确认了 MIGA 的代位求偿权。

在双边和区域性投资规则[①]中,以相互承认对方国家海外投资保险机构的代位求偿权为主要内容:若缔约一方或其指定的机构对其投资者在缔约另一方境内的某项投资提供了担保,并据此向投资者作了支付,缔约另一方应承认该投资者的权利和请求权依照法律或合法交易转让给了该缔约一方或其指定机构,并承认该缔约一方或其指定机构对上述权利和请求权的代位。[②] 一般而言,各缔约方会约定将代位权限定在该投资者的原有权利范围内,事实上这种限制是没有必要的,因为海外投资保险机构对投资者的赔偿不是在原有权利范围内 100% 赔偿,而是按比例赔偿,海外投资保险机构能请求的代位权只能在该范围内,不能超出现有范围。

值得注意的是,美国 BIT 范本、NAFTA 中没有代位条款,但在 USMCA 中存在[③],原因是美国实行双重双边投资保护,即相互促进与保护投资协定(The Encouragement and Reciprocal Protection of Investment)、投资保险与保证协定(The Investment Insurance and Guarantee Agreement)。前者是实体性和程序性条款合二为一的投资条约类型;后者是程序性的条约类型,主要涉及美国海外投资保险机构 OPIC 的代位求偿问题。我国于 1980 年和美国签订了《关于投资保险和投资保证的鼓励投资的协定及有关

---

① 例如 CAFTAI 第 12 条,RCEP 第 12 条,CPTPP 第 9.13 条。
② 例如 2003 年中德 BIT 第 7 条。
③ USMCA 第 14.5 条。

问题的换文》,主要内容是我国承认 OPIC 的代位求偿权。[1] 由于当时我国没有海外投资保险机构,因此该代位权只是中国单方面给予美国的。中美之间至今没有关于承认我国海外投资保险机构——中国出口信用保险公司代位求偿权的相关条约。

2.我国未来取向

我国参与制定多边投资规则时,需要明确以下事项。

第一,总体上接受代位求偿权条款。但需特别注意,对未将代位求偿权单列的国家,需明确海外投资保险机构的代位求偿权,即:若缔约一方或其指定机构对其投资者在缔约另一方领土内投资的非商业风险根据担保或保险合同作了支付,并据此对该投资者进行了支付,缔约另一方应承认该缔约一方依照法律或合法交易通过代位获得了该投资者全部权利和请求权。

第二,对代偿求偿权的权利范围进行限制。海外投资保险机构通过代位获得的权利或者请求权不应超过该投资者原有的权利或者请求权,也不能损害该缔约一方已经获得的该投资者的原有权利或者请求权。

五、投资争端解决条款

本条款是国际投资协定中的重要条款,相对于其他条款,内容详细、具体。学界和实务界非常重视此条款。[2]

(一)争端解决条款的种类

在国际投资规则中,作为救济手段的投资争端解决,一般涉及两种不同性质的争端,

---

① 温先涛:《〈中国投资保护协定范本〉(草案)论稿(二)》,载《国际经济法学刊》2012 年第 1 期。

② 关于此条款或领域的国内外主要研究成果,可参阅黄世席:《可持续发展视角下国际投资争端解决机制的革新》,载《当代法学》2016 年第 2 期;梁咏:《国际投资仲裁机制变革与中国对策研究》,载《厦门大学学报(哲学社会科学版)》2018 年第 3 期;张正怡:《论晚近区域协定中投资争端解决机制的创新及其启示——以 TPP、TTIP、CETA 为例》,载《国际商务(对外经济贸易大学学报)》2018 年第 3 期;Daniel Behn and Malcolm Langford, Trumping the Environment: An Empirical Perspective on the Legitimacy of Investment Treaty Arbitration, *Journal of World Investment & Trade*, 2017, Vol.18, No.1, pp.14-61; Facundo Perez Aznar, Local Litigation Requirements in International Investment Agreements: Their Chartacteristics and Potential in Times of Reform in Latin America, *Journal of World Investment & Trade*, 2016, Vol.17, No.4, pp.536-561; James D. Fry & Juan Ignacio Stampalija, Forged Independence and Impartiality: Conflicts of Interest of International Arbitrators in Investment Disputes, *Arbitration International*, 2014, Vol.30, No.2, pp.189-263; J. Robert Basedow, The Achmea Judgment and the Applicability of the Energy Charter Treaty in Intra-EU Investment Arbitration, *Journal of International Economic Law*, 2020, Vol.23, pp.271-292; J. Christopher Thomas and Harpreet Kaur Dhillon, The Foundations of Investment Treaty Arbitration: The ICSID Convention, Investment Treaties and the Review of Arbitration Awards, *ICSID Review*, 2017, Vol.32, No.3, pp.459-502。

一种是缔约国之间关于投资条约的解释和适用问题的争端,另一种是东道国与外国投资者之间的争端。

1.缔约国间投资争端解决条款的实践

缔约国间争端解决的主要方式是协商和国际仲裁。多数投资协定同时采纳这两种手段,并有先后顺序,即首先通过外交途径解决,外交途径不能解决时再提交仲国际裁。例如,美国 2004 年 BIT 范本第 37 条规定:"任何缔约方之间关于本条约解释和适用的争端不能通过协商或其他外交途径解决的,应当依照国际法规则提交仲裁。"2005 年中国—比利时 BIT 第 9 条第 1 款规定,"与本协定解释或适用有关的任何争端应尽可能通过外交途径协商解决"。我国的"尽可能"表明了外交途径的优先适用和对其他解决手段的保留态度,说明缔约国对国际仲裁手段的谨慎。我国缔结或参加的国际投资规则基本上采用了这种模式。[①]

2.投资者与东道国间投资争端解决条款的理论与实践

投资者与东道国之间的争端是投资争端解决的重点和难点,缘由如下:(1)国际投资规则的目的在于对投资者私权利的保护,限制东道国公权力对其肆意干预,投资争端的解决是投资者利益保护的救济手段,没有救济的权利等于没有权利;(2)该争端通常起源于东道国管理国家的行为,是国家主权的体现,作为私主体的投资者在拥有主权权力的东道国面前,难以与之抗衡,当其利益受到损害时,救济手段的选择直接决定能否得到有效救济;(3)该类争端集中反映了外国投资者与东道国之间的矛盾。投资者的目的在于利益最大化,东道国政府除了经济发展目标,还有公共利益目标;投资者的财产权是私权利,而东道国管理外资行为是公权力的体现;当公权力和私权利冲突时,私权利要服从公权力,当公权力被滥用时,会出现投资者应如何获得救济、由东道国国内救济还是由母国

---

① 关于国家间投资争端仲裁透明度的国外学术成果主要有 Maria Jose Luque Macias, Inter-State Investment Dispute Settlement in Latin America: Is There Space for Transparency, *Journal of World Investment & Trade*, 2016, Vol.17, No.4, pp.634-657.

救济抑或是国际法救济的问题。①

---

① 关于投资者—国家争端解决中存在的主要问题,可参见国内外主要研究成果,如余劲松:《国际投资条约仲裁中投资者与东道国权益保护平衡问题研究》,载《中国法学》2011 年第 2 期;Jacob A. Kuipers, Too Big to Nail: How Investor-State Arbitration Lacks an Appropriate Execution Mechanism for the Largest Awards, *Boston College International and Comparative Review*, 2016, Vol.39, Issue 2, pp.417-451; Katia Fach Gomez, Catharine Titi, The Latin American Challenge to the Current System of Investor-State Dispute Settlement, *Journal of World Investment & Trade*, 2016, Vol.17, No.4, pp. 511-514. 关于投资者—国家争端解决的新发展、新路径或新方法的国内外学术成果主要有:廖凡:《投资者—国家争端解决机制的新发展》,载《江西社会科学》2017 年第 10 期;盛斌、段然:《投资者—东道国争端解决机制的发展及对中国的影响》,载《国际经济合作》2016 年第 3 期;宋俊荣:《欧美投资者与东道国争端解决条款的最新动向》,载《商业研究》2015 年第 12 期;朱明新:《投资者—国家争端解决机制的革新与国家的"回归"》,载《国际法研究》2018 年第 4 期;Dr. Sam Luttrell, ISDS in the Asia-Pacific: A Regional Snap-Shot, *International Trade & Business Law Review*, 2016, Vol.19, pp.20-47; Elsa Sardinha, The New EU-Led Approach to Investor-State Arbitration: The Investment Tribunal System in the Comprehensive Economic Trade Agreement (CETA) and the EU-Vietnam Free Trade Agreement, *ICSID Review*, 2017, Vol.32, No.3, pp.625-672; Ingo Venzke, Investor-State Dispute Settlement in TTIP from the Perspective of a Public Law Theory of International Adjudication, *Journal of World Investment & Trade*, 2016, Vol.17, No.3, pp.374-400; Jose Gustavo Prieto Munoz, The Rise of Common Principles for Investment in Latin America: Proposing a Methodological Shift for Investor-State Dispute Settlement, *Journal of World Investment & Trade*, 2016, Vol.17, No.4, pp. 614-633; Katia Gomez, Catharine Titi, International Investment Law and ISDS: Mapping Contemporary Latin America, *Journal of World Investment & Trade*, 2016, Vol. 17, No. 4, pp. 515-535; Luke Nottage, Rebalancing Investment Treaties and Investor-State Arbitration: Two Approaches, *Journal of World Investment & Trade*, 2016, Vol. 17, No. 6, pp. 1015-1040; Malcolm Langford, etc., The Revolving Door in International Investment Arbitration, *Journal of International Economic Law*, 2017, Vol. 20, pp. 279-300; Mark Feldman, Investment Arbitration Appellate Mechanism Options: Consistency, Accuracy, and Balance of Power, *ICSID Review*, 2017, Vol.32, No.3, pp.528-544; Mark Huber and Greg Tereposky, The WTO Appellate Body: Viability as a Model for an Investor-State Dispute Settlement Appellate Mechanism, *ICSID Review*, 2017, Vol.32, No.3, pp.545-594; N. Jansen Calamita, The (In)Compatibility of Appellate Mechanisms with Existing Instruments of the Investment Treaty Regime, *Journal of World Investment & Trade*, 2017, Vol.18, No.4, pp.585-627; Rodrigo Polanco Lazo, Systems of Legal Defence Used by Latin American Countries in Investment Disputes, *Journal of World Investment & Trade*, 2016, Vol.17, No.4, pp.562-593; Stephen S. Kho, etc., The EU TTIP Investment Court Proposal and the WTO Dispute Settlement System: Comparing Apples and Oranges, *ICSID Review*, 2017, Vol.32, No.2, pp.326-345; Stephan W. Schill, Reforming Investor-State Dispute Settlement: A (Comparative and International) Constitutional Law Framework, *Journal of International Economic Law*, 2017, Vol.20, pp.649-672. 关于投资者—国家争端仲裁透明度的国内外主要学术成果,参见张建:《国际投资条约仲裁的透明度问题探析》,载《保定学院学报》2017 年第 2 期;Esmé Shirlow, Dawn of a new era? The UNCITRAL Rules and UN Convention on Transparency in Treaty-Based Investor-State Arbitration, *ICSID Review*, 2016, Vol.31, No.3 pp.622-654。

此类争端经历了从"政治性争端"向"理性争端"①的进化,其解决经历了从"政治的、外交的、权力导向的解决方式"到"法律的、(准)司法的、规则导向的解决方式""从外交到法律"②的变迁。

在南北矛盾激烈的 20 世纪中后叶,发展中国家强调东道国对外资的管辖权,坚持东道国国内救济手段③,甚至有的国家完全排斥母国或国际法的介入,如著名的卡尔沃主义④,并将这些条款引入国际投资规则中,即卡尔沃条款。但发达国家认为投资者与东道国之间投资争端通常产生于东道国行政和立法决定,在缺乏有效、独立的司法体制的情况下,东道国法院更可能执行当地行政和立法决定,而不是给予外国投资者司法正义,⑤倾向于实施母国外交保护和寻求国际法律手段解决。在发展中国家和发达国家之间难以调和的情况下,世界银行从 1962 年开始研究投资争端的第三方介入解决——仲裁模式,于 1965 年通过了 ICSID 公约,并根据该公约成立了 ICSID。但该中心和其仲裁程序在成立初期未受人们的关注,案件寥寥无几。⑥ 从 1965 年至 1995 年,在 ICSID 登记的案件仅 30 个。⑦ 20 世纪 80 年代以后,发展中国家基于对外资的大量需求,外资政策逐渐放松,很多国家放弃了坚持东道国的国内救济,开始接受发达国家推崇的法律解决手段——主要是国际仲裁,甚至在有卡尔沃主义传统的拉美国家,国际投资仲裁开始得到普遍认可。

在当代,此类争端的主要问题不是是否接受国际仲裁,而是以下问题:(1)国际投资仲裁和东道国国内救济手段的相互关系如何,是强调东道国国内救济优先或用尽当地救济,还是摒弃东道国救济完全采用国际仲裁手段来解决争端。(2)仲裁庭在法律适用问题上是以东道国法律为依据还是以国际法为依据。对于这些问题,不同国家参与制定的不同层次国际投资规则有不同的答案。

在普遍性规则中,ICSID 公约采取了非政治化路线,避开了政治化的外交谈判而采用

---

①　徐崇利:《晚近国际投资争端解决实践之评判:"全球治理"理论的引入》,载《法学家》2010 年第 3 期。

②　王彦志:《国际投资争端解决的法律化:成就与挑战》,载《当代法学》2011 年第 3 期。

③　关于用尽当地救济的国内学术成果,可参见倪小璐:《投资者—东道国争端解决机制中用尽当地救济规则的"衰亡"与"复活"——兼评印度 2015 年 BIT 范本》,载《国际经贸探索》2018 年第 1 期。

④　关于卡尔沃主义的学术成果,可参见韩秀丽:《再论卡尔沃主义的复活——投资者—国家争端解决视角》,载《现代法学》2014 年第 1 期;Rodrigo Polanco Lazo, The No of Tokyo Revisited: Or How Developed Countries Learned to Start Worrying and Love the Calvo Doctrine, *ICSID Review*, 2015, Vol.30, No.1, pp.172-193。

⑤　M. Somarajah, *The Settlement of Foreign Investment Disputes*, Kluwer Law International, 2000, p.254.

⑥　ICSID Secretariat, *Possible Improvements of the Framework for ICSID Arbitration*, 22 April 2004, p.3.

⑦　ICSID, Disputes before the Centre, News from ICSID, 22 February 2005, p.2.

了技术化的法律专家磋商的方式,没有采取协商共识而是采用投票表决通过的方式,[1]加入该公约并不构成仲裁管辖的同意和接受,ICSID 仲裁机制的利用是自愿的,成员国可以自由决定将哪些种类的投资争端同意提交 ICSID 管辖。[2] 该公约的这种开放式态度还表现在处理用尽当地救济与 ICSID 仲裁之间的关系上,其第 26 条"缔约国可以要求以用尽该国行政或司法救济作为其同意根据本公约交付仲裁的条件",表明该公约允许将用尽当地救济作为将争端提交给 ICSID 解决的前置条件。但是有学者对该条文作了进一步解读,认为条文的含义是"如果缔约国在没有明确要求诉诸 ICSID 仲裁之前需要优先采用当地救济,就视为该缔约国放弃了当地救济的要求"。[3] 在 ICSID 公约框架下,如果东道国有意于保留投资争端解决的国内管辖权,则在参与国际投资规则制定时最明智之举是明示地将用尽当地救济作为前置程序。在法律适用问题上,ICSID 公约第 42 条规定,首先适用当事人意思自治原则,在当事人没有选择时,仲裁庭可以适用东道国法律或者国际法。因东道国法律和国际法之间是一种并列关系,具体如何选择由仲裁庭自由裁量。

在 MAI 草案中,可以提起国际仲裁的事项有两类,一是东道国被投资者认为违反了 MAI 的义务引起的争端,二是与一项特定投资合同或一个投资授权的获得有关的争端。MAI 草案的规定不同于 ICSID 的"逐案同意制",所有国家一旦签署 MAI,对根据 MAI 提交仲裁解决的争端是"无条件同意"。在 MAI 体系中,东道国的国内救济完全被摒弃。在法律适用上,MAI 与 ICSID 的规定相似,适用的法律为争端双方同意的法律规则,如果缺乏这类规则,应适用争端缔约国的法律(包括冲突规则)、调整双方协定的法律和可适用的国际法规则。

在区域性投资规则中,NAFTA、美国参与的其他自由贸易区协定投资争端解决条款代表了高标准投资自由化的国际投资规则对争端解决机制的新要求。根据 NAFTA,投资者向 NAFTA 仲裁庭提起仲裁的条件有二:(1)投资者同意遵照本协定规定的程序进行仲裁;(2)投资者放弃由于东道国违反 NAFTA 措施而在东道国国内开始或继续提起的与司法或行政救济程序或其他任何有关的争端解决程序的权利。[4] 缔约国在 NAFTA 协定的签字即表示其愿意将投资争端交由 NAFTA 仲裁庭解决,提起仲裁是投资者的单方权利。该条意味着东道国的国内救济被彻底放弃。在法律适用上,NAFTA 第 1131 条规定,"仲裁应当依据本协定和可适用的国际法规对争议事项进行裁决",表面上不允许当事人选择,但实践中,NAFTA 仲裁的法律适用中允许当事人意思自治的程度和

---

① Andreas F. Lowenfeld. The ICSID Convention—Origins and Transformation, *Georgia Journal of International and Comparative Law*, 2009, Vol.6, p.38.

② Christoph H. Schreuer, Loretta Malintopp, August Reinisch, Anthony Sinclair, *The ICSID Convention—A Commentary* (2nd ed), Cambridge University Press, 2009, p.345.

③ 王海浪:《ICSID 体制内用尽当地救济原则面临的三大挑战及对策》,载《国际经济法学刊》2006年第 3 期。

④ NAFTA 第 1121 条。

ICSID 是相同的。① UNMCA 附件 14-D"墨西哥—美国投资争端"和附件 14-E"墨西哥—美国与涵盖政府合同有关的投资争端"详细规定了投资者—国家争端解决的程序性事项。前者共 14 条,规定了以下事项:定义、磋商与谈判、将请求提交仲裁、同意仲裁、同意的条件与限制、遴选仲裁员、仲裁行为、仲裁进程透明度、准据法、诸附件的解释、专家报告、合并仲裁、裁决、文书送达。与 NAFTA 的规定相比较,本附件的规定有许多重要变化,例如:推定同意仲裁和提交仲裁请求②,准据法为本协定、可适用国际法规则、本协定条款解释委员会的决定③,分别提交仲裁的具有共同的法律或事实问题或其产生于相同事件或客观情况的两项或以上的请求可以经任何争端方申请而合并审理④,等。后者共 6 款,是对前者附件变通后的规定适用于投资者为政府合同当事人的争端解决。

在 ECT 中,投资者可以随时提起国际仲裁,不需事先用尽当地行政或司法救济办法。用尽当地救济被仲裁权所替代,通过要求缔约国无条件同意国际仲裁试图为投资者设立一种权利,能够使投资者直接申请国际仲裁而不需寻求东道国司法救济。⑤ 在法律适用上,仲裁庭应根据 ECT 条款和可适用的国际法规则和原则对争端作出裁决,排除东道国国内法和当事人意思自治的适用。

在以发展中国家为主体的自由贸易区协定中,用尽当地救济仍受到重视,如 CAFTAI 中用尽当地救济被作为和国际仲裁并列的程序存在,投资者享有选择权。⑥ 由于 CAFTAI 没有设立仲裁机构,CAFTAI 中未规定仲裁所适用的法律,法律适用问题留给各个案件的仲裁庭依据仲裁规则解决。在仲裁机构选择上,CAFTAI 采取了相当灵活的做法,即:如果争端所涉缔约方是 ICSID 公约的缔约国,可以提交 ICSID 解决;如果不是其缔约国,则根据《联合国国际贸易法委员会仲裁规则》提交仲裁,或由争端所涉方同意的任何其他仲裁机构或根据任何其他仲裁规则进行仲裁。

CPTPP 第 B 部分专门处理投资者—国家争端解决,尽管其许多规定与上述 USMCA 相同或相近,例如:磋商与谈判、推定已将请求提交仲裁的情形、对缔约方同意仲裁的限制、推定已经提交仲裁的情形、遴选仲裁员、合并审理的条件、仲裁行为、仲裁程序透明度、专家报告、对裁决的要求等,但不乏独特条款,例如:限定提交仲裁的请求范围⑦,申请人选择一种仲裁程序⑧,准据法为本协定、国际法的可适用规则、可适用于相关投资授权的法律规则、被申请方的法律(含其法律冲突规则)、本协定条款解释委员会的

---

① Jan H Dalhuisen,Andrew T. Guzman,The Applicable Law in Foreign Investment Disputes,http://ssrn.com/ abstract=2209503,last visited on 5 Feb.2022.

② UNMCA 附件 14-D 第 14.D.4 条第 2 款。

③ UNMCA 附件 14-D 第 14.D.9 条。

④ UNMCA 附件 14-D 第 14.D.12 条第 1 款。

⑤ James Chalker,Making the Investment Provisions of the Energy Charter Treaty Sustainable DevelopmentFriendly,*International Environmental Agreements*,2006,pp.435-458.

⑥ CAFTAI 第 14 条第 4 款。

⑦ CPTPP 第 9.19 条第 1 款。

⑧ CPTPP 第 9.19 条第 4 款。

决定①,等。

在双边投资协定中,东道国的当地救济不被发达国家主导的 BIT 采纳和肯定。美国 2004 年和 2012 年 BIT 范本中关于投资争端解决,首先肯定了"磋商和谈判",在"磋商和谈判"不能解决时则直接采用国际仲裁手段解决②,完全忽略东道国的救济;在法律适用上,仲裁庭应当适用:"(a)相关投资许可或投资协定中约定,或争议双方另行商定的法律;(b)没有约定或另行商定的:(i)被申请人的法律,包括其冲突规则和(ii)有约束力的国际法规则"③,即基本上是综合了 ICSID 和 NAFTA 的法律适用条款。④ 拉美国家在 20 世纪 90 年代签订了 300 多个双边投资条约,其主要内容之一是对国际投资仲裁管辖权的承认和接受。⑤ 在早期的双边投资协定中,拉美国家有卡尔沃主义痕迹,用尽当地救济是提交国际仲裁的必要前提条件,⑥但在 20 世纪 90 年代以后签订的 BIT 中,用尽当地救济已被抛弃。如在 1991 年美国—阿根廷 BIT 中,用尽当地救济不再是提交国际仲裁的必要前提条件;⑦在法律适用上,投资协定不影响东道国国内法、投资协定与投资许可和"国际法律义务"的法律效力,⑧即仲裁适用的法律主要有东道国国内法、投资协定与投资许可、国际法。中国缔结的双边投资协定基本上经历了有限接受仲裁—全面接受仲裁但东道国国内救济前置—东道国国内救济和仲裁并存的过程。有限接受是根据我国加入 1965 年《华盛顿公约》所做的保留,只将涉及征收或国有化赔偿数额的争端提交国际仲裁。但自 1988 年中国—巴巴多斯 BIT 之后,我国开始全面承认国际仲裁。目前,我国多数 BIT 规定,可以将所有投资争端提交国际仲裁解决。这和我国对外投资强劲,投资母国和东道国双重身份混同日益明显有直接关系。

(二)我国未来取向

从国际投资规则及其运行总体趋势看,国际投资争端的解决日渐法律化,⑨国际仲裁成为主流。虽然此争端解决方式在运行中存在诸多不足和缺陷,被学者们谓为"合法性

---

① CPTPP 第 9.25 条。

② 美国 2004 年和 2012 年 BIT 范本第 23、24 条第 1 款。

③ 美国 2004 年和 2012 年 BIT 范本第 30 条。

④ Jan H Dalhuisen,Andrew T. Guzman,The Applicable Law in Foreign Investment Disputes,http://ssrn.com/abstract=2209503:4,last visited on 25 Feb.2022.

⑤ Jeswald W. Salacuse,BIT by BIT:The Growth of Bilateral Investment Treaties and Their Impact on Foreign Investment in Developing Countries,*International Law*,1990,Vol.24,p.668.

⑥ Bernardo M. Cremades,Disputes Arising out of Foreign Direct Investment in Latin America:A New Look at the Calvo Doctrine and Other Jurisdictional Issue,*Dispute Resolution Journal*,2004,Vol.59,p.80.

⑦ 1991 年美国—阿根廷 BIT 第 7 条。

⑧ 1991 年美国—阿根廷 BIT 第 10 条。

⑨ Susan D. Franck,Foreign Direct Investment,Investment Treaty Arbitration and the Rule of Law,*Mc George Global Business and Development Law Journal*,2007,Vol.19,p.337.

危机"①，但它作为一种第三方解决争端的方式为国际投资良性流动提供了动力。采用国际仲裁方式解决国家间和投资者与国家间的投资争端，已是大势所趋。

我国在参与制定多边投资规则时，须考虑两类不同性质的争端及其各自的解决办法。

对国家间的投资争端，按我国和国际社会的一般做法，先由缔约国间通过政治途径（协商、谈判）解决，政治途径不能解决时，通过国际仲裁庭仲裁解决。

对外国投资者与东道国间的争端，视不同情形的多边投资规则采取不同办法。在制定地缘性、区域性、多边自由贸易区投资规则时，可以将东道国国内救济和国际仲裁并列，不直接规定二者之间的先后关系，由投资者自己选择，还可以考虑在这三类规则体系内建立国际仲裁机构专门用以解决争端。在与上述国家以外的发展中国家制定多边投资规则时，应直接确定用国际仲裁方式解决争端。在与上述国家以外的发达国家制定多边投资规则时，基于我国在很长时期内的资本输入国、资本输出国身份混同以及我国对国际司法手段使用尚不熟练的现状，需要将用尽当地救济和岔道口条款（the fork-in-the-road clause）作为国际仲裁解决的前置条件。

第二节　我国对多边投资规则中特殊条款的取向

在现存国际投资规则中，除了上节中的一般条款，发达国家主导的规则中还有一些

---

① Susan D. Franck., The Legitimacy Crisis in Investment Treaty Arbitration: Privatizing Public International Law through Inconsistent Decisions, *Fordham Law Review*, 2005, Vol.7, p.1572.

特殊条款,主要涉及环境保护①、劳工或健康或人权保护②、一般例外与根本安全例外、投资措施与履行要求③等条款。

---

① 关于投资规则环境条款的国内学术成果,可参阅崔佳文:《国际投资中的环境保护研究——以投资条约为视角》,载《国际商贸》2018 年第 24 期;马迅:《我国国际投资协定中环境条款及其未来进路》,载《生态经济》2016 年第 11 期;宋昕芮:《浅析中国双边投资协定中的环境保护条款》,载《市场研究》2018 年第 7 期。此方面的国外学术成果主要集中在以下三个主题上:(1)环境措施例外,例如 Amelia Keene, The Incorporation and Interpretation of WTO-Style Environmental Exceptions in International Investment Agreements, *Journal of World Investment & Trade*, 2017, Vol.18, No.1, pp.62-99; Arnaud de Nanteuil, Green Latin America—Some Reflections on Environmental Issues in Latin America's New Instruments of Investment Protection, *Journal of World Investment & Trade*, 2016, Vol.17, No.4, pp.594-613; Joshua Paine, Failure to Take Reasonable Environmental Measures as a Breach of Investment Treaty, *Journal of World Investment & Trade*, 2017, Vol.18, No.4, pp.745-754。(2)环境规则与政策,例如 Graham Mayeda, Integrating Environmental Impact Assessments into International Investment Agreements: Global Administrative Law and Transnational Cooperation, *Journal of World Investment & Trade*, 2017, Vol.18, No.1, pp.131-162; Jean Frédéric Morin, etc., The Trade Regime as a Complex Adaptive System: Exploration and Exploitation of Environmental Norms in Trade Agreements, *Journal of International Economic Law*, 2017, Vol.20, pp.365-390; Jeff Sullivan and Valeriya Kirsey, Environmental Policies: A Shield or a Sword in Investment Arbitration, *Journal of World Investment & Trade*, 2017, Vol.18, No.1, pp.100-130。(3)通过投资条约仲裁解决环境争端,例如 Daniel Behn, Ole Kristian Fauchald, Adjudicating Environmental Disputes through Investment Treaty Arbitration: An Introduction, *Journal of World Investment & Trade*, 2017, Vol.18, No.1, pp.9-13。

② 关于劳工或人权保护条款的国内外学术成果主要有梁岿然:《美国双边投资协定范本的劳工保护条款分析——兼论其对我国的影响及我国之对策》,载《河北法学》2014 年第 7 期;梁咏:《2012 年美国 BIT 范本中劳工条款的新发展与中国对策研究——以投资利益与劳工保护平衡为视角》,载《上海商学院学报》2013 年第 4 期;孙玉凤:《国际投资协定中的劳工权保护问题研究》,武汉大学 2014 年博士学位论文;汪玮敏:《双边投资协定中的劳工保护条款研究》,载《国际经贸探索》2015 年第 4 期;Lorenzo Cotula, (Dis)integration in Global Resource Governance: Extractivism, Human Rights, and Investment Treaties, *Journal of International Economic Law*, 2020, Vol. 23, pp. 431-454; Lorenzo Cotula, Human Rights and Investor Obligations in Investor-State Arbitration, *Journal of World Investment & Trade*, 2016, Vol.17, No.1, pp.148-158; Lorenzo Pellegrini, etc., International Investment Agreements, Human Rights, and Environmental Justice: The Texaco/Chevron Case From the Ecuadorian Amazon, *Journal of International Economic Law*, 2020, Vol. 23, pp. 454-468; Tania Voon, Evidentiary Challenges for Public Health Regulation in International Trade and Investment Law, *Journal of International Economic Law*, 2015, Vol.18, pp.795-826。

③ 关于禁止或限制投资措施或履行要求条款的近期国内外主要学术成果如下:李维、冯汉桥:《论"履行要求禁止规则"对外商投资环境的影响》,载《经济研究导刊》2014 年第 30 期;李军:《投资业绩要求禁止规则的新发展及其对中国投资协定谈判的影响》,载《亚太经济》2016 年第 6 期;Joel P. Trachtman, International Legal Control of Domestic Administrative Action, *Journal of International Economic Law*, 2014, Vol.17, pp.753-786。

一、环境保护条款

(一)环境保护条款的国际实践

在世界范围内,首先倡议将环境问题纳入国际投资条约中的是 OECD,并体现在 MAI 草案中。该草案第三部分"投资和投资者的待遇"专设了"关于环境和劳工的附加条款"。该条款被认为是对东道国施加了负担,是对国家主权的限制。

将环境问题正式有效纳入多边投资协定始于 NAFTA,其第 1114 条第 1 款明确规定:"此章任何内容均不得阻止缔约方采取、维持或者强化任何与条约相一致的环境保护措施。"第 2 款更明确表示,"任何缔约方不得放弃或者减损环境保护措施以鼓励投资者在其境内新设、扩大或者保留投资"。在 NAFTA 基础上,东道国不仅可以实施新的环境保护措施,同时负有义务不实施以损害环境为代价的措施来吸引外资。后来的 UNMCA、CPTPP 承袭了此精神[1]。

美国 2012 年 BIT 范本不但在序言中表明环境保护目标,而且第 12 条直接以"投资和环境"为标题,规定:"缔约双方认识到通过降低和减少国内环境保护法律的规定来鼓励投资是不可取的。因此缔约双方承诺不通过放弃或减损这些法律的方式来作为对其境内设立、获取、扩大投资的鼓励……缔约方可以采取、维持或执行其认为与本条约相一致的、能保证其境内投资活动意识到保护环境重要性的措施。"该范本还为环境保护条款设定了磋商程序。该条款给东道国设定了投资措施方面的义务,要求东道国不得采用造成环境损害的投资措施。在发展中国家看来,该条款是给其增加了国际法义务,对其外资管理权进行限制,在很大程度上是为了政治斗争和经济刺激,[2]因此,发展中国家并不看好该条款。

在 ECT 中,考虑到东道国环境保护需求而制定了相关条款,引入了国际环境规则中具有实体性权利的法律规则。其第 24 条第 2 款规定:"不应当排除任何缔约方采取或者强化必要的保护人权、动植物生命或者公众健康相关的措施。"该规定给东道国采取环境保护措施提供了依据。其第 19 条规定:"在公共利益保护和不扭曲投资的情况下,缔约方同意在任何境内的环境污染者应当原则上负担污染费用,包括跨境污染转移的费用。"可见,ECT 中既有环境保护的具体措施,又基本遵循了《里约环境与发展宣言》中的"污染者付费"的原则,使 ECT 对环境保护的广度与深度均相对于其他投资协定更加具体化,而且兼顾了东道国和投资者双方的环境保护义务,而不仅仅是强调东道国的义务。

(二)我国未来取向

在我国目前缔结或参加的投资协定中,涉及环境保护条款的不多。这和我国作为发

---

[1]　UNMCA 第 14.6 条,CPTPP 第 9.16 条。

[2]　Sanford E. Gaines, Environmental Policy Implications of Investor-State Arbitration under NAFTA Chapter 11, http://dx.doi.org/10.2139/ssrn.892438, last visited on 13 Feb. 2022.

展中国家的思维方式有关系,总担心这样的条款会给我国投资管理措施增加国际法上的限制。这种担心的理由有二:一是,有关投资条约中有环境保护条款或在序言中设立环境保护目的,缔约国的国内措施尤其是投资鼓励措施必须考虑到相关的环境保护因素。二是目前大部分发展中国家的投资措施尤其是投资鼓励措施将吸引外资作为基本目标,很少考虑到环保问题,主要体现在两个方面。一方面,为追求利润,西方国家跨国公司转嫁环境危害、故意输出严重污染环境的产业和技术的现象普遍存在;另一方面,资本输入国降低环境标准,一味追求眼前的经济发展速度和规模的现象时有发生。[①]

以降低环境标准为代价追求经济发展速度和规模、先污染后治理的发展模式早已被发展经济学家所否定。在我国参与制定多边投资规则时,应充分考虑到环境保护议题,并规定环境保护条款。虽然这会对东道国的投资措施施加约束,但从可持续发展看,可以促进包括我国在内的发展中国家采取有效措施保护自身环境,并基于环境保护的技术和相关经验有限,不能施加过高的环境保护标准,需要考虑到环境保护和投资利益的协调。

二、劳工保护条款

随着国际社会对人权的关注程度增加,劳工权利作为一种人权存在于国际公约中,劳工权利保护成为国家的义务。企业社会责任进入了全球化时代,劳工权利保护对国际投资产生了重要的经济影响和法律影响:它对工人工资待遇、劳动条件提出了改进的要求,提高了国际投资的生产成本;它使工会的谈判权增强,在投资中的影响力增大,集体劳工权利的行使给国际投资带来了新的风险,例如上汽收购韩国双龙公司案、绵延多年的首钢秘鲁铁矿公司罢工案都是在工会作用下引起的劳资纠纷和投资风险。

(一)劳工保护条款的实践

如前所述,OECD 最早倡议将劳工议题纳入国际投资条约,除了 MAI 草案有"关于环境和劳工的附加条款",还在 MAI 草案序言中声明:"遵守世界峰会哥本哈根声明中提出的承诺,遵守国际上公认的劳工权利,例如结社自由、集体谈判权利、禁止强制劳动、禁止使用童工、采取非歧视政策,以及承认国际劳工组织为制定世界范围核心劳工标准的权威机构。"在正文"不降低标准"一章中规定,"缔约方应认识到通过降低国内健康安全、环境标准或国内劳工标准来吸引外资的做法是不恰当的","缔约一方应努力确保其不免除或以其他方式减损,或提供免除或其他方式减损的机会,来鼓励一国境内投资的设立、收购、扩张或保留"等。MAI 草案还规定了劳工方面的磋商机制。在 MAI 附件中就劳工问题提出了立法建议声明,"多边投资协定并不限制政府非歧视性的正常管理活动,包括健康、安全事项以及设置劳工标准的措施等"。

---

① 刘笋:《国际投资与环境保护的法律冲突与协调——以晚近区域性投资条约及相关案例为研究对象》,载《现代法学》2006 年第 11 期。

国际投资规则中有效引入劳工保护条款依然发端于 NAFTA,其专门就劳工保护问题制定了作为附件的《北美劳工合作协定》(NAALC),要求 NAFTA 所有成员遵循。美国国会甚至将《北美劳工合作协定》的达成作为通过 NAFAT 的条件。NAFTA 率先将劳工问题纳入调整范围,试图通过建立劳工合作机制监督墨西哥劳工法的执行,以逐步提高墨西哥的劳工标准并使之符合美国的利益。这一做法是劳工问题纳入投资议题的开先河之举。该条款的内容不仅涉及具体权利义务还涉及程序性的救济措施和争端解决。

目前有关劳工保护的国际投资规则没有超越 NAFTA 的水平。OECD 2008 年《关于国际投资条约中环境劳工和反腐败事项的研究报告》显示,虽然大部分 OECD 成员国在有关国际投资协定序言中加入了类似条款,只有少数国家在条约中明确写入类似条款。① 即使在同样追求高水平投资待遇的 MAI 中,虽然序言、正文和附件均有涉及劳工问题,但缺乏像 NAFTA 那样的实质性内容和有力的措施。②

我国签订的个别投资协定中涉及劳工保护③,但基本都是在序言中,没有具体的权利义务,也没有具体的实施措施。在 CAFTAI 中有两处:一是序言涉及劳工保护条款,"保护提高和执行工人的基本权利,并加强各缔约方在劳工事项上的共同合作;在各自领域内创造新的就业机会,改善工作条件和生活水平;各缔约方各自建立其在劳工问题上的国际承诺"。二是其第 16 条第 5 款规定,缔约方之间的合作,能促进国际劳工组织宣言和劳工组织第 182 号公约中包含的核心劳工权利的实现,并建立一个劳工合作建设机制来提升劳工标准。但在具体实施措施、劳工权利保护范围等方面,没有更明确的规定。

综观各类投资协定,劳工保护条款多以国际公认的核心劳工标准为基础,采用"不降低标准"和"有权利规定"的用词规定劳工权利,对商谈可接受的工作条件等事项,目前还不具有普遍性。

(二)我国未来取向

在我国,外商投资企业劳务纠纷从未间断,海外投资企业和东道国当地频发劳工冲突,后者如赞比亚—科蓝煤矿劳资纠纷④、首钢秘鲁铁矿公司罢工风波⑤、上汽集团收购

---

① 有关情况可从经合组织网站获取,http://www.oecd.org/document/36/0.3343en264933783766400697961111l.00.html,最后访问日期:2022 年 2 月 23 日。

② James Salzman, Labor Rights, Globalization and Institutions: The Role and Influence of the Organization for Economic Cooperation and Development, *Michigan Journal of International Law*, 2000, Vol.21, p.828.

③ 中国与文莱、泰国、新加坡、圭亚那、多巴哥岛等五个 BIT。

④ 《赞比亚科蓝煤矿发生纠纷　再次警示中资企业》,http://finance.huanqiu.com/data/2012-08/3000273.html,最后访问日期:2022 年 12 月 23 日。

⑤ 《首钢 Hierro 秘鲁公司铁矿工人罢工》,http://finance.qq.com/a/20121010/000344.htm,最后访问日期:2022 年 12 月 23 日。

韩国双龙公司罢工①等,既说明我国海外投资企业在海外投资中处理劳资纠纷时缺乏经验,又说明我国法律在对海外投资行为的指导和约束方面有所缺陷。事实上,如前文所述,我国缔结或参加的国际投资协定中涉及劳工条款的数量较少,表明我国在以前参与制定双边或多边投资规则时未把劳工问题作为一个重要议题来对待。在越来越多的社会问题进入全球治理,国际经济立法和国际社会立法日趋密切联系的背景下,基于我国国际投资中劳资纠纷的现实,我国参与多边投资规则时应在规则中关注劳工议题。但是劳工条件的改善毕竟会增加产品成本,对投资与贸易利益造成损减,因此在我国现阶段关注此条款时不应施加过于严格的条件、实施过高的劳动保护水准。

三、例外条款

例外条款,又称逃避条款或者免责条款,是指在一定条件下排除缔约国行为违法性的条款。例外条款属于一种安全保障安排,发挥着安全阀的作用,对国际协定的存在及运作至关重要。②

该条款最初出现在贸易领域。在GATT/WTO框架下,该条款作为一项义务豁免规则或责任豁免规则存在,成员方可以在违反义务时援引该规则,使自己不承担相应的法律责任。例外条款适用于国际投资领域是晚近才出现的现象。20世纪90年代以来,越来越多的国际投资协定规定例外条款,以确保投资者利益与东道国监管之间的平衡。③

例外条款有一般例外和根本安全例外两种。

(一)一般例外条款

1.一般例外条款的实践

一般例外条款的基本内容是,基于保护人类、动植物生命或健康或者为保护生物或非生物可用竭自然资源的措施而允许采取背离条约义务。加拿大2004年范本第10条规定,在遵守关于此类措施的实施不得在投资之间或投资者之间构成武断或不合理的歧视或者不对国际贸易或投资构成变相歧视的前提下,本协定的任何规定不得解释为阻止缔约一方采取或实施下列必要措施:(a)保护人类、动物或植物生命或健康;(b)为确保遵守与本协定规定不相抵触的法律或法规;(c)为保护生物或非生物可用竭自然资源的措施。CAFTAI第16条规定的一般例外为:(1)为保护公共道德或维护公共秩序所必需的措施。(2)为保护人类、动物或植物的生命或健康所必需的措施。(3)为使与本协定规定不相抵触的法律或规章得到遵守所必需的措施,包括与下列有关的法律或规章:防止欺

---

① 《韩国双龙罢工暴动》,http://www.eeo.com.cn/2009/0805/146721.shtml,最后访问日期:2022年3月6日。

② 刘京莲:《国际投资条约根本安全例外条款研究》,载《国际经济法学刊》2010年第1期。

③ Suzanne A. Spears, *The Quest for Policy Space in a New Generation of International Investment Agreements*, Oxford University Press, 2010, p.23.

骗和欺诈行为或处理服务合同违约所产生的影响；保护与个人信息处理和传播有关个人隐私及保护个人记录和账户的机密性；安全。（4）旨在确保对任何缔约方投资或投资者公平或有效地课征或收取直接税。（5）为保护具有艺术、历史或考古价值的国宝所采取的措施。（6）与保护不可再生自然资源有关的措施，若这些措施与限制国内生产或消费一同实施。

国际投资协定中采用一般例外条款是以更多限制来防止滥用的条件范围为前提的。一般例外条款对援引方更少施加严苛条件，[①]不要求国家证明特定措施是"必需"的，只要求国家证明措施对实现目标是适当的。[②]

2.我国未来取向

一般例外条款涉及社会公共利益，其后果是豁免条约义务，而我国参与相关条款的经验比较缺乏，我国在参与多边投资规则制定时，可以考虑移植美国2004年BIT范本和CAFTAI相关内容，就一般例外可作如下规定，"在此类措施的实施不在类似情形缔约方、缔约方投资者或投资者投资之间构成任意或不合理歧视的手段，或不构成变相限制任何缔约方投资者或其设立投资的前提下，本协定的任何规定不得解释为阻止任何缔约方采取或实施以下措施：（1）为保护公共道德或维护公共秩序所必需的。（2）为保护人类、动物或植物生命或健康所必需的。（3）为使与本协定规定不相抵触的法律或规章得到遵守所必需的，包括与下列有关的法律或规章：（a）防止欺骗和欺诈行为或处理服务合同违约所产生的影响；（b）保护与个人信息处理和传播有关个人隐私及保护个人记录和账户的机密性；和（c）安全。（4）旨在确保对任何缔约方的投资或投资者公平或有效课征或收取直接税。（5）为保护具有艺术、历史或考古价值的国宝所采取的。（6）与保护不可再生自然资源有关的，若这些措施与限制国内生产或消费一同实施"。

（二）根本安全例外条款

该条款是指一国为保护对本国根本安全具有重要意义的利益可以采取的背离条约义务的例外条款。它是国际投资条约中维护国家安全利益的重要条款，但是否将其纳入投资规则，是颇具争议的问题。

1.根本安全例外条款的实践

据统计，截至2008年年底，在2676个双边投资条约中，有大约两百多个包含有该条款，且大部分是在20世纪90年代以后随着ICSID受案量激增而出现的。[③]根据OECD的统计，包含根本安全例外条款的国际投资规则有：NAFTA第2102条、ECT第24条和MAI草案；包含国际安全例外条款的双边投资条约范本主要有：加拿大2004年BIT范

---

① 林一：《简论新一代国际投资协定中的一般例外规则》，载《甘肃政法学院学报》2012年第11期。
② 2002年哥伦比亚BIT第8条。
③ William W. Bruke，White & Andreas Von Staden，Investment Protection in Extraordinary Times：The Implication and Application of Non-Preclude Measures Provisions in Bilateral Investment Treaties，*Virginia Journal of International Law*，2008，Vol.2，p.370.

本、德国 2005 年 BIT 范本、印度 2003 年 BIT 范本、美国 2004 年和 2012 年 BIT 范本、中国 2010 年范本等。①

2.我国未来取向

根本安全例外条款是国际投资规则中对东道国利益进行保护的最后一道阀门,成为保护国家安全利益的最重要条款。只要运用得当,即可将投资协定所制定的一系列对投资者和母国作出的承诺大打折扣,即使在国际投资规则中承诺对投资和投资者给予高水平保护,东道国可以基于国家安全利益理由采取必要措施,即使这些措施对投资者造成损害,也无须赔偿。

我国在国际投资中身份混同日重。作为一个正在成长中的资本输出国,应当为海外投资创造有利的投资环境,提供高水平的法律保护,积极参与国际投资规则的制定,推动投资自由化。作为资本输入国,应充分考虑对国家安全和公共利益的保护。因此,在我国参与制定多边投资规则过程中,应当采用根本安全例外条款,但在运用上应当考虑灵活性,以实现既保护投资者的权益又注重本国安全利益的目的。

四、投资措施和履行要求禁止条款

投资措施和履行要求是东道国政府行使外资管理权,对外资进行限制以实现东道国经济目标的惯常做法。

(一)投资措施与履行要求禁止条款的实践

在以投资自由化为目标的国际投资条约中存在着大量的限制投资措施和履行要求的条款。在区域性投资条约中,NAFTA 第 1106 条和第 1107 条限制涉及以下投资措施和履行要求:出口比例要求、国内成分要求、当地成分要求、外汇平衡要求、贸易平衡要求、技术转让要求、独占性技术许可要求、销售渠道要求、高级管理人员雇用要求等;CPTPP 第 9.10 条和 USMCA 第 14.10 条更详细规定了禁止和限制履行要求的具体情形,前者禁止 9 种、限制 4 种②,后者禁止 9 种、限制 5 种;③RCEP 第 10.6 条则禁止 8 种、限制 4 种。④ 上述限制和禁止不仅适用于准入后的经营运行阶段,还适用于准入前的设立阶段,甚至扩展到收购和扩张阶段。在双边投资条约中,以美国范本为例。美国 2004 年 BIT 范本中禁止的投资措施和履行要求和 NAFTA 如出一辙⑤,2012 年 BIT 范本中增加了技术买卖和使用要求,进一步扩大了禁止和限制的范围⑥。这些区域和双边投资

---

① Essential Security Interests under Investment Law,http://www.oecd.org /data oecd /59/50/4024 34ll.pdf,last visited on 12 Nov. 2012.

② CPTPP 第 9.10 条"履行要求"第 1、2 款。

③ USMCA 第 14.10 条"履行要求"第 1、2 款。

④ RCEP 第 10.6 条"禁止履行要求"第 1、2 款。

⑤ 美国 2004 年 BIT 范本第 8 条。

⑥ 美国 2012 年 BIT 范本第 8 条第 1 款第(h)条。

条约中的禁止和限制条款建立在国民待遇、最惠国待遇和透明度要求的基础上,力图实现消减东道国管理措施和政策措施的影响,实现投资自由化。但这些措施通常是发展中国家普遍采用的投资鼓励或投资管理措施,几乎囊括了发展中国家采取的绝大部分投资措施,对这些措施进行限制或禁止会大大缩减东道国对外资的管理权,因此发展中国对这些条款比较抵触。

为在更广泛范围内实现投资自由化、消除履行要求的障碍,发达国家试图将履行要求禁止引入 GATT 框架中。在乌拉圭回合谈判中,以美国为首的发达国家提出了 13 种投资措施,包括当地股权要求、许可证要求、汇款限制要求、外汇限制要求、制造限制、技术转让要求、国内销售要求、制造方面的要求、产品指令要求、贸易平衡、当地含量、出口要求、进口替代等。经过多方博弈和利益交换,最终达成了协商一致,形成 TRIMs 协定,将禁止的投资措施限于与国际贸易有关的范围内,禁止采取与 GATT 第 4 条"国民待遇"和第 11 条"数量限制"不符的投资措施,禁止采取对贸易造成扭曲的 4 种投资措施,即当地成分要求、贸易平衡要求、外汇平衡要求和当地含量要求。TRIMs 协定基本上实现了对东道国的有损于投资自由化措施的限制,但又考虑到了发展中国家的正常诉求和利益。

(二)我国未来取向

我国既是资本输入国又是资本输出国,在参与制定多边投资规则中,对禁止或限制投资措施和履行要求的态度、具体做法要兼顾这两种地位。

作为资本输入国,我国在对外商投资进行管理时采取了大量的投资措施和履行要求。虽然在 2001 年加入 WTO 前后进行了修订以使国内措施符合 WTO-TRIMs 协定,但若以重要区域投资协定的规定为标准,我国大部分对外资管理的措施将被禁止或限制,会对我国的外资管理和产业政策产生冲击,因此在参与多边投资规则制定时应当慎重对待投资措施和履行要求禁止或限制条款。

作为资本输出国,东道国履行要求的消除将为我国正常投资和贸易提供自由流动的机会,创造有利的发展环境,因此有着消除这些履行要求的内在需求,所以我国在参加多边投资规则制定时,应当对这些投资措施和履行要求禁止和限制予以肯定。

综合我国混同身份所面临的对同一问题不同的立场,基本取向是应当根据不同谈判对象采纳不同的履行要求禁止或限制。例如:在与周边国家、自由贸易区贸易伙伴、区域性或非区域性的发展中国家谈判多边投资规则时,可以采取较窄范围的履行要求禁止或限制。因我国在履行要求禁止和限制方面缺乏经验,且我国外资法中有履行要求,因此在条款设计时宜粗不宜细,可以给条约解释留下余地。在与发达国家或参与普遍性多边投资谈判时,不宜超出 TRIMs 协定所确定的禁止履行要求的范围,在适用阶段上不宜扩展至准入阶段。

第三节　我国参与制定多边投资规则的
谈判条文学者建议稿

　　基于以上对国际投资规则中主要条款及其发展的分析和我国对国际投资条约一般条款和特殊条款取向的研究,结合我国国际投资的现状,考虑到参与不同类型的国际投资规则的特点和不同立场,就我国参与制定多边投资规则提出以下学者建议稿。

一、区域性多边投资规则条文建议稿

(一)建议稿的基础

1.地缘政治和友好相邻关系

　　参与区域性经济合作的国家大多是基于地缘政治和友好相邻关系,在地区间利益相互较量和相互博弈过程中,形成了良好的合作机制,不但在经济利益和贸易利益的实现方面,而且在其他政策层面,非传统利益如政治、外交、安全等也应运而生。[1] 在区域性多边投资规则制定过程中,需要考虑到本地区国家间除经济利益之外的其他利益目标的实现和其他领域的合作因素,还需考虑自由贸易区投资协定和其他区域性投资协定在谈判对象和合作程度方面的区别和差异。

2.推进区域内投资自由化

　　由于参与区域性多边投资规则制定的国家数量较少,谈判成本较低,容易达成一致,投资自由化的推动比较容易达成。我国目前海外投资发展势头迅猛,需要国家通过国际投资条约来保护海外投资,因此可以考虑在区域性投资条约中增加较多的投资自由化的相关内容,推进地区内投资的自由流动。

3.考虑不同发展水平国家的发展需求

　　由于区域内国家的发展水平有差异,要想获得更大范围的认同和推进区域的合作,必须考虑到不同发展水平国家的发展需求,有必要在区域投资协定中增加有关促进、发展的内容。

(二)自由贸易区投资协定范本建议

　　无论是采取“一揽子模式”还是“分立模式”,自由贸易区投资协定都需要考虑投资议题和其他议题的协调,应当在投资协定的序文中增加有关投资同自由贸易区其他协定或

---

　　①　Fernandez and Poters,Returns to Regionalism——An Analysis of Non-Traditional Gains from Regional Trade Agreements,*World Bank Economic Review*,1998,Vol.8,pp.197-220.

议题之间相互关系的内容,在采取分立模式时还需考虑后续签订其他协定的需求,表达出投资协定促进自由贸易区建立的目标和倾向。

拟提出以下建议稿:

中国—××自由贸易区投资协定范本

诸缔约方,

充分认识到为建立中国—××自由贸易区和促进投资,建立一个自由、便利、透明及竞争的投资体制,各缔约方达成一项投资协定,以逐步实现投资体制自由化,加强投资领域的合作,促进投资便利化和提高投资相关法律法规的透明度,并为投资提供保护;

考虑到诸缔约方之间不同的发展阶段和速度,对发展中国家实行特殊和差别待遇的必要性;

考虑到投资与环境、人权特别是劳工权利之间的相互关系,诸缔约方应当尽量以符合环境目标和国际社会认可的劳工权利保护的方式促进投资。

兹达成条款如下。

第一条　定义

1.投资者,指正在或已在缔约一方境内从事投资的缔约另一方自然人或法人。其中:自然人,指根据该缔约另一方法律拥有其国籍、公民身份或永久居民权的任何自然人;法人,指根据该缔约另一方法律组建或组织的任何法律实体,无论其是否以营利为目的,属私人所有还是政府所有,且在该缔约另一方境内具有实质性经营,包括任何公司、信托、合伙企业、合资企业、个人独资企业或社团。

2.**方案一:以国际货币基金组织投资定义为基准**

投资,指具有缔约一方居民对缔约另一方居民企业实施管理上的控制或重要影响之特征的投资,包括带来控制或影响的股权和与此股权关系有关的投资,含投资于间接影响或控制的企业联属企业、债务和逆向投资。

方案二:以企业为基础之投资定义为基准

投资,指缔约一方投资者在缔约另一方领土内设立、获取或扩大的一企业,包括该投资者通过设立、维持或获取一法人,或获取该企业股份、债券或其他所有权文书,条件是该企业根据该缔约另一方法律建立或获取并按其法律要求被注册、批准、承认。此等企业可以拥有以下资产:

(a)该企业或另一企业的股份、股票、债券和其他权益文书;

(b)另一企业的债务担保;

(c)对一企业的贷款;

(d)动产或不动产和诸如抵押、留置或典当之类的其他财产权;

(e)金钱请求权,或对合同项下具有金融价值的任何履行的请求权;

(f)按该缔约另一方法律认可范围内的版权、专有技术、信誉和诸如专利、商标、工业设计、商号之类的知识产权;

(g)法律或按合同赋予的权利,包括种植、提炼或开发自然资源的许可。

投资不包括：

(i)政府发行的债务证券，或对政府的贷款；

(ii)组合投资；

(iii)仅产生于缔约一方领土内国民或企业向缔约另一方企业销售货物或服务之商事合同的金钱请求权，或者与商事交易有关的信用扩张，或对不涉及上述(a)至(g)项中所列各种利益的金钱请求权。

方案三：以资产为基础之投资定义为基准(一)

投资，指根据缔约一方法律规章准许或准入的下列资产：

(1)一企业。

(2)一企业的一项权益担保。

(3)以下情形的一企业的一债务担保：

(a)该企业是投资者的一附属企业；或

(b)该债务担保初始期限至少3年，但不包括一国家或国家企业的一项债务担保，不考虑其初始期限。

(4)对以下情形的一企业的贷款：

(a)该企业是投资者的一附属企业，或

(b)贷款初始期限至少3年，但不包括对一国家企业的贷款，不考虑其初始期限。

(5)在使所有权人有权利分享收入或利润的一企业中的一项利益。

(6)在使所有权人有权利分享解散企业资产中的一项利益，但不是被上述第(3)项或第(4)项中排除的债务担保或贷款。

(7)预期获得的或为了经济利益或其他经营目的使用的有形或无形的不动产或其他财产。

(8)在缔约另一方领土内对其境内经济活动承诺资本或其他资源所产生的利益，诸如：

(a)涉及投资者在该缔约另一方领土内财产所存在的合同，包括总控钥匙合同或建筑合同，或特许权，或

(b)回报实质上依赖一企业之生产、收益或利润的合同。

(9)投资不包括仅具有以下性质的资产：组合投资；信誉；不论是否基于源自缔约一方之贸易的市场份额或贸易权；仅衍生于向缔约另一方领土或从缔约一方向缔约另一方领土销售货物或服务之商事合同的金钱请求权，或仅衍生于向缔约另一方或其国家企业贷款的金钱请求权；银行信用证；与诸如贸易融资之类商事交易有关的信用扩张；或对缔约另一方或其国家企业的贷款，或缔约一方或其国家企业对此等贷款发出的债务担保。

(10)一项资产必须具有诸如承诺资本或其他资源投入、期望获利、承担风险和对本国发展具有重要性的投资特性。投资或再投资的资产在形式上的任何改变，不应当影响其作为投资的特性。

方案四：以资产为基础之投资定义为基准(二)

投资，指根据东道国缔约方法律规章准许或形成的任何资产，包括：

（1）动产、不动产和诸如抵押、留置和典当之类的其他相关财产权。

（2）对货币、货物、服务或具有经济价值的其他履行的请求权。

（3）诸企业的股票、股份、债券和此等企业财产中的利益。

（4）与东道国缔约方领土内经营业务关联的知识产权、技术工艺、专有技术、信誉和其他利益或益处。

（5）法律或按合同赋予的商业特许权，包括：

（a）建设、营运、拥有/移交、改造、扩大、重建和/或改善基础设施的合同；和

（b）研究、种植、提炼或开发自然资源的特许权。

（6）投资不包括仅具有以下性质的资产：组合投资；信誉；不论是否基于源自缔约一方之贸易的市场份额或贸易权；仅衍生于向或从缔约一方领土向缔约另一方领土销售货物或服务之商事合同的金钱请求权，或向该缔约另一方或其国家企业贷款的金钱请求权；银行信用证；与诸如贸易融资之类商事交易有关的信用扩张。

（7）一项资产必须具有诸如承诺资本或其他资源投入、期望获利、承担风险和对东道国发展具有重要性的投资特性。投资或再投资的资产在形式上的任何改变，不应当影响其作为投资的特性。

3.措施，包括缔约一方采取的影响投资者和/或投资的普遍适用的任何法律、法规、规章、规则、程序、行政决定或行政行为。

4.收益，指获利于或源自一项投资的总金额，其中包括但不限于利润、利息、资本所得、红利、版税或酬金。投资收益和再投资时的那些再投资收益，享有与投资相同的保护。

5.政府采购，指政府为公共目的获取商品和服务的过程。政府采购不得以商业销售或转售为目的，或被用于商业销售或转售产品、服务的生产和供应。

6.ICSID 公约，指 1965 年 3 月 18 日在华盛顿开放签署的《解决国家与他国国民间投资争端公约》。

7.ICSID，指依据 ICSID 公约设立的"解决投资争端国际中心"。

第二条　适用范围

1.本协定适用于缔约一方采取和维持的以下措施：

（a）与缔约他方的投资者有关；

（b）与涵盖投资有关。

2.本协定不适用于本协定生效前发生的任何缔约方的行为或事实，或曾经存在但已终止的其他情形。

第三条　国民待遇

缔约一方应当给予缔约他方投资者及其投资在其境内设立、获取、扩大、管理、运营、转让、出售或其他处置方面的待遇，不低于该缔约一方在同等情况下给予其本国投资者及其投资的待遇。

第四条　最惠国待遇

缔约一方给予缔约他方投资者及其投资在其境内设立、获取、扩大、管理、运营、出售

或其他处置方面的待遇,不应当低于其在同等情况下给予任何第三国投资者或其投资的待遇。但是,本条规定的义务不应当包含要求给予缔约他方投资者除本条规定以外的争端解决程序。

第五条 公平公正待遇

1.各缔约方应当按照国际习惯法的要求,赋予涵盖投资公平公正待遇和充分保护与安全。

2.为避免歧义,第1款规定的待遇水平应当将国际习惯法外国人最低待遇标准作为对涵盖投资的最低待遇标准。"公平公正待遇"和"充分保护与安全"的概念既不能超出最低待遇标准,也不创设额外实体权利。第1款下规定的各缔约方以下义务:

(a)"公平公正待遇"包含保证刑事、民事或行政裁决程序符合世界主要法律体系中正当程序和正义要求的各项义务;和

(b)"充分保护与安全"要求各缔约方根据国际习惯法要求标准给予的治安保护水平。国际习惯法,指源自各缔约方产生于法律义务感的普遍和一致实践。

3.对本协定其他条款或其他国际条约的违反不构成对本条的违反。

4.尽管本协定有任何规定,任何缔约方应当保证遵守其对缔约另一方投资者的投资作出的任何承诺。

第六条 利益拒绝

若作为缔约另一方企业的投资者是由非缔约方和拒绝给予利益的缔约方的投资者所拥有或控制,且拒绝给予利益的缔约方与该非缔约方之间没有正常经济关系,缔约一方可以拒绝将本协定的利益给予该缔约另一方的投资者。

第七条 征收

1.各缔约方不应当直接或间接通过征收、国有化或类似措施对涵盖投资进行征收或国有化,但符合以下者除外:

(a)为公共目的;

(b)以非歧视的方式;

(c)给予本条第2款所述的补偿;和

(d)符合法律正当程序和第五条"公平公正待遇"规定。

2.补偿应以征收公布时或征收发生时被征收投资的公平市场价值计算,以较早者为准。补偿应当允许以可自由兑换货币从东道国自由转移。补偿的偿清和支付不应当不合理延迟。公平市场价值不应当因征收事先被公众知悉而发生任何价值变化。

3.若发生延迟,补偿应当包括按主要商业利率计算的自征收发生日至支付日之间的利息。包括应付利息在内的补偿,应当以原投资货币或应投资者请求以可自由兑换货币进行支付。

4.对征收和类似措施的解释

(1)通过正式移转所有权或直接没收形式进行的直接征收或国有化除外,征收措施包括缔约一方为达到使投资者的投资陷于实质上无法产生收益或不能产生回报境地而故意采取的一项或一系列措施,但不涉及正式移转所有权或直接没收。

(2)在一特定情形下确定缔约一方的一项或一系列措施是否构成上述第1项所述措施,需进行以事实为依据的个案审查,该审查应当考虑以下各因素:

a.该项或一系列措施的经济影响,但仅有缔约一方的一项或一系列措施负面影响投资的经济价值的事实,不足以推断已经发生了征收或国有化;

b.该项或一系列措施在范围或适用上歧视某一缔约方或某一投资者或某一企业的程度;

c.该项或一系列措施违背明显、合理、以投资为依据的预期之程度;

d.该项或一系列措施的性质和目的,是不是为了善意公共利益目标而采取,以及在该等措施和征收目的之间是否存在合理联系。

(3)特殊情形除外,缔约一方采取的旨在保护公共利益的非歧视管制措施,包括根据司法机关作出的具有普遍适用效力的裁决所采取的措施,不构成间接征收或国有化。

第八条　利润汇回

1.缔约一方应当确保缔约他方的投资者在其境内与投资有关的资金毫不迟延地转移出其领土,这些转移特别包括但不限于:

(1)建立、维持和扩大投资所必需的款项;

(2)利润、利息、股息、资本收益、版税和其他费用;

(3)基于合同所得的偿付,包括根据贷款协议的偿付;

(4)全部或部分出售或清算资产获得的款项;

(5)根据第七条所得的偿付;

(6)根据第二十一条因争端解决所得的偿付;

(7)在缔约一方领土内从事与投资有关活动的缔约他方的国民的收入和其他报酬。

2.除非本协定有相反规定,任何缔约方不当应阻碍以可自由兑换货币按转移日该货币通行市场汇率毫不迟延地实施转移。

3.尽管存在上述第1款和第2款规定,缔约一方可以通过公平、非歧视、善意适用其与以下有关的法律迟延或阻止转移:

(1)破产、倒闭或者保护债权人权利;

(2)证券或衍生工具的发行、买卖或交易;

(3)犯罪或触犯刑法,或者保证遵循司法程序中的判决或命令;

(4)在协助执法或金融监管当局所必要时对转移的金融报告或保存记录。

4.尽管存在本协定其他条款,各缔约方可以在以下情况下根据其法律规章,采取或维持与本条义务不一致的措施:

(1)存在收支平衡和外部财政方面的严重困难或有此等困难威胁;或

(2)例外情况下,资本转移引起特别是金融和汇率政策方面宏观经济管理的严重困难或者此等困难威胁。

5.上述第4款所述的措施必须:

(1)符合《国际货币基金协定》条款,各缔约方作出保留的除外;

(2)不超过处理上述第4款中情形所必要;

(3)是临时的且在条件许可时被取消;

(4)即刻通知给缔约他方。

第九条 代位

1.若任何缔约方或其指定的任何代理人、机构、法定机构或公司,依照保险向其本国投资者就有关投资或其任何部分按本协定形成的请求权进行了支付,其他相关缔约方应当承认此缔约方或其指定的任何代理人、机构、法定机构或公司有资格代位行使其投资者的权利和请求权。代位的权利或请求权不应当超出投资者的原始权利或请求权。

2.若缔约一方或其指定的任何代理人、机构、法定机构或公司已向其投资者进行了支付且已接管了该投资者的权利和请求权,该投资者不应当向缔约他方主张这些权利或请求权,除非该投资者被授权代表该缔约一方或进行了支付的代理机构采取行动。

第十条 透明度

1.各缔约方应当保证其与本协定所涉及事项有关的下列者被适当公开且可供公众查询:

(a)法律、法规、工作程序和具有普遍拘束力的行政规章;和

(b)司法判决。

2.本条所称"具有普遍拘束力的行政规章",是在其管辖范围内普遍适用且作为行为准则的一项行政规定或解释,但不包括:

(a)在特定情况下,行政或准司法程序针对缔约他方特定投资或其投资者的决定或裁定;

(b)针对特定行为或事实作出的规定。

3.建立或指定一个咨询点,缔约他方的任何自然人、法人或任何人可以要求并及时获得第1款和第2款下要求公布的与措施有关的全部信息。

4.各缔约方同意定期举行谈判,以提高投资法律规章的透明度。

第十一条 不适用措施

1.第三条"国民待遇"、第四条"最惠国待遇"不适用于:

(1)任何现存的在其境内维持的不符措施;

(2)上述第(1)项所述任何不符措施的延续;

(3)对上述第(1)项所述任何不符措施的修改,只要这种修改不增加该措施在修改前已存在的不符此等义务的程度。

不符措施不应当超过现有水平,并将努力逐渐消除这些不符措施。

2.第三条"国民待遇"、第四条"最惠国待遇"不适用于:

(a)政府采购;或

(b)缔约一方的补贴或拨款,包括政府贷款、保证和保险。

第十二条 税收

1.本条另有规定除外,本协定不适用于税收措施。

2.本协定不应当影响各缔约方在任何税收协定下的权利和义务。若本协定的规定与任何税收条约的规定不一致,此税收条约的规定应当在不一致的范围内予以适用。若各

缔约方同为一税收条约的缔约国,该条约规定的相关税收当局应当对其决定本协定与该条约是否存在不一致负责。

3.本协定第七条的规定应当适用于涉嫌具有征收性质的税收措施。

4.本协定的争端解决条款适用于本条第3款规定的税收措施。

5.投资者援引第七条作为根据第二十一条提请仲裁请求的依据,应当适用下述程序:

该投资者应当将该税收措施是否与征收有关,提交给东道国税收主管机关。各缔约方税收主管机关应当举行磋商。自提交之日起6个月后,若各缔约方税收主管机关未能达成一致协议而认定该措施与征收无关,或各缔约方税收主管机关未举行相互磋商,该投资者有权利根据第二十一条规定提起仲裁请求。

第十三条　履行要求的限制

各缔约方应当尽可能不采取与本协定第三条"国民待遇"、第四条"最惠国待遇"、第十条"透明度"相违背的对贸易或投资造成扭曲和变相限制的措施。各缔约方承诺不采取与 WTO-TRIMs 协定相冲突的措施。

第十四条　反腐败与反非法行为的措施

1.各缔约方应采取或维持措施,尽力防止和打击与本协定所涉事项有关的腐败、洗钱和恐怖主义融资。

2.本协定中的任何规定不应当强制任何缔约方保护以非法来源资本或非法来源资产进行的投资,或保护其设立或营运经证实有因资产流失或腐败行为而遭受过制裁的非法行为的投资。

第十五条　社会责任政策

1.各缔约方认识到促进在其境内营运或受其管辖的公司实施可持续性和社会责任政策并促进东道国发展的重要性。

2.投资者及其投资应当尽最大努力遵守经济合作与发展组织的《跨国企业准则》,特别是:

(a)以可持续发展视角提升经济、社会、环境的发展;

(b)尊重参与公司活动的人员的国际公认人权;

(c)通过与本地社区密切合作,促进发展当地能力;

(d)鼓励发展人力资本,特别是通过创造就业机会,并为员工提供培训;

(e)避免寻求或接受与人权、环境、健康、安全、工作、税收制度、财政激励或其他事项相关的法律或监管框架中未考虑的豁免;

(f)支持和捍卫良好公司治理原则,并制定和实施良好的公司治理实践;

(g)制定和实施自律且有效的管理制度,促进公司与其开展活动的社区之间的相互信任关系;

(h)通过适当传播公司政策,包括通过培训计划,促进员工对公司政策的了解和遵守;

(i)不得对善意准备向管理层或在适当情况下向公共主管部门报告违反法律或公司政策的行为的员工采取歧视或纪律措施;

(j)尽可能鼓励其商业合作伙伴,包括供应商和承包商,采用符合本条所述原则的商业行为准则;和

(k)避免干预当地政治活动。

第十六条 环境

1.各缔约方确认多边环境公约和各自国内环境保护法律规章在环境保护中的重要作用。

2.各缔约方承认通过降低和减少国内环境保护法律的规定来鼓励投资是不可取的。因此,各缔约方承诺,不通过放弃或减损这些法律的方式或者不能有效地执行这些环境法律规章的作为或不作为来作为对其境内设立、获取、扩大投资的鼓励。

3.各缔约方可以采取、维持或执行其认为与本协定相符的能保证其境内投资活动意识到保护环境重要性的措施。

4.对任何缔约方就本条任何规定作出的书面磋商请求,缔约他方应当在30个工作日内给予书面回复,以示收到了此磋商请求。此后各缔约方应当举行磋商并达成均满意的解决办法。

第十七条 劳工

1.各缔约方重申作为国际劳工组织成员国的义务,并重申《国际劳工组织关于工作中的基本原则和权利宣言》下的承诺。

2.各缔约方认识到通过降低和减少国内劳工保护法的规定来鼓励投资是不合适的。因此,各缔约方承诺,不通过放弃或减损这些法律与国际公认的劳工权利的一致性来作为对其境内设立、获取、扩大投资的鼓励。若缔约一方认为缔约另一方采取了类似鼓励措施,可以请求与该缔约另一方磋商。各缔约方应当力求避免采取类似措施。

3.本条所称"劳工保护法",指各缔约方与以下国际公认的劳工权利直接相关的法律或规章:

(a)集会的自由;

(b)组织和集体谈判的权利;

(c)禁止使用暴力或强迫劳动的权利;

(d)有效保护儿童和未成年劳工的权利,包括最低工作年龄和禁止使用、虐待童工;

(e)有效消除雇用和职业歧视;

(f)关于最低工资、工作时间和职业安全健康方面的正常工作条件。

4.对任何缔约方就本条任何规定作出的书面磋商请求,缔约他方应当在30个工作日内给予书面回复,以示收到了该磋商请求。此后各缔约方应当举行磋商并达成均满意的解决办法。

5.各缔约方确认,各缔约方视情况而定,对本条下的任何事项提供公众参与机会。

第十八条 一般例外

在有关措施的实施不在类似情形的缔约方、缔约方投资者或其投资之间构成任意或不合理歧视的手段,或不构成变相限制任何缔约方投资者或其设立的投资的前提下,本协定的任何规定不应当解释为阻止任何缔约方采取或实施以下措施:

（1）为保护公共道德或维护公共秩序所必要的。

（2）为保护人类、动植物的生命或健康所必要的。

（3）为使与本协定规定不抵触的法律或规章得到遵守所必要的，包括与下列有关的法律或规章：

a.防止欺骗和欺诈行为或处理服务合同违约所产生的影响；

b.保护与个人信息处理和传播有关个人隐私以及保护个人记录与账户的机密性；和

c.安全。

（4）旨在确保对任何缔约方的投资或投资者公平或有效课征或收取直接税的。

（5）为保护具有艺术、历史或考古价值的国宝所采取的。

（6）与保护不可再生自然资源相关的，若这些措施与限制国内生产或消费一同实施。

第十九条 根本安全例外

1.本协定的任何规定不应当解释为要求各缔约方提供其认为若披露则会违背其根本安全利益的任何信息。

2.本协定的任何规定不应当解释为阻止缔约一方为了保护本国根本安全利益、根据本国法律、在非歧视的基础上采取其认为必要的措施。除非缔约一方采取的措施与所维护的根本安全利益之间严重不成比例，缔约一方对由此给投资者造成的损失不负责任。若缔约一方采取的措施与所维护的根本安全利益之间严重不成比例，该缔约方应当承担责任，但应当充分考虑该缔约方采取讼争措施时所处的情势。

3.本协定的任何规定不应当解释为阻止缔约一方为了履行维护国际和平与安全义务所采取的其认为必要的任何措施。该缔约方对由此给投资者造成的损失不承担责任。

第二十条 缔约方之间争端的解决

1.若任何缔约方请求解决与本协定有关的任何争端，或者请求讨论与本协定的解释或适用、本协定目标的实现等有关的事项，各争端缔约方应当立刻通过外交途径举行磋商。

2.若争端未在6个月内解决，应当根据任一争端缔约方的请求，将此争端提交专设仲裁庭解决。

3.仲裁庭由3名仲裁员组成。各争端缔约方应当自收到请求仲裁的书面通知之日起2个月内共同任命3名仲裁员，并共同选定其中1位与争端各方均有外交关系的非争端缔约方的国民担任首席仲裁员。

4.若仲裁庭自收到请求仲裁的书面通知之日起4个月内未组成，且各争端缔约方之间无其他协议，任何争端缔约方可以提请国际法院院长作出必要任命。若国际法院院长是任一争端缔约方的国民或因其他原因不能履行此项任命，应当提请国际法院中非任何缔约方国民且无其他不胜任原因的最资深法官履行此项必要任命。

5.仲裁庭应当决定其自身程序。仲裁庭应当依据本协定、各缔约方共同认可的国际法原则、全体缔约方共同作出的决定作出裁决。

6.仲裁庭应以多数票作出裁决。裁决应当自仲裁庭组成之日起10个月内作出。裁决是终局的，对各缔约方均有拘束力。应任何缔约方的请求，仲裁庭应解释其作出裁决的理由。

7.各争端缔约方应当各自承担其出席仲裁程序的费用,仲裁员和仲裁庭的相关费用应由争端各方平均承担。

第二十一条 投资者与缔约一方争端的解决

1.为了本条目的,本条所称争端,指缔约一方与缔约他方投资者之间的指控该缔约一方违反本协定造成或导致了缔约他方投资者投资的损害和损失的争端。

2.若发生争端,该争端应当尽可能通过协商或谈判解决。若协商或谈判未解决,投资者应当将该争端提交以下途径之一解决:

(1)投资所在地有管辖权的法院;

(2)在争端被争端任何一方提请协商之日起4个月后,国际仲裁。

3.在国际仲裁的情况下,根据投资者的选择,可以将争端提交至:

(1)依据1965年3月18日在华盛顿签署的ICSID公约设立的ICSID;或者

(2)根据《联合国国际贸易法委员会仲裁规则》或者经争端各方同意的其他任何仲裁规则设立的仲裁庭。

争端缔约方可以要求相关投资者在提交国际仲裁之前用尽该缔约方的法律规章规定的国内行政复议程序。国内行政复议程序,包括要求提交文件的时间,自复议申请提交日起算,不得超过4个月。若在4个月内没有完成此程序,它将被视为已经完成,投资者可以提起国际仲裁。投资者可以在本条第2款第(2)项规定的4个月期间,提起行政复议程序。

各缔约方同意,争端投资者将争端提交至有拘束力的国际仲裁解决。

4.若投资者将争端提交给有管辖权的投资所在地法院、ICSID或者依本条第3款第(2)项组成的仲裁庭,三种程序中的任一程序选择,应当是终局的。

5.根据本条第3款提起争端解决的投资者应当在提出请求之前至少90日向争端缔约方发出书面通知,说明其提起争端解决的意向。此通知应当列明:

(1)争端投资者的名称和地址;

(2)争端缔约方的具体争议措施、能充分清楚说明争议事项的事实和法律根据的摘要,包括指控争端缔约方所违反的本协定条款;

(3)寻求的救济措施,包括必要的请求赔偿大约额;和

(4)争端投资者寻求本条第3款(1)(2)项中所列的争端解决程序。

6.仲裁裁决应当基于本协定、各缔约方对本协定的共同解释或共同决定、各缔约方共同接受的国际法原则、争端缔约方的法律(包括冲突法规则)。

7.尽管有本条第3款的规定,若自投资者首次知道或者应当知道其遭受损失或损害之日起已超过3年,投资者不得根据本条第3款提出请求。

8.仲裁裁决是终局的,对争端各方具有拘束力。各缔约方有义务根据其相关法律执行裁决。

9.各争端缔约方应当各自承担其出席仲裁程序的费用。仲裁员和仲裁庭的相关费用应由争端各方平均承担,但仲裁庭有权决定败诉方承担此等费用的全部或大部分。

第二十二条　与其他协定的关系

本协定不应当减损任何缔约方作为其他任何国际协定缔约方的现有权利和义务。

第二十三条　发展中国家的特殊待遇

发展中国家缔约方和最不发达国家缔约方,可以采取清单方式列明不适用第三条"国民待遇"、第四条"最惠国待遇"、第十三条"履行要求的限制"和其他条款的具体领域及其事项。

第二十四条　工作机制安排

设立中国—××自由贸易区委员会,负责本协定的管理、监督、指导、协调并审议本协定的实施。

第二十五条　生效

本协定自各缔约方完成使国际条约生效的全部国内法律手续的最后日起第 3 个月第 1 日生效。

(三)其他区域性投资协定主要条文建议稿

在建立自由贸易区的条件不成熟时,可考虑制定某一区域多边投资规则。各方参与制定此类投资规则,通常是基于地缘政治因素,政治、地区安全因素的考量多于经济因素,且谈判伙伴并非国际投资互动频繁的国家或地区,因此在谈判时就高水平的投资自由化达成一致的可能性较小。与自由贸易区投资协定相比,此类投资规则在投资自由化程度上应当有所降低和减弱,一些体现投资自由化的主要条款应当有灵活性。

以下以上述自由贸易区投资协定范本建议稿为基础,就区域性投资协定可变动条款提出建议稿:

中国—×××区域投资协定

（以自由贸易区投资协定范本为基础的可变动条款）

一、序言

各缔约方,

认识到本区域内各国之间相互团结合作对促进本区域和平发展和各国经济社会发展的重要性;

认识到有必要为鼓励缔约一方投资者在缔约他方领土内投资创造有利条件;

认识到相互鼓励和保护投资将有助于激励本区域内的经营积极性和促进本地区各国的繁荣;

考虑到环境、劳工权利与国际投资之间的相互关系,希望通过与保护国民健康、安全、自然环境和推动国际认可的劳工权利相一致的方式实现以上目标。

二、第三条　国民待遇

缔约一方给予缔约他方投资者及其投资在其境内经营、管理、运营、出售、清算或其他处置方面的待遇,应当不低于该缔约一方在同等情况下给予其本国投资者及其投资的待遇。

三、第八条　利润汇回

缔约一方应当确保缔约他方投资者在其境内投资有关的资金不迟延地转移进出其领土。

四、第十条　透明度

各缔约方有必要及时并至少每年向缔约他方通报明显影响其境内投资或本协定下承诺的任何新法律与规章或现行法律规章的任何变化。各缔约方应当保证其与本协定所涉事项的以下者予以适当公开并可供公众查询:(a)法律、法规、工作程序和有普遍拘束力的行政规章;和(b)司法判决。

五、第十一条　投资措施与履行要求禁止

任何缔约方不应当采取或维持违背 WTO-TRIMs 协定的任何投资措施或履行要求。

六、第十六条　环境

各缔约方应当认识到多边环境公约和各自国内环境保护法律规章在环境保护中的重要作用,尽量不使用对环境保护造成损害的投资措施。各缔约方可以采取、维持或执行其认为与本协定一致的、能保证其境内投资活动意识到保护环境重要性的措施。

七、第十七条　劳工

各缔约方应当认识到通过降低和减少国内劳工保护法的规定来鼓励投资是不合适的。各缔约方承担作为国际劳工组织成员国的义务,并重申各缔约方在《国际劳工组织关于工作中的基本原则和权利宣言》下的承诺。

八、第二十一条　投资者与缔约方争端的解决

1.缔约一方投资者和缔约他方之间的与本协定范围内投资有关的任何争端,应尽可能由争端当事方通过友好协商解决。

2.争端当事方未能在 6 个月内友好协商解决争端的,经争端各方当事人共同同意,可以将争端提交至:

(1)根据接受投资的缔约方的法律,该缔约方有管辖权的司法、仲裁或行政机构解决,若可以提交此等机构解决;或

(2)根据《联合国国际贸易法委员会调解规则》进行国际调解;

(3)若争端当事方未能就本款规定的争端解决程序达成一致或争端虽被提交国际调解但调解程序被终止且未能达成和解协议,可将此争端提交国际仲裁。国际仲裁程序如下:

a.投资者所属的缔约方和缔约他方均为 1965 年 ICSID 公约的缔约方,且投资者书面同意将该争端提交 ICSID,此争端应提交 ICSID 解决;或

b.若争端当事方均同意,依照 ICSID 附设机构进行调解、仲裁和查明事实程序;或

c.由争端任何一方根据 1976 年《联合国国际贸易法委员会仲裁规则》提交专设仲裁庭,但受限于对该规则的下列修改:(i)该规则第七条下的任命机构应当是非缔约任何一方国民的国际法院之院长、副院长或其他资深法官。首席仲裁员不应当是任何争端缔约

方的国民。(ii)各争端当事方应当在 2 个月内任命其仲裁员。(iii)仲裁裁决应根据本协定、各缔约方对本协定的共同解释或共同决定、各缔约方共同接受的国际法原则、争端缔约方的法律作出。(iv)仲裁庭应当陈述其裁决的基础并根据争端任何一方要求,说明其裁决的理由。

3.争端缔约方可以要求争端投资者在根据第二十一条第 2 款第(2)项规定将争端提交国际调解或根据第二十一条第 2 款第(3)项提交国际仲裁前,先行用尽争端缔约方的国内救济程序。

二、对经合组织《多边投资协定》的主要条文建议稿

经合组织《多边投资协定》草案虽然在 1998 年流产,但其提供了一个高标准的、高度自由化的多边投资协定框架,代表了投资自由化的方向和发达国家的利益。我国作为新兴市场经济国家和最大发展中投资国,在与经合组织成员进行《多边投资协定》谈判时,应当尽可能争取作为发展中国家的利益,实现投资利益和东道国利益的平衡。以 MAI 草案为基础,在以下方面提出我国利益诉求,形成相应建议条文。

(一)序言

各缔约方,

意识到相互鼓励、保护投资将有助于激励投资者经营积极性、促进资本国际流动和增进各国、世界繁荣;

考虑到加强投资领域的合作,促进投资便利化和提高投资相关法律规章的透明度,并为投资提供保护;

考虑到投资对东道国经济社会发展的重要影响,重申以符合东道国社会利益、环境目标和国际社会认可的劳工权利保护的方式促进投资;

考虑到诸缔约方之间不同的发展阶段和速度,对发展中国家实行特殊和差别待遇的必要性。

(二)国民待遇和最惠国待遇

缔约一方应当给予缔约他方投资者及其投资在本国境内经营、管理、运营、出售、清算或其他处置方面的待遇,不低于该缔约一方在同等情况下给予其本国投资者及其投资的待遇。

缔约一方应当给予缔约他方投资者或其投资在本国境内设立、获取、扩大、管理、运营、出售或其他处置方面的待遇,不低于该缔约方在同等情况下给予非缔约方投资者或其投资的待遇。但是,本款规定的义务不包含要求给予缔约他方投资者除本款规定以外的争端解决程序。

国民待遇和最惠国待遇不适用于:a.在东道国境内维持的任何现存不符措施;b.第 a 项所述任何不符措施的延续;c.对第 a 项所述任何不符措施的修改,但是这种修改不应当增加该措施在修改前存在的不符此等义务的程度。不符措施不应超过现有水平且将努

力逐渐消除这些不符措施。

（三）公平公正待遇

1.各缔约方应当按照国际习惯法的要求赋予涵盖投资公平公正待遇。

2.为避免歧义,第 1 款规定的待遇水平应当以国际习惯法外国人最低待遇标准作为对涵盖投资的最低待遇标准。"公平公正待遇"既不能超出最低待遇标准,也不创设额外实体权利。各缔约方第 1 款下的义务包括:

a.保证刑事、民事或行政裁决程序符合世界主要法律体系中正当程序和正义要求的义务;

b.要求各缔约方根据国际习惯法要求的标准给予治安保护水平。

3.对本协定其他条款或其他国际条约的违反不构成对本条的违反。

（四）透明度

1.各缔约方应当公布或者在其他情况下公开其影响本协定的法律、法令、法规、规则、行政规章、工作程序、法院判决。若不包括在此处所列种类中但影响到本协定实施的各缔约方政策,应当予以公开或公布。

2.缔约方应予以回复缔约他方就上述第 1 款所述公开或公布提出的具体问题、质询和咨询。

3.在发展中缔约方履行本条所列义务有困难时,缔约他方应当给予技术支持和给予一定合理宽限期,以帮助其履行第 1 款规定的义务。

（五）禁止履行要求

缔约一方针对缔约他方的投资措施或履行要求的禁止范围不应当超出世界贸易组织《与贸易有关的投资措施协定》规定的范围。

（六）遵守对投资者投资的承诺

任何缔约方应保证遵守其就缔约另一方投资者的投资作出的任何承诺。

（七）投资者与东道国之间争端的解决

1.缔约一方和缔约他方投资者之间发生的投资争端,应先行协商、谈判解决。协商、谈判不成的,投资者应当在该争端缔约方境内寻求行政或/和司法救济。

2.缔约一方自投资者首次提出司法或行政救济之日起 6 个月内未解决的,投资者可将该争端提交至争端当事方共同认可的仲裁机构仲裁解决。

（其他条款依 MAI 草案）

三、普遍性投资规则的主要条文建议稿

（一）说明

本处所称普遍性投资规则,是指除现存国际投资公约、WTO 框架内有关投资的协定以外的普遍性投资规则,主要指普遍性综合投资规则。

在普遍性投资规则的谈判中,参与主体多,各自发展水平差异大,国家间的相互关系有亲疏远近。

我国目前和未来相当长时期内处于资本输入和资本输出大国地位。

我国参与制定普遍性投资规则,对投资自由化应采取适当保守的态度,对东道国利益和投资者利益的平衡不宜过分强调,应当采取一种较为中庸的态度。

(二)普遍性综合投资协定主要条文建议稿

各缔约方,

认识到经济全球化不断深化使各国经济社会发展的相互依存越来越明显;

认识到各国在世界经济发展中具有其优势和互补性;

认识到相互鼓励、促进和保护投资有助于资本国际流动、增进各国和世界繁荣;

考虑到加强投资领域合作、促进投资便利化和提高投资相关法律法规的透明度,并为投资提供充分保护;

认识到以符合环境目标和国际社会认可的劳工权利保护的方式促进投资的必要性和重要性;

考虑到各缔约方之间不同的发展阶段及其利益需求,对发展中国家实行特殊和差别待遇的必要性;

声明《建立世界贸易组织协定》或其他国际条约的成员的缔约方应当享有该等国际条约规定的权利、履行其规定的义务。

兹达成如下条款:

第一条　定义

1.投资者,指正在或已在缔约一方境内投资的缔约另一方自然人或法人。自然人,指根据该缔约另一方法律拥有该缔约方国籍、公民身份或永久居民权的任何自然人;法人,指根据该缔约另一方法律组建或设立的任何法律实体,无论其是否以营利为目的,无论私人所有还是政府所有,并在该缔约另一方境内具有实质经营,包括任何公司、信托、合伙企业、合资企业、个人独资企业或社团。

2.**方案一:以国际货币基金组织投资定义为基准**

投资,指具有缔约一方居民对缔约另一方居民企业实施管理上的控制或重要影响之特征的投资,包括带来控制或影响的股权和与此股权关系有关的投资,含投资于间接影响或控制的企业联属企业、债务和逆向投资。

方案二:以企业为基础之投资定义为基准

投资,指缔约一方投资者在缔约另一方领土内设立、获取或扩大的一企业,包括投资者通过设立、维持或获取一法人,或获取该企业股份、债券或其他所有权文书,条件是该企业根据缔约另一方法律建立或获取并按该缔约另一方法律要求被注册、批准、承认。此等企业可以拥有以下资产:

(a)该企业或另一企业的股份、股票、债券和其他权益文书;

(b)另一企业的债务担保;

(c)对一企业的贷款;

(d)动产或不动产和诸如抵押、留置或典当之类的其他财产权；

(e)金钱请求权，或对合同项下具有金融价值的任何履行的请求权；

(f)按东道国法律认可范围内的版权、专有技术、信誉和诸如专利、商标、工业设计、商号之类的知识产权；

(g)法律或按合同赋予的权利，包括种植、提炼或开发自然资源的许可。

投资不包括：

(i)政府发行的债务证券，或对政府的贷款；

(ii)组合投资；

(iii)仅产生于缔约一方领土内国民或企业向缔约另一方企业销售货物或服务之商事合同的金钱请求权，或者与商事交易有关的信用扩张，或对不涉及上述(a)至(g)项中所列各种利益的金钱请求权。

方案三：以资产为基础之投资定义为基准(一)

投资，指根据东道缔约国法律规章准许或准入的下列资产：

(1)一企业。

(2)一企业的一项权益担保。

(3)以下情形的一企业的一债务担保：

(a)该企业是投资者的一附属企业；或

(b)该债务担保初始期限不低于3年，但不包括一国家或国家企业的一项债务担保，不考虑其初始期限。

(4)对以下情形的一企业的贷款：

(a)该企业是投资者的一附属企业，或

(b)贷款初始期限不低于3年，但不包括对一国家企业的贷款，不考虑其初始期限。

(5)在使所有权人有权利分享收入或利润的一企业中的一项利益。

(6)在使所有权人有权利分享解散企业资产中的一项利益，但不是上述第(3)项或第(4)项中排除的债务担保或贷款。

(7)预期获得的或为了经济利益或其他经营目的使用的有形或无形不动产或其他财产。

(8)在东道国缔约方领土内对其境内经济活动承诺资本或其他资源投入所产生的利益，诸如：

(a)涉及投资者在东道国缔约方领土内财产所存在的合同，包括总控钥匙合同或建筑合同，或特许权，或

(b)回报实质上依赖一企业之生产、收益或利润的合同。

(9)投资不包括仅具有以下性质的资产：组合投资；信誉；不论是否基于源自缔约一方之贸易的市场份额或贸易权；仅衍生于向东道国缔约方领土或从缔约一方向东道国缔约方领土销售货物或服务之商事合同的金钱请求权，或仅衍生于向东道国缔约方或其国家企业贷款的金钱请求权；银行信用证；与诸如贸易融资之类商事交易有关的信用扩张；或对东道国缔约方或其国家企业的贷款，或缔约一方或其国家企业对此等贷款发出的债务担保。

（10）一项资产必须具有诸如承诺资本或其他资源投入、期望获利、承担风险和对东道国发展具有重要性的投资特性。投资或再投资的资产在形式上的任何改变，不应当影响其作为投资的特性。

方案四：以资产为基础之投资定义为基准（二）

投资，指根据东道国缔约方法律规章准许或形成的任何资产，包括：

（1）动产、不动产和诸如抵押、留置和典当之类的其他相关财产权。

（2）对货币、货物、服务或具有经济价值的其他履行的请求权。

（3）诸企业的股票、股份、债券和此等企业财产中的利益。

（4）与东道国缔约方领土内经营业务关联的知识产权、技术工艺、专有技术、信誉和其他利益或益处。

（5）法律或按合同赋予的商业特许权，包括：

（a）建设、营运、拥有/移交、改造、扩大、重建和/或改善基础设施的合同；和

（b）研究、种植、提炼或开发自然资源的特许权。

（6）投资不包括仅具有以下性质的资产：组合投资；信誉；不论是否基于源自缔约一方之贸易的市场份额或贸易权；仅衍生于向东道国缔约方或从缔约一方领土向东道国缔约方领土销售货物或服务之商事合同的金钱请求权，或向东道国缔约方或其国家企业贷款的金钱请求权；银行信用证；与诸如贸易融资之类商事交易有关的信用扩张。

（7）一项资产必须具有诸如承诺资本或其他资源投入、期望获利、承担风险和对东道国发展具有重要性的投资特性。投资或再投资的资产在形式上的任何改变，不应当影响其作为投资的特性。

3.措施，指缔约一方采取的、影响投资者和/或投资的、普遍适用的任何法律、法规、规章、规则、程序、政策、行政决定或行政行为。

4.收益，是指获利于或源自一项投资的总金额，特别是，包括但不限于利润、利息、资本收益、红利、版税或酬金。投资收益和再投资时的再投资收益享有与投资相同的保护。

5.政府采购，指政府为了公共目的获取商品和服务的过程。政府采购不得以商业销售或转售为目的，或被用于商业销售或转售产品、服务的生产和供应。

6.ICSID公约，指1965年3月18日在华盛顿开放签署的《解决国家与他国国民间投资争端公约》。

7.ICSID，指依照ICSID公约设立的"解决投资争端国际中心"。

第二条　适用范围

1.本协定适用于缔约一方采取和维持的以下措施：

（a）与缔约另一方投资者有关的；

（b）与涵盖投资有关的。

2.本协定不适用于在本协定生效前发生的任何缔约方的行为或事实，或曾经存在但已经终止的其他情形。

第三条　国民待遇

缔约一方应当给予缔约另一方的投资者及其投资在其境内经营、管理、运营、清算、

出售或其他投资处置方面的待遇,不低于该缔约一方在类似情况下给予其本国投资者及其投资的待遇。

第四条　最惠国待遇

1.缔约一方应当给予缔约另一方的投资者及其投资在其境内设立、获取、扩大、管理、运营、清算出售或其他投资处置方面的待遇,不低于该缔约一方在类似情况下给予任何非缔约方投资者或其投资的待遇。

2.本条规定的义务不包含要求给予缔约另一方投资者本协定规定以外的争端解决程序。

第五条　公平公正待遇

1.各缔约方应当按照国际习惯法要求赋予涵盖投资公平公正待遇。

2.为了更加明确,第1款规定的待遇水平应当以国际习惯法外国人最低待遇标准作为对涵盖投资的最低待遇标准。各缔约方第1款下的义务包括:

(a)保证刑事、民事或行政程序符合世界主要法律体系中正当程序和正义要求的义务;

(b)要求各缔约方根据国际习惯法要求的标准给予治安保护水平。

3. 违反本协定其他条款或其他国际条约,不构成违反本条。

第六条　利益拒绝

若作为缔约另一方企业的投资者是由非缔约方和拒绝给予利益的缔约方的投资者拥有或控制,且拒绝给予利益的缔约方与该非缔约方之间没有正常经济关系,缔约一方可以拒绝将本协定的利益给予该缔约另一方投资者。

第七条　征收

1.各缔约方不应当直接或间接通过征收、国有化或类似措施对涵盖投资进行征收或国有化(简称"征收"),但符合以下者除外:

(a)为公共利益目的;

(b)以非歧视方式;

(c)给予本条第2款所述的补偿;和

(d)符合正当法律程序和第5条"公平公正待遇"规定。

2.补偿应以征收公布时或征收发生时被征收投资的公平市场价值计算,以较早者为准。补偿应当允许用可自由兑换货币从东道国自由转移。补偿的偿清和支付不应当不合理延迟。公平市场价值不应当因公众事先知悉征收所发生的任何价值变化。

3.若发生延迟,补偿应当包括按通行商业利率计算的自征收日起至支付日止的利息。包括应付利息在内的补偿应当以原投资货币或应投资者请求以可自由兑换货币进行支付。

4.第1款中"类似措施"应当解释为:

(1)通过正式移转所有权或直接没收形式进行的直接征收或国有化除外,征收措施包括缔约一方为了达到使投资者投资陷于实质上无法产生收益或不能产生回报的境地而有意采取的一项或一系列措施,但不涉及正式移转所有权或直接没收。

(2)在一特定情形下确定缔约一方的一项或一系列措施是否构成第1款所述的类似措施,需进行以事实为根据的个案审查,该审查应当考虑以下各因素:

a.该项或系列措施的经济影响,但是仅有缔约一方的一项或一系列措施负面影响投资的经济价值这一事实,不足以推断已经发生了征收或国有化;

b.该项或系列措施在范围或适用上歧视某一缔约方或某一投资者或某一企业的程度;

c.该项或系列措施违背明显、合理、以投资为依据的预期程度;

d.该项或系列措施的性质和目的,是不是为了善意公共利益目标所采取,和在该等措施和征收目的之间是否存在合理联系。

(3)除非在特殊情况下,缔约一方采取的旨在保护公共利益的非歧视管制措施,包括根据司法机关作出的具有普遍适用效力的裁决所采取的措施,不构成间接征收或国有化。

第八条　收益汇回

1.缔约一方应当确保缔约另一方投资者与在其境内投资有关的资金毫不迟延地转移进出其领土,这些转移特别包括但不限于:

(1)建立、维持和扩大投资所必需的资本;

(2)利润、利息、股息、资本收益、版税和其他费用;

(3)基于合同所得的偿付,包括根据贷款协议的偿付;

(4)全部或部分出售或清算资产的所得;

(5)根据第七条和第九条获得的补偿或赔偿;

(6)根据第二十一条因争端解决所得的赔偿;

(7)在缔约一方领土内从事与投资有关活动的缔约另一方国民的收入和其他报酬。

2.除非本协定有相反规定,任何缔约方不应当阻碍用可自由兑换货币、按转移日该货币通行市场汇率不迟延地实施转移。

3.尽管有第1款和第2款,缔约一方可以通过公平、非歧视、善意方式适用与以下有关的法律,迟延或者阻止转移:

(1)破产、倒闭或者保护债权人权利;

(2)证券或衍生工具的发行、买卖或交易;

(3)犯罪或者触犯刑法,或保证遵守司法程序中的判决或命令;

(4)为了协助执法或金融监管当局所进行的关于转移的金融报告或保存记录。

4.尽管有本协定其他条款,各缔约方可以在以下情况下根据其法律与规章,采取或维持与本条义务不一致的措施:

(1)存在国际收支平衡和外部财政方面的严重困难或者严重困难威胁;或

(2)例外情况下,资金转移引起特别是金融和汇率政策方面的宏观经济管理严重困难或者严重困难威胁。

5.第4款所述的措施必须:

(1)符合《国际货币基金协定》,但各缔约方作出保留的除外;

(2)不超出为处理上述第4款描述情形所必要;

(3)是临时的并在条件许可时被取消;

(4)即刻通知缔约他方。

第九条　战乱损害及其赔偿

1.若缔约一方投资者在缔约另一方领土内的投资因战争、全国紧急状态、武装冲突、暴乱或其他类似事件遭受损失,该缔约另一方在恢复原状、赔偿、补偿或采取其他措施方面,应当给予该投资者的待遇不低于该缔约另一方给予其本国投资者或任何第三国投资者的待遇。

2.在不损害第1款的情况下,缔约一方投资者在缔约另一方领土内遭受的损害或损失是由于:

(1)该国军队或当局征用其财产;

(2)该国军队或当局非因战斗行动或情势必需毁坏了其财产。

在财产被征用期间或因毁坏财产导致的损害或损失,应得到公平合理和非歧视的赔偿。由此所发生的款项应当以可兑换货币支付并自由转移。

第十条　遵守对投资者投资的承诺

任何缔约方应保证遵守其就缔约另一方投资者的投资作出的任何承诺。

第十一条　代位

1.若任何缔约方或其指定的任何代理人、机构、法定机构或公司,就有关投资或其任何部分,依照保险、依据本协定形成的请求权,向其本国投资者进行了支付,其他相关缔约方应当承认该缔约方或其指定的任何代理人、机构、法定机构或公司有资格代位履行该投资者的权利和请求权。代位的权利或请求权不应当超出该投资者的原始权利或请求权。

2.若缔约一方或其指定的任何代理人、机构、法定机构或公司已向其投资者进行了支付,并已接管该投资者的权利与请求权,该投资者不应当向缔约另一方主张这些权利或请求权,除非该投资者被授权代表该缔约一方或进行了支付的代理机构采取行动。

第十二条　透明度

1.各缔约方应当保证其与本条协定所涉事项有关的法律、法令、法规、规则、行政规章、工作流程、行政行为、政策、司法判决适当公开并供公众查询。

2.各缔约方应当回复缔约他方就第1款所述公开或公布事项提出的具体问题、质询和咨询。

3.发展中缔约方履行本条所列义务有困难时,缔约他方应当给予技术支持和3年宽限期,以帮助其履行第1款规定的义务。

第十三条　履行要求的禁止和限制

各缔约方承诺不采取与WTO-TRIMs协定相冲突的履行要求或投资措施。

第十四条　反腐败、反非法行为的措施

1.各缔约方应当采取或保持措施,尽力防止和打击与本协定所涉事项有关的腐败、洗钱和恐怖主义融资。

2.本协定中的任何规定均不应当强制任何缔约方保护以非法来源资本或非法来源资产进行的投资,或保护其设立或运作经证实有因资产流失或腐败行为而遭到过制裁的非法行为的投资。

第十五条　健康、环境、劳工问题和其他监管目标的投资与措施

1.各缔约方可以采取、维持或执行其认为适当的任何措施,以确保其境内投资活动符合本协定规定,并考虑该缔约方的劳动、环境或健康方面的法律。

2.各缔约方认识到,通过降低其劳动、环境或卫生法的标准来鼓励投资是不恰当的。因此,各缔约方不应当放弃适用或以任何其他方式废除、放宽或提出放弃、放宽或废除上述措施,作为鼓励其领土内建立、维持或扩大投资的手段。

第十六条　不适用措施

1.本协定第三条"国民待遇"和第四条"最惠国待遇"不适用于:

(1)在其境内维持的任何现存不符措施;

(2)上述第(1)项所述任何不符措施的延续;

(3)对上述第(1)项述任何不符措施的修改,但是此种修改不应当提高该措施在修改前存在的不符此等义务的程度。

2.第1款所述的不符措施不应当超过现有水平,各缔约方应当努力逐渐消除这些不符措施。

3.本协定第三条"国民待遇"和第四条"最惠国待遇"不适用于:

(a)政府采购;或

(b)缔约一方的补贴或拨款,包括政府贷款、保证和保险。

第十七条　税收

1.本条另有规定除外,本协定不适用于税收措施。

2.本协定的任何规定不应当影响各缔约方在任何税收协定下的权利和义务。若本协定的规定和任何税收协定的规定相抵触,该税收协定的规定应当在不一致的范围内予以适用。若各缔约方同为某一税收协定缔约方,该税收协定规定的有关税收当局应当对其决定本协定与该税收协定是否存在不一致负责。

3.本协定第七条"征收"的规定适用于具有征收性质的税收措施。

4.本协定第二十条"缔约方之间争端的解决"、第二十一条"投资者与缔约一方争端的解决"适用于本条第3款所述的税收措施。

5.若投资者援引第七条"征收"作为根据第二十一条"投资者与缔约一方争端的解决"提请仲裁请求的依据,应适用下述程序:

(1)投资者应当首先将涉及的该税收措施是否与征收有关,提交东道国税收主管机关;

(2)争端缔约方税收主管机关应当举行磋商。若争端缔约方税收主管机关自投资者提交日起6个月内认定该措施与征收无关且不能达成一致,或者争端缔约方税收主管机关未举行磋商,该投资者可以根据第二十一条"投资者与缔约一方争端的解决"规定提出仲裁请求。

第十八条　一般例外

在依本协定实施措施不应当在类似情形的缔约方、缔约方投资者或投资者投资之间构成任意或不合理歧视的手段,或不构成变相限制任何缔约方投资者或其设立的投资的前提下,本协定的任何规定不应当解释为阻止任何缔约方采取或实施以下措施:

（1）为保护公共道德或维护公共秩序所必需的。

（2）为保护人类、动植物的生命或健康所必需的。

（3）为遵守与本协定规定不抵触的法律或规章所必需的，包括与以下有关的法律或规章：

a.防止欺骗和欺诈行为或处理违反服务合同而产生的影响；

b.保护与个人信息处理和传播有关个人隐私、保护个人记录与账户的机密性；和

c.安全。

（4）旨在确保对任何缔约方的投资或其投资者公平或有效课征或收取直接税。

（5）为保护具有艺术、历史或考古价值的国宝所采取的。

（6）与保护不可再生自然资源有关的，若这些措施与限制国内生产或消费一同实施。

第十九条　安全例外

1.本协定的任何规定不应当解释为要求各缔约方提供其认为一旦披露会违背其根本安全利益的任何信息。

2.本协定的任何规定不应当解释为阻止缔约一方为了保护本国根本安全利益、根据本国法律、在非歧视基础上采取其认为必要的措施。除非缔约一方采取的措施与所维护的根本安全利益之间严重不成比例，该缔约一方对由此给投资者造成的损失不负责任。若缔约一方采取的措施与所维护的根本安全利益之间严重不成比例，该缔约一方应当承担责任，但应当充分考虑缔该约一方采取讼争措施时所处的情势。

3.本协定的任何规定不应当解释为阻止东道国为了履行维护国际和平与安全义务采取其认为必要的任何措施。东道国对由此给投资者造成的损失，不承担责任。

第二十条　缔约方之间争端的解决

1.若任何缔约一方请求解决与本协定有关的任何争端，或者要求讨论与本协定的解释或适用、本协定目标的实现等有关的事项，争端各方应当立刻通过外交途径举行磋商。

2.若争端未在6个月内解决，经任一争端缔约方请求，应当将争端提交专设仲裁庭仲裁解决。

3.仲裁庭由3名仲裁员组成。自收到请求仲裁的书面通知之日起2个月内，各争端缔约方应当共同任命3名仲裁员，并指定其中一位与各缔约方均有外交关系的第三国国民担任首席仲裁员。

4.仲裁庭未在收到请求仲裁的书面通知起4个月内组成，争端各方间又无其他协议，争端任何缔约方可以提请国际法院院长作出必要任命。若国际法院院长是争端任何缔约一方的国民，或由于其他原因不能履行此项任命，应提请国际法院中是非争端缔约方国民且无其他不胜任原因的最资深法官履行此必要任命。

5.仲裁庭应当决定其自身程序。仲裁庭应当根据本协定和争端方共同认可的国际法原则作出裁决。

6.仲裁庭应以多数票作出裁决。裁决在仲裁庭组成之日起10个月内作出。该裁决是终局的，对争端各方均有拘束力。应任何缔约一方的请求，仲裁庭应解释其作裁决的理由。

7.争端各方应当各自承担其出席仲裁程序的费用。仲裁员和仲裁庭的相关费用应当由争端各方平均承担,但仲裁庭有权决定败诉缔约方承担此等费用的大部分。

第二十一条　投资者与缔约一方争端的解决

1.为了本条目的,争端系指缔约一方与缔约另一方投资者之间的指控该缔约一方违反本协定造成或导致了缔约另一方投资者投资的损害和损失的争端。

2.第1款规定的争端应当尽可能在东道国国内解决。争端缔约方可以要求用尽本国一切可以采取的救济措施。若用尽本国一切救济手段仍未解决,或者自案件首次提交争端缔约方国内解决之日起18个月内未解决,投资者可以将此争端提交至争端各方共同认可的国际仲裁解决。

3.在国际仲裁情况下,按投资者的选择,可以将争端提交至:

(1)依据1965年3月18日在华盛顿签署的ICSID公约设立的ICSID;或者

(2)根据《联合国国际贸易法委员会仲裁规则》或者经争端各方同意的其他任何仲裁规则设立的专设仲裁庭。

4.投资者将争端提交给ICSID或者依照本条第3款第(2)项组成的专设仲裁庭,两种程序中的任一选择是终局的。

5.根据本条第3款提交争端的投资者应当在提起诉求之前至少90日向争端缔约方发送书面通知,说明其提起争端解决的意向。该通知应当列明:

(1)争端投资者的名称和地址;

(2)争端缔约方的具体争议措施、能充分清楚说明与此争端有关事项的事实和法律根据的摘要,包括指控争端缔约方违反本协定的具体条款;

(3)寻求的救济措施,包括必要的请求赔偿大约额;和

(4)争端投资者寻求本条第3款(1)(2)项所列的争端解决程序。

6.仲裁裁决应当以本协定、各缔约方对本协定的共同解释或共同决定、各缔约方共同接受的国际法原则、争端缔约方的法律(包括冲突法规则)为基础。

7.尽管有第3款规定,若自投资者首次知道或者应当知道其遭受损失或损害之日起已届满3年,投资者不得根据本条第3款提起请求。

8.仲裁裁决是终局的,对争端各方具有拘束力。各缔约方有义务根据其相关法律执行裁决。

9.争端各方应当各自承担其出席仲裁程序的费用。仲裁员和仲裁庭的相关费用应当由争端各方平均承担,但仲裁庭可以决定败诉方承担此等费用的全部或大部分。

第二十二条　与其他协定的关系

本协定不应当损害任何缔约方作为其他任何国际协定缔约方的现有权利和义务。

第二十三条　发展中国家的特殊待遇

考虑到发展中国家的发展水平和本协定义务可能对其造成的影响,本协定的第十二条"透明度"、第十三条"履行要求的禁止和限制"、第十五条"健康、环境、劳工问题和其他监管目标的投资与措施"的实施,应给予发展中国家3～5年过渡期,必要时可由第二十四条"机制安排"下的××委员会对其提供帮助和技术指导。

第二十四条　机制安排

根据本协定设立××委员会,负责本协定的解释、监督、指导、协调,并审议本协定的实施。

××委员会下设秘书局,负责处理与本协定有关的日常事务。

第二十五条　生效

各缔约方承诺完成使本协定生效的全部国内法律程序,并向秘书局交存完成国内批准程序的证书。

本协定自第 15 个缔约方向秘书局交存批准证书的第三个月首日起生效。

本章小结

本章以现有国际投资规则中一般条款和特殊条款及其发展为蓝本,结合我国在国际投资中的地位,就我国制定参与多边投资规则时对一般条款和特殊条款的选择和未来取向进行了论证,并以此为依据,提出了我国参与制定区域性和普遍性多边投资规则主要条款的谈判条文学者建议稿。

参考文献

一、中文类

(一)著作

1.《2007年世界贸易报告》,中国世界贸易组织研究会、对外经济贸易大学中国WTO研究院译,中国商务出版社2008年版。

2.陈安:《国际经济法学专论》,高等教育出版社2007年第2版。

3.博温托·桑托斯:《迈向新的法律常识——法律、全球化和解放》,刘坤轮、叶传星译,中国人民大学出版社2009年版。

4.陈业宏、张庆麟、刘笋主编:《国际经济法新论》,华中科技大学出版社2010年版。

5.陈叔红:《经济全球化趋势下的国家经济安全研究》,湖南人民出版社2005年版。

6.陈坤等编:《国际投资法》,哈尔滨工程大学出版社2003年版。

7.高凛等:《国际经济法热点问题研究》,中国民主法制出版社2007年版。

8.郭飞等:《贸易自由化与投资自由化互动关系研究》,人民出版社2006年版。

9.黄东黎:《国际经济法》,社会科学文献出版社2006年版。

10.李斯:《WTO规则对中国农业的影响评价与发展对策实用手册》,世图电子音像出版社2002年版。

11.李杨:《多边贸易体制的博弈机制》,对外经济贸易大学出版社2010年版。

12.金成华:《国际投资立法发展现状与展望》,中国法制出版社2009年版。

13.杰里尔·A.罗塞蒂:《美国对外政策的政治学》,周启明等译,世界知识出版社1997年版。

14.卢进勇等主编:《国际投资条约与协定新论》,人民出版社2007年版。

15.陆建人主编:《亚太经合组织与中国》,经济管理出版社2007年版。

16.刘笋:《国际投资保护的国际法制——若干重要法律问题》,法律出版社2001年版。

17.刘笋:《WTO 法律规则体系对国际投资法的影响》,中国法制出版社 2001 年版。

18.刘笋:《国际投资保护的国际法制》,法律出版社 2002 年版。

19.刘文秀:《欧盟的超国家治理》,社会科学文献出版社 2003 年版。

20.刘文秀等:《欧洲联盟政策及政策过程研究》,法律出版社 2003 年版。

21.迈克尔·波特:《国家竞争优势》,李明轩、邱如美译,华夏出版社 2002 年版。

22.欧共体官方出版局编:《欧洲共同体条约集》,戴炳然译,复旦大学出版社 1993 年版。

23.孙哲:《左右未来:美国国会的制度创新和决策行为》,复旦大学出版社 2001 年版。

24.邵景春:《欧洲联盟的法律与制度》,人民法院出版社 1999 年版。

25.孙昂:《美国对外事务法律机制》,国际文化出版公司 2008 年版。

26.苏旭霞:《国际直接投资自由化与中国外资政策:以 WTO 多边投资框架谈判为背景》,中国商务出版社 2005 年版。

27.蒲罗尔:《美帝国主义论》,陈羽纶译,五十年代出版社 1953 年版。

28.徐泉:《国际贸易投资自由化法律规制研究》,中国检察出版社 2004 年版。

29.徐泉:《国家经济主权论》,人民出版社 2006 年版。

30.薛荣久、樊瑛:《WTO 多哈回合与中国》,对外经济贸易大学出版社 2004 年版。

31.王贵国:《国际投资法》,北京大学出版社 2001 年版。

32.吴承明编:《帝国主义在中国的投资》,人民出版社 1955 年版。

33.杨光斌主编:《政治学导论》,中国人民大学出版社 2000 年版。

34.杨树明等:《国际投资法原理》,重庆大学出版社 1992 年版。

35.姚梅镇:《国际投资法》,武汉大学出版社 1998 年版。

36.张磊:《多哈回合谈判的最新进展——2010 年度报告》,法律出版社 2012 年版。

37.张庆麟:《国际投资法问题专论》,武汉大学出版社 2007 年版。

38.张彤等:《欧盟法概论》,中国人民大学出版社 2011 年版。

39.张向晨:《发展中国家与 WTO 的政治经济关系》,法律出版社 2000 年版。

40.张严方主编:《与贸易有关的投资措施协定解读》,湖南科学技术出版社 2005 年版。

41.曾华群主编:《国际投资法学》,北京大学出版社 1999 年版。

(二)期刊论文

1.陈畅东:《国际投资立法自由化趋势及我国的对策》,载《民主与法治》2008 年第 8 期。

2.陈辉萍:《美国投资者与东道国争端解决机制的晚近发展及其对发展中国家的启示》,载《国际经济法学刊》2007 年第 14 卷第 3 期。

3.陈辉萍:《多边投资法律框架发展的历史与现状——WTO 多边投资规则谈判争论的视角》,载《厦门大学法律评论》第 2 期,厦门大学出版社 2001 年版。

4.陈洁蓓、张二震:《从分歧到融合——国际贸易与投资理论的发展趋势综述》,载《经济学研究》2003 年第 3 期。

5.东艳:《深度一体化:中国自由贸易区战略的新趋势》,载《当代亚太》2009 年第 4 期。

6.高鸿钧:《美国法全球化:典型例证与发法理反思》,载《中国法学》2011 年第 1 期。

7.向铁梅:《国际贸易与直接投资的关系及其中国情况的实证分析》,载《世界经济研究》2003 年第 3 期。

8.古尔默·阿布杜罗:《非洲与中国:新殖民主义还是新型战略伙伴关系?》,马京鹏译,载《国外理论动态》2012 年第 9 期。

9.龚斌恩:《金砖五国合作政策》,载《中国外资》2011 年第 6 期。

10.方流芳:《中西公司法律地位历史考察》,载《中国社会科学》1992 年第 4 期。

11.冯军:《从多哈回合议程谈中国多边投资框架谈判立场》,载《政治与法律》2005 年第 2 期。

12.樊静:《经济全球化趋势下的国家主权原则》,载《法学杂志》2002 年第 6 期。

13.田海:《我国应对 TPP 的策略思考》,载《中国国情国力》2012 年第11 期。

14.华晓红、庄芮、杨立强:《中国参与周边区域经济合作的实践与策略》,载《云南师范大学学报(哲社版)》2011 年第 2 期。

15.季烨:《国际投资条约中投资定义的扩展及其限度》,载《北大法律评论》2011 年第 1 期。

16.金学凌、赵红梅:《国际投资法制多边化发展趋势研究》,载《河南司法警官职业学院学报》2011 年第 9 卷第 1 期。

17.李本:《对国际多边投资立法从回应到参与——中国外商投资立法的嬗变分析》,载《法学杂志》2009 年第 8 期。

18.李宏岳:《中国参与国际区域经济合作的战略思考》,载《经济问题探索》2010 年第 1 期。

19.李靖宇、韩青:《中俄两国边境区域合作开发文件落实问题探讨》,载《俄罗斯中亚东欧市场》2011 年第 4 期。

20.李强:《中国周边的地缘政治经济环境》,载《世界经济与政治》2007 年第 8 期。

21.李荣林:《国际贸易和直接投资的关系:文献综述》,载《世界经济》2002 年第 1 期。

22.林一:《简论新一代国际投资协定中的一般例外规则》,载《甘肃政法学院学报》2012 年第 11 期。

23.梁丹妮:《国际投资条约最惠国待遇条款适用问题研究》,载《法商研究》2012 年第 2 期。

24.刘勇:《WTO 坎昆会议的失败及其相关思考》,载《环球经贸》2003 年第 11 期。

25.刘重力、王丽华:《2011 年 APEC 重要议题评析及中国策略》,载《亚太经济》2011 年第 6 期。

26.刘京莲:《国际投资仲裁体制的困境与出路》,载《福建论坛》2011 年第 5 期。

27.刘京莲:《国际投资仲裁正当性危机之投资仲裁员独立性研究》,载《河北法学》2011 年第 9 期。

28.刘京莲:《国际投资条约根本安全例外条款研究》,载《国际经济法学刊》2010 年第 1 期。

29.刘笋:《国际投资仲裁裁决的不一致性及其解决》,载《法商研究》2009 年第 6 期。

中国参与制定多边投资规则问题研究

30.刘笋：《从多边投资协定草案看国际投资多边法制的走向》，载《比较法研究》2003年第2期。

31.刘笋：《关于"与贸易有关的"问题及WTO调整范围的思考》，载《法商研究》2003年第5期。

32.刘笋：《从MAI看综合性国际投资多边立法的困境和出路》，载《中国法学》2001年第5期。

33.刘笋：《国际投资与环境保护的法律冲突与协调——以晚近区域性投资条约及相关案例为研究对象》，载《现代法学》2006年第11期。

34.刘笋：《从多边投资协定草案看国际投资多边法制的走向》，载《比较法研究》2003年第2期。

35.卢进勇、杨立强：《多边投资框架谈判与中国》，载《国际商务（对外经济贸易大学学报）》2004年第5期。

36.路建人：《APEC20年：回顾与展望》，载《国际贸易问题》2010年第1期。

37.路宇立：《APEC合作的理论基础：新区域主义的视角分析》，载《国际贸易问题》2011年第4期。

38.潘忠岐、黄仁伟：《中国的地缘经济战略》，载《清华大学学报（哲社版）》2008年第5期。

39.漆彤：《论国际投资协定中的利益拒绝条款》，载《政治与法律》2012年第9期。

40.綦建红、陈东：《关于多边投资框架的经济学分析》，载《学习与探索》2005年第3期。

41.盛斌：《国际投资协定：多边安排是唯一的途径吗?》，载《南开经济研究》2003年第3期。

42.孙哲、李巍：《美国贸易代表办公室与美国贸易政策》，载《美国研究》2007年第1期。

43.田海：《TPP背景下中国的选择策略思考——基于与APEC的比较分析》，载《亚太经济》2012年第4期。

44.王毅：《中国与周边国家外交关系综述：与邻为善以邻为伴》，载《求是》2013年第2期。

45.王海浪：《ICSID体制内用尽当地救济原则面临的三大挑战及对策》，载《国际经济法学刊》2006年第3期。

46.王彦志：《国际投资争端解决的法律化：成就与挑战》，载《当代法学》2011年第3期。

47.温先涛：《〈中国投资保护协定范本〉（草案）论稿（一）》，载《国际经济法学刊》2011年第4期。

48.温先涛：《〈中国投资保护协定范本〉（草案）论稿（二）》，载《国际经济法学刊》2012年第1期。

49.冼国明、方友林：《发展中国家加入多边投资框架的利弊及当前的抉择》，载《世界经济与政治》2004年第1期。

50.徐崇利:《经济全球化与国际经济条约谈判方式的创新》,载《比较法研究》2001年第3期。

51.徐崇利:《晚近国际投资争端解决实践之评判:"全球治理"理论的引入》,载《法学家》2010年第3期。

52.徐崇利:《从实体到程序:最惠国待遇适用范围之争》,载《法商研究》2007年第2期。

53.徐泉:《美国外贸政策决策机制的变革——美国〈1934年互惠贸易协定法〉述评》,载《法学家》2008年第1期。

54.许海云:《对〈范登堡案〉的历史反思》,载《史学月刊》2007年第3期。

55.闫永红、梁洪杰:《外资准入自由化趋势下中国外资准入立法取向》,载《辽东学院学报(社会科学版)》2006年第1期。

56.杨国华:《异曲同工——美国对华贸易政策》,载《国际经济法学刊》2008年第3期。

57.叶兴平:《外国直接投资最新趋势与变迁中的国际投资规则——宏观考察》,载《法学评论》2002年第4期。

58.叶兴平:《WTO内多边投资规则谈判的利弊分析》,载《深圳大学学报》2006年第8期。

59.易卜拉欣·F.I.西哈塔:《多边投资担保机构形成的早期历史(上、下)》,黎晖译,载《南京大学法学评论》1996年春、秋季号。

60.张艾妮:《中国应对多边投资协定谈判的策略研究》,载《广东海洋大学学报》2009年第2期。

61.张庆麟、彭忠波:《晚近多边投资规则谈判的新动向——兼论我国多边投资谈判策略的选择》,载《国际经济法学刊》2005年第3期。

62.张庆麟:《论国际投资协定中的投资性质与扩大化的意义》,载《法学家》2011年第6期。

63.张庆麟、张惟威:《〈里斯本条约〉对欧盟国际投资法律制度的影响》,载《武汉大学国际法评论》2011年第1期。

64.朱凯兵:《中国维护与发展中国家合作关系的战略前瞻》,载《南京政治学院学报》2012年第3期。

65.周升起:《中国对外直接投资:现状、趋势与政策》,载《东亚论文》2009年第75期。

(三)其他文献

1.Karl P.Sauvant、陈辉萍:《中美双边投资协定:多边投资框架的范本?》,载《哥伦比亚国际直接投资展望》,2012年12月17日No.85。

2.联合国贸易与发展会议:《2020年世界投资报告——疫情后的国际生产》(要旨和概述)(中文版)。

3.《区域全面经济伙伴关系协定》(中译本),2020年。

4.联合国贸易与发展会议:《2012 年世界投资报告》(中文版)。

5.联合国贸易与发展会议:《2008 年世界投资报告》(中文版)。

6.联合国贸易与发展会议:《2004 年世界投资报告》(中文版)。

7.陈辉萍:《论多边投资法律框架发展的新动向》,厦门大学 1999 年学位博士论文。

8.董跃:《MAI:构建多边投资规则的未来之路》,北大法律信息网,http://article.chinalawinfo.com/。

9.郭丽梅:《国际投资法中投资定义研究》,厦门大学 2009 年硕士学位论文。

10.郭莉莉:《非洲示范投资法述评》,湘潭大学 2011 年法律硕士(法学)学位论文。

11.李喆:《间接征收认定问题的法律研究》,载《中国国际经济法学会 2011 年年会》第三卷。

12.李荣林:《国际贸易和直接投资的替代性和互补性》,载《2001 年中国经济学年会论文集》,北京大学中国经济研究中心。

13.刘力韻:《试论"旋转门"现象对美国外交的影响》,中国外交学院 2012 年硕士学位论文。

14.商务部、国家统计局、国家外汇管理局:《2009 年度对外直接投资统计公报》。

15.商务部、国家统计局、国家外汇管理局:《2010 年度中国对外直接投资统计公报》。

16.商务部、国家统计局、国家外汇管理局:《2011 年度中国对外直接投资统计公报》。

17.商务部、国家统计局、国家外汇管理局:《2019 年度中国对外直接投资统计公报》。

18.商务部:《2012 年 1—12 月全国吸收外商直接投资情况》,http://www.mofcom.gov.cn/article/。

19.商务部:《中国对外投资合作发展报告(2011—2012)》。

20.尚妍:《〈反假冒贸易协定〉研究》,西南政法大学 2013 年博士学位论文。

21.王健:《上海合作组织发展进程》,上海社会科学院世界经济研究所 2012 年博士论文。

22.许宁宁:《中国与东盟经贸合作 2012 年—2013 年度报告》,http://news.hexun.com/。

23.詹晓宁、葛顺奇:《2012 年世界投资报告:迈向新一代的投资政策》,载《第一财经日报》2012 年 7 月 9 日。

24.张庆麟:《评晚近国际投资协定中"投资"定义的扩大趋势》,载《全球化时代的国际经济法:中国的视角国际研讨会论文集(上)》,2008 年。

25.张云燕:《社会建构主义与东亚区域经济合作》,复旦大学 2004 年博士学位论文。

二、外文类

(一)著作

1. Alina Kaczorowska, *European Union Law*, Routledge-Cavendish Press, 2008.

2. Andrea K. Bjorklund，*Yearbook on International Investment Law and Policy 2014—2015*，Oxford University Press，2016.

3. Andrew Newcombe，Lluis Paradell，*Law and Practice of Investment Treaties—Standards of Treatment*，Wolters Kluwer Press，2009.

4. Arnaud de Nantruil，*International Investment Law*，Edward Elgar Publishing limited，2020.

5. Christoph H. Schreuer，Loretta Malintopp，August Reinisch，Anthony Sinclair，*The ICSID Convention：A Commentary*（2nd ed），Cambridge University Press，2009.

6. Crina baltag，*The Energy Charter Treaty—the Notion of Investor*，Kluwer Law Press，2012.

7. Donatella Alessandrini，*Value Making in International Economic Law and Regulation：Alternative Possibilities*，Routledge Press，2016.

8. Eamon Doyle，*Tariffs and the Future of Trade*，Greenhaven Publishing，2020.

9. Freya Baetens and José Caiado，*Frontiers of International Economic Law：Legal Tools to Confront Interdisciplinary Challenges*，Brill Nijhoff Publishing，2014.

10. Flavia Marisi，*Environmental Interests in Investment Arbitration—Challenges and Direction*，Wikters Kluwer，2020.

11. Goldsmith Bradley，*Foreign Relations Law—Cases and Materials*，Wolter Kluwer Press，2003.

12. I. M. Destler，*American Trade Politics*（4th ed.），Peterson Institute press，2005.

13. I. D. Michalak and J. W. Salacuse，*Social Legislation in the Contemporary Middle East*，University of California International & Area Studies Press，2009.

14. Ignaz Seidl-Hohenveldern，*International Economic Law*，Kluwer Law International Press，1999.

15. Indira Carr and Peter Stone，*Internatioanl Trade Law*，6th ed.，Routledge Press，2018.

16. Jacqueline D. Krikorian，*International Trade Law and Domestic Policy：Canada，the United States，and the WTO*，UBC Press，2012.

17. Jagdish Bhagwati，*The World Trade System at Risk*，Prentice Hall-Harvester Wheatsheaf Publishers Press，1991.

18. Janet Laible，*Separatism and Sovereignty in the New Europe-Party Politics and the Meanings of Statehood in a Supranational Context*，Palgrave and Macmillan Press，2008.

19. Jean Ho，*State Reponsibility for Breaches of Investment Contracts*，Cambridge University Press，2018.

20. Jeswald W. Salacuse，*The Law of Investment Treaties*，Oxford University Press，2010.

21. Joanna Jemielniak，etc.，Establishing Judicial Authority in International Economic Law，Cambridge University Press，2016.

22. Joern Griebel and Steffen Hindelang，*International Investment Law and EU Law*，Springer Press，2011.

23. Jorun Baumgartner，*Treaty Shopping in International Investment Law*，Oxford University Press，2017.

24. Kenneth J. Vandevelde，*U.S. International Investment Agreements*，Oxford University Press，2009.

25. M. Sornarajah，*The International Law on Foreign Investment*，Cambridge University press，1996.

26. M. Sornarajah，*The Settlement of Foreign Investment Disputes*，Kluwer Law International，2000.

27. M. Sornarajah，*The International Law on Foreign Investment*，Cambridge University Press，2010.

28. Marc Bungenberg，Jörn Griebel，Teffen Hindelang，*International Investment Law and EU Law*，Springer press，2011.

29. Mavluda Sattorova，*The Impact of Investment Treaty Law on Host States：Enabling Good Governance?*，Hart Publishing，2018.

30. Monique Sasson，*Substantive Law in Investment Treaty Arbitration—The Unsettled Relationship between International Law and Municipal Law*，2nd ed.，Wolters Kluwer，2017.

31. Muchlinski Peter，Ortino Federico，Schreuer Christoph，*The Oxford Handbook of International Investment Law*，Oxford university press，2008.

32. Peter D. Cameron，*International Energy Investment Law*，Oxford University Press，2010.

33. Peter Quayle，Xuan Gao，*International Organizations and the Promotion of Effective Dispute Resolution：AIIB Yearbook of International Law 2019*，Brill Nijhoff Press，2019.

34. Petros C. Mavroidis，*The Regulation of International Trade*，Volume 1：*GATT*，MIT Press，2016.

35. Petros C. Mavroidis，*The Regulation of International Trade*，Volume 2：*The WTO Agreements on Trade in Goods*，MIT Press，2016.

36. R. C. Van Caenegem，*European Law in the Past and the Future—Unity and Diversity over Two Millennia*，Cambridge University Press，2004.

37. Richard Baldwin，Patrick Low，*Multilateralizing Regionalism*，Cambridge

University Press，2009.

38. Rodrigo Polanco，*The Return of the Home State to Investor-State Disputes*，Cambridge Unversity Press，2019.

39. Rudolph Dolzer，Christoph Schreuer，*Principles of International Investment Law*，2nd ed.，Oxford University Press，2012.

40. Sanam Salem Haghighi，*Energy Security—The External Legal Relations of the European Union with Major Oil and Gas Supplying Country*，Hart Publishing Press，2007.

41. Sarah Joseph，*Blame it on the WTO: A Human Rights Critique*，Oxford university press，2011.

42. Stephan W. Schill，*The Multilateralization of International Investment Law*，Cambridge University Press，2009.

43. Stephan W. Schill，etc.，*International Investment Law and History*，Edward Elgar Publishing，2018.

44. Suzanne A. Spears，*The Quest for Policy Space in a New Generation of International Investment Agreements*，Oxford University Press，2010.

45. William A. Lovett，Alfred E. Eckes and Richard L.Brinkman，*U.S. Trade Policy—History，Theory and the WTO*，E. Sharpe Press，1999.

46. Zachary Douglas，*The International Law of Investment Claims*，Cambridge University Press，2009.

（二）期刊论文

1. A. Konoplyanik，Energy Charter Plus-Russia to Take the Lead Role in Modernizing ECT?，*OGEL Journal*，2008,Vol.7.

2. A. Konoplyanik，Russia-Eu Summit，WTO，The Energy Charter and the Issue of Energy Transit，*International Energy Law and Taxation Review*,2005，No.2.

3. ABA，American Bar Association Section of International Law and Practice Report to the House of Delegates—Multilateral Agreement on Investment，*The International Lawyer*，1999,Vol.30.

4. A. V. Ganesan，Strategic Options Available to Developing Countries with regard to a Multilateral Agreement on Investment，*International Monetary and Financial Issues for the 1990s*，1999,Vol.10.

5. Andreas F. Lowenfeld. The ICSID Convention: Origins and Transformation，*Georgia Journal of International and Comparative Law*,2009,Vol.6.

6. Azlan Mohamed Noh，Establishing Jurisdiction through A Most-Favoured-Nation Clause，*Int'l Trade & Bus. L. Rev.*，2012,Vol.15.

7. Bernardo M. Cremades，Disputes Arising out of Foreign Direct Investment in

Latin America: A New Look at the Calvo Doctrine and other Jurisdictional Issue, *Dispute Resolution Journal*, 2004, Vol.59.

8. Cardwell, P. J.& French, D., The European Union and a Global Investment Partner —Law, Policy and Rhetoric of the Attainment of Development Assistance and Market Liberalization?, in C. Brown and K.Miles, ed., *Evolution in Investment Treaty Law and Arbitration*, Cambridge University Press, 2011.

9. Daniel M. Price, An Overview of the NAFTA Investment Chapter—Substantive Rules and Investor-State Dispute Settlement, *The International Lawyer*, 2018, Vol.27.

10. Dattu, A Journey from Havana to Paris, *Fordham International Law Journal*, 2000, Vol.24.

11. Dimopoulos, The Common Commercial Policy After the Lisbon Treaty-Establishing Parallelism Between Internal and External Economic Relations, *Yearbook European Law and Policy*, 2008.

12. Dolzer, Rudolf, Indirect Expropriations: New Developments?, *New York University Environmental Law Journal*, 2002, Vol.11.

13. Erhraim Clark, Valuing of Political Risk, *Journal of International Money and Finance*, 1997, Vol.1.

14. Errc M. Burt, Developing Countries and the Framework for Negotiations on Foreign Direct Investment in the World Trade Organization, *American University Journal of International Law & Policy*, 1997, Vol.12.

15. Fernandez and Poters, Returns to Regionalism: An Analysis of Non-Traditional Gains from Regional Trade Agreements, *the World Bank Economic Review*, 1998, Vol.8.

16. Fortier, L.yves & Drymer, Stephen L, Indirect Expropriation in the Law of International Investment: I Know It When I See It, or Caveat Investor, *ICSID Review—Foreign Investment Law Journal*, 2004, Vol.19.

17. Herman Walker Jr, Provisions on Companies in United States Commercial Treaties, *American Journal of International Law*, 1956, Vol.50.

18. I. Seidl-Hoheveldern, Subrogation under the MIGA Convention, 2 *ICSID Review—Foreign Law Journal*, 1987.

19. J. W. Salacuse, BIT by BIT—The Growth of Bilateral Investment Treaties and Their Impact of Foreign Investment in Developing Countries, *Int'l Law*, 1990, Vol.24.

20. James Chalker, Making the Investment Provisions of the Energy Charter Treaty Sustainable Development Friendly, *International Environmental Agreements*, 2006.

21. James Salzman, Labor Rights, Globalization and Institutions—The Role and Influence of the Organization for Economic Cooperation and Development, *Michigan Journal of International Law*, 2000, Vol.21.

22. John H. Jackson，Perspectives on Regionalism in Trade Relations，*Law and Policy in International Business*，1996，Vol.27.

23. Julie A. Maupin，MFN-based Jurisdiction in Investor-State Arbitration：Is There any Hope for a Consistent Approach，*Journal of International Economic Law*，2011，Vol.14.

24. Kenneth J. Vandevelde，A Brief History of International Investment Agreements，*U.C. Davis Journal of International Law and Policy*，2005，Vol.12.

25. A. Konoplyanik，T. Walde，Energy Charter Treaty and Its Role in International Energy，*Journal of Energy and Natural Resources Law*，2007，Vol.24.

26. Kojo Yelpaala，Fundamentalism in Public Health and Safety in Bilateral Investment Treaties（Part Ⅰ），*AJWH*，2008，Vol.3.

27. Rafael Leal-Arcas，The Multilateralization of International Investment Law，*North Carolina Journal of International Law*，2009，Vol.35，Iss.1.

28. Richard H. Steinberg，Antidotes to Regionalism：Responses to Trade Diversion Effects of the North American Free Trade Agreement，*Stanford Journal of International Law*，1993，Vol.29.

29. S. Fietta，Most Favored Nation Treatment and Dispute Resolution under Bilateral Investment Treaties：A Turing Point，*International Arbitration Law Review*，2005，Vol.5.

30. Scott Vesel，Clearing a Path through a Tangled Jurisprudence：Most-Favored-Nation Clauses and Dispute Settlement Provisions in Bilateral Investment Treaties，*Yale Journal of International Law*，2007，Vol.32.

31. Sol Picciotto，Linkage in International Investment Regulation：The Antinomies of the Draft Multilateral Agreement on Investment，*University of Pennsylvania Journal of International Economic Law*，1998，Vol.19.

32. Stephen Woolcock，The Potential Impact of lisbon Treaty on European Union External Trade Policy，*European Policy Analysis*，June Issue，2008.

33. Susan D. Franck，Foreign Direct Investment，Investment Treaty Arbitration and the Rule of Law，*Mc George Global Business and Development Law Journal*，2007，Vol.19.

34. Susan D. Franck，The Legitimacy Crisis in Investment Treaty Arbitration：Privatizing Public International Law through Inconsistent Decisions，*Fordham Law Review*，2005，Vol.7.

35. Tim Buthe，Helen V. Milner，The Politics of Foreign Direct Investment into Developing Countries：Increasing FDI through International Trade Agreements?，*American Journal of Political Science*，2008，Vol.52，No.4.

36. Thomas W.Waelde，International Investment under the 1994 Energy Charter

Treaty: Legal Negotiation and Policy Implication for International Investors within Western and Commonwealth of Independent States/Eastern Countries, *Journal of World Trade*, 1995, Vol.29,

37. Wesley Scholz, International Regulation of Foreign Direct Investment, *International Law Journal*, 1998, Vol.31, No.3.

38. William W. Bruke, White & Andreas Von Staden, Investment Protection in Extraordinary Times : The Implication and Application of Non-preclude Measures Provisions in Bilateral Investment Treaties, *Virginia Journal of international law*, 2008, Vol.2.

39. Wouters, Coppens and De Meester, The European Union's External Relations after the Lisbon Treaty, in S. Griller and J. Ziller ed., *The Lisbon Treaty—EU Constitutionalism without a Constitutional Treaty?* European Community Studies Association of Austria Publication Series, 2008, Vol.11.

40. Yannick Radi, The Application of the Most-Favoured-Nation Clause to the Dispute Settlement Provisions of Bilateral Investment Treaties—Domesticating the "Trojan Horse", *The European Journal of International Law*, 2007, Vol.18, Iss.4.

(三)其他

1. Benno Ferrarini, A Multilateral Framework for Investment? Research Fellow, World Trade Institute, University of Bern, http://www.wti.org/.

2. Carolinn Hjalmroth, Stefan Westerberg, A Common Investment Policy for the EU, http://www.kommers.se/In-English/Analyses/.

3. Drabek Z., *A Multilateral Agreement on Investment—Convincing the Skeptics*, WTO Staff Working Paper, 1998.

4. European Commission, Global Europe: Competing in the World, COM (2006) 567 final, 4 October 2006.

5. E. K. Fitz Gerald, R. Cubero-Brealey and A. Lehmann, *The Development Implications of the Multilateral Agreement on Investment*, A Report Commissioned by the Department for International Development, 2010.

6. Katia Tieleman, The Failure of the Multilateral Agreement on Investment and the Absence of a Global Public Policy Network, http://www.gppi.net/fileadmin/gppi.

7. ICSID, *History of the ICSID Convention*, 1968, Vol.2.

8. ICSID Secretariat, *Possible Improvements of the Framework for ICSID Arbitration.*, April 22, 2004.

9. ICSID, *Disputes before the Centre*, News from ICSID, February 22, 2005.

10. IMF, *World Economic Outlook*, October 2012.

11. *Indirect Expropriation: Is the Right to Regulate at Risk? Symposium Co-*

organised by ICSID，OECD and UNCTAD：Making the Most of International Investment Agreements—A Common Agenda，12 December，2005.

12. OECD，*FDI in Figures*，July 2012，http://www. oecd. org/redirect/investment/.

13. OECD，Harnessing Freedom of Investment for Green Growth，5 May 2011，http://www.oecd.org/investment/.

14. OECD，*Launch of the Negotiations of a Multilateral Agreement on Investment*，DAFFE/CMIT/CIME(95)13/FINAL，5 May 1995.

15. Stephen Young，Ana Teresa Tavares，Multilateral Rules on FDI：Do We Need Them? Will We Get Them? A Developing Country Perspective，http://findarticles.com/p/articles/mi_6790/.

16. UNCTAD，*International Investment Instruments—A Compendium*，UNCTAD/DITE/4(Vol.V)，2000.

17. UNCTAD，*Investor-State Dispute Settlement and Impact on Investment Rulemaking*，Sales No. E.07.11.D. 10，2007.

18. UNCTAD，*International Investment Rule-making—Stocktaking*，*Challenges and the Way Forward*，UNCTAD/ITE/IIT/2007/3，2008.

19. UNCTAD，*World Investment Report* 2012：*Towards a New Generation of Investment Policies—the Regional Trends in FDI*，UNCTAD/E.12.II.D.3，2012.

20. UNCTAD，*Foreign Direct Investment and Performance Requirement—New Evidence Form Selected Countries*，UNCTAD/ITE/IIA/2003/7.

21. UNCTAD，*World Investment Report* 2012，July 7，2012.

22. UNCTAD，*World Investment Report* 2020，June 2020.

23. UNCTAD，*Lessons from the MAI*，UNCTAD Series on Issues in International Investment Agreements，United Nations，1999.

24. UNCTC，*Bilateral Investment Treaties*，1988.

25. U.S. Foreign Affairs Manual，http://www.state.gov/m/a/dir/regs/fam/.

26. U.S. CRS Report，Declaration of War and Authorization for the Use of Military Force—Historical Background and Legal Implications，2007.

27. Whilhelm Lehmann，*Lars Bosche*，*Lobbying in the European Union*，*Current Rules and Practices*，European Parliament，Directorate-General for Research，Working Paper，AFCO 104 EN，04-2003.

28. WTO，*Doha WTO Ministerial* 2001—*Ministerial Declaration*，WT/MIN(01)/DEC/1.

29. WTO，Doha Development Agenda—Doha Work Programme.

30. WTO，*Report of the Working Group on the Relationship between Trade and Investment to the General Council*，WT/WGTI/4，2000.

31. WTO，*Working Group on the Relationship between Trade and Investment*，*Communication from Korea*，WT/WGTI/W/70，30 March 1999.

32. WTO，*Working Group on the Relationship between Trade and Investment*，*Communication from China*，WT/WGTI/W/160，15 April 2003.

33. WTO，*Working Group on the Relationship between Trade and Investment*，*Communication from Japan*，WT/WGTI/W/121，27 July 2002.

34. WTO，*Working Group on the Relationship between Trade and Investment*，*Communication from EUROPEAN Community and Its Members*，WT/WGTI/W/125，28 June 2002.

35. WTO，*Working Group on the Relationship between Trade and Investment*，*Communication from EUROPEAN Community and Its Members*，WT/WGTI/W/150，7 October 2002.

附　录

Ⅰ. AGREEMENT ON TRADE-RELATED INVESTMENT MEASURES
(MARRAKESH AGREEMENT ESTABLISHING THE WORLD TRADE ORGANIZATION ANNEX 1A: MULTILATERAL AGREEMENTS ON TRADE IN GOODS)

Members,

Considering that Ministers agreed in the Punta del Este Declaration that "Following an examination of the operation of GATT Articles related to the trade-restrictive and distorting effects of investment measures, negotiations should elaborate, as appropriate, further provisions that may be necessary to avoid such adverse effects on trade";

Desiring to promote the expansion and progressive liberalisation of world trade and to facilitate investment across international frontiers so as to increase the economic growth of all trading partners, particularly developing country Members, while ensuring free competition;

Taking into account the particular trade, development and financial needs of developing country Members, particularly those of the least-developed country Members;

Recognizing that certain investment measures can cause trade-restrictive and distorting effects;

Hereby *agree* as follows:

Article 1　*Coverage*

This Agreement applies to investment measures related to trade in goods only (referred to in this Agreement as "TRIMs").

Article 2　*National Treatment and Quantitative Restrictions*

1. Without prejudice to other rights and obligations under GATT 1994, no Member shall apply any TRIM that is inconsistent with the provisions of Article Ⅲ or Article Ⅺ of GATT 1994.

2. An illustrative list of TRIMs that are inconsistent with the obligation of national treatment provided for in paragraph 4 of Article Ⅲ of GATT 1994 and the obligation of general elimination of quantitative restrictions provided for in paragraph 1 of Article Ⅺ of GATT 1994 is contained in the Annex to this Agreement.

Article 3　*Exceptions*

All exceptions under GATT 1994 shall apply, as appropriate, to the provisions of this Agreement.

Article 4　*Developing Country Members*

A developing country Member shall be free to deviate temporarily from the provisions of Article 2 to the extent and in such a manner as Article ⅩⅧ of GATT 1994, the Understanding on the Balance-of-Payments Provisions of GATT 1994, and the Declaration on Trade Measures Taken for Balance-of-Payments Purposes adopted on 28 November 1979 (BISD 26S/205-209) permit the Member to deviate from the provisions of Articles Ⅲ and Ⅺ of GATT 1994.

Article 5　*Notification and Transitional Arrangements*

1. Members, within 90 days of the date of entry into force of the WTO Agreement, shall notify the Council for Trade in Goods of all TRIMs they are applying that are not in conformity with the provisions of this Agreement. Such TRIMs of general or specific application shall be notified, along with their principal features.[①]

2. Each Member shall eliminate all TRIMs which are notified under paragraph 1 within two years of the date of entry into force of the WTO Agreement in the case of a developed country Member, within five years in the case of a developing country Member, and within seven years in the case of a least-developed country Member.

3. On request, the Council for Trade in Goods may extend the transition period for the elimination of TRIMs notified under paragraph 1 for a developing country Member, including a least-developed country Member, which demonstrates particular difficulties

---

① ［原文脚注 1］ In the case of TRIMs applied under discretionary authority, each specific application shall be notified. Information that would prejudice the legitimate commercial interests of particular enterprises need not be disclosed.

in implementing the provisions of this Agreement. In considering such a request, the Council for Trade in Goods shall take into account the individual development, financial and trade needs of the Member in question.

4. During the transition period, a Member shall not modify the terms of any TRIM which it notifies under paragraph 1 from those prevailing at the date of entry into force of the WTO Agreement so as to increase the degree of inconsistency with the provisions of Article 2. TRIMs introduced less than 180 days before the date of entry into force of the WTO Agreement shall not benefit from the transitional arrangements provided in paragraph 2.

5. Notwithstanding the provisions of Article 2, a Member, in order not to disadvantage established enterprises which are subject to a TRIM notified under paragraph 1, may apply during the transition period the same TRIM to a new investment (i) where the products of such investment are like products to those of the established enterprises, and (ii) where necessary to avoid distorting the conditions of competition between the new investment and the established enterprises. Any TRIM so applied to a new investment shall be notified to the Council for Trade in Goods. The terms of such a TRIM shall be equivalent in their competitive effect to those applicable to the established enterprises, and it shall be terminated at the same time.

Article 6　*Transparency*

1. Members reaffirm, with respect to TRIMs, their commitment to obligations on transparency and notification in Article X of GATT 1994, in the undertaking on "Notification" contained in the Understanding Regarding Notification, Consultation, Dispute Settlement and Surveillance adopted on 28 November 1979 and in the Ministerial Decision on Notification Procedures adopted on 15 April 1994.

2. Each Member shall notify the Secretariat of the publications in which TRIMs may be found, including those applied by regional and local governments and authorities within their territories.

3. Each Member shall accord sympathetic consideration to requests for information, and afford adequate opportunity for consultation, on any matter arising from this Agreement raised by another Member. In conformity with Article X of GATT 1994 no Member is required to disclose information the disclosure of which would impede law enforcement or otherwise be contrary to the public interest or would prejudice the legitimate commercial interests of particular enterprises, public or private.

Article 7　*Committee on Trade-Related Investment Measures*

1. A Committee on Trade-Related Investment Measures (referred to in this Agreement as the "Committee") is hereby established, and shall be open to all Members. The Committee shall elect its own Chairman and Vice-Chairman, and shall

meet not less than once a year and otherwise at the request of any Member.

2. The Committee shall carry out responsibilities assigned to it by the Council for Trade in Goods and shall afford Members the opportunity to consult on any matters relating to the operation and implementation of this Agreement.

3. The Committee shall monitor the operation and implementation of this Agreement and shall report thereon annually to the Council for Trade in Goods.

Article 8　Consultation and Dispute Settlement

The provisions of Articles XII and XXIII of GATT 1994, as elaborated and applied by the Dispute Settlement Understanding, shall apply to consultations and the settlement of disputes under this Agreement.

Article 9　Review by the Council for Trade in Goods

Not later than five years after the date of entry into force of the WTO Agreement, the Council for Trade in Goods shall review the operation of this Agreement and, as appropriate, propose to the Ministerial Conference amendments to its text. In the course of this review, the Council for Trade in Goods shall consider whether the Agreement should be complemented with provisions on investment policy and competition policy.

ANNEX

Illustrative List

1. TRIMs that are inconsistent with the obligation of national treatment provided for in paragraph 4 of Article III of GATT 1994 include those which are mandatory or enforceable under domestic law or under administrative rulings, or compliance with which is necessary to obtain an advantage, and which require:

(a) the purchase or use by an enterprise of products of domestic origin or from any domestic source, whether specified in terms of particular products, in terms of volume or value of products, or in terms of a proportion of volume or value of its local production; or

(b) that an enterprise's purchases or use of imported products be limited to an amount related to the volume or value of local products that it exports.

2. TRIMs that are inconsistent with the obligation of general elimination of quantitative restrictions provided for in paragraph 1 of Article XI of GATT 1994 include those which are mandatory or enforceable under domestic law or under administrative rulings, or compliance with which is necessary to obtain an advantage, and which restrict:

(a) the importation by an enterprise of products used in or related to its local production, generally or to an amount related to the volume or value of local production that it exports;

(b) the importation by an enterprise of products used in or related to its local production by restricting its access to foreign exchange to an amount related to the foreign exchange inflows attributable to the enterprise; or

(c) the exportation or sale for export by an enterprise of products, whether specified in terms of particular products, in terms of volume or value of products, or in terms of a proportion of volume or value of its local production.

Ⅱ. GENERAL AGREEMENT ON TRADE IN SERVICES

(MARRAKESH AGREEMENT ESTABLISHING THE WORLD TRADE ORGANIZATION ANNEX 1B: GENERAL AGREEMENT ON TRADE IN SERVICES AND MINISTERIAL DECISIONS RELATING TO THE GENERAL AGREEMENT ON TRADE IN SERVICES)

Content

Members,

Recognizing the growing importance of trade in services for the growth and development of the world economy;

Wishing to establish a multilateral framework of principles and rules for trade in services with a view to the expansion of such trade under conditions of transparency and progressive liberalization and as a means of promoting the economic growth of all trading partners and the development of developing countries;

Desiring the early achievement of progressively higher levels of liberalization of trade in services through successive rounds of multilateral negotiations aimed at promoting the interests of all participants on a mutually advantageous basis and at securing an overall balance of rights and obligations, while giving due respect to national policy objectives;

Recognizing the right of Members to regulate, and to introduce new regulations, on the supply of services within their territories in order to meet national policy objectives and, given asymmetries existing with respect to the degree of development of services regulations in different countries, the particular need of developing countries to exercise this right;

Desiring to facilitate the increasing participation of developing countries in trade in services and the expansion of their service exports including, *inter alia*, through the strengthening of their domestic services capacity and its efficiency and competitiveness;

Taking particular account of the serious difficulty of the least-developed countries in view of their special economic situation and their development, trade and financial needs;

Hereby *agree* as follows:

PART Ⅰ SCOPE AND DEFINITION

Article Ⅰ Scope and Definition

1. This Agreement applies to measures by Members affecting trade in services.

2. For the purposes of this Agreement, trade in services is defined as the supply of a service:

(a) from the territory of one Member into the territory of any other Member;

(b) in the territory of one Member to the service consumer of any other Member;

(c) by a service supplier of one Member, through commercial presence in the territory of any other Member;

(d) by a service supplier of one Member, through presence of natural persons of a Member in the territory of any other Member.

3. For the purposes of this Agreement:

(a) "measures by Members" means measures taken by:

(i) central, regional or local governments and authorities; and

(ii) non-governmental bodies in the exercise of powers delegated by central, regional or local governments or authorities;

In fulfilling its obligations and commitments under the Agreement, each Member shall take such reasonable measures as may be available to it to ensure their observance by regional and local governments and authorities and non-governmental bodies within its territory;

(b) "services" includes any service in any sector except services supplied in the exercise of governmental authority;

(c) "a service supplied in the exercise of governmental authority" means any service which is supplied neither on a commercial basis nor in competition with one or more service suppliers.

PART Ⅱ GENERAL OBLIGATIONS AND DISCIPLINES

Article Ⅱ *Most-Favoured-Nation Treatment*

1. With respect to any measure covered by this Agreement, each Member shall accord immediately and unconditionally to services and service suppliers of any other Member treatment no less favourable than that it accords to like services and service suppliers of any other country.

2. A Member may maintain a measure inconsistent with paragraph 1 provided that such a measure is listed in, and meets the conditions of, the Annex on Article Ⅱ Exemptions.

3. The provisions of this Agreement shall not be so construed as to prevent any Member from conferring or according advantages to adjacent countries in order to facilitate exchanges limited to contiguous frontier zones of services that are both locally produced and consumed.

Article Ⅲ *Transparency*

1. Each Member shall publish promptly and, except in emergency situations, at the latest by the time of their entry into force, all relevant measures of general application which pertain to or affect the operation of this Agreement. International agreements pertaining to or affecting trade in services to which a Member is a signatory shall also be published.

2. Where publication as referred to in paragraph 1 is not practicable, such information shall be made otherwise publicly available.

3. Each Member shall promptly and at least annually inform the Council for Trade in Services of the introduction of any new, or any changes to existing, laws, regulations or administrative guidelines which significantly affect trade in services covered by its specific commitments under this Agreement.

4. Each Member shall respond promptly to all requests by any other Member for specific information on any of its measures of general application or international agreements within the meaning of paragraph 1. Each Member shall also establish one or more enquiry points to provide specific information to other Members, upon request, on all such matters as well as those subject to the notification requirement in paragraph 3.

Such enquiry points shall be established within two years from the date of entry into force of the Agreement Establishing the WTO (referred to in this Agreement as the "WTO Agreement"). Appropriate flexibility with respect to the time-limit within which such enquiry points are to be established may be agreed upon for individual developing country Members. Enquiry points need not be depositories of laws and regulations.

5. Any Member may notify to the Council for Trade in Services any measure, taken by any other Member, which it considers affects the operation of this Agreement.

Article Ⅲ *bis Disclosure of Confidential Information*

Nothing in this Agreement shall require any Member to provide confidential information, the disclosure of which would impede law enforcement, or otherwise be contrary to the public interest, or which would prejudice legitimate commercial interests of particular enterprises, public or private.

Article Ⅳ *Increasing Participation of Developing Countries*

1. The increasing participation of developing country Members in world trade shall be facilitated through negotiated specific commitments, by different Members pursuant to Parts Ⅲ and Ⅳ of this Agreement, relating to:

(a) the strengthening of their domestic services capacity and its efficiency and competitiveness,*inter alia* through access to technology on a commercial basis;

(b) the improvement of their access to distribution channels and information networks; and

(c) the liberalization of market access in sectors and modes of supply of export interest to them.

2. Developed country Members, and to the extent possible other Members, shall establish contact points within two years from the date of entry into force of the WTO Agreement to facilitate the access of developing country Members' service suppliers to information, related to their respective markets, concerning:

(a) commercial and technical aspects of the supply of services;

(b) registration, recognition and obtaining of professional qualifications; and

(c) the availability of services technology.

3. Special priority shall be given to the least-developed country Members in the implementation of paragraphs 1 and 2. Particular account shall be taken of the serious difficulty of the least-developed countries in accepting negotiated specific commitments in view of their special economic situation and their development, trade and financial needs.

Article Ⅴ *Economic Integration*

1. This Agreement shall not prevent any of its Members from being a party to or entering into an agreement liberalizing trade in services between or among the parties to

such an agreement, provided that such an agreement:

(a) has substantial sectoral coverage①, and

(b) provides for the absence or elimination of substantially all discrimination, in the sense of Article XVII, between or among the parties, in the sectors covered under subparagraph (a), through:

(i) elimination of existing discriminatory measures, and/or

(ii) prohibition of new or more discriminatory measures, either at the entry into force of that agreement or on the basis of a reasonable time-frame, except for measures permitted under Articles XI, XII, XIV and XIV bis.

2. In evaluating whether the conditions under paragraph 1 (b) are met, consideration may be given to the relationship of the agreement to a wider process of economic integration or trade liberalization among the countries concerned.

3. (a) Where developing countries are parties to an agreement of the type referred to in paragraph 1, flexibility shall be provided for regarding the conditions set out in paragraph 1, particularly with reference to subparagraph (b) thereof, in accordance with the level of development of the countries concerned, both overall and in individual sectors and subsectors.

(b) Notwithstanding paragraph 6, in the case of an agreement of the type referred to in paragraph 1 involving only developing countries, more favourable treatment may be granted to juridical persons owned or controlled by natural persons of the parties to such an agreement.

4. Any agreement referred to in paragraph 1 shall be designed to facilitate trade between the parties to the agreement and shall not in respect of any Member outside the agreement raise the overall level of barriers to trade in services within the respective sectors or subsectors compared to the level applicable prior to such an agreement.

5. If, in the conclusion, enlargement or any significant modification of any agreement under paragraph 1, a Member intends to withdraw or modify a specific commitment inconsistently with the terms and conditions set out in its Schedule, it shall provide at least 90 days advance notice of such modification or withdrawal and the procedure set forth in paragraphs 2, 3 and 4 of Article XXI shall apply.

6. A service supplier of any other Member that is a juridical person constituted under the laws of a party to an agreement referred to in paragraph 1 shall be entitled to treatment granted under such agreement, provided that it engages in substantive

---

① ［本协定原文脚注 1］ This condition is understood in terms of number of sectors, volume of trade affected and modes of supply. In order to meet this condition, agreements should not provide for the *a priori* exclusion of any mode of supply.

business operations in the territory of the parties to such agreement.

7. (a) Members which are parties to any agreement referred to in paragraph 1 shall promptly notify any such agreement and any enlargement or any significant modification of that agreement to the Council for Trade in Services. They shall also make available to the Council such relevant information as may be requested by it. The Council may establish a working party to examine such an agreement or enlargement or modification of that agreement and to report to the Council on its consistency with this Article.

(b) Members which are parties to any agreement referred to in paragraph 1 which is implemented on the basis of a time-frame shall report periodically to the Council for Trade in Services on its implementation. The Council may establish a working party to examine such reports if it deems such a working party necessary.

(c) Based on the reports of the working parties referred to in subparagraphs (a) and (b), the Council may make recommendations to the parties as it deems appropriate.

8. A Member which is a party to any agreement referred to in paragraph 1 may not seek compensation for trade benefits that may accrue to any other Member from such agreement.

Article V bis Labour Markets Integration Agreements

This Agreement shall not prevent any of its Members from being a party to an agreement establishing full integration① of the labour markets between or among the parties to such an agreement, provided that such an agreement:

(a) exempts citizens of parties to the agreement from requirements concerning residency and work permits;

(b) is notified to the Council for Trade in Services.

Article VI Domestic Regulation

1. In sectors where specific commitments are undertaken, each Member shall ensure that all measures of general application affecting trade in services are administered in a reasonable, objective and impartial manner.

2. (a) Each Member shall maintain or institute as soon as practicable judicial, arbitral or administrative tribunals or procedures which provide, at the request of an affected service supplier, for the prompt review of, and where justified, appropriate remedies for, administrative decisions affecting trade in services. Where such procedures are not independent of the agency entrusted with the administrative decision concerned, the Member shall ensure that the procedures in fact provide for an objective

---

① ［本协定原文脚注 2］ Typically, such integration provides citizens of the parties concerned with a right of free entry to the employment markets of the parties and includes measures concerning conditions of pay, other conditions of employment and social benefits.

and impartial review.

(b) The provisions of subparagraph (a) shall not be construed to require a Member to institute such tribunals or procedures where this would be inconsistent with its constitutional structure or the nature of its legal system.

3. Where authorization is required for the supply of a service on which a specific commitment has been made, the competent authorities of a Member shall, within a reasonable period of time after the submission of an application considered complete under domestic laws and regulations, inform the applicant of the decision concerning the application. At the request of the applicant, the competent authorities of the Member shall provide, without undue delay, information concerning the status of the application.

4. With a view to ensuring that measures relating to qualification requirements and procedures, technical standards and licensing requirements do not constitute unnecessary barriers to trade in services, the Council for Trade in Services shall, through appropriate bodies it may establish, develop any necessary disciplines. Such disciplines shall aim to ensure that such requirements are, inter alia:

(a) based on objective and transparent criteria, such as competence and the ability to supply the service;

(b) not more burdensome than necessary to ensure the quality of the service;

(c) in the case of licensing procedures, not in themselves a restriction on the supply of the service.

5. (a) In sectors in which a Member has undertaken specific commitments, pending the entry into force of disciplines developed in these sectors pursuant to paragraph 4, the Member shall not apply licensing and qualification requirements and technical standards that nullify or impair such specific commitments in a manner which:

(i) does not comply with the criteria outlined in subparagraphs 4(a), (b) or (c); and

(ii) could not reasonably have been expected of that Member at the time the specific commitments in those sectors were made.

(b) In determining whether a Member is in conformity with the obligation under paragraph 5 (a), account shall be taken of international standards of relevant international organizations① applied by that Member.

6. In sectors where specific commitments regarding professional services are undertaken, each Member shall provide for adequate procedures to verify the

---

① [本协定原文脚注 3] The term "relevant international organizations" refers to international bodies whose membership is open to the relevant bodies of at least all Members of the WTO.

competence of professionals of any other Member.

Article VII *Recognition*

1. For the purposes of the fulfilment, in whole or in part, of its standards or criteria for the authorization, licensing or certification of services suppliers, and subject to the requirements of paragraph 3, a Member may recognize the education or experience obtained, requirements met, or licenses or certifications granted in a particular country. Such recognition, which may be achieved through harmonization or otherwise, may be based upon an agreement or arrangement with the country concerned or may be accorded autonomously.

2. A Member that is a party to an agreement or arrangement of the type referred to in paragraph 1, whether existing or future, shall afford adequate opportunity for other interested Members to negotiate their accession to such an agreement or arrangement or to negotiate comparable ones with it. Where a Member accords recognition autonomously, it shall afford adequate opportunity for any other Member to demonstrate that education, experience, licenses, or certifications obtained or requirements met in that other Member's territory should be recognized.

3. A Member shall not accord recognition in a manner which would constitute a means of discrimination between countries in the application of its standards or criteria for the authorization, licensing or certification of services suppliers, or a disguised restriction on trade in services.

4. Each Member shall:

(a) within 12 months from the date on which the WTO Agreement takes effect for it, inform the Council for Trade in Services of its existing recognition measures and state whether such measures are based on agreements or arrangements of the type referred to in paragraph 1;

(b) promptly inform the Council for Trade in Services as far in advance as possible of the opening of negotiations on an agreement or arrangement of the type referred to in paragraph 1 in order to provide adequate opportunity to any other Member to indicate their interest in participating in the negotiations before they enter a substantive phase;

(c) promptly inform the Council for Trade in Services when it adopts new recognition measures or significantly modifies existing ones and state whether the measures are based on an agreement or arrangement of the type referred to in paragraph 1.

5. Wherever appropriate, recognition should be based on multilaterally agreed criteria. In appropriate cases, Members shall work in cooperation with relevant intergovernmental and non-governmental organizations towards the establishment and adoption of common international standards and criteria for recognition and common international standards for the practice of relevant services trades and professions.

Article Ⅷ Monopolies and Exclusive Service Suppliers

1.Each Member shall ensure that any monopoly supplier of a service in its territory does not, in the supply of the monopoly service in the relevant market, act in a manner inconsistent with that Member's obligations under Article Ⅱ and specific commitments.

2. Where a Member's monopoly supplier competes, either directly or through an affiliated company, in the supply of a service outside the scope of its monopoly rights and which is subject to that Member's specific commitments, the Member shall ensure that such a supplier does not abuse its monopoly position to act in its territory in a manner inconsistent with such commitments.

3. The Council for Trade in Services may, at the request of a Member which has a reason to believe that a monopoly supplier of a service of any other Member is acting in a manner inconsistent with paragraph 1 or 2, request the Member establishing, maintaining or authorizing such supplier to provide specific information concerning the relevant operations.

4. If, after the date of entry into force of the WTO Agreement, a Member grants monopoly rights regarding the supply of a service covered by its specific commitments, that Member shall notify the Council for Trade in Services no later than three months before the intended implementation of the grant of monopoly rights and the provisions of paragraphs 2, 3 and 4 of Article ⅩⅡ shall apply.

5. The provisions of this Article shall also apply to cases of exclusive service suppliers, where a Member, formally or in effect, (*a*) authorizes or establishes a small number of service suppliers and (*b*) substantially prevents competition among those suppliers in its territory.

Article Ⅸ Business Practices

1. Members recognize that certain business practices of service suppliers, other than those falling under Article Ⅷ, may restrain competition and thereby restrict trade in services.

2. Each Member shall, at the request of any other Member, enter into consultations with a view to eliminating practices referred to in paragraph 1. The Member addressed shall accord full and sympathetic consideration to such a request and shall cooperate through the supply of publicly available non-confidential information of relevance to the matter in question. The Member addressed shall also provide other information available to the requesting Member, subject to its domestic law and to the conclusion of satisfactory agreement concerning the safeguarding of its confidentiality by the requesting Member.

Article Ⅹ Emergency Safeguard Measures

1. There shall be multilateral negotiations on the question of emergency safeguard

measures based on the principle of non-discrimination. The results of such negotiations shall enter into effect on a date not later than three years from the date of entry into force of the WTO Agreement.

2. In the period before the entry into effect of the results of the negotiations referred to in paragraph 1, any Member may, notwithstanding the provisions of paragraph 1 of Article XXI, notify the Council on Trade in Services of its intention to modify or withdraw a specific commitment after a period of one year from the date on which the commitment enters into force; provided that the Member shows cause to the Council that the modification or withdrawal cannot await the lapse of the three-year period provided for in paragraph 1 of Article XXI.

3. The provisions of paragraph 2 shall cease to apply three years after the date of entry into force of the WTO Agreement.

Article XI *Payments and Transfers*

1. Except under the circumstances envisaged in Article XII, a Member shall not apply restrictions on international transfers and payments for current transactions relating to its specific commitments.

2. Nothing in this Agreement shall affect the rights and obligations of the members of the International Monetary Fund under the Articles of Agreement of the Fund, including the use of exchange actions which are in conformity with the Articles of Agreement, provided that a Member shall not impose restrictions on any capital transactions inconsistently with its specific commitments regarding such transactions, except under Article XII or at the request of the Fund.

Article XII *Restrictions to Safeguard the Balance of Payments*

1. In the event of serious balance-of-payments and external financial difficulties or threat thereof, a Member may adopt or maintain restrictions on trade in services on which it has undertaken specific commitments, including on payments or transfers for transactions related to such commitments. It is recognized that particular pressures on the balance of payments of a Member in the process of economic development or economic transition may necessitate the use of restrictions to ensure, *inter alia*, the maintenance of a level of financial reserves adequate for the implementation of its programme of economic development or economic transition.

2. The restrictions referred to in paragraph 1:

(a) shall not discriminate among Members;

(b) shall be consistent with the Articles of Agreement of the International Monetary Fund;

(c) shall avoid unnecessary damage to the commercial, economic and financial interests of any other Member;

(d) shall not exceed those necessary to deal with the circumstances described in paragraph 1;

(e) shall be temporary and be phased out progressively as the situation specified in paragraph 1 improves.

3. In determining the incidence of such restrictions, Members may give priority to the supply of services which are more essential to their economic or development programmes. However, such restrictions shall not be adopted or maintained for the purpose of protecting a particular service sector.

4. Any restrictions adopted or maintained under paragraph 1, or any changes therein, shall be promptly notified to the General Council.

5. (a) Members applying the provisions of this Article shall consult promptly with the Committee on Balance-of-Payments Restrictions on restrictions adopted under this Article.

(b) The Ministerial Conference shall establish procedures[①] for periodic consultations with the objective of enabling such recommendations to be made to the Member concerned as it may deem appropriate.

(c) Such consultations shall assess the balance-of-payment situation of the Member concerned and the restrictions adopted or maintained under this Article, taking into account, *inter alia*, such factors as:

(i) the nature and extent of the balance-of-payments and the external financial difficulties;

(ii) the external economic and trading environment of the consulting Member;

(iii) alternative corrective measures which may be available.

(d) The consultations shall address the compliance of any restrictions with paragraph 2, in particular the progressive phase out of restrictions in accordance with paragraph 2(e).

(e) In such consultations, all findings of statistical and other facts presented by the International Monetary Fund relating to foreign exchange, monetary reserves and balance of payments, shall be accepted and conclusions shall be based on the assessment by the Fund of the balance-of-payments and the external financial situation of the consulting Member.

6. If a Member which is not a member of the International Monetary Fund wishes to apply the provisions of this Article, the Ministerial Conference shall establish a review procedure and any other procedures necessary.

---

① ［本协定原文脚注 4］ It is understood that the procedures under paragraph 5 shall be the same as the GATT 1994 procedures.

Article XⅢ *Government Procurement*

1. Articles Ⅱ, ⅩⅥ and ⅩⅦ shall not apply to laws, regulations or requirements governing the procurement by governmental agencies of services purchased for governmental purposes and not with a view to commercial resale or with a view to use in the supply of services for commercial sale.

2. There shall be multilateral negotiations on government procurement in services under this Agreement within two years from the date of entry into force of the WTO Agreement.

Article XⅣ *General Exceptions*

Subject to the requirement that such measures are not applied in a manner which would constitute a means of arbitrary or unjustifiable discrimination between countries where like conditions prevail, or a disguised restriction on trade in services, nothing in this Agreement shall be construed to prevent the adoption or enforcement by any Member of measures:

(a) necessary to protect public morals or to maintain public order; ①

(b) necessary to protect human, animal or plant life or health;

(c) necessary to secure compliance with laws or regulations which are not inconsistent with the provisions of this Agreement including those relating to:

(i) the prevention of deceptive and fraudulent practices or to deal with the effects of a default on services contracts;

(ii) the protection of the privacy of individuals in relation to the processing and dissemination of personal data and the protection of confidentiality of individual records and accounts;

(iii) safety;

(d) inconsistent with Article ⅩⅦ, provided that the difference in treatment is aimed

---

① ［本协定原文脚注 5］ The public order exception may be invoked only where a genuine and sufficiently serious threat is posed to one of the fundamental interests of society.

at ensuring the equitable or effective① imposition or collection of direct taxes in respect of services or service suppliers of other Members;

(e) inconsistent with Article Ⅱ, provided that the difference in treatment is the result of an agreement on the avoidance of double taxation or provisions on the avoidance of double taxation in any other international agreement or arrangement by which the Member is bound.

Article ⅩⅣ bis Security Exceptions

1. Nothing in this Agreement shall be construed:

(a) to require any Member to furnish any information, the disclosure of which it considers contrary to its essential security interests; or

(b) to prevent any Member from taking any action which it considers necessary for the protection of its essential security interests:

(i) relating to the supply of services as carried out directly or indirectly for the purpose of provisioning a military establishment;

(ii) relating to fissionable and fusionable materials or the materials from which they are derived;

(iii) taken in time of war or other emergency in international relations; or

(c) to prevent any Member from taking any action in pursuance of its obligations under the United Nations Charter for the maintenance of international peace and security.

---

① ［本协定原文脚注 6］Measures that are aimed at ensuring the equitable or effective imposition or collection of direct taxes include measures taken by a Member under its taxation system which:

(i) apply to non-resident service suppliers in recognition of the fact that the tax obligation of non-residents is determined with respect to taxable items sourced or located in the Member's territory; or

(ii) apply to non-residents in order to ensure the imposition or collection of taxes in the Member's territory; or

(iii) apply to non-residents or residents in order to prevent the avoidance or evasion of taxes, including compliance measures; or

(iv) apply to consumers of services supplied in or from the territory of another Member in order to ensure the imposition or collection of taxes on such consumers derived from sources in the Member's territory; or

(v) distinguish service suppliers subject to tax on worldwide taxable items from other service suppliers, in recognition of the difference in the nature of the tax base between them; or

(vi) determine, allocate or apportion income, profit, gain, loss, deduction or credit of resident persons or branches, or between related persons or branches of the same person, in order to safeguard the Member's tax base.

Tax terms or concepts in paragraph (d) of Article ⅩⅣ and in this footnote are determined according to tax definitions and concepts, or equivalent or similar definitions and concepts, under the domestic law of the Member taking the measure.

2. The Council for Trade in Services shall be informed to the fullest extent possible of measures taken under paragraphs 1(b) and (c) and of their termination.

Article XV *Subsidies*

1. Members recognize that, in certain circumstances, subsidies may have distortive effects on trade in services. Members shall enter into negotiations with a view to developing the necessary multilateral disciplines to avoid such trade-distortive effects.[①] The negotiations shall also address the appropriateness of countervailing procedures. Such negotiations shall recognize the role of subsidies in relation to the development programmes of developing countries and take into account the needs of Members, particularly developing country Members, for flexibility in this area. For the purpose of such negotiations, Members shall exchange information concerning all subsidies related to trade in services that they provide to their domestic service suppliers.

2. Any Member which considers that it is adversely affected by a subsidy of another Member may request consultations with that Member on such matters. Such requests shall be accorded sympathetic consideration.

PART Ⅲ　SPECIFIC COMMITMENTS

Article XVI *Market Access*

1. With respect to market access through the modes of supply identified in Article I, each Member shall accord services and service suppliers of any other Member treatment no less favourable than that provided for under the terms, limitations and conditions agreed and specified in its Schedule.[②]

2. In sectors where market-access commitments are undertaken, the measures which a Member shall not maintain or adopt either on the basis of a regional subdivision or on the basis of its entire territory, unless otherwise specified in its Schedule, are defined as:

(a) limitations on the number of service suppliers whether in the form of numerical quotas, monopolies, exclusive service suppliers or the requirements of an economic needs test;

---

① ［本协定原文脚注 7］ A future work programme shall determine how, and in what time-frame, negotiations on such multilateral disciplines will be conducted.

② ［本协定原文脚注 8］ If a Member undertakes a market-access commitment in relation to the supply of a service through the mode of supply referred to in subparagraph 2(a) of Article I and if the cross-border movement of capital is an essential part of the service itself, that Member is thereby committed to allow such movement of capital. If a Member undertakes a market-access commitment in relation to the supply of a service through the mode of supply referred to in subparagraph 2(c) of Article I, it is thereby committed to allow related transfers of capital into its territory.

(b) limitations on the total value of service transactions or assets in the form of numerical quotas or the requirement of an economic needs test;

(c) limitations on the total number of service operations or on the total quantity of service output expressed in terms of designated numerical units in the form of quotas or the requirement of an economic needs test; [1]

(d) limitations on the total number of natural persons that may be employed in a particular service sector or that a service supplier may employ and who are necessary for, and directly related to, the supply of a specific service in the form of numerical quotas or the requirement of an economic needs test;

(e) measures which restrict or require specific types of legal entity or joint venture through which a service supplier may supply a service; and

(f) limitations on the participation of foreign capital in terms of maximum percentage limit on foreign share holding or the total value of individual or aggregate foreign investment.

Article XVII *National Treatment*

1. In the sectors inscribed in its Schedule, and subject to any conditions and qualifications set out therein, each Member shall accord to services and service suppliers of any other Member, in respect of all measures affecting the supply of services, treatment no less favourable than that it accords to its own like services and service suppliers. [2]

2. A Member may meet the requirement of paragraph 1 by according to services and service suppliers of any other Member, either formally identical treatment or formally different treatment to that it accords to its own like services and service suppliers.

3. Formally identical or formally different treatment shall be considered to be less favourable if it modifies the conditions of competition in favour of services or service suppliers of the Member compared to like services or service suppliers of any other Member.

Article XVIII *Additional Commitments*

Members may negotiate commitments with respect to measures affecting trade in services not subject to scheduling under Articles XVI or XVII, including those regarding qualifications, standards or licensing matters. Such commitments shall be inscribed in a

---

① ［本协定原文脚注 9］Subparagraph 2(c) does not cover measures of a Member which limit inputs for the supply of services.

② ［本协定原文脚注 10］Specific commitments assumed under this Article shall not be construed to require any Member to compensate for any inherent competitive disadvantages which result from the foreign character of the relevant services or service suppliers.

Member's Schedule.

PART IV　PROGRESSIVE LIBERALIZATION

Article XIX Negotiation of Specific Commitments

1. In pursuance of the objectives of this Agreement, Members shall enter into successive rounds of negotiations, beginning not later than five years from the date of entry into force of the WTO Agreement and periodically thereafter, with a view to achieving a progressively higher level of liberalization. Such negotiations shall be directed to the reduction or elimination of the adverse effects on trade in services of measures as a means of providing effective market access. This process shall take place with a view to promoting the interests of all participants on a mutually advantageous basis and to securing an overall balance of rights and obligations.

2. The process of liberalization shall take place with due respect for national policy objectives and the level of development of individual Members, both overall and in individual sectors. There shall be appropriate flexibility for individual developing country Members for opening fewer sectors, liberalizing fewer types of transactions, progressively extending market access in line with their development situation and, when making access to their markets available to foreign service suppliers, attaching to such access conditions aimed at achieving the objectives referred to in Article IV.

3. For each round, negotiating guidelines and procedures shall be established. For the purposes of establishing such guidelines, the Council for Trade in Services shall carry out an assessment of trade in services in overall terms and on a sectoral basis with reference to the objectives of this Agreement, including those set out in paragraph 1 of Article IV. Negotiating guidelines shall establish modalities for the treatment of liberalization undertaken autonomously by Members since previous negotiations, as well as for the special treatment for least-developed country Members under the provisions of paragraph 3 of Article IV.

4. The process of progressive liberalization shall be advanced in each such round through bilateral, plurilateral or multilateral negotiations directed towards increasing the general level of specific commitments undertaken by Members under this Agreement.

Article XX Schedules of Specific Commitments

1. Each Member shall set out in a schedule the specific commitments it undertakes under Part III of this Agreement. With respect to sectors where such commitments are undertaken, each Schedule shall specify:

(a) terms, limitations and conditions on market access;

(b) conditions and qualifications on national treatment;

中国参与制定多边投资规则问题研究

(c) undertakings relating to additional commitments;

(d) where appropriate the time-frame for implementation of such commitments; and

(e) the date of entry into force of such commitments.

2. Measures inconsistent with both Articles XVI and XVII shall be inscribed in the column relating to Article XVI. In this case the inscription will be considered to provide a condition or qualification to Article XVII as well.

3. Schedules of specific commitments shall be annexed to this Agreement and shall form an integral part thereof.

Article XXI Modification of Schedules

1. (a) A Member (referred to in this Article as the "modifying Member") may modify or withdraw any commitment in its Schedule, at any time after three years have elapsed from the date on which that commitment entered into force, in accordance with the provisions of this Article.

(b) A modifying Member shall notify its intent to modify or withdraw a commitment pursuant to this Article to the Council for Trade in Services no later than three months before the intended date of implementation of the modification or withdrawal.

2. (a) At the request of any Member the benefits of which under this Agreement may be affected (referred to in this Article as an "affected Member") by a proposed modification or withdrawal notified under subparagraph 1(b), the modifying Member shall enter into negotiations with a view to reaching agreement on any necessary compensatory adjustment. In such negotiations and agreement, the Members concerned shall endeavour to maintain a general level of mutually advantageous commitments not less favourable to trade than that provided for in Schedules of specific commitments prior to such negotiations.

(b) Compensatory adjustments shall be made on a most-favoured-nation basis.

3. (a) If agreement is not reached between the modifying Member and any affected Member before the end of the period provided for negotiations, such affected Member may refer the matter to arbitration. Any affected Member that wishes to enforce a right that it may have to compensation must participate in the arbitration.

(b) If no affected Member has requested arbitration, the modifying Member shall be free to implement the proposed modification or withdrawal.

4. (a) The modifying Member may not modify or withdraw its commitment until it has made compensatory adjustments in conformity with the findings of the arbitration.

(b) If the modifying Member implements its proposed modification or withdrawal and does not comply with the findings of the arbitration, any affected Member that participated in the arbitration may modify or withdraw substantially equivalent benefits

222

in conformity with those findings. Notwithstanding Article II, such a modification or withdrawal may be implemented solely with respect to the modifying Member.

5. The Council for Trade in Services shall establish procedures for rectification or modification of Schedules. Any Member which has modified or withdrawn scheduled commitments under this Article shall modify its Schedule according to such procedures.

PART Ⅴ　INSTITUTIONAL PROVISIONS

Article ⅩⅫ Consultation

1. Each Member shall accord sympathetic consideration to, and shall afford adequate opportunity for, consultation regarding such representations as may be made by any other Member with respect to any matter affecting the operation of this Agreement. The Dispute Settlement Understanding (DSU) shall apply to such consultations.

2. The Council for Trade in Services or the Dispute Settlement Body (DSB) may, at the request of a Member, consult with any Member or Members in respect of any matter for which it has not been possible to find a satisfactory solution through consultation under paragraph 1.

3. A Member may not invoke Article ⅩⅦ, either under this Article or Article ⅩⅩⅢ, with respect to a measure of another Member that falls within the scope of an international agreement between them relating to the avoidance of double taxation. In case of disagreement between Members as to whether a measure falls within the scope of such an agreement between them, it shall be open to either Member to bring this matter before the Council for Trade in Services.① The ouncil shall refer the matter to arbitration. The decision of the arbitrator shall be final and binding on the Members.

Article ⅩⅩⅢ Dispute Settlement and Enforcement

1. If any Member should consider that any other Member fails to carry out its obligations or specific commitments under this Agreement, it may with a view to reaching a mutually satisfactory resolution of the matter have recourse to the DSU.

2. If the DSB considers that the circumstances are serious enough to justify such action, it may authorize a Member or Members to suspend the application to any other Member or Members of obligations and specific commitments in accordance with Article 22 of the DSU.

3. If any Member considers that any benefit it could reasonably have expected to

---

①　［本协议原文脚注 11］With respect to agreements on the avoidance of double taxation which exist on the date of entry into force of the WTO Agreement, such a matter may be brought before the Council for Trade in Services only with the consent of both parties to such an agreement.

accrue to it under a specific commitment of another Member under Part Ⅲ of this Agreement is being nullified or impaired as a result of the application of any measure which does not conflict with the provisions of this Agreement, it may have recourse to the DSU. If the measure is determined by the DSB to have nullified or impaired such a benefit, the Member affected shall be entitled to a mutually satisfactory adjustment on the basis of paragraph 2 of Article ⅩⅪ, which may include the modification or withdrawal of the measure. In the event an agreement cannot be reached between the Members concerned, Article 22 of the DSU shall apply.

Article ⅩⅩⅣ *Council for Trade in Services*

1. The Council for Trade in Services shall carry out such functions as may be assigned to it to facilitate the operation of this Agreement and further its objectives. The Council may establish such subsidiary bodies as it considers appropriate for the effective discharge of its functions.

2. The Council and, unless the Council decides otherwise, its subsidiary bodies shall be open to participation by representatives of all Members.

3. The Chairman of the Council shall be elected by the Members.

Article ⅩⅩⅤ *Technical Cooperation*

1. Service suppliers of Members which are in need of such assistance shall have access to the services of contact points referred to in paragraph 2 of Article Ⅳ.

2. Technical assistance to developing countries shall be provided at the multilateral level by the Secretariat and shall be decided upon by the Council for Trade in Services.

Article ⅩⅩⅥ *Relationship with Other International Organizations*

The General Council shall make appropriate arrangements for consultation and cooperation with the United Nations and its specialized agencies as well as with other intergovernmental organizations concerned with services.

PART Ⅵ FINAL PROVISIONS

Article ⅩⅩⅦ *Denial of Benefits*

A Member may deny the benefits of this Agreement:

(a) to the supply of a service, if it establishes that the service is supplied from or in the territory of a non-Member or of a Member to which the denying Member does not apply the WTO Agreement;

(b) in the case of the supply of a maritime transport service, if it establishes that the service is supplied:

(i) by a vessel registered under the laws of a non-Member or of a Member to which the denying Member does not apply the WTO Agreement, and

(ii) by a person which operates and/or uses the vessel in whole or in part but which is of a non-Member or of a Member to which the denying Member does not apply the WTO Agreement;

(c) to a service supplier that is a juridical person, if it establishes that it is not a service supplier of another Member, or that it is a service supplier of a Member to which the denying Member does not apply the WTO Agreement.

Article XXVIII Definitions

For the purpose of this Agreement:

(a) "measure" means any measure by a Member, whether in the form of a law, regulation, rule, procedure, decision, administrative action, or any other form;

(b) "supply of a service" includes the production, distribution, marketing, sale and delivery of a service;

(c) "measures by Members affecting trade in services" include measures in respect of

(i) the purchase, payment or use of a service;

(ii) the access to and use of, in connection with the supply of a service, services which are required by those Members to be offered to the public generally;

(iii) the presence, including commercial presence, of persons of a Member for the supply of a service in the territory of another Member;

(d) "commercial presence" means any type of business or professional establishment, including through

(i) the constitution, acquisition or maintenance of a juridical person, or

(ii) the creation or maintenance of a branch or a representative office, within the territory of a Member for the purpose of supplying a service;

(e) "sector" of a service means,

(i) with reference to a specific commitment, one or more, or all, subsectors of that service, as specified in a Member's Schedule,

(ii) otherwise, the whole of that service sector, including all of its subsectors;

(f) "service of another Member" means a service which is supplied,

(i) from or in the territory of that other Member, or in the case of maritime transport, by a vessel registered under the laws of that other Member, or by a person of that other Member which supplies the service through the operation of a vessel and/or its use in whole or in part; or

(ii)in the case of the supply of a service through commercial presence or through the presence of natural persons, by a service supplier of that other Member;

（g）"service supplier" means any person that supplies a service；[①]

（h）"monopoly supplier of a service" means any person, public or private, which in the relevant market of the territory of a Member is authorized or established formally or in effect by that Member as the sole supplier of that service；

（*i*）"service consumer" means any person that receives or uses a service；

（j）"person" means either a natural person or a juridical person；

（k）"natural person of another Member" means a natural person who resides in the territory of that other Member or any other Member, and who under the law of that other Member：

（i）is a national of that other Member；or

（ii）has the right of permanent residence in that other Member, in the case of a Member which：

（1）does not have nationals；or

（2）accords substantially the same treatment to its permanent residents as it does to its nationals in respect of measures affecting trade in services, as notified in its acceptance of or accession to the WTO Agreement, provided that no Member is obligated to accord to such permanent residents treatment more favourable than would be accorded by that other Member to such permanent residents. Such notification shall include the assurance to assume, with respect to those permanent residents, in accordance with its laws and regulations, the same responsibilities that other Member bears with respect to its nationals；

（l）"juridical person" means any legal entity duly constituted or otherwise organized under applicable law, whether for profit or otherwise, and whether privately-owned or governmentally-owned, including any corporation, trust, partnership, joint venture, sole proprietorship or association；

（m）"juridical person of another Member" means a juridical person which is either：

（i）constituted or otherwise organized under the law of that other Member, and is engaged in substantive business operations in the territory of that Member or any other Member；or

（ii）in the case of the supply of a service through commercial presence, owned or controlled by：

---

① ［本协定原文脚注 12］Where the service is not supplied directly by a juridical person but through other forms of commercial presence such as a branch or a representative office, the service supplier (i.e. the juridical person) shall, nonetheless, through such presence be accorded the treatment provided for service suppliers under the Agreement. Such treatment shall be extended to the presence through which the service is supplied and need not be extended to any other parts of the supplier located outside the territory where the service is supplied.

(1) natural persons of that Member; or

(2) juridical persons ofthatother Memberidentifiedunder subparagraph (i);

(n) a juridical person is:

(i) "owned" by persons of a Member if more than 50 per cent of the equity interest in it is beneficially owned by persons of that Member;

(ii) "controlled" by persons of a Member if such persons have the power to name a majority of its directors or otherwise to legally direct its actions;

(iii) "affiliated" with another person when it controls, or is controlled by, that other person; or when it and the other person are both controlled by the same person; and

(o) "direct taxes" comprise all taxes on total income, on total capital or on elements of income or of capital, including taxes on gains from the alienation of property, taxes on estates, inheritances and gifts, and taxes on the total amounts of wages or salaries paid by enterprises, as well as taxes on capital appreciation.

Article XIII Annexes

The Annexes to this Agreement are an integral part of this Agreement.

* * *

ANNEXES

Annex on Article II Exemptions

Scope

1. This Annex specifies the conditions under which a Member, at the entry into force of this Agreement, is exempted from its obligations under paragraph 1 of Article II.

2. Any new exemptions applied for after the date of entry into force of the WTO Agreement shall be dealt with under paragraph 3 of Article IX of that Agreement.

Review

3. The Council for Trade in Services shall review all exemptions granted for a period of more than 5 years. The first such review shall take place no more than five years after the entry into force of the WTO Agreement.

4. The Council for Trade in Services in a review shall:

(a) examine whether the conditions which created the need for the exemption still prevail; and

(b) determine the date of any further review.

Termination

5. The exemption of a Member from its obligations under paragraph 1 of Article II

of the Agreement with respect to a particular measure terminates on the date provided for in the exemption.

6. In principle, such exemptions should not exceed a period of 10 years. In any event, they shall be subject to negotiation in subsequent trade-liberalizing rounds.

7. A Member shall notify the Council for Trade in Services at the termination of the exemption period that the inconsistent measure has been brought into conformity with paragraph 1 of Article Ⅱ of the Agreement.

Lists of Article Ⅱ Exemptions

[The agreed lists of exemptions under paragraph 2 of Article Ⅱ appear as part of this Annex in the treaty copy of the WTO Agreement.]

* * *

Annex on Movement of Natural Persons Supplying Services under the Agreement

1. This Annex applies to measures affecting natural persons who are service suppliers of a Member, and natural persons of a Member who are employed by a service supplier of a Member, in respect of the supply of a service.

2. The Agreement shall not apply to measures affecting natural persons seeking access to the employment market of a Member, nor shall it apply to measures regarding citizenship, residence or employment on a permanent basis.

3. In accordance with Parts Ⅲ and Ⅳ of the Agreement, Members may negotiate specific commitments applying to the movement of all categories of natural persons supplying services under the Agreement. Natural persons covered by a specific commitment shall be allowed to supply the service in accordance with the terms of that commitment.

4. The Agreement shall not prevent a Member from applying measures to regulate the entry of natural persons into, or their temporary stay in, its territory, including those measures necessary to protect the integrity of, and to ensure the orderly movement of natural persons across, its borders, provided that such measures are not applied in such a manner as to nullify or impair the benefits accruing to any Member under the terms of a specific commitment.①

* * *

Annex on Air Transport Services

1. This Annex applies to measures affecting trade in air transport services, whether

---

① ［本协定原文脚注 13］The sole fact of requiring a visa for natural persons of certain Members and not for those of others shall not be regarded as nullifying or impairing benefits under a specific commitment.

scheduled or non-scheduled, and ancillary services. It is confirmed that any specific commitment or obligation assumed under this Agreement shall not reduce or affect a Member's obligations under bilateral or multilateral agreements that are in effect on the date of entry into force of the WTO Agreement.

2. The Agreement, including its dispute settlement procedures, shall not apply to measures affecting:

(a) traffic rights, however granted; or

(b) services directly related to the exercise of traffic rights, except as provided in paragraph 3 of this Annex.

3. The Agreement shall apply to measures affecting:

(a) aircraft repair and maintenance services;

(b) the selling and marketing of air transport services;

(c) computer reservation system (CRS) services.

4. The dispute settlement procedures of the Agreement may be invoked only where obligations or specific commitments have been assumed by the concerned Members and where dispute settlement procedures in bilateral and other multilateral agreements or arrangements have been exhausted.

5. The Council for Trade in Services shall review periodically, and at least every five years, developments in the air transport sector and the operation of this Annex with a view to considering the possible further application of the Agreement in this sector.

6. Definitions:

(a) "Aircraft repair and maintenance services" mean such activities when undertaken on an aircraft or a part thereof while it is withdrawn from service and do not include so-called line maintenance.

(b) "Selling and marketing of air transport services" mean opportunities for the air carrier concerned to sell and market freely its air transport services including all aspects of marketing such as market research, advertising and distribution. These activities do not include the pricing of air transport services nor the applicable conditions.

(c) "Computer reservation system (CRS) services" mean services provided by computerized systems that contain information about air carriers' schedules, availability, fares and fare rules, through which reservations can be made or tickets may be issued.

(d) "Traffic rights" mean the right for scheduled and non-scheduled services to operate and/or to carry passengers, cargo and mail for remuneration or hire from, to, within, or over the territory of a Member, including points to be served, routes to be operated, types of traffic to be carried, capacity to be provided, tariffs to be charged and their conditions, and criteria for designation of airlines, including such criteria as number, ownership, and control.

* * *

Annex on Financial Services

1. *Scope and Definition*

(a) This Annex applies to measures affecting the supply of financial services. Reference to the supply of a financial service in this Annex shall mean the supply of a service as defined in paragraph 2 of Article I of the Agreement.

(b) For the purposes of subparagraph 3(b) of Article I of the Agreement, "services supplied in the exercise of governmental authority" means the following:

(i) activities conducted by a central bank or monetary authority or by any other public entity in pursuit of monetary or exchange rate policies;

(ii) activities forming part of a statutory system of social security or public retirement plans; and

(iii) other activities conducted by a public entity for the account or with the guarantee or using the financial resources of the Government.

(c) For the purposes of subparagraph 3(b) of Article I of the Agreement, if a Member allows any of the activities referred to in subparagraphs (b)(ii) or (b)(iii) of this paragraph to be conducted by its financial service suppliers in competition with a public entity or a financial service supplier, "services" shall include such activities.

(d) Subparagraph 3(c) of Article I of the Agreement shall not apply to services covered by this Annex.

2. *Domestic Regulation*

(a) Notwithstanding any other provisions of the Agreement, a Member shall not be prevented from taking measures for prudential reasons, including for the protection of investors, depositors, policy holders or persons to whom a fiduciary duty is owed by a financial service supplier, or to ensure the integrity and stability of the financial system. Where such measures do not conform with the provisions of the Agreement, they shall not be used as a means of avoiding the Member's commitments or obligations under the Agreement.

(b) Nothing in the Agreement shall be construed to require a Member to disclose information relating to the affairs and accounts of individual customers or any confidential or proprietary information in the possession of public entities.

3. *Recognition*

(a) A Member may recognize prudential measures of any other country in determining how the Member's measures relating to financial services shall be applied. Such recognition, which may be achieved through harmonization or otherwise, may be based upon an agreement or arrangement with the country concerned or may be accorded autonomously.

(b) A Member that is a party to such an agreement or arrangement referred to in subparagraph (a), whether future or existing, shall afford adequate opportunity for other interested Members to negotiate their accession to such agreements or arrangements, or to negotiate comparable ones with it, under circumstances in which there would be equivalent regulation, oversight, implementation of such regulation, and, if appropriate, procedures concerning the sharing of information between the parties to the agreement or arrangement. Where a Member accords recognition autonomously, it shall afford adequate opportunity for any other Member to demonstrate that such circumstances exist.

(c) Where a Member is contemplating according recognition to prudential measures of any other country, paragraph 4(b) of Article VII shall not apply.

4. *Dispute Settlement*

Panels for disputes on prudential issues and other financial matters shall have the necessary expertise relevant to the specific financial service under dispute.

5. *Definitions*

For the purposes of this Annex:

(a) A financial service is any service of a financial nature offered by a financial service supplier of a Member. Financial services include all insurance and insurance-related services, and all banking and other financial services (excluding insurance). Financial services include the following activities:

Insurance and insurance-related services

(i) Direct insurance (including co-insurance):

(A) life,

(B) non-life;

(ii) Reinsurance and retrocession;

(iii) Insurance intermediation, such as brokerage and agency;

(iv) Services auxiliary to insurance, such as consultancy, actuarial, risk assessment and claim settlement services.

Banking and other financial services (excluding insurance)

(v) Acceptance of deposits and other repayable funds from the public;

(vi) Lending of all types, including consumer credit, mortgage credit, factoring and financing of commercial transaction;

(vii) Financial leasing;

(viii) All payment and money transmission services, including credit, charge and debit cards, travellers cheques and bankers drafts;

(ix) Guarantees and commitments;

(x) Trading for own account or for account of customers, whether on an exchange, in an over-the-counter market or otherwise, the following:

(A) money market instruments (including cheques, bills, certificates of deposits);

(B) foreign exchange;

(C) derivative products including, but not limited to, futures and options;

(D) exchange rate and interest rate instruments, including products such as swaps, forward rate agreements;

(E) transferable securities;

(F) other negotiable instruments and financial assets, including bullion.

(xi) Participation in issues of all kinds of securities, including underwriting and placement as agent (whether publicly or privately) and provision of services related to such issues;

(xii) Money broking;

(xiii) Asset management, such as cash or portfolio management, all forms of collective investment management, pension fund management, custodial, depository and trust services;

(xiv) Settlement and clearing services for financial assets, including securities, derivative products, and other negotiable instruments;

(xv) Provision and transfer of financial information, and financial data processing and related software by suppliers of other financial services;

(xvi) Advisory, intermediation and other auxiliary financial services on all the activities listed in subparagraphs (v) through (xv), including credit reference and analysis, investment and portfolio research and advice, advice on acquisitions and on corporate restructuring and strategy.

(b) A financial service supplier means any natural or juridical person of a Member wishing to supply or supplying financial services but the term "financial service supplier" does not include a public entity.

(c) "Public entity" means:

(i) a government, a central bank or a monetary authority, of a Member, or an entity owned or controlled by a Member, that is principally engaged in carrying out governmental functions or activities for governmental purposes, not including an entity principally engaged in supplying financial services on commercial terms; or

(ii) a private entity, performing functions normally performed by a central bank or monetary authority, when exercising those functions.

* * *

Second Annex on Financial Services

1. Notwithstanding Article Ⅱ of the Agreement and paragraphs 1 and 2 of the Annex on Article Ⅱ Exemptions, a Member may, during a period of 60 days beginning four months after the date of entry into force of the WTO Agreement, list in that Annex measures relating to financial services which are inconsistent with paragraph 1 of Article Ⅱ of the Agreement.

2. Notwithstanding Article ⅩⅪ of the Agreement, a Member may, during a period of 60 days beginning four months after the date of entry into force of the WTO Agreement, improve, modify or withdraw all or part of the specific commitments on financial services inscribed in its Schedule.

3. The Council for Trade in Services shall establish any procedures necessary for the application of paragraphs 1 and 2.

* * *

Annex on Negotiations on Maritime Transport Services

1. Article Ⅱ and the Annex on Article Ⅱ Exemptions, including the requirement to list in the Annex any measure inconsistent with most-favoured-nation treatment that a Member will maintain, shall enter into force for international shipping, auxiliary services and access to and use of port facilities only on:

(a) the implementation date to be determined under paragraph 4 of the Ministerial Decision on Negotiations on Maritime Transport Services; or,

(b) should the negotiations not succeed, the date of the final report of the Negotiating Group on Maritime Transport Services provided for in that Decision.

2. Paragraph 1 shall not apply to any specific commitment on maritime transport services which is inscribed in a Member's Schedule.

3. From the conclusion of the negotiations referred to in paragraph 1, and before the implementation date, a Member may improve, modify or withdraw all or part of its specific commitments in this sector without offering compensation, notwithstanding the provisions of Article ⅩⅪ.

* * *

Annex on Telecommunications

1. *Objectives*

Recognizing the specificities of the telecommunications services sector and, in particular, its dual role as a distinct sector of economic activity and as the underlying transport means for other economic activities, the Members have agreed to the following Annex with the objective of elaborating upon the provisions of the Agreement with respect to measures affecting access to and use of public telecommunications transport networks and services. Accordingly, this Annex provides notes and supplementary provisions to the Agreement.

2. *Scope*

(a) This Annex shall apply to all measures of a Member that affect access to and use of public telecommunications transport networks and services.[①]

(b) This Annex shall not apply to measures affecting the cable or broadcast distribution of radio or television programming.

(c) Nothing in this Annex shall be construed:

(i) to require a Member to authorize a service supplier of any other Member to establish, construct, acquire, lease, operate, or supply telecommunications transport networks or services, other than as provided for in its Schedule; or

(ii) to require a Member (or to require a Member to oblige service suppliers under its jurisdiction) to establish, construct, acquire, lease, operate or supply telecommunications transport networks or services not offered to the public generally.

3. *Definitions*

For the purposes of this Annex:

(a) "Telecommunications" means the transmission and reception of signals by any electromagnetic means.

(b) "Public telecommunications transport service" means any telecommunications transport service required, explicitly or in effect, by a Member to be offered to the public generally. Such services may include, *inter alia*, telegraph, telephone, telex, and data transmission typically involving the real-time transmission of customer-supplied information between two or more points without any end-to-end change in the form or content of the customer's information.

(c) "Public telecommunications transport network" means the public telecommunications infrastructure which permits telecommunications between and among defined network termination points.

(d) "Intra-corporate communications" means telecommunications through which a company communicates within the company or with or among its subsidiaries, branches and, subject to a Member's domestic laws and regulations, affiliates. For these purposes, "subsidiaries", "branches" and, where applicable, "affiliates" shall be as

---

① ［本协定原文脚注 14］ This paragraph is understood to mean that each Member shall ensure that the obligations of this Annex are applied with respect to suppliers of public telecommunications transport networks and services by whatever measures are necessary.

defined by each Member. "Intra-corporate communications" in this Annex excludes commercial or non-commercial services that are supplied to companies that are not related subsidiaries, branches or affiliates, or that are offered to customers or potential customers.

(e) Any reference to a paragraph or subparagraph of this Annex includes all subdivisions thereof.

4. *Transparency*

In the application of Article Ⅲ of the Agreement, each Member shall ensure that relevant information on conditions affecting access to and use of public telecommunications transport networks and services is publicly available, including: tariffs and other terms and conditions of service; specifications of technical interfaces with such networks and services; information on bodies responsible for the preparation and adoption of standards affecting such access and use; conditions applying to attachment of terminal or other equipment; and notifications, registration or licensing requirements, if any.

5. *Access to and Use of Public Telecommunications Transport Networks and Services*

(a) Each Member shall ensure that any service supplier of any other Member is accorded access to and use of public telecommunications transport networks and services on reasonable and non-discriminatory terms and conditions, for the supply of a service included in its Schedule. This obligation shall be applied, *inter alia*, through paragraphs (b) through (f).①

(b) Each Member shall ensure that service suppliers of any other Member have access to and use of any public telecommunications transport network or service offered within or across the border of that Member, including private leased circuits, and to this end shall ensure, subject to paragraphs (e) and (f), that such suppliers are permitted:

(i) to purchase or lease and attach terminal or other equipment which interfaces with the network and which is necessary to supply a supplier's services;

(ii) to interconnect private leased or owned circuits with public telecommunications transport networks and services or with circuits leased or owned by another service supplier; and

(iii) to use operating protocols of the service supplier's choice in the supply of any

---

① ［本协定原文脚注 15］ The term "non-discriminatory" is understood to refer to most-favoured-nation and national treatment as defined in the Agreement, as well as to reflect sector-specific usage of the term to mean "terms and conditions no less favourable than those accorded to any other user of like public telecommunications transport networks or services under like circumstances".

service, other than as necessary to ensure the availability of telecommunications transport networks and services to the public generally.

(c) Each Member shall ensure that service suppliers of any other Member may use public telecommunications transport networks and services for the movement of information within and across borders, including for intra-corporate communications of such service suppliers, and for access to information contained in data bases or otherwise stored in machine-readable form in the territory of any Member. Any new or amended measures of a Member significantly affecting such use shall be notified and shall be subject to consultation, in accordance with relevant provisions of the Agreement.

(d) Notwithstanding the preceding paragraph, a Member may take such measures as are necessary to ensure the security and confidentiality of messages, subject to the requirement that such measures are not applied in a manner which would constitute a means of arbitrary or unjustifiable discrimination or a disguised restriction on trade in services.

(e) Each Member shall ensure that no condition is imposed on access to and use of public telecommunications transport networks and services other than as necessary:

(i) to safeguard the public service responsibilities of suppliers of public telecommunications transport networks and services, in particular their ability to make their networks or services available to the public generally;

(ii) to protect the technical integrity of public telecommunications transport networks or services; or

(iii) to ensure that service suppliers of any other Member do not supply services unless permitted pursuant to commitments in the Member's Schedule.

(f) Provided that they satisfy the criteria set out in paragraph (e), conditions for access to and use of public telecommunications transport networks and services may include:

(i) restrictions on resale or shared use of such services;

(ii) a requirement to use specified technical interfaces, including interface protocols, for inter-connection with such networks and services;

(iii) requirements, where necessary, for the inter-operability of such services and to encourage the achievement of the goals set out in paragraph 7(a);

(iv) type approval of terminal or other equipment which interfaces with the network and technical requirements relating to the attachment of such equipment to such networks;

(v) restrictions on inter-connection of private leased or owned circuits with such networks or services or with circuits leased or owned by another service supplier; or （vi）notification, registration and licensing.

（g）Notwithstanding the preceding paragraphs of this section, a developing country Member may, consistent with its level of development, place reasonable conditions on access to and use of public telecommunications transport networks and services necessary to strengthen its domestic telecommunications infrastructure and service capacity and to increase its participation in international trade in telecommunications services. Such conditions shall be specified in the Member's Schedule.

6. *Technical Cooperation*

（a）Members recognize that an efficient, advanced telecommunications infrastructure in countries, particularly developing countries, is essential to the expansion of their trade in services. To this end, Members endorse and encourage the participation, to the fullest extent practicable, of developed and developing countries and their suppliers of public telecommunications transport networks and services and other entities in the development programmes of international and regional organizations, including the International Telecommunication Union, the United Nations Development Programme, and the International Bank for Reconstruction and Development.

（b）Members shall encourage and support telecommunications cooperation among developing countries at the international, regional and sub-regional levels.

（c）In cooperation with relevant international organizations, Members shall make available, where practicable, to developing countries information with respect to telecommunications services and developments in telecommunications and information technology to assist in strengthening their domestic telecommunications services sector.

（d）Members shall give special consideration to opportunities for the least-developed countries to encourage foreign suppliers of telecommunications services to assist in the transfer of technology, training and other activities that support the development of their telecommunications infrastructure and expansion of their telecommunications services trade.

7. *Relation to International Organizations and Agreements*

（a）Members recognize the importance of international standards for global compatibility and inter-operability of telecommunication networks and services and undertake to promote such standards through the work of relevant international bodies, including the International Telecommunication Union and the International Organization for Standardization.

（b）Members recognize the role played by intergovernmental and non-governmental organizations and agreements in ensuring the efficient operation of domestic and global telecommunications services, in particular the International Telecommunication Union.

Members shall make appropriate arrangements, where relevant, for consultation with such organizations on matters arising from the implementation of this Annex.

* * *

Annex on Negotiations on Basic Telecommunications

1. Article Ⅱ and the Annex on Article Ⅱ Exemptions, including the requirement to list in the Annex any measure inconsistent with most-favoured-nation treatment that a Member will maintain, shall enter into force for basic telecommunications only on:

(a) the implementation date to be determined under paragraph 5 of the Ministerial Decision on Negotiations on Basic Telecommunications; or,

(b) should the negotiations not succeed, the date of the final report of the Negotiating Group on Basic Telecommunications provided for in that Decision.

2. Paragraph 1 shall not apply to any specific commitment on basic telecommunications which is inscribed in a Member's Schedule.

* * *

FOURTH PROTOCOL TO THE GENERAL AGREEMENT ON TRADE IN SERVICES
[excerpts]
(WORLD TRADE ORGANIZATION)

Members of the World Trade Organization (hereinafter referred to as the "WTO") whose Schedules of Specific Commitments and Lists of Exemptions from Article Ⅱ of the General Agreement on Trade in Services concerning basic telecommunications are annexed to this Protocol (hereinafter referred to as "Members concerned"),

Having carried out negotiations under the terms of the Ministerial Decision on Negotiations on Basic Telecommunications adopted at Marrakesh on 15 April 1994,

Having regard to the Annex on Negotiations on Basic Telecommunications,

Agree as follows:

Upon the entry into force of this Protocol, a Schedule of Specific Commitments and a List of Exemptions from Article Ⅱ concerning basic telecommunications annexed to this Protocol relating to a Member shall, in accordance with the terms specified therein, supplement or modify the Schedule of Specific Commitments and the List of Article Ⅱ Exemptions of that Member.

This Protocol shall be open for acceptance, by signature or otherwise, by the Members concerned until 30 November 1997.

The Protocol shall enter into force on 1 January 1998 provided it has been accepted by all Members concerned. If by 1 December 1997 the Protocol has not been accepted by all Members concerned, those Members which have accepted it by that date may decide, prior to 1 January 1998, on its entry into force.

This Protocol shall be deposited with the Director-General of the WTO. The Director- General of the WTO shall promptly furnish to each Member of the WTO a certified copy of this Protocol and notifications of acceptances thereof.

This Protocol shall be registered in accordance with the provisions of Article 102 of the Charter of the United Nations.

Done at Geneva on 15 April, One thousand nine hundred and ninety-seven, in a single copy in the English, French and Spanish languages, each text being authentic, except as otherwise provided for in respect of the Schedules annexed hereto.

* * *

FIFTH PROTOCOL TO THE GENERAL AGREEMENT ON
TRADE IN SERVICES
[excerpts]
(WORLD TRADE ORGANIZATION)

Members of the World Trade Organization (hereinafter referred to as the "WTO") whose Schedules of Specific Commitments and Lists of Exemptions from Article Ⅱ of the General Agreement on Trade in Services concerning financial services are annexed to this Protocol (hereinafter referred to as "Members concerned"),

Having carried out negotiations under the terms of the Second Decision on Financial Services adopted by the Council for Trade in Services on 21 July 1995 (S/L/ 9),

Agree as follows:

[1] A Schedule of Specific Commitments and a List of Exemptions from Article Ⅱ concerning financial services annexed to this Protocol relating to a Member shall, upon the entry into force of this Protocol for that Member, replace the financial services sections of the Schedule of Specific Commitments and the List of Article Ⅱ Exemptions of that Member.

[2] This Protocol shall be open for acceptance, by signature or otherwise, by the Members concerned until 29 January 1999.

[3] This Protocol shall enter into force on the 30th day following the date of its acceptance by all Members concerned. If by 30 January 1999 it has not been accepted by all Members concerned, those Members which have accepted it before that date may, within a period of 30 days thereafter, decide on its entry into force.

[4] This Protocol shall be deposited with the Director-General of the WTO. The Director- General of the WTO shall promptly furnish to each Member of the WTO a

certified copy of this Protocol and notifications of acceptances thereof pursuant to paragraph 3.

[5] This Protocol shall be registered in accordance with the provisions of Article 102 of the Charter of the United Nations.

Done at Geneva this [—] day of [month] one thousand nine hundred and ninety [—], in a single copy in English, French and Spanish languages, each text being authentic, except as otherwise provided for in respect of the Schedules annexed hereto.

III. FRAMEWORK AGREEMENT ON THE PROMOTION, PROTECTION AND LIBERALIZATION OF INVESTMENT IN APTA PARTICIPATING STATES
(ECONOMIC AND SOCIAL COMMISSION FOR ASIA AND THE PACIFIC: ASIA-PACIFIC TRADE AGREEMENT)

FRAMEWORK AGREEMENT ON THE PROMOTION, PROTECTION AND LIBERALIZATION OF INVESTMENT IN APTA PARTICIPATING STATES
(hereinafter referred to as "this Agreement")

The Governments of the People's Republic of Bangladesh, the People's Republic of China, the Republic of India, the Lao People's Democratic Republic, the Republic of Korea and the Democratic Socialist Republic of Sri Lanka, Participating States of the Asia-Pacific Trade Agreement (APTA) (hereinafter referred to as "Participating States");

AFFIRMING the importance of sustaining economic growth and development in all Participating States through joint efforts in liberalizing trade and promoting intra-APTA trade and investment flows;

RECOGNIZING that investment is an important source of knowledge and finance for sustaining the pace of economic, industrial, infrastructure and technology development;

FURTHER RECOGNIZING the need to take action to attract higher and sustainable levels of investment in Participating States;

RECALLING the decision of the APTA Ministers in their Ministerial Declaration adopted at the Second Session of the Ministerial Council in Goa, India on 26 October 2007 to direct the Standing Committee to adopt modalities for the extension of negotiations into other areas, such as non-tariff measures, trade facilitation, services, and investment, as soon as possible;

DETERMINED to further strengthen the position of Participating States as competitive investment destinations through a more liberal and transparent investment environment;

REFERRING to Article 11 of APTA, which states that Participating States shall explore future areas of cooperation with regard to border and non-border measures to supplement and complement the liberalization of trade; and further referring to Article 26 of APTA on Amendments to the Asia-Pacific Trade Agreement;

HAVE AGREED AS FOLLOWS:

Article 1　Definitions

For the purposes of this Agreement,

1. "APTA investor" means:

(a) a natural person having the citizenship of a Participating State in accordance with its applicable laws; or

(b) any legal entity duly constituted or otherwise organized under applicable law of a Participating State, whether for profit or otherwise, and whether privately-owned or government-owned, including any corporation, trust, partnership, joint venture, sole proprietorship or association; or

(c) any legal entity duly constituted or otherwise organized under applicable law of any State, whether for profit or otherwise, including any corporation, trust, partnership, joint venture, sale proprietorship or association and owned or controlled, directly or indirectly, by natural persons or legal entities as defined in (a) and (b) above.

2. (a) "Investment" means every kind of asset invested or acquired by an APTA investor in accordance with the laws of the Participating State in whose territory the investment is made and includes, though not exclusively:

(i) movable and immovable property and other property rights such as mortgage, liens or pledges;

(ii) shares, stocks, debentures and similar forms of participation;

(iii) bonds, loans and other forms of debt instruments;

(iv) rights to money or any performance under contract having a financial value;

(v) intellectual property rights, goodwill, technical processes and know-how as conferred by law;

(vi) business concessions conferred by law or under contract, including concessions to search for, extract or exploit oil and other minerals and other natural resources.

(b) For the purposes of paragraph 1, returns that are invested shall be treated' as investments and any alteration in the form in which assets are invested or reinvested shall not affect their character as investments.

3. "Returns" means the amounts, monetary or in kind, yielded by investments and, in particular, though not exclusively, includes profits, interest, capital gains, dividends, royalties or payments in connection with intellectual property rights, and all kinds of fees.

4. "Secretariat" means the secretariat of the United Nations Economic and Social Commission for Asia and the Pacific (ESCAP).

Article 2   Objectives

The objectives of this Agreement are to:

(a) substantially increase the flow of investments into Participating States;

(b) jointly promote Participating States as attractive investment destinations;

(c) strengthen and increase the competitiveness of Participating States' economic sectors;

(d) progressively reduce or eliminate investment regulations and conditions which may impede investment flows and the operation of investment projects in Participating States;

(e) progressively strive towards a harmonized investment regime among all Participating States;

(f) promote the free flow of investments and transfer of technology among Participating States.

Article 3   Programmes and Action Plans

1. Participating States shall, for the implementation of the obligations under this Agreement, initiate negotiations no later than a date to be decided by the Standing Committee, for the joint development and implementation of the following programmes within a timeframe to be decided:

(a) cooperation and facilitation programme as specified in Schedule I;

(b) promotion and awareness programme as specified in Schedule II;

(c) liberalization programme as specified in Schedule III; and

(d) protection programme as specified in Schedule N.

2. Participating States shall submit Action Plans for the implementation of the programmes through the secretariat by a date to be decided by the Standing Committee.

3. The Action Plans shall be reviewed every two years by the Ministerial Council after consideration by the Standing Committee to ensure that the objectives of this Agreement are achieved.

Article 4　Transparency

1. Each Participating State shall make available to the Standing Committee through the secretariat all laws, regulations; procedures, administrative rulings of general application which pertain to, or affect, the operation of this Agreement. This shall also apply to international agreements pertaining to or affecting investment to which a Participating State is also a signatory.

2. Each Participating State shall promptly and at least annually inform the Standing Committee through the secretariat of the introduction of any new or any changes to existing matters set out in paragraph 1 of this article which affect investments or its commitments under this Agreement.

3. Nothing in this Agreement shall require any Participating State to provide confidential information, the disclosure of which would impede law enforcement, or otherwise be contrary to the public interest, or which would prejudice legitimate commercial interests of particular enterprises, public or private.

Article 5　General Exceptions

Subject to the requirement that such measures are not applied in a manner which would constitute a means of arbitrary or unjustifiable discrimination between Participating States where like conditions prevail, or a disguised restriction on investment flows, nothing in this Agreement shall be construed to prevent any Participating State from adopting and implementing measures:

1. which it considers necessary for the protection of its national security, the protection of public morals and maintenance of public order[①], the protection of human, animal and plant life and health, and the protection of articles of artistic, historical and archaeological value;

2. which are aimed at ensuring the equitable or effective imposition or collection of direct taxes in respect of investments or investors of Participating States; or

3. which it considers necessary to secure compliance with laws and regulations which are not inconsistent with the provisions of this Agreement including those relating to:

（a）the prevention of deceptive and fraudulent practices;

（b）the protection of the privacy of individuals in relation to the processing and dissemination of personal data and the protection of confidentiality of individual records

---

① ［本协定原文脚注 1］ The public order exception may be invoked only where a genuine and sufficiently serious threat is posed to one of the fundamental interest of society.

and accounts;

(c) Safety.

Article 6　Institutional Arrangements

1. The Ministerial Council shall review the implementation of this Agreement every two years. For this purpose, the MinisterialCouncil shall comprise the Ministers authorized to review this Agreement by the Heads of Government of each Participating State.

2. The Standing Committee shall supervise and coordinate the implementation of this Agreement and submit its recommendations for review to the Ministerial Council.

3. For the purpose of implementing paragraph 2, the Standing Committee shall establish a Working Group on Investment (WGI) comprising senior officials from relevant governments of the Participating States.

4. The Working Group on Investment shall meet at least twice yearly and report to the Ministerial Council through the Standing Committee.

5. The ESCAP secretariat shall be the secretariat of the Working Group on Investment.

Article 7　Settlement of Disputes among Participating States

1. A specific dispute settlement mechanism may be established for the purposes of this Agreement which shall form an integral part of this Agreement.

2. Unless a specific dispute settlement mechanism is established under paragraph 1 of this article, with regard to any dispute among Participating States arising out of the interpretation or implementation of this Agreement, articles 20 and 21 of APTA shall apply mutatis mutandis.

Article 8　Special Consideration

1. Least developed country Participating States shall be provided flexibility in the submission and implementation of all Schedules and Action Plans under this Agreement. The Participating States shall provide special concessions to these countries in their Schedules and Action Plans.

2. Special consideration shall be given by Participating States to requests from least developed country Participating States for technical assistance and cooperation arrangements designed to assist them in expanding their investment relations with other Participating States.

3. Special consideration in accordance with paragraph 1 hereof shall also be extended to Sri Lanka.

Article 9　Modifications and Amendments

The provisions, Schedules and Action Plans of this Agreement may be amended or modified through the consent of all the Participating States and such amendments shall become effective upon acceptance by all Participating States.

Article 10　Supplementary Agreements or Arrangements

The Schedules, Action Plans, Annexes and any other arrangement or agreements arising under this Agreement shall form an integral part of this Agreement.

Article 11　Contact Point

1. Each Participating State shall designate a contact point to facilitate communications between the Participating States on any matter covered by this Agreement, including the exchange of information relevant to the implementation and operation of this Agreement.

2. At the r quest of any Participating State, the contact point of the requested Participating State shall identify thc office or official responsible for the matter and assist in facilitating communication with the requesting Participating State.

Article 12　Final Provisions

1. In the event of inconsistency between this Agreement and the APTA Framework Agreement on the Promotion and Liberalization of Trade in Services, the relevant provisions of the APTA Framework Agreement on the Promotion and Liberalization of Trade in Services shall apply with regard to liberalization of trade in services as defined in Article I, Paragraph 2 (c) of the General Agreement on Trade in Services ("commercial presence") of the World Trade Organization and the relevant provisions of this Agreement shall apply with regard to the investment protection measures to be stipulated according to Schedule Ⅳ of this Agreement.

2. This Agreement shall enter into force upon the deposit of instruments of ratification or acceptance by all signatory Governments with the Executive Secretary of ESCAP, who shall promptly furnish a certified copy thereof to each Participating State. The signatory Governments undertake to deposit their instruments of ratification or acceptance within six months after the date of signing of this Agreement.

3. In accordance with Articles 11 and 26 of APTA, this Agreement shall form an integral part of APTA, by becoming Annex III-C thereto.

IN WITNESS WHEREOF the undersigned, duly authorized representatives of the signatory States, have signed the present Agreement on behalf of their respective

Governments. Done at Seoul, this fifteenth day of December two thousand and nine, in one single copy in the English language.

SCHEDULE I   COOPERATION AND FACILITATION PROGRAMME

In respect of the Cooperation and Facilitation Programme, Participating States, with the assistance of the secretariat where relevant, shall take:

1. Individual initiatives to:

(a) increase transparency of the Participating State's investment rules, regulations, policies and procedures through the publication of such information on a regular basis and by making such information widely available;

(b) simplify and expedite procedures for applications, approvals and implementation of investment projects at all levels; and

(c) expand the number of bilateral agreements for the avoidance of double taxation among the Participating States.

2. Collective initiatives to:

(a) establish a database for APTA Supporting Industries and APTA Technology suppliers;

(b) establish a database to enhance the flow of APTA investment data and information on investment opportunities in APTA;

(c) promote public-private sector linkages through regular dialogues with the APTA business community and other international-organizations to identify investment impediments within and outside APTA and propose ways to improve the APTA investment environment;

(d) identify target areas for technical cooperation, e. g. development of human resources, infrastructure, supporting industries, small, and medium-sized enterprises, information technology, industrial technology, R & D and coordinate efforts within APTA with other international organizations involved in technical cooperation;

(e) examine the possibility of an APTA Agreement for the avoidance of double taxation.

SCHEDULE II   PROMOTION AND AWARENESS PROGRAMME

In respect of the Promotion and Awareness Programme, Participating States, in cooperation with the secretariat where relevant, shall:

1. Organize joint investment promotion . activities, e. g. seminars, workshops, roadshows, investment forums;

2. Conduct regular consultations among investment agencies of Participating States on investment promotion matters;

3. Organize investment-related training programmes for officials of investment

agencies of Participating States;

4. Exchange lists of promoted sectors /industries where Participating States could encourage investments from other Participating States and initiate promotional activities;

5. Examine possible ways by which the investment agencies and apex chambers of commerce and industry of Participating States can support the promotion efforts of other Participating States; and

6. Establish a Joint Investment Promotion Committee to facilitate the promotional activities.

SCHEDULE Ⅲ　LIBERALIZATION PROGRAMME

In respect of the Liberalization Programme, Participating States agree to enter into negotiations to progressively improve their investment regime with a view to promoting freer investment among the APTA Participating States.

SCHEDULE Ⅳ　PROTECTION PROGRAMME

In respect of the Protection Programme, Participating States shall:

1. Formulate and conclude an APTA Agreement for the Promotion and Protection of Investments. That Agreement shall include, at a minimum, provisions related to the following issues:

(a) post-establishment national treatment and Most-Favoured Nation treatment to APTA investors;

(b) full security and protection of the investments made in accordance with the legislation of the host country by APTA investors and protection against unreasonable or discriminatory measures impairing the operation, management, maintenance, use, enjoyment, extension, 1 disposition or liquidation of such investments;

(c) protection against expropriation and nationalization, except for public use, or public purpose, or in the public interest, and under due process of law, on a non-discriminatory basis and upon payment of prompt, adequate and effective compensation;

(d) transfer of the capital, net profits, dividends, royalties, technical assistance and technical fees, interests and other income, accruing from any investments of APTA investors, including a provision for safeguarding the balance of payments;

(e) dispute settlement procedures in cases of dispute relating to an investment between any Participating State and an investor of another Participating State or between Participating States;

(f) the imposition or enforcement of performance requirements.

2. Protect and uphold the principles of intellectual property rights, at a minimum in accordance with the principles and rules of the WTO Agreement on Trade-Related Aspects of Intellectual Property rights.

Ⅳ. AGREEMENT ON INVESTMENT OF THE FRAMEWORK AGREEMENT ON COMPREHENSIVE ECONOMIC CO-OPERATION BETWEEN THE PEOPLE'S REPUBLIC OF CHINA AND THE ASSOCIATION OF SOUTHEAST ASIAN NATIONS

The Government of the People's Republic of China ("China") and the Governments of Brunei Darussalam, the Kingdom of Cambodia ("Cambodia"), the Republic of Indonesia ("Indonesia"), the Lao People's Democratic Republic ("Lao PDR"), Malaysia, the Union of Myanmar ("Myanmar"), the Republic of the Philippines ("Philippines"), the Republic of Singapore, the Kingdom of Thailand ("Thailand") and the Socialist Republic of Viet Nam ("Viet Nam"), Member States of the Association of Southeast Asian Nations (collectively, "ASEAN" or "ASEAN Member States", or individually, "ASEAN Member State");

RECALLING the Framework Agreement on Comprehensive Economic Co-operation ("the Framework Agreement") between China and ASEAN (collectively, "the Parties", or individually referring to China or to an ASEAN Member State as a "Party") signed by the Heads of Government/State of China and ASEAN Member States in Phnom Penh, Cambodia on the 4th day of November 2002;

RECALLING further Article 5 and Article 8 of the Framework Agreement, where in order to establish a China-ASEAN Free Trade Area and to promote investments and create a liberal, facilitative, transparent and competitive investment regime, the Parties agreed to negotiate and conclude as expeditiously as possible an investment agreement in order to progressively liberalise the investment regime, strengthen co-operation in investment, facilitate investment and improve transparency of investment rules and regulations, and provide for the protection of investments;

NOTING that the Framework Agreement recognised the different stages and pace of development among the Parties and the need for special and differential treatment and flexibility for the newer ASEAN Member States of Cambodia, Lao PDR, Myanmar and Viet Nam;

REAFFIRMING the Parties' commitment to establish the China-ASEAN Free

Trade Area within the specified timeframes, while allowing flexibility to the Parties to address their sensitive areas as provided in the Framework Agreement, in the realisation of the sustainable economic growth and development goals on the basis of equality and mutual benefits so as to achieve a win-win outcome;

REAFFIRMING further the rights, obligations and undertakings of each Party under the World Trade Organization ("WTO"), and other multilateral, regional and bilateral agreements and arrangements,

HAVE AGREED AS FOLLOWS:

Article 1　Definitions

1. For the purpose of this Agreement:

(a) "AEM" means ASEAN Economic Ministers;

(b) "freely usable currency" means any currency designated as such by the International Monetary Fund ("IMF") under its Articles of Agreement and any amendments thereto;

(c) "GATS" means the General Agreement on Trade in Services in Annex 1B to the WTO Agreement;

(d) "investment" means every kind of asset invested by the investors of a Party in accordance with the relevant laws, regulations and policies[①] of another Party in the territory of the latter including, but not limited to, the following:

(i) movable and immovable property and any other property rights such as mortgages, liens or pledges;

(ii) shares, stocks and debentures of juridical persons or interests in the property of such juridical persons;

(iii) intellectual property rights, including rights with respect to copyrights, patents and utility models, industrial designs, trademarks and service marks, geographical indications, layout designs of integrated circuits, trade names, trade secrets, technical processes, know-how and goodwill;

(iv) business concessions[②] conferred by law, or under contract, including concessions to search for, cultivate, extract, or exploit natural resources; and

---

① ［本协定原文脚注 1］For greater certainty, policies shall refer to those affecting investment that are endorsed and announced by the Government of a Party, and made publicly available in a written form.

② ［本协定原文脚注 2］Business concessions include contractual rights such as those under turnkey, construction or management contracts, production or revenue sharing contracts, concessions, or other similar contracts and can include investment funds for projects such as Build-Operate and Transfer (BOT) and Build-Operate and Own (BOO) schemes.

(v) claims to money or to any performance having financial value.

For the purpose of the definition of investment in this Sub-paragraph, returns that are invested should be treated as investments and any alteration of the form in which assets are invested or reinvested shall not affect their character as investments;

(e) "investor of a Party" means a natural person of a Party or a juridical person of a Party that is making① or has made an investment in the territories of the other Parties;

(f) "juridical person of a Party" means any legal entity duly constituted or otherwise organised under the applicable law of a Party, whether for profit or otherwise, and whether privately-owned or governmentally-owned, and engaged in substantive business operations in the territory of that Party, including any corporation, trust, partnership, joint venture, sole proprietorship or association;

(g) "measure" means any law, regulation, rule, procedure, or decision or administrative action of general application, affecting investors and/or investments, taken by a Party including its:

(i) central, regional or local governments and authorities; and

(ii) non-governmental bodies in the exercise of powers delegated by central, regional or local governments and authorities;

(h) "MOFCOM" means Ministry of Commerce of the People's Republic of China;

(i) "natural person of a Party" means any natural person possessing the nationality or citizenship of, or right of permanent residence in the Party in accordance with its laws and regulations;②

(j) "returns" means amounts yielded by or derived from an investment particularly, though not exclusively, profits, interests, capital gains, dividends, royalties or fees;

(k) "SEOM" means ASEAN Senior Economic Officials Meetings;

---

① ［本协定原文脚注 3］ For greater certainty, the phrase "is making" shall refer only to Article 5 (Most-Favoured-Nation Treatment) and Article 10 (Transfers and Repatriation of Profits).

② ［本协定原文脚注 4］ In the case of Indonesia, Lao PDR, Myanmar, Thailand and Viet Nam, which do not grant rights of permanent residence to foreigners or do not accord its permanent residents the same benefits as its nationals or citizens, they shall not be legally obliged to accord the benefits of this Agreement to permanent residents of any of the other Parties, or claim the aforesaid benefits for its permanent residents, if applicable, from any of the other Parties. In the case of China, until such time when China enacts its domestic law on the treatment of permanent residents of foreign countries, the permanent residents of the other Parties shall, provided there is reciprocity from those other Parties, be treated no less favourably than those of third countries, in like circumstances, if such permanent residents waive their rights that may be derived from provisions of dispute resolution under any other investment agreements or arrangements concluded between China and any third country.

(l) "WTO Agreement" means the Marrakesh Agreement Establishing the World Trade Organization, done at Marrakesh, Morocco on the 15th of April 1994, as may be amended.

2. The definitions of each of the above terms shall apply unless the context otherwise requires, or where a Party has specifically defined any of the above terms for application to its commitments or reservations.

3. In this Agreement, all words used in the singular shall include the plural, and all words in the plural shall include the singular, unless the context otherwise requires.

Article 2　Objectives

The objectives of this Agreement are to promote investment flows and to create a liberal, facilitative, transparent and competitive investment regime in China and ASEAN through the following:

(a) progressively liberalising the investment regimes of China and ASEAN;

(b) creating favourable conditions for the investment by the investor of a Party in the territory of another Party;

(c) promoting the cooperation between a Party and the investor who has investment in the territory of that Party on a mutually beneficial basis;

(d) encouraging and promoting the flow of investment among the Parties and cooperation among the Parties on investment-related matters;

(e) improving the transparency of investment rules conducive to increased investment flows among the Parties; and

(f) providing for the protection of investments in China and ASEAN.

Article 3　Scope of Application

1. This Agreement shall apply to measures adopted or maintained by a Party relating to:

(a) investors of another Party; and

(b) investments of investors of another Party in its territory, which shall be:

(i) in respect of China, the entire customs territory according to the WTO definition at the time of her accession to the WTO on the 11th day of December 2001. For this purpose, for China, "territory" in this Agreement refers to the customs territory of China; and

(ii) in respect of ASEAN Member States, their respective territories.

2. Unless otherwise provided in this Agreement, this Agreement shall apply to all investments made by investors of a Party in the territory of another Party, whether made before or after the entry into force of this Agreement. For greater certainty, the

provisions of this Agreement do not bind any Party in relation to any act or fact that took place or any situation that ceased to exist before the date of entry into force of this Agreement.

3. In the case of Thailand，this Agreement shall apply only in cases where the investment by an investor of another Party in the territory of Thailand has been admitted，and specifically approved in writing for protection by its competent authorities①, in accordance with its domestic laws，regulations and policies.

4. This Agreement shall not apply to：

（a）any taxation measure. This Sub-paragraph shall not undermine the Parties' rights and obligations with respect to taxation measures：

（i）where corresponding rights or obligations are also granted or imposed under the WTO Agreement；

（ii）under Article 8（Expropriation）and Article 10（Transfers and Repatriation of Profits）；

（iii）under Article 14（Investment Disputes between a Party and an Investor），only when the dispute arises from Article 8（Expropriation）；and

（iv）under any tax convention relating to the avoidance of double taxation；

（b）laws，regulations，policies or procedures of general application governing the procurement by government agencies of goods and services purchased for governmental purposes（government procurement）and not with a view to commercial resale or with a view to use in the production of goods or the supply of services for commercial sale；

（c）subsidies or grants provided by a Party or to any conditions attached to the receipt or the continued receipt of such subsidies or grants，whether or not such subsidies or grants are offered exclusively to domestic investors and investments；

（d）services supplied in the exercise of governmental authority by the relevant body or authority of a Party. For the purposes of this Agreement，a service supplied in the exercise of governmental authority means any service which is supplied neither on a commercial basis nor in competition with one or more service suppliers；and

（e）measures adopted or maintained by a Party affecting trade in services.

5. Notwithstanding Sub-paragraph 4（e），Article 7（Treatment of Investment），Article 8（Expropriation），Article 9（Compensation for Losses），Article 10（Transfers and Repatriation of Profits），Article 12（Subrogation）and Article 14（Investment Disputes between a Party and an Investor）shall apply，mutatis mutandis，to any measure affecting the supply of a service by a service supplier of a Party through

---

① ［本协定原文脚注 5］The name and contact details of the competent authorities responsible for granting such approval shall be informed to the other Parties through the ASEAN Secretariat.

commercial presence in the territory of another Party, but only to the extent that they relate to an investment and an obligation under this Agreement, regardless of whether or not such a service sector is scheduled in the Party's Schedule of Specific Commitments made under the Agreement on Trade in Services of the Framework Agreement on Comprehensive Economic Co-operation between the People's Republic of China and the Association of Southeast Asian Nations signed in Cebu, Philippines on the 14th day of January 2007.

Article 4　National Treatment

Each Party shall, in its territory, accord to investors of another Party and their investments treatment no less favourable than it accords, in like circumstances, to its own investors and their investments with respect to management, conduct, operation, maintenance, use, sale, liquidation, or other forms of disposal of such investments.

Article 5　Most-Favoured-Nation Treatment

1. Each Party shall accord to investors of another Party and their investments treatment no less favourable than that it accords, in like circumstances, to investors of any other Party or third country and/or their respective investments with respect to admission, establishment, acquisition, expansion, management, conduct, operation, maintenance, use, liquidation, sale, and other forms of disposal of investments.

2. Notwithstanding Paragraph 1, if a Party accords more favourable treatment to investors of another Party or third country and their investments by virtue of any future agreements or arrangements to which that Party is a party, it shall not be obliged to accord such treatment to investors of another Party and their investments. However, upon request from another Party, it shall accord adequate opportunity to negotiate the benefits granted therein.

3. The treatment, as set forth in Paragraph 1 and Paragraph 2, shall not include:

(a) any preferential treatment accorded to investors and their investments under any existing bilateral, regional or international agreements, or any forms of economic or regional cooperation with any non-Party; and

(b) any existing or future preferential treatment accorded to investors and their investments in any agreement or arrangement between or among ASEAN Member States or between any Party and its separate customs territories.

4. For greater certainty, the obligation in this Article does not encompass a requirement for a Party to extend to investors of another Party dispute resolution procedures other than those set out in this Agreement.

Article 6　Non-Conforming Measures

1. Article 4 (National Treatment) and Article 5 (Most-Favoured-Nation Treatment) shall not apply to:

(a) any existing or new non-conforming measures maintained or adopted within its territory;

(b) the continuation or amendment of any non-conforming measures referred to in Sub-paragraph (a).

2. The Parties will endeavour to progressively remove the non-conforming measures.

3. The Parties shall enter into discussions pursuant to Article 24 (Review) with a view to furthering the objectives in Article 2(a) and Article 2(e). The Parties will endeavour to achieve the objectives to be overseen by the institution under Article 22 (Institutional Arrangement).

Article 7　Treatment of Investment

1. Each Party shall accord to investments of investors of another Party fair and equitable treatment and full protection and security.

2. For greater certainty:

(a) fair and equitable treatment refers to the obligation of each Party not to deny justice in any legal or administrative proceedings; and

(b) full protection and security requires each Party to take such measures as may be reasonably necessary to ensure the protection and security of the investment of investors of another Party.

3. A determination that there has been a breach of another provision of this Agreement, or of a separate international agreement, shall not establish that there has been a breach of this Article.

Article 8　Expropriation

1. A Party shall not expropriate, nationalise or take other similar measures ("expropriation") against investments of investors of another Party, unless the following conditions are met:

(a) for a public purpose;

(b) in accordance with applicable domestic laws, including legal procedures;

(c) carried out in a non-discriminatory manner; and

(d) on payment of compensation in accordance with Paragraph 2.

2. Such compensation shall amount to the fair market value of the expropriated

investment at the time when expropriation was publicly announced or when expropriation occurred, whichever is earlier, and it shall be freely transferable in freely usable currencies from the host country. The fair market value shall not reflect any change in market value occurring because the expropriation had become publicly known earlier.

3. The compensation shall be settled and paid without unreasonable delay. In the event of delay, the compensation shall include interest at the prevailing commercial interest rate from the date of expropriation until the date of payment[①]. The compensation, including any accrued interest, shall be payable either in the currency in which the investment was originally made or, if requested by the investor, in a freely usable currency.

4. Notwithstanding Paragraph 1, Paragraph 2 and Paragraph 3, any measure of expropriation relating to land shall be as defined in the expropriating Party's existing domestic laws and regulations and any amendments thereto, and shall be for the purposes of and upon payment of compensation in accordance with the aforesaid laws and regulations.

5. Where a Party expropriates the assets of a juridical person which is incorporated or constituted under its laws and regulations, and in which investors of another Party own shares, it shall apply the provisions of the preceding Paragraphs so as to ensure that compensation is paid to such investors to the extent of their interest in the assets expropriated.

6. This Article shall not apply to the issuance of compulsory licences granted to intellectual property rights in accordance with the Agreement on Trade-Related Aspects of Intellectual Property Rights in Annex 1C to the WTO Agreement.

Article 9　Compensation for Losses

Investors of a Party whose investments in the territory of another Party suffer losses owing to war or other armed conflict, revolution, a state of emergency, revolt, insurrection or riot in the territory of the latter Party shall be accorded by the latter Party treatment, as regard restitution, indemnification, compensation or other settlement, no less favourable than that which the latter Party accords, in like

---

① ［本协定原文脚注 6］For Malaysia, Myanmar, Philippines, Thailand and Viet Nam, in the event of delay, the rate and payment of interest of compensation for expropriation of investments of investors of another Party shall be determined in accordance with their laws, regulations and policies provided that such laws, regulations and policies are applied on a non-discriminatory basis to investments of investors of another Party or a non-Party.

circumstances, to investors of any third country or its own nationals, whichever is more favourable.

Article 10   Transfers and Repatriation of Profits

1. Each Party shall allow all transfers in respect of investments in its territory of an investor of any other Party to be made in any freely usable currency at the prevailing market rate of exchange on the date of transfer, and allow such transfers to be freely transferred into and out of its territory without delay. Such transfers shall include:

(a) the initial capital, plus any additional capital used to maintain or expand the investments[①];

(b) net profits, capital gains, dividends, royalties, licence fees, technical assistance and technical and management fees, interest and other current income accruing from any investment of the investors of any other Party;

(c) proceeds from the total or partial sale or liquidation of any investment made by investors of any other Party;

(d) funds in repayment of borrowings or loans given by investors of a Party to the investors of any other Party which the respective Parties have recognised as investment;

(e) net earnings and other compensations of natural persons of any other Party, who are employed and allowed to work in connection with an investment in its territory;

(f) payments made under a contract entered into by the investors of any other Party, or their investments including payments made pursuant to a loan transaction; and

(g) payments made pursuant to Article 8 (Expropriation) and Article 9 (Compensation for Losses).

2. Each Party undertakes to accord to the transfer referred to in Paragraph 1, treatment as favourable as that accorded, in like circumstances, to the transfer originating from investments made by investors of any other Party or third country.

3. Notwithstanding Paragraph 1 and Paragraph 2, a Party may prevent or delay a transfer through the equitable, non-discriminatory and good faith application of its laws and regulations relating to:

(a) bankruptcy, loss of ability or capacity to make payments, or protection of the right of creditors;

(b) non-fulfilment of the host Party's transfer requirements in respect of trading or

---

① [本协定原文脚注 7] The Parties understand that the reference to "the initial capital, plus any additional capital used to maintain or expand the investments" only applies following the successful completion of the approval procedures for inward investment.

dealing in securities, futures, options or derivatives;

(c) non-fulfilment of tax obligations;

(d) criminal or penal offences and the recovery of the proceeds of crime;

(e) social security, public retirement or compulsory saving schemes;

(f) compliance with judgements in judicial or administrative proceedings;

(g) workers' retrenchment benefits in relation to labour compensation relating to, amongst others, foreign investment projects that are closed down; and

(h) financial reporting or record keeping of transfers when necessary to assist law enforcement or financial regulatory authorities.

4. For greater certainty, the transfers referred to in the preceding Paragraphs shall comply with relevant formalities stipulated by the host Party's domestic laws and regulations relating to exchange administration, insofar as such laws and regulations are not to be used as a means of avoiding a Party's obligations under this Agreement.

5. Nothing in this Agreement shall affect the rights and obligations of the Parties as members of the IMF under the Articles of Agreement of the IMF, including the use of exchange actions which are in conformity with the Articles of Agreement of the IMF, provided that a Party shall not impose restrictions on any capital transactions inconsistently with its specific commitments under this Agreement regarding such transactions, except:

(a) under Article 11 (Measures to Safeguard the Balance of Payments); or

(b) at the request of the IMF; or

(c) where, in exceptional circumstances, movements of capital cause, or threaten to cause, serious economic or financial disturbance in the Party concerned, provided such restrictions do not affect the rights and obligations of the Parties as members of the WTO under Paragraph 1 of Article XI of GATS, and the measures are taken in accordance with paragraph 2 of Article 11 of this Agreement, mutatis mutandis.

Article 11　Measures to Safeguard the Balance of Payments

1. In the event of serious balance of payments and external financial difficulties or threat thereof, a Party may adopt or maintain restrictions on investments, including payments or transfers related to such investments. It is recognised that particular pressures on the balance of payments of a Party in the process of economic development may necessitate the use of restrictions to ensure, inter alia, the maintenance of a level of financial reserves adequate for the implementation of its programme of economic development.

2. The restrictions referred to in Paragraph 1 shall:

(a) be consistent with the Articles of Agreement of the IMF;

(b) not discriminate among the Parties;

(c) avoid unnecessary damage to the commercial, economic and financial interests of any other Party;

(d) not exceed those necessary to deal with the circumstances described in Paragraph 1;

(e) be temporary and be phased out progressively as the situation specified in Paragraph 1 improves; and

(f) be applied such that any other Party is treated no less favourably than any third country.

3. Any restrictions adopted or maintained by a Party under Paragraph 1 or any changes therein, shall be promptly notified to the other Parties.

Article 12   Subrogation

1. In the event that any Party or any agency, institution, statutory body or corporation designated by it, as a result of an indemnity it has given in respect of an investment or any part thereof, makes payment to its own investors in respect of any of their claims under this Agreement, the other Parties concerned shall acknowledge that the former Party or any agency, institution, statutory body or corporation designated by it is entitled by virtue of subrogation to exercise the rights and assert the claims of its own investors. The subrogated rights or claims shall not be greater than the original rights or claims of the said investor.

2. Where a Party or any agency, institution, statutory body or corporation designated by it has made a payment to an investor of that Party and has taken over the rights and claims of the investor, that investor shall not, unless authorised to act on behalf of the Party or the agency, institution, statutory body or corporation designated by it making the payment, pursue those rights and claims against the other Party.

Article 13   Dispute between Parties

The provisions of the Agreement on Dispute Settlement Mechanism of the Framework Agreement on Comprehensive Economic Co-operation between the People's Republic of China and the Association of Southeast Asian Nations signed in Vientiane, Lao PDR on the 29th day of November 2004 shall apply to the settlement of disputes between or amongst the Parties under this Agreement.

Article 14   Investment Disputes between a Party and an Investor

1. This Article shall apply to investment disputes between a Party and an investor of another Party concerning an alleged breach of an obligation of the former Party under

Article 4 （National Treatment）, Article 5 （Most-Favoured-Nation Treatment ）, Article 7 （Treatment of Investment）, Article 8 （Expropriation）, Article 9 （Compensation for Losses） and Article 10 （Transfers and Repatriation of Profits）, which causes loss or damage to the investor in relation to its investment with respect to the management, conduct, operation, or sale or other disposition of an investment.

2. This Article shall not apply:

（a） to investment disputes arising out of events which occurred, or to investment disputes which had been settled, or which were already under judicial or arbitral process, prior to the entry into force of this Agreement;

（b） in cases where the disputing investor holds the nationality or citizenship of the disputing Party.

3. The parties to the dispute shall, as far as possible, resolve the dispute through consultations.

4. Where the dispute cannot be resolved as provided for under Paragraph 3 within six（6） months from the date of written request for consultations and negotiations, unless the parties to the dispute agree otherwise, it may be submitted at the choice of the investor:

（a） to the courts or administrative tribunals of the disputing Party, provided such courts or administrative tribunals have jurisdiction; or

（b） under the International Centre for Settlement of Investment Disputes （ICSID） Convention and the ICSID Rules of Procedure for Arbitration Proceedings[1], provided that both the disputing Party and the non-disputing Party are parties to the ICSID Convention; or

（c） under the ICSID Additional Facility Rules, provided that either of the disputing Party or non-disputing Party is a party to the ICSID Convention; or

（d） to arbitration under the rules of the United Nations Commission on International Trade Law; or

（e） if the disputing parties agree, to any other arbitration institution or under any other arbitration rules.

5. In case a dispute has been submitted to a competent domestic court, it may be submitted to international disputesettlement, provided that the investor concerned has withdrawn its case from the domestic court before a final judgement has been reached in the case. In the case of Indonesia, Philippines, Thailand, and Viet Nam, once the

---

[1] ［本协定原文脚注 8］ In the case of Philippines, submission of a claim under the ICSID Convention and the ICSID Rules of Procedure for Arbitration Proceedings shall be subject to a written agreement between the disputing parties in the event that an investment dispute arises.

investor has submitted the dispute totheirrespective competent courtsor administrative tribunals or to one of the arbitration procedures stipulated in Sub-paragraphs 4(b), 4 (c), 4(d) or 4(e), the choice of the procedure is final.

6. Thesubmission ofa disputeto conciliationor arbitration under Sub-paragraphs 4 (b), 4(c), 4(d) or 4(e) in accordance with the provisions of this Article, shall be conditional upon:

(a) the submission of the dispute to such conciliation or arbitration taking place within three (3) years of the time at which the disputing investor became aware, or should reasonably have become aware, of a breach of an obligation under this Agreement causing loss or damage to the investor or its investment; and

(b) the disputing investor providing written notice, which shall be submitted at least ninety (90) days before the claim is submitted, to the disputing Party of his or her intent to submit the dispute to such conciliation or arbitration. Upon the receipt of the notice, the disputing Party may require the disputing investor to go through any applicable domestic administrative review procedure specified by its domestic laws and regulations before the submission of the dispute under Sub-paragraphs 4(b), 4(c), 4 (d) or 4(e). The notice shall:

(i) nominate either Sub-paragraphs 4(b), 4(c), 4(d) or 4(e) as the forum for dispute settlement and, in the case of Sub-paragraph 4(b), nominate whether conciliation or arbitration is being sought;

(ii) waive the right to initiate or continue any proceedings, excluding proceedings for interim measures of protection referred to in Paragraph 7, before any of the other dispute settlement fora referred to in Paragraph 4 in relation to the matter under dispute; and

(iii) briefly summarise the alleged breach of the disputing Party under this Agreement, including the Articles alleged to have been breached, and the loss or damage allegedly caused to the investor or its investment.

7. No Party shall prevent the disputing investor from seeking interim measures of protection, not involving the payment of damages or resolution of the substance of the matter in dispute before the courts or administrative tribunals of the disputing Party, prior to the institution of proceedings before any of the dispute settlement fora referred to in Paragraph 4, for the preservation of its rights and interests.

8. No Party shall give diplomatic protection, or bring an international claim, in respect of a dispute which one of its investors and any one of the other Parties shall have consented to submit or have submitted to conciliation or arbitration under this Article, unless such other Party has failed to abide by and comply with the award rendered in such dispute. Diplomatic protection, for the purposes of this Paragraph, shall not

include informal diplomatic exchanges for the sole purpose of facilitating a settlement of the dispute.

9. Where an investor claims that the disputing Party has breached Article 8 (Expropriation) by the adoption or enforcement of a taxation measure, the disputing Party and the non-disputing Party shall, upon request from the disputing Party, hold consultations with a view to determining whether the taxation measure in question has an effect equivalent to expropriation or nationalisation. Any tribunal that may be established under this Article shall accord serious consideration to the decision of both Parties under this Paragraph.

10. If both Parties fail either to initiate such consultations, or to determine whether such taxation measure has an effect equivalent to expropriation or nationalisation within the period of one hundred eighty (180) days from the date of receipt of the request for consultation referred to in Paragraph 4, the disputing investor shall not be prevented from submitting its claim to arbitration in accordance with this Article.

Article 15   Denial of Benefits

1. Subject to prior notification and consultation, a Party may deny the benefits of this Agreement to:

(a) investors of another Party where the investment is being made by a juridical person that is owned or controlled by persons of a non-Party and the juridical person has no substantive business operations in the territory of another Party; or

(b) investors of another Party where the investment is being made by a juridical person that is owned or controlled by persons of the denying Party.

2. Notwithstanding Paragraph 1, in the case of Thailand, it may, under its applicable laws and/or regulations, deny the benefits of this Agreement relating to the admission, establishment, acquisition and expansion of investments to an investor of the other Party that is a juridical person of such Party and to investments of such an investor where Thailand establishes that the juridical person① is owned or controlled by natural persons or juridical persons of a non-Party or the denying Party.

3. Without prejudice to Paragraph 1, Philippines may deny the benefits of this Agreement to investors of another Party and to investments of that investor, where it

---

①　［本协定原文脚注 9］(a) In the case of Thailand, a juridical person referred to in this Article is: (i)"owned" by natural persons or juridical persons of a Party or a non-Party if more than fifty (50) percent of the equity interests in it is beneficially owned by such persons; (ii) "controlled" by natural persons or juridical persons of a Party or non-Party if such persons have the power to name a majority of its directors or otherwise to legally direct its actions. (b) In the case of Indonesia, Myanmar, Philippines and Viet Nam, ownership and control shall be defined in its domestic laws and regulations.

establishes that such investor has made an investment in breach of the provisions of Commonwealth Act No.108, entitled "An Act to Punish Acts of Evasion of Laws on the Nationalisation of Certain Rights, Franchises or Privileges", as amended by Presidential Decree No.715, otherwise known as "The Anti-Dummy Law", as may be amended.

Article 16　General Exceptions

1. Subject to the requirement that such measures are not applied in a manner which would constitute a means of arbitrary or unjustifiable discrimination between the Parties, their investors or their investments where like conditions prevail, or a disguised restriction on investors of any Party or their investments made by investors of any Party, nothing in this Agreement shall be construed to prevent the adoption or enforcement by any Party of measures:

(a) necessary to protect public morals or to maintain public order①;

(b) necessary to protect human, animal or plant life or health;

(c) necessary to secure compliance with laws or regulations which are not inconsistent with the provisions of this Agreement including those relating to:

(i) the prevention of deceptive and fraudulent practices to deal with the effects of a default on a contract;

(ii) the protection of the privacy of individuals in relation to the processing and dissemination of personal data and the protection of confidentiality of individual records and accounts; and

(iii) safety;

(d) aimed at ensuring the equitable or effective② imposition or collection of direct taxes in respect of investments or investors of any Party;

(e) imposed for the protection of national treasures of artistic, historic or archaeological value; or

(f) relating to the conservation of exhaustible natural resources if such measures are made effective in conjunction with restrictions on domestic production or consumption.

2. Insofar as measures affecting the supply of financial services are concerned, paragraph 2 (Domestic Regulation) of the Annex on Financial Services of GATS shall be incorporated into and form an integral part of this Agreement, mutatis mutandis.

---

① ［本协定原文脚注 10］For the purpose of this Sub-paragraph, footnote 5 of Article XIV of the GATS is incorporated into and forms part of this Agreement, *mutatis mutandis*.

② ［本协定原文脚注 11］For the purpose of this Sub-paragraph, footnote 6 of Article XIV of the GATS is incorporated into and forms part of this Agreement, *mutatis mutandis*.

Article 17　Security Exceptions

Nothing in this Agreement shall be construed:

(a) to require any Party to furnish any information, the disclosure of which it considers contrary to its essential security interests; or

(b) to prevent any Party from taking any action which it considers necessary for the protection of its essential security interests, including but not limited to:

(i) action relating to fissionable and fusionable materials or the materials from which they derived;

(ii) action relating to the traffic in arms, ammunition and implements of war and to such traffic in other goods and materials as is carried on directly or indirectly for the purpose of supplying a military establishment;

(iii) action taken so as to protect critical public infrastructure from deliberate attempts intended to disable or degrade such infrastructure;

(iv) action taken in time of war or other emergency in domestic or international relations; or

(c) to prevent any Party from taking any action in pursuance of its obligations under the United Nations Charter for the maintenance of international peace and security.

Article 18　Other Obligations

1. If the legislation of any Party or international obligations existing at the time of entry into force of this Agreement or established thereafter between or among the Parties result in a position entitling investments by investors of another Party to a treatment more favourable than is provided for by this Agreement, such position shall not be affected by this Agreement.

2. Each Party shall observe any commitments it may have entered into with the investors of another Party as regards to their investments.

Article 19　Transparency

1. In order to achieve the objectives of this Agreement, each Party shall:

(a) make available through publication, all relevant laws, regulations, policies and administrative guidelines of general application that pertain to, or affect investments in its territory.

(b) promptly and at least annually notify the other Parties of the introduction of any new law or any changes to its existing laws, regulations, policies or administrative guidelines, which significantly affect investments in its territory, or its commitments under this Agreement.

(c) establish or designate an enquiry point where, upon request of any natural person, juridical person or any one of the other Parties, all information relating to the measures required to be published or made available under Sub-paragraphs (a) and (b) may be promptly obtained.

(d) notify the other Parties through the ASEAN Secretariat at least once annually of any future investment-related agreements or arrangements which grants any preferential treatment and to which it is a party.

2. Nothing in this Agreement shall require a Party to furnish or allow access to confidential information, the disclosure of which would impede law enforcement, or otherwise contrary to the public interest, or which would prejudice legitimate commercial interests of particular juridical persons, public or private.

3. All notifications and communications made pursuant to Paragraph 1 shall be in the English language.

Article 20　Promotion of Investment

The Parties shall cooperate in promoting and increasing awareness of China-ASEAN as an investment area through, amongst others:
(a) increasing China-ASEAN investments;
(b) organising investment promotion activities;
(c) promoting business matching events;
(d) organising and supporting the organisation of various briefings and seminars on investment opportunities and on investment laws, regulations and policies; and
(e) conducting information exchanges on other issues of mutual concern relating to investment promotion and facilitation.

Article 21　Facilitation of Investment

Subject to their laws and regulations, the Parties shall cooperate to facilitate investments amongst China and ASEAN through, amongst others:
(a) creating the necessary environment for all forms of investment;
(b) simplifying procedures for investment applications and approvals;
(c) promoting dissemination of investment information, including investment rules, regulations, policies and procedures; and
(d) establishing one-stop investment centres in the respective host Parties to provide assistance and advisory services to the business sectors including facilitation of operating licences and permits.

Article 22　Institutional Arrangements

1. Pending the establishment of a permanent body, the AEM-MOFCOM, supported and assisted by the SEOM-MOFCOM, shall oversee, supervise, coordinate and review the implementation of this Agreement.

2. The ASEAN Secretariat shall monitor and report to the SEOM-MOFCOM on the implementation of this Agreement. All Parties shall cooperate with the ASEAN Secretariat in the performance of its duties.

3. Each Party shall designate a contact point to facilitate communications between the Parties on any matter covered by this Agreement. On the request of a Party, the contact point of the requested Party shall identify the office or official responsible for the matter and assist in facilitating communication with the requesting Party.

Article 23　Relations with Other Agreements

Nothing in this Agreement shall derogate from the existing rights and obligations of a Party under any other international agreements to which it is a party.

Article 24　General Review

The AEM-MOFCOM or their designated representatives shall meet within a year from the date of entry into force of this Agreement and then biennially or otherwise as appropriate to review this Agreement with a view to furthering the objectives set out in Article 2 (Objectives).

Article 25　Amendments

This Agreement may be amended by agreement in writing by the Parties and such amendments shall enter into force on such date or dates as may be agreed by the Parties.

Article 26　Depositary

For the ASEAN Member States, this Agreement shall be deposited with the Secretary-General of ASEAN, who shall promptly furnish a certified copy thereof, to each ASEAN Member State.

Article 27　Entry into Force

1. This Agreement shall enter into force six (6) months from the date of signing of this Agreement.

2. The Parties undertake to complete their internal procedures for the entry into force of this Agreement.

3. Where a Party is unable to complete its internal procedures for the entry into force of this Agreement within six（6）months from the date of signing of this Agreement，the rights and obligations of that Party under this Agreement shall commence thirty（30）days after the date of notification of completion of such internal procedures.

4. A Party shall upon the completion of its internal procedures for the entry into force of this Agreement notify the other Parties in writing.

IN WITNESS WHEREOF，the undersigned，being duly authorised by their respective Governments，have signed this Agreement on Investment of the Framework Agreement on Comprehensive Economic Co-operation between the People's Republic of China and the Association of Southeast Asian Nations.

DONE at Bangkok，Thailand this Fifteenth Day of August in the Year Two Thousand and Nine，in duplicate copies in the English Language.

Ⅴ. AGREEMENT AMONG THE GOVERNMENT OF JAPAN, THE GOVERNMENT OF THE REPUBLIC OF KOREA AND THE GOVERNMENT OF THE PEOPLE'S REPUBLIC OF CHINA FOR THE PROMOTION, FACILITATION AND PROTECTION OF INVESTMENT

The Government of Japan，the Government of the Republic of Korea and the Government of the People's Republic of China，

Desiring to further promote investment in order to strengthen the economic relationship among Japan，the Republic of Korea and the People's Republic of China （hereinafter referred to in this Agreement as "the Contracting Parties"）；

Intending to create stable，favorable and transparent conditions for investment by investors of one Contracting Party in the territory of the other Contracting Parties；

Recognizing that the reciprocal promotion，facilitation and protection of such investment and the progressive liberalization of investment will be conducive to stimulating business initiative of the investors and increase prosperity among the Contracting Parties；

Recognizing that these objectives can be achieved without relaxing health，safety and environmental measures of general application；

Recognizing the importance of investors' complying with the laws and regulations of a Contracting Party in the territory of which the investors are engaged in investment activities, which contribute to the economic, social and environmental progress; and

Bearing in mind their respective rights and obligations under the WTO Agreement and other multilateral instruments of cooperation;

Have agreed as follows:

Article 1　Definitions

For the purposes of this Agreement:

(1) the term "investments" means every kind of asset that an investor owns or controls, directly or indirectly, which has the characteristics of an investment, such as the commitment of capital or other resources, the expectation of gain or profit, or the assumption of risk. Forms that investments may take include:

(a) an enterprise and a branch of an enterprise;

(b) shares, stocks or other forms of equity participation in an enterprise, including rights derived therefrom;

(c) bonds, debentures, loans and other forms of debt, including rights derived therefrom;

(d) rights under contracts, including turnkey, construction, management, production or revenue-sharing contracts;

(e) claims to money and claims to any performance under contract having a financial value associated with investment;

(f) intellectual property rights, including copyrights and related rights, patent rights and rights relating to utility models, trademarks, industrial designs, layout-designs of integrated circuits, new varieties of plants, trade names, indications of source or geographical indications and undisclosed information;

(g) rights conferred pursuant to laws and regulations or contracts such as concessions, licenses, authorizations and permits; and

(h) any other tangible and intangible, movable and immovable property, and any related property rights, such as leases, mortgages, liens and pledges;

Note: Investments also include the amounts yielded by investments, in particular, profit, interest, capital gains, dividends, royalties and fees.

A change in the form in which assets are invested does not affect their character as investments.

(2) the term "investor of a Contracting Party" means a natural person or an enterprise of a Contracting Party that makes investments in the territory of another Contracting Party;

(3) the term "natural person of a Contracting Party" means a natural person that

has the nationality of that Contracting Party in accordance with its applicable laws and regulations;

（4）the term "enterprise of a Contracting Party" means any legal person or any other entity constituted or organized under the applicable laws and regulations of that Contracting Party, whether or not for profit, and whether private-or government-owned or controlled, and includes a company, corporation, trust, partnership, sole proprietorship, joint venture, association or organization;

Note:For greater certainty, a branch of an enterprise is not, in and by itself, deemed to be an enterprise.

（5）the term "investment activities" means management, conduct, operation, maintenance, use, enjoyment and sale or other disposition of investments;

（6）the term "freely usable currencies" means freely usable currencies as defined under the Articles of Agreement of the International Monetary Fund;

（7）the term "ICSID Convention" means the Convention on the Settlement of Investment Disputes between States and Nationals of Other States, done at Washington, March 18, 1965;

（8）the term "UNCITRAL Arbitration Rules" means the arbitration rules of the United Nations Commission on International Trade Law;

（9）the term "WTO Agreement" means the Marrakesh Agreement Establishing the World Trade Organization, done at Marrakesh, April 15, 1994;

（10）the term "ICSID Additional Facility Rules" means the Rules Governing the Additional Facility for the Administration of Proceedings by the Secretariat of the International Centre for Settlement of Investment Disputes.

Article 2 Promotion and Protection of Investments

1. Each Contracting Party shall encourage and create favorable conditions for investors of the other Contracting Parties to make investments in its territory.

2. Each Contracting Party shall, subject to its rights to exercise powers in accordance with the applicable laws and regulations, including those with regard to foreign ownership and control, admit investment of investors of another Contracting Party.

Article 3 National Treatment

1. Each Contracting Party shall in its territory accord to investors of another Contracting Party and to their investments treatment no less favorable than that it accords in like circumstances to its own investors and their investments with respect to investment activities.

2. Paragraph 1 shall not apply to non-conforming measures, if any, existing at the date of entry into force of this Agreement maintained by each Contracting Party under its laws and regulations or any amendment or modification to such measures, provided that the amendment or modification does not decrease the conformity of the measure as it existed immediately before the amendment or modification.

Treatment granted to investment once admitted shall in no case be less favorable than that granted at the time when the original investment was made.

3. Each Contracting Party shall take, where applicable, all appropriate steps to progressively remove all the non-conforming measures referred to in paragraph 2.

Note: The People's Republic of China confirms that its measures referred to in paragraph 2 shall not be inconsistent with paragraph 2 of Article 3 of, and paragraph 3 of the Protocol to, the Agreement between Japan and the People's Republic of China Concerning the Encouragement and Reciprocal Protection of Investment, signed at Beijing, August 27, 1988.

Article 4　Most-Favored-Nation Treatment

1. Each Contracting Party shall in its territory accord to investors of another Contracting Party and to their investments treatment no less favorable than that it accords in like circumstances to investors of the third Contracting Party or of a non-Contracting Party and to their investments with respect to investment activities and the matters relating to the admission of investment in accordance with paragraph 2 of Article 2.

2. Paragraph 1 shall not be construed so as to oblige a Contracting Party to extend to investors of another Contracting Party and to their investments any preferential treatment resulting from its membership of:

（a）any customs union, free trade area, monetary union, similar international agreement leading to such union or free trade area, or other forms of regional economic cooperation;

（b）any international agreement or arrangement for facilitating small scale trade in border areas; or

（c）any bilateral and multilateral international agreements involving aviation, fishery and maritime matters including salvage.

3. It is understood that the treatment accorded to investors of the third Contracting Party or any non-Contracting Party and to their investments as referred to in paragraph 1 does not include treatment accorded to investors of the third Contracting Party or any non-Contracting Party and to their investments by provisions concerning the settlement of investment disputes between a Contracting Party and investors of the third

Contracting Party or between a Contracting Party and investors of any non-Contracting Party that are provided for in other international agreements.

Note: For the purposes of this Article, the term "non-Contracting Parties" shall not include any separate customs territory within the meaning of the General Agreement on Tariffs and Trade or of the WTO Agreement that is a member of the World Trade Organization as of the date of entry into force of this Agreement.

Article 5　General Treatment of Investments

1. Each Contracting Party shall accord to investments of investors of another Contracting Party fair and equitable treatment and full protection and security. The concepts of "fair and equitable treatment" and "full protection and security" do not require treatment in addition to or beyond any reasonable and appropriate standard of treatment accorded in accordance with generally accepted rules of international law. A determination that there has been a breach of another provision of this Agreement, or of a separate international agreement, does not *ipso facto* establish that there has been a breach of this paragraph.

2. Each Contracting Party shall observe any written commitments in the form of an agreement or contract it may have entered into with regard to investments of investors of another Contracting Party.

Article 6　Access to the Courts of Justice

Each Contracting Party shall in its territory accord to investors of another Contracting Party treatment no less favorable than that it accords in like circumstances to its own investors, investors of the third Contracting Party or of a non-Contracting Party, with respect to access to the courts of justice and administrative tribunals and agencies in all degrees of jurisdiction, both in pursuit and in defense of such investors' rights.

Article 7　Prohibition of Performance Requirements

1. The provisions of the Agreement on Trade-Related Investment Measures in Annex 1A to the WTO Agreement are incorporated into and made part of this Agreement, *mutatis mutandis* and shall apply with respect to all investments under this Agreement.

2. No Contracting Party shall, in its territory, impose unreasonable or discriminatory measures on investment by investors of another Contracting Party concerning performance requirements on export or transfer of technology.

Article 8　Entry of Personnel

Each Contracting Party shall endeavor, to the extent possible, in accordance with its applicable laws and regulations, to facilitate the procedures for the entry, sojourn and residence of natural persons of another Contracting Party who wish to enter the territory of the former Contracting Party and to remain therein for the purpose of conducting business activities in connection with investments.

Article 9　Intellectual Property Rights

1. (a) Each Contracting Party shall, in accordance with its laws and regulations, protect intellectual property rights.

(b) Each Contracting Party shall establish and maintain transparent intellectual property rights regimes, and will, under the existing consultation mechanism on intellectual property, promote cooperation and communications among the Contracting Parties in the intellectual property field.

2. Nothing in this Agreement shall be construed so as to derogate from the rights and obligations under international agreements in respect of protection of intellectual property rights to which two or more Contracting Parties are parties.

3. Nothing in this Agreement shall be construed so as to oblige a Contracting Party to extend to investors of another Contracting Party and their investments treatment accorded to investors of the third Contracting Party or of a non-Contracting Party and their investments by virtue of international agreements in respect of protection of intellectual property rights, to which, respectively, the first-mentioned Contracting Party and the third Contracting Party and the first-mentioned Contracting Party and the non-Contracting Party are parties.

Article 10　Transparency

1. Each Contracting Party shall promptly publish, or otherwise make publicly available, its laws, regulations, administrative procedures and administrative rulings and judicial decisions of general application as well as international agreements to which the Contracting Party is a party and which pertain to or affect investment activities. The Government of each Contracting Party shall make easily available to the public, the names and addresses of the competent authorities responsible for such laws, regulations, administrative procedures and administrative rulings.

2. When a Contracting Party introduces or changes its laws or regulations that significantly affect the implementation and operation of this Agreement, the Contracting Party shall endeavor to provide a reasonable interval between the time when

such laws or regulations are published or made publicly available and the time when they enter into force, except for those laws or regulations involving national security, foreign exchange rates or monetary policies and other laws or regulations the publication of which would impede law enforcement.

3. Each Contracting Party shall, upon the request by another Contracting Party, within a reasonable period of time and through existing bilateral channels, respond to specific questions from, and provide information to, the latter Contracting Party with respect to any actual or proposed measure of the former Contracting Party, which might materially affect the interests of the latter Contracting Party and its investors under this Agreement.

4. Each Contracting Party shall, in accordance with its laws and regulations:

(a) make public in advance regulations of general application that affect any matter covered by this Agreement; and

(b) provide a reasonable opportunity for comments by the public for those regulations related to investment and give consideration to those comments before adoption of such regulations.

5. The provisions of this Article shall not be construed so as to oblige any Contracting Party to disclose confidential information, the disclosure of which:

(a) would impede law enforcement;

(b) would be contrary to the public interest; or

(c) could prejudice privacy or legitimate commercial interests.

Article 11   Expropriation and Compensation

1. No Contracting Party shall expropriate or nationalize investments in its territory of investors of another Contracting Party or take any measure equivalent to expropriation or nationalization (hereinafter referred to in this Agreement as "expropriation") except:

(a) for a public purpose;

(b) on a non-discriminatory basis;

(c) in accordance with its laws and international standard of due process of law; and

(d) upon compensation pursuant to paragraphs 2, 3 and 4.

2. The compensation shall be equivalent to the fair market value of the expropriated investments at the time when the expropriation was publicly announced or when the expropriation occurred, whichever is the earlier. The fair market value shall not reflect any change in market value occurring because the expropriation had become publicly known earlier.

3. The compensation shall be paid without delay and shall include interest at a commercially reasonable rate, taking into account the length of time from the time of expropriation to the time of payment. It shall be effectively realizable and freely transferable and shall be freely convertible, at the market exchange rate prevailing on the date of expropriation, into the currency of the Contracting Party of the investors concerned, and into freely usable currencies.

4. Without prejudice to the provisions of Article 15, the investors affected by expropriation shall have a right of access to the courts of justice or the administrative tribunals or agencies of the Contracting Party making the expropriation to seek a prompt review of the investors' case and the amount of compensation in accordance with the principles set out in this Article.

Article 12　Compensation for Losses or Damages

1. Each Contracting Party shall accord to investors of another Contracting Party that have suffered loss or damage relating to their investments in the territory of the former Contracting Party due to armed conflict or a state of emergency such as revolution, insurrection, civil disturbance or any other similar event in the territory of that former Contracting Party, treatment, as regards restitution, indemnification, compensation or any other settlement, that is no less favorable than that it accords to its own investors, to investors of the third Contracting Party or to investors of a non-Contracting Party, whichever is more favorable to the investors of another Contracting Party.

2. Any payments as a means of settlement referred to in paragraph 1 shall be effectively realizable, freely transferable and freely convertible at the market exchange rate into the currency of the Contracting Party of the investors concerned and into freely usable currencies.

Article 13　Transfers

1. Each Contracting Party shall ensure that all transfers relating to investments in its territory of an investor of another Contracting Party may be made freely into and out of its territory without delay. Such transfers shall include, in particular, though not exclusively:

(a) the initial capital and additional amounts to maintain or increase investments;

(b) profits, capital gains, dividends, royalties, interests, fees and other current account incomes accruing from investments;

(c) proceeds from the total or partial sale or liquidation of investments;

(d) payments made under a contract including loan payments in connection with investments;

(e) earnings and remuneration of personnel from the latter Contracting Party who work in connection with investments in the territory of the former Contracting Party;

(f) payments made in accordance with Articles 11 and 12; and

(g) payments arising out of the settlement of a dispute under Article 15.

2. Each Contracting Party shall further ensure that such transfers may be made in freely usable currencies at the market exchange rate prevailing on the date of each transfer.

3. Notwithstanding paragraphs 1 and 2, a Contracting Party may delay or prevent such transfers through the equitable, non-discriminatory and good faith application of its laws relating to:

(a) bankruptcy, insolvency or the protection of the rights of creditors;

(b) issuing, trading or dealing in securities, futures, options or other derivatives;

(c) criminal or penal offenses;

(d) ensuring compliance with orders or judgments in adjudicatory proceedings; or

(e) reports of transfers of currency or other monetary instruments.

4. The transfers referred to in this Article shall comply with relevant formalities stipulated by the laws and regulations, if any, of each Contracting Party relating to exchange administration which are in force at the time of investment by investors of another Contracting Party.

These formalities include, but are not limited to those related to:

(a) overseas investment;

(b) liquidation, transfer of ownership and registered capital reduction, including those related to reinvestment of funds derived therefrom;

(c) the repayment of principal and interest of registered external debts (including loans from foreign investors); or

(d) external guarantee provided by domestic guarantors.

5. The period required for the completion of the formalities referred to in paragraph 4 shall commence on the day on which a written request for each transfer with necessary documentation is submitted by the investor referred to in paragraph 1 to the foreign exchange authorities of the Contracting Party in the territory of which the investor's investments exist. The necessary authorizations should be granted in a period of approximately one month, which shall not exceed two months, from the submission of the request. Such formalities shall not be used as a means of avoiding the obligations of the Contracting Party under this Agreement.

Article 14　Subrogation

1. If a Contracting Party or its designated agency makes a payment to any of its investors pursuant to an indemnity, guarantee or insurance contract, pertaining to investments of that investor in the territory of another Contracting Party, the latter Contracting Party shall:

(a) recognize the assignment, to the former Contracting Party or its designated agency, of any right or claim of the investor that formed the basis of such payment; and

(b) recognize the right of the former Contracting Party or its designated agency to exercise by virtue of subrogation such right or claim to the same extent as the original right or claim of the investor.

2. If a Contracting Party or its designated agency has made a payment to its investors and thereby entered into the rights of the investor, the investor may not make a claim based on these rights against another Contracting Party without the consent of the former Contracting Party or its designated agency making the payment.For greater certainty, the investor shall continue to be entitled to exercise its rights that have not been subrogated pursuant to paragraph 1.

3. Articles 11, 12 and 13 shall apply *mutatis mutandis* as regards payment to be made to the Contracting Party or its designated agency referred to in paragraph 1 by virtue of such assignment of right or claim, and the transfer of such payment.

Article 15　Settlement of Investment Disputes Between a Contracting Party and an Investor of Another Contracting Party

1. For the purposes of this Article, an investment dispute is a dispute between a Contracting Party and an investor of another Contracting Party that has incurred loss or damage by reason of, or arising out of, an alleged breach of any obligation of the former Contracting Party under this Agreement with respect to the investor or its investments in the territory of the former Contracting Party.

2. Any investment dispute shall, as far as possible, be settled amicably through consultation between the investor who is a party to the investment dispute (hereinafter referred to in this Article as "disputing investor") and the Contracting Party that is a party to the investment dispute (hereinafter referred to in this Article as "disputing Contracting Party"). A written request for consultation shall be submitted to the disputing Contracting Party by the disputing investor before the submission of the investment dispute to the arbitration set out in paragraph 3. Such a written request shall specify:

(a) the name and address of the disputing investor;

(b) the obligations under this Agreement alleged to have been breached;

(c) a brief summary of the facts of the investment dispute; and

(d) the relief sought and the approximate amount of damages.

Note: The written consultation request shall be delivered to the following competent authorities of the disputing Contracting Party:

(a) in the case of the People's Republic of China, the Treaty and Law Department, Ministry of Commerce;

(b) in the case of Japan, the Ministry of Foreign Affairs or the entity in lieu of or replacing the aforementioned; and

(c) in the case of the Republic of Korea, International Legal Affairs Division, Ministry of Justice.

3. The investment dispute shall at the request of the disputing investor be submitted to either:

(a) a competent court of the disputing Contracting Party;

(b) arbitration in accordance with the ICSID Convention, if the ICSID Convention is available;

(c) arbitration under the ICSID Additional Facility Rules, if the ICSID Additional Facility Rules are available;

(d) arbitration under the UNCITRAL Arbitration Rules; or

(e) if agreed with the disputing Contracting Party, any arbitration in accordance with other arbitration rules, provided that, for the purposes of subparagraphs (b) through (e):

(i) the investment dispute cannot be settled through the consultation referred to in paragraph 2 within four months from the date of the submission of the written request for consultation to the disputing Contracting Party; and

(ii) the requirement concerning the domestic administrative review procedure set out in paragraph 7, where applicable, is met.

Note: For the purposes of subparagraph (a), this paragraph shall not be construed to prevent, where applicable, preliminary trial by administrative tribunals or agencies.

4. Each Contracting Party hereby gives its consent to the submission of an investment dispute by a disputing investor to the arbitration set out in paragraph 3 in accordance with the provisions of this Article.

5. Once the disputing investor has submitted an investment dispute to the competent court of the disputing Contracting Party or to one of the arbitrations set out in paragraph 3, the choice of the disputing investor shall be final and the disputing investor may not submit thereafter the same dispute to the other arbitrations set out in paragraph 3.

6. Notwithstanding paragraphs 3 and 4, no claim may be submitted to the

arbitration set out in paragraph 3 unless the disputing investor gives the disputing Contracting Party written waiver of any right to initiate before any competent court of the disputing Contracting Party with respect to any measure of the disputing Contracting Party alleged to constitute a breach referred to in paragraph 1.

7. When the disputing investor submits a written request for consultation to the disputing Contracting Party under paragraph 2, the disputing Contracting Party may require, without delay, the investor concerned to go through the domestic administrative review procedure specified by the laws and regulations of that Contracting Party before the submission to the arbitration set out in paragraph 3.

The domestic administrative review procedure shall not exceed four months from the date on which an application for the review is filed. If the procedure is not completed by the end of the four months, it shall be deemed to be completed and the disputing investor may submit the investment dispute to the arbitration set out in paragraph 3. The investor may file an application for the review unless the four months consultation period as provided in paragraph 3 has elapsed.

Note: It is understood that any decision made under the domestic administrative review procedure shall not prevent the disputing investor from submitting the investment dispute to the arbitration set out in paragraph 3.

8. The applicable arbitration rules shall govern the arbitration set out in paragraph 3 except to the extent modified in this Article.

9. The award rendered by an arbitral tribunal established under paragraph 3 (hereinafter referred to in this Article as the "Tribunal") shall include:

(a) a finding whether or not there has been a breach by the disputing Contracting Party of any obligation under this Agreement with respect to the disputing investor and its investments; and

(b) one or both of the following remedies, only if the disputing investor's loss or damage is attributed to such breach:

(i) monetary damages and applicable interest; and

(ii) restitution of property, in which case the award shall provide that the disputing Contracting Party may pay monetary damages and any applicable interest, in lieu of restitution.

10. The award which is rendered by the Tribunal shall be final and binding upon both parties to the investment dispute. This award shall be executed in accordance with the applicable laws and regulations concerning the execution of award in force, in the country in whose territory such execution is sought.

11. Notwithstanding paragraph 3, no claim may be submitted to the arbitration set out in that paragraph, if more than three years have elapsed from the date on which the

disputing investor first acquired, or should have first acquired, whichever is the earlier, the knowledge that the disputing investor had incurred the loss or damage referred to in paragraph 1.

12. Paragraph 3 (except subparagraph (a)) and paragraph 4 shall not apply to any investment dispute with respect to:

(a) the obligations of a Contracting Party under subparagraph 1(b) of Article 9; and

(b) the measures of a Contracting Party that fall within the scope of Article 20.

Article 16　Special Formalities and Information Requirements

1. Nothing in Article 3 shall be construed to prevent a Contracting Party from adopting or maintaining a measure that prescribes special formalities in connection with investment activities by investors of another Contracting Party in its territory, such as the requirement that investments be legally constituted under the laws or regulations of the former Contracting Party, provided that such formalities are consistent with this Agreement and do not materially impair the protections afforded by the former Contracting Party to investors of the latter Contracting Party and their investments pursuant to this Agreement.

2. Notwithstanding Articles 3 and 4, a Contracting Party may require an investor of another Contracting Party, in its territory, to provide information concerning its investments solely for informational or statistical purposes. The former Contracting Party shall protect such information that is confidential from any disclosure that would prejudice the competitive position of the investor of the latter Contracting Party or its investments. Nothing in this paragraph shall be construed so as to prevent a Contracting Party from otherwise obtaining or disclosing information in connection with the equitable and good faith application of its law.

Article 17　Settlement of Disputes among Contracting Parties

1. Any Contracting Party may request in writing consultations with another Contracting Party to resolve any dispute relating to the interpretation or application of this Agreement. The former Contracting Party (hereinafter referred to in this Article as "the complaining Party") shall at the time of the request deliver to the third Contracting Party a copy of that request. Where the third Contracting Party considers that it has a substantial interest in the dispute, it shall be entitled to participate in such consultations.

2. (a) Where the consultations referred to in paragraph 1 do not satisfactorily resolve the dispute within six months after the date of receipt of the request referred to

in that paragraph, the complaining Party or the Contracting Party to which such request was addressed (hereinafter collectively referred to in this Article as "the disputing Parties") may, upon written request to the other disputing Party, submit the dispute to an arbitral tribunal.

(b) The disputing Party that submits the dispute to an arbitral tribunal under subparagraph (a) shall deliver to the third Contracting Party a copy of the request for arbitration under that subparagraph.

(c) The third Contracting Party may make submissions to the arbitral tribunal referred to in subparagraph (a) on a question of the interpretation of this Agreement, upon written notice to the disputing Parties.

(d) Where the third Contracting Party considers that it has a substantial interest in the dispute, it shall be entitled to participate in the arbitration proceedings by joining either of the disputing Parties on delivery of a written notice of its intention to participate to the disputing Parties and to the arbitral tribunal referred to in subparagraph (a). Such written notice shall be delivered to the disputing Parties at the earliest possible time and in any event no later than seven days after the date of delivery of the copy of the request under subparagraph (b).

3. Unless otherwise provided for in this Article, or in the absence of an agreement by the disputing Parties to the contrary, the UNCITRAL Arbitration Rules shall apply *mutatis mutandis* to the proceedings of the arbitral tribunal. However, these rules may be modified by the disputing Parties or modified by the arbitrators appointed pursuant to paragraph 4, provided that none of the disputing Parties objects to the modification. The arbitral tribunal may, for its part, determine its own rules and procedures.

4. Within sixty days from the date of receipt of the request under subparagraph 2 (a), each disputing Party shall appoint an arbitrator. The two arbitrators shall, in consultation with the disputing Parties, select a third arbitrator as the chairperson, who shall be a national of a non-Contracting Party. The UNCITRAL Arbitration Rules applicable to appointing members of three-member panels shall apply *mutatis mutandis* to other matters relating to the appointment of the arbitrators of the arbitral tribunal provided that the appointing authority referenced in those rules shall be the President of the International Court of Justice.If the President is a national of any Contracting Party or otherwise prevented from discharging the said function, the Vice-President shall be invited to make the appointment. If the Vice-President also is a national of any Contracting Party or otherwise prevented from discharging the said function, the member of the International Court of Justice next in seniority who is not a national of any Contracting Party shall be invited to make the appointment.

5. Unless otherwise agreed by the disputing Parties, all submissions of documents

shall be made and all hearings shall be completed within a period of one hundred and eighty days from the date of selection of the third arbitrator. The arbitral tribunal shall render its award, in accordance with the provisions of this Agreement and the rules of international law applicable to the disputing Parties, within sixty days from the date of the final submissions of documents or the date of the closing of the hearings, whichever is the later. Such award shall be final and binding upon the disputing Parties.

6. The third Contracting Party that is not participating in the arbitration proceedings in accordance with subparagraph 2(d) shall, on delivery of a written notice to the disputing Parties and to the arbitral tribunal, be entitled to attend all hearings, to make written and oral submissions to the arbitral tribunal and to receive a copy of the written submissions of the disputing Parties to the arbitral tribunal.

7. Unless otherwise agreed by the disputing Parties, expenses incurred by the chairperson and other arbitrators, and other costs of the proceedings, shall be borne equally by the disputing Parties.

Article 18   Security Exceptions

1. Notwithstanding any other provisions in this Agreement other than the provisions of Article 12, each Contracting Party may take any measure:

(a) which it considers necessary for the protection of its essential security interests;

(i) taken in time of war, or armed conflict, or other emergency in that Contracting Party or in international relations; or

(ii) relating to the implementation of national policies or international agreements respecting the non-proliferation of weapons;

(b) in pursuance of its obligations under the United Nations Charter for the maintenance of international peace and security.

2. In cases where a Contracting Party takes any measure, pursuant to paragraph 1, that does not conform with the obligations of the provisions of this Agreement other than the provisions of Article 12, that Contracting Party shall not use such measure as a means of avoiding its obligations.

Article 19   Temporary Safeguard Measures

1. A Contracting Party may adopt or maintain measures not conforming with its obligations under Article 3 relating to cross-border capital transactions and Article 13:

(a) in the event of serious balance-of-payments and external financial difficulties or threat thereof; or

(b) in cases where, in exceptional circumstances, movements of capital cause or threaten to cause serious difficulties for macroeconomic management, in particular, monetary and exchange rate policies.

2. The measures referred to in paragraph 1:

(a) shall be consistent with the Articles of Agreement of the International Monetary Fund, so long as the Contracting Party taking the measures is a party to the said Articles;

(b) shall not exceed those necessary to deal with the circumstances set out in paragraph 1;

(c) shall be temporary and eliminated as soon as conditions permit;

(d) shall be promptly notified to the other Contracting Parties in an appropriate manner;

(e) shall ensure that any of the other Contracting Parties is treated as favorably as the third Contracting Party and any non-Contracting Party; and

(f) shall be adopted or maintained endeavoring to avoid unnecessary damage to the commercial, economic and financial interests of the other Contracting Parties.

3. Nothing in this Agreement shall be regarded as altering the rights enjoyed and obligations undertaken by a Contracting Party as a party to the Articles of Agreement of the International Monetary Fund.

Article 20　Prudential Measures

1. Notwithstanding any other provisions of this Agreement, a Contracting Party shall not be prevented from taking measures relating to financial services for prudential reasons, including measures for the protection of investors, depositors, policy holders or persons to whom a fiduciary duty is owed by an enterprise supplying financial services, or to ensure the integrity and stability of the financial system.

2. Where the measures referred to in paragraph 1 do not conform with the provisions of this Agreement, they shall not be used as a means of avoiding the Contracting Party's obligations under this Agreement.

Article 21　Taxation

1. Nothing in this Agreement shall apply to taxation measures except as expressly provided for in paragraphs 3, 4 and 5.

2. Nothing in this Agreement shall affect the rights and obligations of any Contracting Party under any tax convention. In the event of any inconsistency between this Agreement and any such convention, that convention shall prevail to the extent of the inconsistency.

Note: In resolving issues relating to taxes, the competent authorities of each Contracting Party under the relevant tax convention shall determine whether or not such convention governs such issues.

3. Article 11 shall apply to taxation measures.

4. Article 15 shall apply to disputes under paragraph 3.

5. (a) No investor may invoke Article 11 as the basis for the submission of an investment dispute to the arbitration set out in paragraph 3 of Article 15, where it has been determined pursuant to subparagraph (b) the taxation measure in question is not an expropriation.

(b) The disputing investor shall refer the issue, at the time of the submission of a written request for consultation to the disputing Contracting Party under paragraph 2 of Article 15, to the competent authorities of the Contracting Party of the disputing investor and the disputing Contracting Party to determine whether such measure is not an expropriation. If the competent authorities of both Contracting Parties do not consider the issue or, having considered it, fail to determine that the measure is not an expropriation within six months from the date on which the written request for consultation is submitted to the disputing Contracting Party under paragraph 2 of Article 15, the investor may submit its claim to the arbitration set out in paragraph 3 of Article 15.

(c) For the purposes of subparagraph (b), the term "competent authorities" means:

(i) in the case of the People's Republic of China, the Ministry of Finance and State Administration of Taxation or their authorized representatives;

(ii) in the case of Japan, the Minister of Finance or his or her authorized representatives, who shall consider the issue in consultation with the Minister for Foreign Affairs or his or her authorized representatives; and

(iii) in the case of the Republic of Korea, the Deputy Minister for Tax and Customs Office of the Ministry of Strategy and Finance or his or her authorized representatives.

Article 22　Denial of Benefits

1. A Contracting Party may deny the benefits of this Agreement to an investor of another Contracting Party that is an enterprise of the latter Contracting Party and to its investments if the enterprise is owned or controlled by an investor of a non-Contracting Party and the denying Contracting Party:

(a) does not maintain normal economic relations with the non-Contracting Party; or

(b) adopts or maintains measures with respect to the non-Contracting Party that prohibit transactions with the enterprise or that would be violated or circumvented if the benefits of this Agreement were accorded to the enterprise or to its investments.

2. A Contracting Party may deny the benefits of this Agreement to an investor of another Contracting Party that is an enterprise of the latter Contracting Party and to its investments if the enterprise is owned or controlled by an investor of a non-Contracting Party or of the denying Contracting Party, and the enterprise has no substantial business activities in the territory of the latter Contracting Party.

Note: For the purposes of this Article, the term "non- Contracting Parties" shall not include any separate customs territory within the meaning of the General Agreement on Tariffs and Trade or of the WTO Agreement that is a member of the World Trade Organization as of the date of entry into force of this Agreement.

Article 23　Environmental Measures

Each Contracting Party recognizes that it is inappropriate to encourage investment by investors of another Contracting Party by relaxing its environmental measures. To this effect each Contracting Party should not waive or otherwise derogate from such environmental measures as an encouragement for the establishment, acquisition or expansion of investments in its territory.

Article 24　Joint Committee

1. The Contracting Parties shall establish a Joint Committee (hereinafter referred to in this Article as the "Committee") with a view to accomplishing the objectives of this Agreement. The functions of the Committee shall be:

(a) to discuss and review the implementation and operation of this Agreement; and

(b) to discuss other investment-related matters concerning this Agreement, including the scope of the existing non-conforming measures referred to in paragraphs 2 and 3 of Article 3.

2. The Committee may, as necessary, decide to make appropriate recommendations to the Contracting Parties for the more effective functioning or the attainment of the objectives of this Agreement.

3. The Committee shall be composed of representatives of the Governments of the Contracting Parties and may decide to invite representatives of relevant entities other than the Governments of the Contracting Parties with the necessary expertise relevant to the issues to be discussed. The Committee shall decide on the modalities of its operation as necessary.

4. Any decision of the Committee shall be made by consensus.

5. Unless otherwise decided by the Contracting Parties, the Committee shall convene once a year.

Article 25   Relation to Other Agreements

Nothing in this Agreement shall affect the rights and obligations of a Contracting Party, including those relating to treatment accorded to investors of another Contracting Party, under any bilateral investment agreement between those two Contracting Parties existing on the date of entry into force of this Agreement, so long as such a bilateral agreement is in force.

Note: It is confirmed that, when an issue arises between an investor of a Contracting Party and another Contracting Party, nothing in this Agreement shall be construed so as to prevent the investor from relying on the bilateral investment agreement between those two Contracting Parties which is considered by the investor to be more favorable than this Agreement.

Article 26   Headings

The headings of the Articles of this Agreement are inserted for convenience of reference only and shall not affect the interpretation of this Agreement.

Article 27   Final Provisions

1. The Governments of the Contracting Parties shall notify one another, through diplomatic channels, of the completion of their respective internal procedures necessary for the entry into force of this Agreement. This Agreement shall enter into force on the thirtieth day after the latest of the dates of receipt of the notifications.

2. This Agreement shall remain in force for a period of ten years after its entry into force and shall continue in force thereafter except as provided in paragraphs 5 and 6. This Agreement shall also apply to all investments of investors of any Contracting Party acquired in the territory of another Contracting Party in accordance with the applicable laws and regulations of the latter Contracting Party prior to the entry into force of this Agreement.

3. The Contracting Parties shall undertake a general review of this Agreement, as well as a review of its implementation and operation, so as to further facilitate investment and create more open investment environment in the Contracting Parties, every three years after the entry into force of this Agreement or upon the request of any Contracting Party, unless otherwise agreed by the Contracting Parties.

4. The Contracting Parties shall, at the request of any Contracting Party, enter into negotiations through appropriate channels for the purpose of amending this Agreement. This Agreement may be amended by agreement among the Contracting Parties. Such amendment shall be accepted by the Contracting Parties in accordance with

their respective legal procedures, and shall enter into force on the date to be agreed upon by the Contracting Parties.Amendments shall not affect the rights and obligations of the Contracting Parties provided for under this Agreement until the amendments enter into force.

5. A Contracting Party may, by giving one year's advance notice in writing to the other Contracting Parties, withdraw from this Agreement at the end of the initial ten year period or at any time thereafter.If a Contracting Party withdraws, this Agreement shall remain in force for the remaining Contracting Parties. In respect of investments acquired prior to the date of withdrawal from this Agreement, the provisions of this Agreement shall continue to be effective for that withdrawing Contracting Party for a period of ten years from the date of such withdrawal.

6. This Agreement shall terminate when either of the remaining Contracting Parties as are stipulated in paragraph 5 withdraws in accordance with that paragraph. In respect of investments acquired prior to the date of termination of this Agreement, the provisions of this Agreement shall continue to be effective for those remaining Contracting Parties for a period of ten years from the date of termination of this Agreement.

7. This Agreement shall not apply to claims arising out of events which occurred, or to claims which had been settled, prior to its entry into force.

IN WITNESS WHEREOF, the undersigned, being duly authorized by their respective Governments, have signed this Agreement.

DONE in triplicate at Beijing, on this day of May, 2012, in the English language.

PROTOCOL

At the time of signing the Agreement among the Government of Japan, Government of the Republic of Korea and the Government of the People's Republic of China for the Promotion, Facilitation and Protection of Investment (hereinafter referred to as "the Agreement"), the undersigned have agreed upon the following provisions which shall form an integral part of the Agreement:

1. Paragraph 1 of Article 4 of the Agreement shall not apply to matters related to the acquisition of land property.

2. (a) The Contracting Parties confirm their shared understanding that paragraph 1 of Article 11 of the Agreement addresses the following two situations:

(i) the first situation is direct expropriation, where investments are nationalized or otherwise directly expropriated through formal transfer of title or outright seizure; and

(ii) the second situation is indirect expropriation, where an action or a series of actions by a Contracting Party has an effect equivalent to direct expropriation without formal transfer of title or outright seizure.

(b) The determination of whether an action or a series of actions by a Contracting Party, in a specific fact situation, constitutes an indirect expropriation requires a case-by-case, fact-based inquiry that considers, among other factors:

(i) the economic impact of the action or series of actions, although the fact that such action or series of actions has an adverse effect on the economic value of investments, standing alone, does not establish that an indirect expropriation has occurred;

(ii) the extent to which the action or series of actions interferes with distinct and reasonable expectations arising out of investments; and

(iii) the character and objectives of the action or series of actions, including whether such action is proportionate to its objectives.

(c) Except in rare circumstances, such as when an action or a series of actions by a Contracting Party is extremely severe or disproportionate in light of its purpose, non-discriminatory regulatory actions adopted by the Contracting Party for the purpose of legitimate public welfare do not constitute indirect expropriation.

IN WITNESS WHEREOF, the undersigned, being duly authorized by their respective Governments, have signed the present Protocol.

DONE in triplicate at Beijing, on this [—] day of May, 2012, in the English language.

Ⅵ. REGIONAL COMPREHENSIVE ECONOMIC PARTNERSHIP AGREEMENT, CHAPTER 10 INVESTMENT

Article 10.1 Definitions

For the purposes of this Chapter:

(a) **covered investment** means, with respect to a Party, an investment in its territory of an investor of another Party in existence as of the date of entry into force of this Agreement or established, acquired, or expanded thereafter, and which, where applicable, has been admitted①②, by the host Party, subject to its relevant laws, regulations, and policies;③

(b) **freely usable currency** means a freely usable currency as determined by the IMF under the IMF Articles of Agreement as may be amended;

(c) **investment** means every kind of asset that an investor owns or controls, directly or indirectly, and that has the characteristics of an investment, including such characteristics as the commitment of capital or other resources, the expectation of gains or profits, or the assumption of risk. Forms that an investment may take include:

(i) shares, stocks, and other forms of equity participation in a juridical person, including rights derived therefrom;

(ii) bonds, debentures, loans④, and other debt instruments of a juridical person and rights derived therefrom;⑤

(iii) rights under contracts, including turnkey, construction, management, production, or revenue-sharing contracts;

(iv)intellectual property rights and goodwill, which are recognised pursuant to the laws and regulations of the host Party;

(v)claims to money or to any contractual performance related to a business and having financial value;⑥

(vi) rights conferred pursuant to the laws and regulations of the host Party or contracts, such as concessions, licences, authorisations, and permits, including those for the exploration and exploitation of natural resources; and

---

① ［本章原文脚注 1］ For Malaysia and Thailand, protection under this Chapter shall be accorded to covered investments which, where applicable, have been specifically approved in writing for protection by their respective competent authorities in accordance with their respective laws, regulations, and policies.

② ［本章原文脚注 2］ For Cambodia, Indonesia, and Viet Nam, "has been admitted" means "has been specifically registered or approved in writing, as the case may be".

③ ［本章原文脚注 3］ For the purposes of this definition, "policies" means those policies affecting an investment that are endorsed and announced by the government of a Party in a written form and made publicly available in a written form.

④ ［本章原文脚注 4］ A loan issued by a Party to another Party is not an investment.

⑤ ［本章原文脚注 5］ Some forms of debt, such as bonds, debentures, and long-term notes, are more likely to have the characteristics of an investment, while other forms of debt, such as claims to payment that are immediately due and result from the sale of goods or services, are less likely to have such characteristics.

⑥ ［本章原文脚注 6］ For greater certainty, investment does not mean claims to money that arise solely from:

(a)commercial contracts for the sale of goods or services; or

(b)the extension of credit in connection with such commercial contracts.

(vii)movable and immovable property, and other property rights, such as leases, mortgages, liens, or pledges.①

The term "investment" does not include an order or judgment entered in a judicial or administrative action or an arbitral proceeding.

For the purposes of the definition of investment in this subparagraph, returns that are invested shall be treated as an investment and any alteration of the form in which assets are invested or reinvested shall not affect their character as an investment;

(d) investor of a non-Party means, with respect to a Party, an investor that seeks to make②, is making, or has made an investment in the territory of that Party, that is not an investor of a Party;

(e) investor of a Party means a natural person of a Party or a juridical person of a Party that seeks to make,③ is making, or has made an investment in the territory of another Party;

(f) juridical person means any entity constituted or organised under applicable law, whether or not for profit, and whether private or governmental, including any corporation, trust, partnership, joint venture, sole proprietorship, association or similar organisation, and a branch of a juridical person;④⑤⑥

(g) juridical person of a Party means a juridical person constituted or organised under the law of that Party, and a branch located in the territory of that Party and

① [本章原文脚注 7] For greater certainty, market share, market access, expected gains, and opportunities for profit-making are not, by themselves, investments.

② [本章原文脚注 8] For greater certainty, the Parties understand that an investor "seeks to make" an investment when that investor has taken concrete action or actions to make an investment. Where a notification or approval process is required for making an investment, an investor that "seeks to make" an investment refers to an investor that has initiated such notification or approval process.

③ [本章原文脚注 9] For greater certainty, the Parties understand that an investor "seeks to make" an investment when that investor has taken concrete action or actions to make an investment. Where a notification or approval process is required for making an investment, an investor that "seeks to make" an investment refers to an investor that has initiated such notification or approval process.

④ [本章原文脚注 10] For greater certainty, a branch of a juridical person does not have any right to make any claim against any Party under this Agreement.

⑤ [本章原文脚注 11] For greater certainty, the inclusion of a "branch" in the definition of "juridical person" is without prejudice to a Party's ability to treat a branch under its law as an entity that has no independent legal existence and is not separately organised.

⑥ [本章原文脚注 12] A branch of a legal entity of a non-Party shall not be considered as a juridical person of a Party.

carrying out business activities there; ①②③

(h) measure by a Party means any measure adopted or maintained by:

(i)central, regional, or local governments and authorities of that Party; and

(ii) non-governmental bodies in the exercise of powers delegated by central, regional, or local governments or authorities of that Party; and

(*i*) natural person of a Party means, for the purposes of subparagraph (e), a natural person who under the law of that Party:

(i)is a national or citizen of that Party; or

(ii)has the right of permanent residence in that Party, where both that Party and another Party recognise permanent residents and accord substantially the same treatment to their respective permanent residents as they accord to their respective nationals in respect of measures affecting investment.

Article 10.2　Scope

1. This Chapter shall apply to measures adopted or maintained by a Party relating to:

(a) investors of another Party; and

(b) covered investments.

2. This Chapter shall not apply to:

(a) government procurement;

(b) subsidies or grants provided by a Party;

(c) services supplied in the exercise of governmental authority by the relevant body or authority of a Party. For the purposes of this Chapter, "service supplied in the exercise of governmental authority" means any service which is supplied neither on a commercial basis nor in competition with one or more service suppliers;

(d) measures adopted or maintained by a Party to the extent that they are covered by Chapter 8 (Trade in Services); and

(e) measures adopted or maintained by a Party to the extent that they are covered by Chapter 9 (Temporary Movement of Natural Persons).

For greater certainty, this Chapter does not bind any Party in relation to any act or

---

① ［本章原文脚注 13］For greater certainty, a branch of a juridical person does not have any right to make any claim against any Party under this Agreement.

② ［本章原文脚注 14］For greater certainty, the inclusion of a "branch" in the definition of "juridical person of a Party" is without prejudice to a Party's ability to treat a branch under its law as an entity that has no independent legal existence and is not separately organised.

③ ［本章原文脚注 15］A branch of a legal entity of a non-Party shall not be considered as a juridical person of a Party.

fact that took place or any situation that ceased to exist before the date of entry into force of this Agreement.

3. Notwithstanding subparagraph 2(d), Article 10.5 (Treatment of Investment), Article 10.7 (Senior Management and Board of Directors)[1], Article 10.9 (Transfers), Article 10.11 (Compensation for Losses), Article 10.12 (Subrogation), and Article 10.13 (Expropriation) shall apply, mutatis mutandis, to any measure affecting the supply of a service by a service supplier of a Party through commercial presence in the territory of any other Party within the meaning of Chapter 8 (Trade in Services), but only to the extent that any such measure relates to a covered investment and an obligation under this Chapter.

Article 10.3　National Treatment[2]

1. Each Party shall accord to investors of another Party, and to covered investments, treatment no less favourable than that it accords, in like circumstances, to its own investors and their investments with respect to the establishment, acquisition, expansion, management, conduct, operation, and sale or other disposition of investments in its territory.

2. For greater certainty, the treatment to be accorded by a Party under paragraph 1 means, with respect to a government other than at the central level, treatment no less favourable than the most favourable treatment accorded, in like circumstances, by that government to investors, and to the investments of investors, of the Party of which it forms a part.

---

① ［本章原文脚注 16］Article 10.7 (Senior Management and Board of Directors) shall apply to measures affecting the supply of a service only for a Party making commitments in accordance with Article 8.8 (Schedules of Non-Conforming Measures).

② ［本章原文脚注 17］For greater certainty, whether the treatment is accorded in "like circumstances" under this Article depends on the totality of the circumstances, including whether the relevant treatment distinguishes between investors or investments on the basis of legitimate public welfare objectives.

Article 10.4　Most-Favoured-Nation Treatment [①][②]

1. Each Party shall accord to investors of another Party treatment no less favourable than that it accords, in like circumstances, to investors of any other Party or non-Party with respect to the establishment, acquisition, expansion, management, conduct, operation, and sale or other disposition of investments in its territory.

2. Each Party shall accord to covered investments treatment no less favourable than that it accords, in like circumstances, to investments in its territory of investors of any other Party or non-Party with respect to the establishment, acquisition, expansion, management, conduct, operation, and sale or other disposition of investments.

3. For greater certainty, the treatment referred to in paragraphs 1 and 2 does not encompass any international dispute resolution procedures or mechanisms under other existing or future international agreements.

Article 10.5　Treatment of Investment[③]

1. Each Party shall accord to covered investments fair and equitable treatment and full protection and security, in accordance with the customary international law minimum standard of treatment of aliens.

2. For greater certainty:

(a) fair and equitable treatment requires each Party not to deny justice in any legal or administrative proceedings;

(b) full protection and security requires each Party to take such measures as may be reasonably necessary to ensure the physical protection and security of the covered investment; and

(c) the concepts of fair and equitable treatment and full protection and security do not require treatment to be accorded to covered investments in addition to or beyond that which is required under the customary international law minimum standard of treatment of aliens, and do not create additional substantive rights.

---

① ［本章原文脚注 18］This Article shall not apply to Cambodia, Lao PDR, Myanmar, and Viet Nam. The treatment under this Article shall not be accorded to investors of Cambodia, Lao PDR, Myanmar, and Viet Nam, and to covered investments of such investors.

② ［本章原文脚注 19］For greater certainty, whether the treatment is accorded in "like circumstances" under this Article depends on the totality of the circumstances, including whether the relevant treatment distinguishes between investors or investments on the basis of legitimate public welfare objectives.

③ ［本章原文脚注 20］This Article shall be interpreted in accordance with Annex 10A (Customary International Law).

3. A determination that there has been a breach of another provision of this Agreement, or of a separate international agreement, does not establish that there has been a breach of this Article.

Article 10.6　Prohibition of Performance Requirements

1. No Party shall impose or enforce, as a condition for establishment, acquisition, expansion, management, conduct, operation, or sale or other disposition of an investment in its territory of an investor of any other Party, any of the following requirements:[①]

(a) to export a given level or percentage of goods;

(b) to achieve a given level or percentage of domestic content;

(c) to purchase, use, or accord a preference to goods produced in its territory, or to purchase goods from persons in its territory;

(d) to relate the volume or value of imports to the volume or value of exports or to the amount of foreign exchange inflows associated with investments of that investor;

(e) to restrict sales of goods in its territory that such investments produce by relating such sales to the volume or value of its exports or foreign exchange earnings;

(f) to transfer a particular technology, a production process, or other proprietary knowledge to a person in its territory;

(g) to supply exclusively from the territory of the Party the goods that such investments produce to a specific regional market or to the world market; or

(h) to adopt a given rate or amount of royalty under a licence contract, in regard to any licence contract in existence at the time the requirement is imposed or enforced, or any future licence contract freely entered into between the investor and a person in its territory, provided that the requirement is imposed or enforced in a manner that constitutes direct interference with that licence contract by an exercise of non-judicial governmental authority of a Party.[②] For greater certainty, this subparagraph does not apply when the licence contract is concluded between the investor and a Party.

Notwithstanding this Article, subparagraphs (f) and (h) shall not apply to Cambodia, Lao PDR, and Myanmar.

2. No Party shall condition the receipt or continued receipt of an advantage, in

---

① ［本章原文脚注 21］For greater certainty, each Party may maintain existing measures or adopt new or more restrictive measures that do not conform with obligations under this Article, as set out in List A and List B of its Schedule in Annex Ⅲ (Schedules of Reservations and Non-Conforming Measures for Services and Investment).

② ［本章原文脚注 22］For the purposes of this subparagraph, a "licence contract" means any contract concerning the licensing of technology, a production process, or other proprietary knowledge.

connection with the establishment, acquisition, expansion, management, conduct, operation, or sale or other disposition of an investment in its territory of an investor of any other Party on compliance with any of the following requirements:

(a) to achieve a given level or percentage of domestic content;

(b) to purchase, use, or accord a preference to goods produced in its territory, or to purchase goods from persons in its territory;

(c) to relate the volume or value of imports to the volume or value of exports or to the amount of foreign exchange inflows associated with investments of that investor; or

(d) to restrict sales of goods in its territory that such investments produce by relating such sales to the volume or value of its exports or foreign exchange earnings.

3. (a) Nothing in paragraph 2 shall be construed to prevent a Party from conditioning the receipt or continued receipt of an advantage, in connection with an investment in its territory of an investor of any other Party, on compliance with a requirement to locate production, supply a service, train or employ workers, construct or expand particular facilities, or carry out research and development, in its territory.

(b) Subparagraphs 1(f) and (h) shall not apply:

(i) if a Party authorises use of an intellectual property right in accordance with Article 31 or Article 31 bis of the TRIPS Agreement[①], or to measures requiring the disclosure of proprietary information that fall within the scope of, and are consistent with, Article 39 of the TRIPS Agreement; or

(ii) if the requirement is imposed or enforced by a court, administrative tribunal, or competition authority to remedy a practice determined after judicial or administrative process to be anti-competitive under the Party's competition laws and regulations.

(c) Subparagraph 1(h) shall not apply if the requirement is imposed or enforced by a tribunal or competent authority as equitable remuneration under the Party's copyright laws and regulations.

(d) Subparagraphs 1(a) through (c), 2(a), and 2(b) shall not apply to qualification requirements for goods with respect to export promotion and foreign aid programmes.

(e) Subparagraphs 2(a) and (b) shall not apply to requirements imposed by an importing Party relating to the content of goods necessary to qualify for preferential tariffs or preferential quotas.

4. For greater certainty, paragraphs 1 and 2 shall not apply to any requirement

---

① ［本章原文脚注 23］This includes any amendment to the TRIPS Agreement implementing paragraph 6 of the Doha Declaration on the TRIPS Agreement and Public Health (WT/MIN(01)/DEC/2) adopted at Doha on 14 November 2001.

other than those set out in those paragraphs.

Article 10.7   Senior Management and Board of Directors

1. No Party shall require that a juridical person of that Party that is a covered investment appoint to a senior management position a natural person of any particular nationality.

2. A Party may require that a majority of the board of directors, or any committee thereof, of a juridical person of that Party that is a covered investment, be of a particular nationality or resident in the territory of that Party, provided that the requirement does not materially impair the ability of the investor to exercise control over its investment.

Article 10.8   Reservations and Non-Conforming Measures

1. Article 10. 3 (National Treatment), Article 10.4 (Most-Favoured- Nation Treatment), Article 10.6 (Prohibition of Performance Requirements), and Article 10.7 (Senior Management and Board of Directors) shall not apply to:

(a) any existing non-conforming measure that is maintained by a Party at:

(i) the central level of government, as set out by that Party in List A of its Schedule in Annex Ⅲ (Schedules of Reservations and Non-Conforming Measures for Services and Investment);

(ii) a regional level of government, as set out by that Party in List A of its Schedule in Annex Ⅲ (Schedules of Reservations and Non-Conforming Measures for Services and Investment); or

(iii) a local level of government;

(b) the continuation or prompt renewal of any non-conforming measure referred to in subparagraph (a); and

(c) an amendment to any non-conforming measure referred to in subparagraph (a) to the extent that the amendment does not decrease the conformity of the measure:

(i) for Cambodia, Indonesia, Lao PDR, Myanmar, and the Philippines, as it existed at the date of entry into force of this Agreement; and

(ii) for Australia, Brunei, China, Japan, Korea, Malaysia, New Zealand, Singapore, Thailand, and Viet Nam, as it existed immediately before the amendment,

with Article 10. 3 (National Treatment), Article 10. 4 (Most-Favoured-Nation Treatment), Article 10.6 (Prohibition of Performance Requirements), and Article 10.7 (Senior Management and Board of Directors).

2. Article 10. 3 (National Treatment), Article 10. 4 (Most-Favoured-Nation Treatment), Article 10.6 (Prohibition of Performance Requirements), and Article 10.7

(Senior Management and Board of Directors) shall not apply to any measure that a Party adopts or maintains with respect to sectors, subsectors, or activities, as set out by that Party in List B of its Schedule in Annex Ⅲ (Schedules of Reservations and Non-Conforming Measures for Services and Investment).

3. Notwithstanding subparagraph 1(c)(ii), for five years after the date of entry into force of this Agreement, Article 10.3 (National Treatment), Article 10.4 (Most-Favoured-Nation Treatment), Article 10.6 (Prohibition of Performance Requirements), and Article 10.7 (Senior Management and Board of Directors) shall not apply to an amendment to any non-conforming measure referred to in subparagraph 1(a) to the extent that the amendment does not decrease the conformity of the measure as it existed at the date of entry into force of this Agreement with Article 10.3 (National Treatment), Article 10.4 (Most-Favoured-Nation Treatment), Article 10.6 (Prohibition of Performance Requirements), and Article 10.7 (Senior Management and Board of Directors).

4. No Party shall, under any measure adopted after the date of entry into force of this Agreement and covered by List B of its Schedule in Annex Ⅲ (Schedules of Reservations and Non-Conforming Measures for Services and Investment), require an investor of another Party, by reason of its nationality, to sell or otherwise dispose of an investment that exists at the time the measure becomes effective, unless otherwise specified in the initial approval by the relevant authorities.

5. Article 10.3 (National Treatment) and Article 10.4 (Most-Favoured-Nation Treatment) shall not apply to any measure that falls within Article 5 of the TRIPS Agreement, and any measure that is covered by an exception to, or derogation from, the obligations imposed by Article 11.7 (National Treatment), or imposed by Article 3 or 4 of the TRIPS Agreement.

Article 10.9　Transfers

1. Each Party shall allow all transfers relating to a covered investment to be made freely and without delay into and out of its territory. Such transfers include:

(a) contributions to capital, including the initial contribution;

(b) profits, capital gains, dividends, interest, royalty payments, technical assistance and technical and management fees, licence fees, and other current income accruing from the covered investment;

(c) proceeds from the sale or liquidation of all or any part of the covered investment;

(d) payments made under a contract, including a loan agreement;

(e) payments made pursuant to Article 10.11 (Compensation for Losses) and

Article 10.13 (Expropriation);

(f) payments arising out of the settlement of a dispute by any means including adjudication, arbitration, or the agreement of the parties to the dispute; and

(g) earnings and other remuneration of personnel engaged from abroad in connection with the covered investment.

2. Each Party shall allow such transfers relating to a covered investment to be made in any freely usable currency at the market rate of exchange prevailing at the time of transfer.

3. Notwithstanding paragraphs 1 and 2, a Party may prevent or delay a transfer through the equitable, non-discriminatory, and good faith application of its laws and regulations relating to:

(a) bankruptcy, insolvency, or the protection of the rights of creditors including employees;

(b) issuing, trading, or dealing in securities, futures, options, or derivatives;

(c) criminal or penal offences and the recovery of the proceeds of crime;

(d) financial reporting or record keeping of transfers when necessary to assist law enforcement or financial regulatory authorities;

(e) ensuring compliance with awards or orders or judgments in judicial or administrative proceedings;

(f) taxation;①

(g) social security, public retirement, superannuation, compulsory savings schemes, or other arrangements to provide pension or similar retirement benefits;

(h) severance entitlement of employees; and

(i) requirements to register and satisfy other formalities imposed by the central bank and other relevant authorities of that Party.

4. Nothing in this Chapter shall affect the rights and obligations of a Party as a member of the IMF under the IMF Articles of Agreement as may be amended, including the use of exchange actions which are in conformity with the IMF Articles of Agreement as may be amended, provided that the Party shall not impose restrictions on any capital transactions inconsistently with the obligations under this Chapter regarding such transactions, except under Article 17.15 (Measures to Safeguard the Balance of Payments) or on request of the IMF.

---

① ［本章原文脚注 24］For greater certainty, this also includes the adoption or enforcement of any taxation measure aimed at ensuring the equitable or effective imposition or collection of taxes including any taxation measure that differentiates between persons based on their place of residence or incorporation.

Article 10.10　Special Formalities and Disclosure of Information

1. Nothing in Article 10.3（National Treatment）shall be construed to prevent a Party from adopting or maintaining a measure that prescribes special formalities in connection with covered investments, including a requirement that covered investments be legally constituted under its laws or regulations, provided that such formalities do not materially impair the protections afforded by that Party to investors of another Party and covered investments pursuant to this Chapter.

2. Notwithstanding Article 10.3（National Treatment）and Article 10.4（Most-Favoured-Nation Treatment）, a Party may require an investor of another Party or its covered investment to provide information concerning that investment solely for informational or statistical purposes. The Party shall protect, to the extent possible, any confidential information which has been provided from any disclosure that would prejudice the legitimate commercial interests or the competitive position of the investor or the covered investment. Nothing in this paragraph shall be construed to prevent a Party from otherwise obtaining or disclosing information in connection with the equitable and good faith application of its laws and regulations.

Article 10.11　Compensation for Losses

Each Party shall accord to investors of another Party, and their covered investments, with respect to measures it adopts or maintains relating to losses suffered by investments in its territory owing to armed conflict, civil strife, or state of emergency, treatment no less favourable than that it accords, in like circumstances, to:

(a) its own investors and their investments; and

(b) investors of any other Party or non-Party, and their investments.

Article 10.12　Subrogation

1. If a Party, or an agency designated by a Party, makes a payment to an investor of that Party under a guarantee, a contract of insurance or other form of indemnity that it has granted in respect of a covered investment, the other Party in whose territory the covered investment was made shall recognise the subrogation or transfer of any right or claim in respect of such covered investment. The subrogated or transferred right or claim shall not be greater than the original right or claim of the investor.

2. Where a Party or an agency designated by a Party has made a payment to an investor of that Party and has taken over any right or claim of the investor, that investor shall not pursue that right or claim against the other Party in whose territory the covered investment was made, unless that investor is authorised to act on behalf of

the Party making the payment or the agency designated by that Party.

3. In the exercise of subrogated or transferred right or claim, a Party or an agency designated by a Party exercising such right or claim shall disclose the coverage of the claims arrangement with its investors to the relevant Party.

Article 10.13 Expropriation①

1. No Party shall expropriate or nationalise a covered investment either directly or through measures equivalent to expropriation or nationalisation (hereinafter referred to as "expropriation" in this Chapter), except:

(a) for a public purpose;

(b) in a non-discriminatory manner;

(c) onpaymentofcompensationinaccordancewith paragraphs 2 and 3; and

(d) in accordance with due process of law.

2. The compensation referred to in subparagraph 1(c) shall:

(a) be paid without delay;②

(b) be equivalent to the fair market value of the expropriated investment at the time when the expropriation was publicly announced③, or when the expropriation occurred, whichever is earlier (hereinafter referred to as the "date of expropriation" in this Chapter);④⑤⑥

(c) not reflect any change in value occurring because the intended expropriation had become known earlier; and

(d) be effectively realisable and freely transferable.

3. In the event of delay, the compensation shall include an appropriate interest in

---

① ［本章原文脚注 25］This Article shall be interpreted in accordance with Annex 10B (Expropriation).

② ［本章原文脚注 26］The Parties understand that there may be legal and administrative processes that need to be observed before payment can be made.

③ ［本章原文脚注 27］For the Philippines, the time when the expropriation was publicly announced for the purpose of calculating the fair market value of the expropriated investment refers to the date of filing of the Petition for Expropriation.

④ ［本章原文脚注 28］For Australia, Brunei Darussalam, Korea, Malaysia, New Zealand, and Singapore, the date of expropriation for the purpose of calculating the fair market value of the expropriated investment means the date immediately before the expropriation occurs.

⑤ ［本章原文脚注 29］For Cambodia, Lao PDR, Myanmar, and Viet Nam, the date of expropriation for the purpose of calculating the fair market value of the expropriated investment means the date when the expropriation decision is issued by the competent authority.

⑥ ［本章原文脚注 30］For Thailand, the date of expropriation for the purpose of calculating the fair market value of the expropriated investment means the date when the expropriation occurs.

accordance with the expropriating Party's laws, regulations, and policies provided that such laws, regulations, and policies are applied on a non-discriminatory basis.

4. This Article does not apply to the issuance of compulsory licences granted in relation to intellectual property rights, or to the revocation, limitation, or creation of intellectual property rights, to the extent that such issuance, revocation, limitation, or creation is consistent with Chapter 11 (Intellectual Property) and the TRIPS Agreement.①

5. Notwithstanding paragraphs 1 through 3, any measure of expropriation relating to land shall be as defined in the existing laws and regulations of the expropriating Party, and shall be, for the purposes of and on payment of compensation, in accordance with the aforesaid laws and regulations. Such compensation shall be subject to any subsequent amendments to the aforesaid laws and regulations relating to the amount of compensation where such amendments follow the general trends in the market value of the land.

Article 10.14　Denial of Benefits②

1. A Party may deny the benefits of this Chapter to an investor of another Party that is a juridical person of that other Party and to investments of that investor if the juridical person:

(a) is owned or controlled by a person of a non-Party or of the denying Party; and

(b) has no substantial business activities in the territory of any Party other than the denying Party.

2. A Party may deny the benefits of this Chapter to an investor of another Party that is a juridical person of that other Party and to investments of that investor if persons of a non-Party own or control the juridical person and the denying Party adopts or maintains measures with respect to the non-Party or a person of the non-Party that prohibit transactions with the juridical person or that would be violated or circumvented if the benefits of this Chapter were accorded to the juridical person or to its investments.

3. A Party may deny the benefits of this Chapter to an investor of another Party that is a juridical person of that other Party and to investments of that investor if persons of a non-Party own or control the juridical person and the denying Party does

---

① ［本章原文脚注 31］For greater certainty, the Parties recognise that, for the purposes of this Article, the "revocation" of intellectual property rights includes the cancellation or nullification of such rights, and the "limitation" of intellectual property rights includes exceptions to such rights.

② ［本章原文脚注 32］A Party's right to deny the benefits of this Chapter as provided for in this Article may be exercised at any time.

not maintain diplomatic relations with the non-Party.

4. Notwithstanding paragraph 1, Thailand may, under its applicable laws and regulations, deny the benefits of this Chapter relating to the admission, establishment, acquisition, and expansion of investments to an investor of another Party that is a juridical person of such Party and to investments of such an investor where Thailand establishes that the juridical person is owned or controlled by natural persons or juridical persons of a non-Party or of Thailand.

5. For the purposes of this Article, for Thailand, a juridical person is:

(a) "owned" by natural persons or juridical persons of a Party or of a non-Party if more than 50 per cent of the equity interest in it is beneficially owned by such persons; and

(b) "controlled" by natural persons or juridical persons of a Party or of a non-Party if such persons have the power to name a majority of its directors or otherwise to legally direct its actions.

6. The Philippines may deny the benefits of this Chapter to investors of another Party and to investments of that investor where it establishes that such investor has made an investment in breach of the provisions of Commonwealth Act No.108, entitled An Act to Punish Acts of Evasion of Laws on the Nationalization of Certain Rights, Franchises or Privileges, as amended by Presidential Decree No.715, otherwise known as The Anti-Dummy Law, as may be amended.

7. A Party may deny the benefits of this Chapter to an investor of another Party or of a non-Party and to investments of that investor where such an investor has made an investment in breach of the provisions of the denying Party's laws and regulations that implement the Financial Action Task Force Recommendations.

Article 10.15   Security Exceptions

Notwithstanding Article 17.13 (Security Exceptions), nothing in this Chapter shall be construed to:

(a) require a Party to furnish or allow access to any information the disclosure of which it determines to be contrary to its essential security interests; or

(b) preclude a Party from applying measures that it considers necessary for:

(i)the fulfilment of its obligations with respect to the maintenance or restoration of international peace or security; or

(ii)the protection of its own essential security interests.

Article 10.16   Promotion of Investment

The Parties shall endeavour to promote and increase awareness of the region as an investment area including through:

(a) encouraging investments among the Parties;

(b) organising joint investment promotion activities between or among Parties;

(c) promoting business matching events;

(d) organising and supporting the organisation of various briefings and seminars on investment opportunities and on investment laws, regulations, and policies; and

(e) conducting information exchanges on other issues of mutual concern relating to investment promotion.

Article 10.17　Facilitation of Investment

1. Subject to its laws and regulations, each Party shall endeavour to facilitate investments among the Parties, including through:

(a) creating the necessary environment for all forms of investment;

(b) simplifying its procedures for investment applications and approvals;

(c) promoting the dissemination of investment information, including investment rules, laws, regulations, policies, and procedures; and

(d) establishing or maintaining contact points, one-stop investment centres, focal points, or other entities in the respective Party to provide assistance and advisory services to investors, including the facilitation of operating licences and permits.

2. Subject to its laws and regulations, a Party's activities under subparagraph 1(d) may include, to the extent possible, assisting investors of any other Party and covered investments to amicably resolve complaints or grievances with government bodies which have arisen during their investment activities by:

(a) receiving and, where appropriate, considering referring or giving due consideration to complaints raised by investors relating to government activities impacting their covered investment; and

(b) providing assistance, to the extent possible, in resolving difficulties experienced by the investors in relation to their covered investments.

3. Subject to its laws and regulations, each Party may, to the extent possible, consider establishing mechanisms to make recommendations to its relevant government bodies addressing recurrent issues affecting investors of another Party.

4. The Parties shall endeavour to facilitate meetings between their respective competent authorities aimed at exchanging knowledge and approaches to better facilitate investment.

5. Nothing in this Article shall be subject to, or otherwise affect, any dispute resolution proceedings under this Agreement.

Article 10.18　Work Programme

1. The Parties shall, without prejudice to their respective positions, enter into discussions on:

(a) the settlement of investment disputes between a Party and an investor of another Party; and

(b) the application of Article 10.13 (Expropriation) to taxation measures that constitute expropriation,

no later than two years after the date of entry into force of this Agreement, the outcomes of which are subject to agreement by all Parties.

2. The Parties shall conclude the discussions referred to in paragraph 1 within three years from the date of commencement of the discussions.

* * * * *

ANNEX 10A
CUSTOMARY INTERNATIONAL LAW

The Parties confirm their shared understanding that "customary international law" generally and as specifically referenced in Article 10.5 (Treatment of Investment), including in relation to the customary international law minimum standard of treatment of aliens, results from a general and consistent practice of States that they follow from a sense of legal obligation.

* * * * *

ANNEX 10B
EXPROPRIATION

The Parties confirm their shared understanding that:

1. An action or a series of related actions by a Party cannot constitute an expropriation unless it interferes with a tangible or intangible property right or property interest[1]1 in a covered investment.

2. Article 10.13 (Expropriation) addresses two situations:

(a) the first situation is direct expropriation, where a covered investment is nationalised or otherwise directly expropriated through formal transfer of title or outright seizure; and

(b) the second situation is where an action or a series of related actions by a Party

---

① ［本附件原文脚注 1］ For the purposes of this Annex, "property interest" refers to such property interest as may be recognised under the laws and regulations of that Party.

has an effect equivalent to direct expropriation without formal transfer of title or outright seizure.

3. The determination of whether an action or series of related actions by a Party, in a specific fact situation, constitutes an expropriation of the type referred to in subparagraph 2(b) requires a case-by-case, fact-based inquiry that considers, among other factors:

(a) the economic impact of the government action, although the fact that an action or a series of related actions by a Party has an adverse effect on the economic value of an investment, standing alone, does not establish that such an expropriation has occurred;

(b) whether the government action breaches the government's prior binding written commitment to the investor, whether by contract, licence, or other legal document; and

(c) the character of the government action, including its objective and context.[①]

4. Non-discriminatory regulatory actions by a Party that are designed and applied to achieve legitimate public welfare objectives, such as the protection of public health, safety, public morals, the environment, and real estate price stabilisation, do not constitute expropriation of the type referred to in subparagraph 2(b).

---

① ［本附件原文脚注 2］For Korea, a relevant consideration could include whether the investor bears a disproportionate burden, such as a special sacrifice that exceeds what the investor or investment should be expected to endure for the public interest. This footnote does not prejudice the determination of the character of the government action of any other Party.

后　记

　　本书是在笔者主持的中国法学会 2012 年度部级法学研究重大课题"中国参与多边投资规则制定问题研究"(课题组成员:徐泉、杨国华、刘笋、周亚光、何芳、寇顺萍)结项成果(研究报告,结项等级优秀)基础上,做重大删减、修改、补充而成,也属笔者主持的西南大学 2017 年党的十九大精神研究重大科研专项资金项目"构建新时代中国特色对外投资法律制度研究"(项目批准号 SWU1709733)和笔者主持的西南大学 2018 年度中央高校基本科研业务费专项资金项目(博士启动项目)"金砖国家国际投资法研究"(项目批准号 SWU1809682)的阶段性研究成果。

　　本书以章为序,执笔人分工如下:

　　引言、第一章:邓瑞平(西南大学法学院);

　　第二章、第三章:寇顺萍(西南大学经济管理学院)、邓瑞平;

　　第四章、第五章:邓瑞平、周亚光(西北政法大学);

　　第六章、第七章:周亚光、邓瑞平;

　　第八章:何芳(西安工程大学)、邓瑞平。

　　本书的出版得益于厦门大学出版社编辑李宁、甘世恒等同志的大力支持和西南大学的出版资助。

　　对以上单位和个人,一并致以诚挚谢意!

　　本书附录了我国缔结或参加的重要多边投资协定英文本,以便读者深入理解本书相关内容和相关规则。

　　书中难免存在不当或错误之处,敬请读者批评指正。

邓瑞平

2022 年 12 月 25 日

重庆缙云山麓